CRAZY WOMAN CREEK

CRAZY WOMAN CREEK

WOMEN REWRITE
THE AMERICAN WEST

EDITED BY

LINDA M. HASSELSTROM,
GAYDELL COLLIER, AND NANCY CURTIS

A MARINER BOOK

HOUGHTON MIFFLIN COMPANY

BOSTON · NEW YORK

2004

For information about permission to reproduce selections
from this book, write to Permissions, Houghton Mifflin Company,
215 Park Avenue South, New York, New York 10003.

Visit our Web site: www.houghtonmifflinbooks.com.

ISBN-13: 978-0-618-24933-6
ISBN-10: 0-618-24933-8

Library of Congress Cataloging-in-Publication Data

Crazy Woman Creek : women rewrite the American West / edited by
Linda M. Hasselstrom, Gaydell Collier, and Nancy Curtis.
p. cm.
"A Mariner Book."
Includes index.
ISBN 0-618-24933-8
1. American literature—West (U.S.) 2. Women—West (U.S.)—Literary
collections. 3. American literature—Women authors. 4. West (U.S.)—
Literary collections. 5. American literature—21st century. I. Hasselstrom,
Linda M. II. Collier, Gaydell. III. Curtis, Nancy, date.
PS561.C83 2004
810.8'03278'082—dc22 2003056893

Book design by Melissa Lotfy
Frontispiece illustration by Gertrud Goetz

Printed in the United States of America

QUM 10 9 8 7 6 5 4 3 2 1

*To all women who have the wild idea
they can make community work,
in the West or anywhere else*

Our community . . . was armed with words,
woven together because women know the value of
 collected stories.

Connection lives inside the words . . .

What weaves us all together into community
is our vulnerability,
the uncertainties that find us all in wilderness places.

— JANE KIRKPATRICK

Contents

II ✑ *HALLELUJAH AND A SHOW OF HANDS*

III ✦ *COWGIRL UP, CUPCAKES*

Introduction:
Beyond Crazy Woman Creek

"We celebrate community and stories."
—JANE KIRKPATRICK

One hot day not long ago, the three editors of this collection were bouncing along a two-lane highway between Recluse and Story, Wyoming. One of us was driving; we all own beat-up SUVs with enough cargo space to haul the boxes of books and fliers we take to readings. The windows were down, so we inhaled the zest of sagebrush and tasted the difference in dust from plateaus or creek bottoms. Two of us visited in front while the third, nesting among our luggage in the back seat, leaned forward to make remarks.

The tires rumbled as we crossed a bridge. "Crazy Woman Creek," one of us snarled. "Why isn't it ever Samantha Wilson Creek?"

"Or," said the beautiful and brilliant editor, "Wonderful Woman Creek?"

"Or even," said the serious one, "First Woman Doctor Creek."

"Strangers must think all the memorable women in the Old West were nuts," said the cynical one, "or prostitutes like Mother Featherlegs."

"Or nameless," said the thoughtful one. "And what does that tell you about the men who did the naming?"

"My home state was just full of places with 'squaw' in the name until pretty recently," said the one from South Dakota.

"And Wyoming still has those little sharp-pointed hills called Maggie's Nipples," said the one who collects maps.

"Squaw Hill, Old Woman Creek, Crazy Mountains," mumbled somebody from the back seat.

"Is anything important named after ordinary women?" said the ex-librarian. "Like rivers or mountains? Are there any memorials to women homesteaders?"

"I guess you could count the Tetons," said the one who shoots a muzzle loader, "thanks to some lonely French fur trapper; they never looked like breasts to me."

"My grandmother," mentioned the oldest one, "always said a decent woman's name appeared in public only three times: at birth, at her marriage, and at her death. I guess our tombstones are supposed to be our monuments."

"The good news is, we have to die first," snapped the grouchy one.

> *"What knits us are the rhythms of our female lives."*
> —ROSEMERRY WAHTOLA TROMMER

Nearly everyone has a favorite, and different, image of the West, where myth and reality gallop into the same sunset. Maybe you had to be crazy to settle here, especially if you were a woman. Both legend and history record extremes in temperature, elevation, snowfall, drought, fire, and flood. Lyric and chronicle celebrate courage and cowardice, profusion and famine, beauty and monotony, peace and lawlessness. Pioneers heading west from Europe or the Eastern states were often called lunatics by their relatives.

Conflict and change are inherent in the West, though Westerners are perceived to be mostly honest, hard-working, independent lovers of freedom, who are tough or tender, depending on the need. Westerners are renowned for building friendly settlements in the middle of hardship. This book stands solidly on a tradition that cherishes paradox.

The editors of *Crazy Woman Creek* think women furnished more to the Western character than their labor feeding campfires and rearing children. So why weren't more mountains, statues, or government buildings named for women?

Perhaps Westerners thought anyone could do women's work, and maybe some of us accepted that judgment. The contrary West has always had room for both the minister's wife and the mistress; sometimes they worked together toward a common goal. And maybe naming features of the landscape after shady ladies is further evidence of the puzzle that is the West.

Many modern Western women, including some of the writers of this collection, still live remote from what passes for modern civilization, but they are also part of a cooperative community. Like their foremothers, they work hard, respect themselves, and can laugh at their mistakes. They may burst into song in the middle of a cattle drive or turn the air blue with curses while fixing a flat tire. Outrageous behavior may be the key to survival; our history sparkles with tales of women who prevailed because they were unpredictable enough to outsmart the bad guys.

Westerners have always admired these crazy women, knowing that every good idea was once considered mad. Near my home, a statue celebrates Esther Hobart Morris, the first woman judge in America. Wyoming was still a territory when Esther joined a group of women who had the out-

rageous idea that they should be able to vote and hold public office; woman suffrage passed here in 1869.

Still, modern Western women are tired of being nameless. *Crazy Woman Creek* presents ordinary women from west of the Mississippi River telling personal—and true—stories about their connections to the rest of the world. The writers in these pages accept some traditional Western views and renounce others. Carving their own images on the land in deed, word, and thought, they are rewriting history for all of us.

> *"We are most aware of the inevitable tug of time."*
> —SARAH BYRN RICKMAN

This collection of writing by contemporary Western women is a conversation in prose and poetry for readers and writers. Modern Western women keep house, do outside chores, haul children and horses to 4-H meetings and rodeos. They learned from their mothers and grandmothers, but they are also absorbing new ideas: how to hold a job in town, or travel the Internet as well as gravel roads. Their work has rarely been acknowledged publicly or permanently. A bawdy-house madam was more likely to be remembered in myth and on maps than an ordinary housewife, but both were overshadowed by male adventurers who wrote the history books. This book is one way to recognize the ways women have shaped and sustained Western communities and contributed, sometimes silently, to the true legacy of the West.

Crazy Woman Creek also portrays the new story we are writing, as strangers move West to inhabit the land differently. As a contributor to this volume notes, "What each of these groups can't see is that at the core, they . . . love the same place and want the same thing." (Unless otherwise credited, quotations in this introduction are from contributors' writing in *Crazy Woman Creek*.)

We may not always realize or acknowledge the likeness, but each individual is linked to every other by similar experiences, interests, attitudes, and beliefs. A crisis may bring us together, but it is easy to forget those bonds when our opinions clash. These days, "the natives . . . are a little bitter" toward "the newcomers, 'those damn environmentalists.'" Old-timers wonder, sometimes in loud outrage, what will happen to the neighborhoods we have cherished. We are afraid that as the places change, we will lose the values we esteem—honesty, friendliness, self-sufficiency, moral courage.

The Native Americans probably said the same things as immigrant wagons rumbled across the buffalo grass—yet the descendants of people who bickered and brawled in different languages are now accepted as native Westerners. We think the true stories in *Crazy Woman Creek* will continue to inspire intelligent conversations about community.

In the Old West, both men and women sometimes used force to get their way. Though we favor peaceful negotiation, we don't want to forget those tough old broads rudely memorialized in our place-names. Moving beyond Crazy Woman Creek doesn't mean forgetting their legacy. We'll offer new neighbors coffee and banana bread. But if some newcomer doesn't think the name Maggie's Nipples is politically correct, we might resist changing the name to Margaret's Mammaries.

> *"Until we find meaning in the stories of our lives, we're destined to wander in the wilderness, even though we're in a promised land."*
> —JANE KIRKPATRICK

We three editors have known one another for more than twenty years. Collecting writing by Western women in two previous anthologies taught us that "we could count on each other," and working together has made us friends.

Gaydell, a librarian before she retired, writes and operates Backpocket Books from a small ranch near Sundance. Nancy helps manage the family ranch near Glendo and directs High Plains Press, publishing books about Wyoming and the West. Linda lives in Cheyenne and owns a South Dakota ranch where she conducts writing retreats for women.

All three of the anthologies we have edited together, including *Crazy Woman Creek*, grew out of the Western landscape and the women who inhabit it. During the past decade, the editors have driven thousands of miles together, speculating about how each collection might develop, while discussing a zillion other topics. When we traveled to promote the books through readings and autograph parties, we inevitably came home feeling invigorated.

Our first partnership grew out of conversations about strong women who helped form the Western communities where we grew up. We encouraged women from six Western states to tell us how they survived in troubled times. Though we'd heard these stories all our lives, we weren't sure women would reveal them to readers who live mostly in cities. Would urban dwellers appreciate these Western truths?

Western women sent a stack of submissions taller than any of us, proving that the tough, shrewd women of the real West aren't all in cemeteries as hard to find as the Mother Featherlegs Monument. (Yes, she was probably a prostitute. Local cowboys nicknamed her for the lacy red pantaloons she wore tied at the ankles when she rode her horse to town, but they seemed to respect her for her grit rather than her profession.)

Teamwork created *Leaning into the Wind: Women Write from the Heart of the West*. Making our selections on the basis of authenticity and quality, we chose 246 essays and poems contributed by 206 women. Some of them had

never before written for publication, but they were—ah—crazy enough to trust us.

Thousands of books sold before the official publication date, thereby demonstrating that we'd found readers as well as writers. The publication party at Devils Tower, Wyoming, in June 1997 created legends. Mindy, an assistant editor for Houghton Mifflin, came from Boston a few days early to meet us, donned a Western hat, and staunchly ate Rocky Mountain oysters at a ranch branding. (She later moved west.)

> *"A small community . . . is a microcosm of the larger world."*
> —MARCIA HENSLEY

On the day of the celebration, we waited nervously at the foot of Devils Tower. As contributors arrived, we handed each a complimentary copy. A gray-haired woman in a red Western suit and riding boots stood a little taller as she said, "It's a real book! I thought it would be mimeographed or something!"

Men leaned on pickups in the parking lot; a father and his children watched deer in the meadow; grandmothers played with babies. At picnic tables in the shade, the contributors read, talked, and signed books. More stories prompted "laughter as we heaped our plates" with a meal provided by the Crook County Cattlewomen. A local woman served three huge cakes; one was decorated with an image of Devils Tower, one with a cowgirl, and one with the book title.

A new association that began to form around the book set the pattern for all three collections. "As subtly as the snow melted into the land, our lives began to melt into the community."

Since we were in Wyoming, the wind was blowing; we duct-taped a box of tissues to the podium, and many women used it as they read and told stories in strong or halting voices. A guitarist sang during intermissions, while the audience limbered up and collected autographs. The reading lasted seven hours, but no one complained. After driving several hours to get there, ranch folks left early, knowing they would have to do chores in the dark. Some of us were reminded of small-town picnics long ago; others, younger or more urban, had never seen anything like that day.

What would such a gathering have been like in Boston? we asked our East Coast editor. Less open, less warm, she said; "the women would have worn less comfortable shoes and tried to stand by the most important person."

Part of the story of the book's creation ended that day, but our lives had become entwined with those of our contributors and readers. Many of us keep in contact, weaving more narratives from the connections we formed, or strengthened, at Devils Tower. Contributors come to read with us every-

where we go; they write books and encourage other women in community efforts. *Leaning,* they say, validates their struggles, encourages them to defend their beliefs. Readers elsewhere realize that these Western women have opinions that must be considered in decisions about the West. Dozens of readers tell us they keep the book on their bedside tables, so they can re-read favorite parts.

Some reviewers didn't realize that the book was written by real women about the hardships and joys to be found in today's West. Befuddled by their own myths, they asked whether these stories by "pioneer women" were really true.

That night, when we editors collapsed, we were already thinking of the next anthology. A reader later wrote, "This isn't a book. It's a communion."

> **"Our lives are a song of communities."**
> —KATHRYN E. KELLEY

As usual, the editors drove around the West promoting the book. Thriftily, we shared motel rooms, discovering that Gaydell writes at sunrise, eats leftover Chinese food for breakfast, and always packs chocolate; that Nancy takes her own coffeepot; that Linda doesn't own a hair dryer. At each stop, we greeted "women we had just met, yet knew to our bones because their stories were our own." Although our opinions sometimes differed wildly—on religion, politics, or agriculture—we found ourselves linked by shared experiences, our worlds expanding with each new acquaintance.

While those first contributors are part of a unique Western population, each is also linked to others in an expanding spiral of influence. Our journeys create widening circles of connection, "interwoven communities" of people who know one another's friends or relatives or home neighborhoods. How many circles, we wonder, swirl around each of us?

As we editors learned to appreciate and trust one another more, we began to talk about women's friendships. We asked one another: What do other Western women value in their friends? The theme of our second anthology, *Woven on the Wind,* had materialized.

> **"I see the process at work—the connections that I did not see and could not value before."**
> —BARBARA JESSING

In *Leaning into the Wind,* contributors wrote about their work, their dogs, their husbands, their work, their horses and goats, their children, work, the weather that complicated their lives, and work.

For the second book, we asked them to write about the one topic they'd avoided: other women. Who were their friends, and why? If they had no

women friends, how did they persevere? We feared that comradeship between women might be too private to publicize, but we were wrong; "in spite of the hard work, or maybe because of it, we found time for fun and friendship."

Women from sixteen Western states and three Canadian provinces told us stories of friendship both fulfilling and disappointing. From more than a thousand manuscripts, we selected essays and poems by 148 women. Houghton Mifflin published *Woven on the Wind: Women Write About Friendship in the Sagebrush West* in 2001.

Tattered Cover, Denver's legendary independent bookstore, generously hosted our May publication party during a typical plains spring blizzard. One writer snowshoed several miles from her mountain home, hoping to hitch a ride—only to find the highway blocked by drifts. Still, dozens of women gathered with our new editor from Boston to read and celebrate. Later, in a newsletter, we joyfully shared the warm reviews with our contributors, strengthening and deepening our bonds with one another. The writing "carries the weight of a communal essay," said one well-known writer, on the book's jacket. Women who live a long way from bookstores and malls exchange copies, celebrating friendship the way our forebears did when they helped each other butcher a buffalo or stitch a quilt.

"Telling stories. Keeping faith."
—MARY SOJOURNER

A community of women has arisen around the three anthologies. With each new project, we refreshed past acquaintance and found new writers. These strong women "nurture not only their families but also their communities," and, like the books, will help preserve the truths of real Western lives for our future.

So the theme of the third collection arose naturally from the writing and connections created by the first two. We believe, with many of these writers, that women who can lead are no more important than women who follow: women who clean the churches, make sandwiches for firefighters and for mourners at funerals. We understand that "as a *group*, we are leaders." On occasion, it is appropriate to act alone, but sometimes our "power to be heard comes through community, not individuality." These books are one way that Western women, some of whom came here from other parts of the world, have united to provide support for one another and to make their voices heard.

We drove all over Nebraska, Colorado, the Dakotas, Montana, and Utah to promote *Woven*, and meanwhile we discussed ideas for a third anthology. We met contributors and readers in bookstores, county libraries, museums, coffee shops, book festivals, and in a huge concrete bunker that was

once an underground water tank but now serves as an art center. Everywhere, we joined a "convergence of women."

We'd planned to meet a Nebraska writer for lunch but arrived late, to find her family's feed store locked. At the local hotel café, a waitress said the woman usually ate lunch at home, and gave us directions. We chuckled at the familiar way a neighborhood keeps track of its residents.

In Billings, Montana, we read with contributors on the sale floor of a cattle auction barn. Many in the audience had never entered a sale barn before, so one contributor's husband, an auctioneer, conducted a mock sale to show how such sales proceed, and to start the performance. We explained that the entire floor of the ring—freshly washed for our appearance—is a scale that weighs the livestock as they are sold and flashes the total onto a large screen, to help buyers calculate their bids. We thanked our hosts for turning off the scale, so that our combined tonnage was not revealed to the audience.

> *"And once we started speaking out, we were never silent again."*
> —MARY ZELINKA

Crazy Woman Creek collects 158 selections in prose or poetry from 153 contributors, portraying diverse communities in twenty-one states and one Canadian province, all west of the Mississippi River.

From the rainy mountains of Oregon to the cornfields of Iowa, from the wheat fields of Saskatchewan to the arid plains of Texas, we solicited women's writing. For the first time in this anthology series, we relied on technology, e-mailing our call for manuscripts to twenty-two states, Mexico, and Canada's Western provinces. We flung our electronic message out to thousands of individuals and organizations focused on writing, reading, storytelling, journalism, rural life, the West, women's studies, and other fields; to radio stations, newspapers, magazines, publishers, and bookstores; to state and regional arts councils, extension services, and on-line discussion groups. Nearly four hundred women responded, sending us almost seven hundred answers in the form of essays and poems.

Though writers were not allowed to submit their contributions by e-mail, we did ask for and receive some submissions on computer disks; in certain cases, we were able to transfer documents directly to our own computers without having to retype them, one of the time-devouring chores of the earlier books. We also worked with some writers on their manuscripts by e-mail. We met to discuss the anthology only once and conducted the rest of our business electronically, despite computer gremlins and outages caused by floods, blizzards, Wyoming wind, and fire.

We cannot say that "we never left anyone out," but we are grateful also to the women who submitted pieces we are not able to publish. Their

thoughts helped shape our perceptions of this book, and their writings inspired agonizing debates. Our most difficult task was deleting pieces we relished, in order to adhere to our contractual word limit.

We delight in the diversity of these texts. Women whose lives differ from ours demonstrate that the West is no fantasy paradise where everyone dresses, votes, and thinks alike. As editors, we must present the truth, because we answer to our contributors. Some of these women are downright cantankerous!

As in our two previous collections, in *Crazy Woman Creek* we allowed submissions to determine content and organization, and we might have created several other books from the available materials. As one contributor writes, "making community is like making rag rugs: it requires a lot of stitching-together, a decision not to regard any one scrap of fabric as essential to the design." Every one of us, and all the brilliant things we say and write, are merely scraps in a crazy quilt. Remove one of us, ten of us, thousands of us, and the design will change, but the creation will be braided anew, the gap filled by another rag or ribbon, so that the community remains strong and beautiful.

> *"People opened their arms . . . gathered us in."*
> —PHYLLIS DUGAN

In "Women Driving Pickups," the writers focus on spontaneous community, groups likely to gather without regular meeting dates, agendas, or officers. Many of these true stories involve a change of perspective: an Alaskan town hosts Vietnamese refugees; a "posse of lesbians" helps a newcomer; San Francisco commuters ignore their squabbles to rally around a larger issue.

Sometimes, cooperation converges on need: a village in Washington conspires to keep a retarded woman safe; Canadian women provide food baskets; a hippie mother in California creatively supports her local library; an Afghan and a Mormon help a new mother of twins. Some women meet in a hot tub to visit, others in pickups or laundromats; a rancher reports on the reactions of cowboys when she chooses horse work over housework.

The title was inspired by Ashley Coats's essay. This part of the book reflects, metaphorically as well as realistically, that "surge of understanding" which may flash between people even when they seem to be speeding down the road in separate vehicles, going different directions.

> *"A unity of women."*
> —GRACE E. REIMERS KYHN

"Hallelujah and a Show of Hands" centers on organized groups, men and women who meet at set times for a specific purpose. Contributors tell

stories of the past and present, and sometimes they consider the future. Here, too, are women impatient with the restrictions of organized groups, women who want to "effect change rather than discuss it," who urge us to "get off the Internet and into the streets." An assortment of societies function or fail in these pages: a New Age commune, gatherings of Buddhists in Nebraska, Benedictine nuns in Colorado, and Hutterites in South Dakota. One writer describes how women ran a Wyoming railroad, until they lost their jobs when the men returned from war. Women recall harmony found at the drugstore, at the beauty parlor, at a powwow, in a sewing circle. Groups cooperate in running races and in saving a historic meeting hall, meet to discuss books or write them, to ride horses, organize funerals, support rape victims.

We found the title in Helen M. Wayman's droll look at a group of church women confronting change, the poem "Hallelujah! Faith Circle!" The bickering "Lutern" women behave in pretty standard fashion for the West, resisting transformation as long as possible—but they also persist until they reach a compromise.

> **"This twist of women, Bonded by our hands, Our hearts."**
> —LORA K. REITER

"Cowgirl Up, Cupcakes" recognizes that whereas we seek membership in some groups, other societies select us. Though the choice of fellowship may not be ours, we often find possibilities we hadn't considered. These writers find humor, despair, admiration, or hope in characters tossed together by circumstance or genetics.

Contributors write of those who build on painful experiences to create joy and who learn to relish the eccentricity of neighbors they never would have chosen. Others scrutinize their families, musing on benefits and obligations gleaned in weeding the garden, harvesting food, teaching an appreciation for language, or "doin' for the less fortunates."

The writers discover communion between saints and spirits in a cemetery; between a hospital patient and the nurses and aides who care for him; among strangers who rally around a cancer patient; between women who are addicted to gambling. Women write of the opportunities inherent in the natural cycles of birth and death, health and illness. Time and memory connect the five-year-old helping her grandmother make tortillas to the grandma passing down tortilla lore. Embracing age, women tell how they learned to create their own companionship. In crises, these women have found an astonishing array of avenues for supporting one another.

The title emerges from Ellen Vayo's story about the efforts of her mother and the Ladies of Charities to combat hardship after World War II. When times were tough, these women didn't put up with whining, but their ef-

forts left a legacy of laughter and toughness their children remember and practice.

"How does a community originate?"
—JUDY ANN

This book began with the real West and its women, and with writing collected in the two previous books, both published by Houghton Mifflin. Instead of erecting monuments, the writers in these pages demonstrate community connections in story form. We expect the books to provide inspiration for our descendants a lot longer than the average fad does, whether it's a trendy bestseller or a marble obelisk.

Traveling together, the editors admired miles of countryside, saw hundreds of *Real Estate for Sale* signs, and noticed malls and subdivisions attempting to encircle small towns. "Like the View?" says one sign; "Buy it!" We discussed the idea that anyone can own nature and asked how this trend will affect the Western communities where we live and work. Moseying along in Flora the Explorer, spitting dust, we pondered the future of Westerners and wannabes in city and country and began this third collaboration.

After all, "woven inside women's ways of knowing" are centuries of survival in spite of tragedy. Whether we live in a subdivision or on a ranch, a logging hamlet or a tourist burg, we want to be in a place where neighbors mourn one another's losses, help each other build new lives, work together to resolve conflicts without rending the fabric of the neighborhood. When we succeed in identifying with fellow citizens, "the community wins," and we all benefit.

Crazy Woman Creek became a wild and crazy gathering of viewpoints as complex as the Western landscape and the women—and men—who inhabit it. Contributors may contradict each other, but they manage to get along as well as folks ever have in the West.

As traditional Western communities are subdivided and expanded, we wonder if new residents can ever settle comfortably into old neighborhoods. To do so, they must banish the myths and see the reality, understand that such places are not static photographs of folks in big hats on horses. We have all seen what one contributor describes as "the ugly face this normally friendly little town can wear." We know that Western communities, like gatherings of people anywhere, can be bleak or cozy.

All three of us editors have lived most of our lives in the kind of traditional rural neighborhoods described by some contributors in the writings that follow. We recognize and love "that hometown sense of belonging, that like-mindedness" some writers report in the pages to follow. But through their writing we've also met women whose backgrounds are entirely dif-

ferent from ours, whose only bond to the land was their grandparents' reminiscences about farm life. They, too, speak in these pages; they care deeply about the West and want to belong. Have they arrived too late? We hope not.

Some of these writers argue that a community can exist only in a particular place and must be composed of people who knew your grandparents and your parents. In many ways, we identify with this opinion, as can many Westerners who grew up in the sheltered assurance of a long and settled family history. But most of us can no longer expect our families to live in one place for several generations.

Are our lively Western communities doomed to exist only as brown photographs of a flat landscape in a dusty book? Will future residents see the West through sepia-toned spectacles?

The stories and poems in *Crazy Woman Creek* offer lively and varied views of the ways people come together in today's West, and ideas that may help us take a fresh look at the idea of community. Perhaps members of Western communities can create new ways of living together in settlements where residents accept the past as well as the future. Those rural settlements where we grew up were founded on the belief that "being part of a community is much more than owning property within its boundaries." Like several other contributors, we don't think that idea is obsolete.

As other writers note, bemoaning our losses and hating newcomers do not improve a community. If folks who can't stand change just move away, they alter more than one neighborhood. Some women write about the challenge of staying in one place, adjusting as it reconstructs itself. Even when we feel most powerless, they say, we are not alone. An Idaho sheep rancher, for example, figured out how to educate newcomers, instead of cursing them. She now says, "In our community, we are all making new friends."

Can neighborliness survive even as our landscape is being bulldozed and paved over? Before we can answer that question, we need to get acquainted. In order to participate as members of any community, we need to exchange our stories, to teach, and to learn. In this book, some women write guidelines for retaining or re-creating the best qualities of old-time Western neighborhoods.

Everyone knows parables that can show us a path when we are lost, can heal us, recall us to our best selves. Telling stories from our lives, say the experts, helps us understand the events that have happened to us, no matter how difficult they have been. Sharing our burdens may assuage our loneliness, allow us to support one another without self-pity.

Will getting to know our neighbors help us arbitrate a better future for our communities? We cannot keep our settlements forever in the past, though our mothers may have lived and died on the banks of Crazy

Woman Creek without complaint, and without considering the implications. But if we invite a new neighbor in for a visit, or help him change a flat tire, we might begin to help people in our neighborhood decide *together* how much change we can accept. Newcomers and longtime residents may learn to live in peace, even if compromise means we must change Bitch Basin to Mountain Meadow Estates.

One contributor remarks, about a tragic story told and retold in her town, that "we needed to draw the suffering of our neighbors into our lives and to claim their pain before we could begin to heal as individuals and as community." Repeating such a story, she implies, is not merely gossip, but a way of learning about each other, one that leads to the discovery of how much we have in common. Human nature tugs us toward one another. To determine the best possible future for Western settlements—or any other neighborhood—we need to get closer than we can by cell phone or a distant wave through the windshield.

Another woman writes that she felt isolated in precisely the kind of subdivision many rural residents fear will replace our wide-open spaces. "Suddenly, community mattered," she writes. Searching for connections, she recalled how her mother and grandmother took casseroles to the bereaved and listened to their sadness. At first, she felt awkward copying her elders' gestures; she thought, "Maybe if I practiced, I would get better at it." And she did.

Creating connections requires work, commitment, and time. Just moving in isn't enough; membership in a group or community has value only if it is earned in those countless rituals that make up our busy days. Offer a lift to a neighbor, visit with the pharmacist; small gestures splice us together, weaving bonds that become friendship and cooperation. A resident of a unique Iowa enclave says, "Those who stay and prosper are the ones who come to cherish Amana for what it is. They join in, take part, and help out." Any group could benefit from such involvement, as could the people who choose to participate—a mutual benefit.

> *"There is no power struggle here; we are all givers."*
> —JUDY ANN

Like the two collections of writing that preceded it, *Crazy Woman Creek: Women Rewrite the American West* has been created by its contributors. We asked women to draw upon their experiences living west of the Mississippi River, to write a good and true story about contemporary women in any community, whether it's a place, an organization, or a spontaneous gathering. Although men were not excluded, we wanted stories focused on women, and on how their actions affect others. Our yardstick would be, as always, authenticity and quality of writing.

Evaluating manuscripts, we were alert for writing that grew out of strong convictions, whether we agreed with the conclusions or not. If a particular subject drew the attention of several writers, we worked to eliminate repetition and to select the most appropriate account. We loved brilliantly written compositions, but we also appreciated the work of less experienced writers whose beliefs and emotions were an important component in the collective voice. We asked ourselves how to balance prose and poetry, how much attention to pay to geographical distribution. Eventually, we agreed, the true stories we chose had to possess a quality we call *heart*.

"Listen up sister."
—SUREVA TOWLER

Historical legends recounting the source of the name of Wyoming's Crazy Woman Creek, running through the wild north-central region, are published at www.travelwyoming.com, but local chronicles are more informal and more vivid.

One Wyoming writer told us that when the family crossed it, her husband always said, "Look, kids! There's your mom's creek: Crazy Woman Creek." He encouraged their kids to call it "Mom Creek." She's not married to him anymore, and she grits her teeth when she tells that story.

Margaret Smith, who lives near the creek, tells us that after the crazy woman of legend died, her spirit inhabited the canyon walls. "For many years, people in the region could point to a woman's face in the rocks," she says. The woman looked as if she were crying—or screaming.

Jane Wells, a contributor to this anthology, also lives nearby, and calls Crazy Woman Canyon "a monument of tumbled granite, rushing snow melt, deep shadows, and brilliant sunlight."

Perhaps the canyon has become a cenotaph to one woman driven mad by grief, and the tales of today's inhabitants are fitting honors for all the nameless women of the West. Recalling the legends, keeping the stories alive can remind us of the power we women share.

Every winter day, Jane Wells leaves her bed before dawn and in the moonlight pitches hay to the horses, breaks ice in the creek with an ax, and does other ranch chores before heading to her day job in town. She's standing behind the information desk at the museum when some tourists from Germany ask if she knows the origin of the name of Crazy Woman Canyon.

She takes a deep breath and looks them straight in the eye. "As a matter of fact," she says, "I do. It was named after me." That's the attitude represented by this book.

"Start learning now *how to make community."*
—LISA HELDKE

A Western woman might be independent enough to kiss a bull or brave enough to tickle a bear, and she tells her own stories. She is part of the tradition that produced *Crazy Woman Creek,* but she's rewriting the West with her words as well as her actions.

If you can't see women in your neighborhood who are creating community, look in the mirror. "You will be held accountable," if not by others, certainly by yourself. Community requires you "to be your sister's keeper, to accept aid when you need it, and to offer help when it is your responsibility—woman to woman." One contributor reminds herself, "A simple, hand-prepared meal is one way back to oneself. I need to remember this." Let us all remember.

Another contributor asserts, "One of the great myths of our age is that community is something you belong to, not something you work for." Why shouldn't the principle apply in families, in city neighborhoods, anywhere? Simply moving our belongings is not joining a community. Being at home requires us to contribute.

Many of us in the rural West, as elsewhere, have "learned that to live near each other meant more than just sharing an address. We also had a responsibility to each other." Being responsible to one another can work in an apartment block, in a subdivision, in any group. Several writers focused precisely and movingly on "the price we pay for alienation and disconnection, the price we pay when a community shuts its eyes." We've all seen examples of this particular expense in our communities.

Let's not wait for a disaster to pull together. Let's gather our energy and purpose, "enter the circle that we may dance." Connections can be woven of few and fragile threads. Remember: "it's your community if you are willing to work for it."

> **"We write into the storm together."**
> —LUCY ADKINS

Cowgirl up, cupcakes, and create community wherever you are, even if you and your confederates are way beyond Crazy Woman Creek.

LINDA M. HASSELSTROM
Cheyenne, Wyoming, 2003

I

WOMEN DRIVING PICKUPS

JENNIFER KAYL SOULE *Banana Bread and Coffee*

Moved by some natural rhythm, they gravitate
in midmorning or midafternoon
toward one home,
these busy women who believe
that banana bread and coffee
are the basic ingredients for communion
in South Dakota, where women hold
together families, neighborhoods,
communities, and each other with food.
The coffee is black like the dirt,
the banana bread warm,
the conversation lively.
This is no Ladies Aid. The women have birthed
and raised dozens of kids, buried,
married, and divorced all combinations
of parents, children, husbands, and grandparents,
sheltered grandchildren and strangers, survived
losses and coped with chronic ailments—
while working as waitresses, teachers,
secretaries, clerks, and office managers.
They have wept rain barrels and laughed
their way through seasons of life as rough
as the weather on the Great Plains—
where friends still circle the wagons
seeking nourishment and strength together.
No need for therapists
or twelve-step programs.
Here an old touchstone—the weekday kitchen—
is going the way of the tall prairie grasses.
But for now the recipes are all shared,
the sorrows all supported, and joys
all passed around with pictures
truly looked at. Visiting daughters welcome.
The society of banana bread and coffee
has a secret it is willing to share:
"At the first sign of trouble, put on the coffee
and break out the banana bread."

KAREN ARMSTRONG ✑ **The Shearing**

Cool fog swirled in a chilling wind as I stepped out of my warm car and pulled up my collar. *What am I doing here?* I thought. The shearer was already busy on a bleating sheep, and thirty more were penned waiting their turn for a spring haircut.

I was there because of my interest in spinning wool into yarn. I wanted to see the whole sequence that started with a woolly sheep in the pasture and ended with a fine hand-spun article. Since I was new to this part of the country, my spinning instructor at the junior college had told me about a shearing at dawn at a woman's nearby ranch.

So there I was, not knowing anyone but determined to help. When I heard, "I need some help with this ram," away I went to join in convincing a large, reluctant ram that he was not going to slaughter, but only to see a nice lady about a new look for spring. The shearer was standing up straight for a minute to rest her back muscles. The talk was quiet and mostly about moving sheep into and out of the pens. But there was also friendly chatter and laughter among people sharing an experience and getting a job done.

As the sun began to break through the fog and the wind slowed, I studied the scene. The entire crew, including the owner, was made up of women doing rough, sometimes bruising, work without a man in sight. This was a new, exhilarating experience for me. I went away from that shearing with a heightened feeling of empowerment, confidence, and companionship I have felt only among women.

To keep the experience alive, I joined a group of spinners, some of whom I met that foggy morning. As we spin, I feel a close bond with these hearty women who so freely share their skills and enthusiasm.

VIRGINIA BENNETT ✑ **Object of Affection**

Her name struck me first. Someone named Daisy Lou had to be a sweetheart. She resides in Twisp, Washington, a small community in the heart of the Methow Valley, guarded by craggy North Cascades peaks and flowing, rounded foothills. Twisp is a secret place, not written about in travel magazines, and Daisy Lou is the secret heart of Twisp.

Riding her one-speed bicycle from drugstore to post office, health food store to library and community center, then back again, Daisy Lou weaves behind her a silken thread to connect them all. Some ignore her presence and importance, but many friends watch over this short, slightly chunky (perfect for hugging), red-haired, smiling lady as she pedals through the streets.

When I first met Daisy Lou, she slid her dancing eyes my way and asked, "When is *your* birthday?"

I answered, "February eighteenth. When is yours?"

"February nineteenth," she answered, as though she had already known. But how could she?

Thus began our friendship, amusingly love-filled on my side, often intense and obsessive on hers. She began to call me regularly. She remembered what went on in my life better than I did.

"Where you going next month?" she might ask.

"I'm not going anywhere next month, Daisy Lou."

"Aren't you going to Denver in January?"

She was right. She remembered what I said because what I say is important to Daisy Lou.

Daisy Lou asks each person she meets about important dates: birthdays, anniversaries, children's birthdays. And then she records the day, month, and year in her miraculous memory. Once, at the small office supplies store, when I mentioned that Daisy Lou remembered my wedding anniversary, a woman responded, "Oh, she knows the birthdays of each one of my five children."

Daisy Lou has the town wrapped around her freckled little finger. Everyone responds to her needs. If I don't phone her when I should, the next time I speak to her, she asks with a pout, why not. When I travel, she always says, "Send me a postcard if you can." She has quite a collection.

An elementary school teacher revealed to me that she was sitting in a faculty lounge one day when Daisy Lou walked in and greeted everyone. When she departed, one woman said, "You know, she calls me every night," to which each person in the room responded, "She calls me every night, too!" The group concluded that Daisy Lou must call thirty people each night. "No wonder," my friend remarked, "she only talks for five minutes."

One woman in Twisp said to me, "I don't mind Daisy Lou calling each night. To me, she represents the epitome of a small, tightly knit community. Daisy Lou never would have been allowed to live on her own in a big city. She would have been institutionalized years ago."

After that, I began to observe how Twisp watched over Daisy Lou. Fran, the postmistress, asked, "Virginia, will you ask Daisy Lou to wear her helmet when she rides her bike? I know she will do whatever you ask her to do." Now Daisy Lou wears her red helmet as she pedals up and down the streets and across the busy state highway. (I worry about that highway; so many people hurrying through do not know our Daisy Lou!)

She has many caregivers—some hired, some volunteers. Daisy Lou picks up the mail for the library, and the librarian helps her select books on horses, cowboy poetry, and California. Daisy Lou shows her gratitude by

threading plastic beads onto stretchy string, forming necklaces for each of her friends. In New Orleans, women are given strands of gaudy beads for baring their breasts. In Twisp, women are given necklaces for showing their hearts.

Daisy Lou loves to have someone sit on the floor with her and look through her photo albums or watch a video. I love the beauty and simple longing of this woman in her mid-sixties, who wants nothing more from life than to have a friend spend time with her.

Daisy Lou is prone to obsess on one person within her world, and she set her fancy on me. In terms of time spent and love shared, I've never given her as much as many others in the community, but when I moved from the valley, she was devastated. Her friends and caregivers were worried. They told me that for the first winter I was away, she sat in her house, on the floor, creating from her red and white Legos a replica of my new house (from pictures I'd sent) and waiting for my phone calls. I tried to call often, and I sent her cards and letters. At Christmas, I sent her toys.

A concerned family member, trying to help, suggested that I cut myself off from Daisy Lou. Although it made some sense, the thought hurt me. I made many long-distance calls to her family, friends, and caregivers asking if this was a good idea, but I finally decided that I could not do it. I am in Daisy Lou's life for the long haul.

As I was building a new life in California, I received many postcards and calls asking me to write to Daisy Lou. I explained to each person that I did call and write Daisy Lou often. Yet Daisy Lou had told all her friends to ask her Virginia to write, and the blessed people of Twisp took the time to let me know. They are the heroes of this story—the folks in Twisp, where Daisy Lou remains, safe and cared for, a symbol of old-fashioned community and family.

MARIAN D. PETERS *At the Line Dance Café*

As on each Monday afternoon
in the Senior Center dining room,
twenty sprightly women
stomp, pivot, pigeon-toe,
spin, hitch, twinkle,
scuff, shuffle, heel-and-toe,
happy to be dancing
even without partners.

Silver-tressed Sophia
fans her denim skirt;

Paulina, in a pewter do,
steps with hands on hips;
Harriet, with golden hair,
flings her arms out wide
as dancers do in *Chorus Line;*
copper-coifed Connie
vines in cowgirl boots.

The strum and twang
of "Sleeping Single in a Double Bed"
dies down. Some women sigh.

"I sleep single in a double bed.
Since my husband died, I sleep
one week on half the bed,
the next week on the other.
I only wash sheets every other week."

"Why doesn't somebody write
'Sleeping Double in a Single Bed'?
I slept that way in the old days."

"Time for 'Let Your Love Flow';
five! six! seven! eight!"

Step right, Vine right, Step right, Kick left,
Step left, Vine left, Step left, Kick right,
Back right, Back left, Back right, Rock right–Hitch left,
Rock left, Rock right, Step left, Pivot left–Clap.

"Good for your arthritis!"

CAROLINE ARLEN *Posse to the Rescue*

The doorbell rings. It's Jake. Who's Jake? Hell if I know. He just shows up in his unbuttoned plaid shirt, with gold chains tangled in his hairy chest. He removes his crisp white cowboy hat and grins. "Howdy. Seen you move in."

I stuff my blistered hands in my pockets. "You watched all that?"

"Yeah, I live over there." He points to the duplex across from mine. "Just moved here from Florida. I have my own business." He puts his hand up on the door frame above my head. "My psychic told me you'd be com-

ing." Jake lets out a sputtering little giggle, then wipes the spittle from his mustache. "You're a Gemini, right?"

"No, a writer."

His brow furrows.

I say, "Listen, I gotta unpack."

He gives me his most practiced smirk. "See ya 'round, then."

When the doorbell rings the next morning, it's Harvey, the plumber. "Gotta crawl under your house, ma'am. Landlord sent me to fix the water heater." Harvey looks at the mudroom, gathers up piles of strewn clothes, and dumps them on the living room floor. Harvey is short and stocky but kind of flattened, as if he is the product of millennia of genetic adaptations to crawlspaces. He tightens his yellow bandanna around the top of his head and disappears through the trapdoor.

A ruckus of clanging tools and verbal abuse ensues. After a while, I realize someone is knocking. It's a woman, probably in her mid-thirties like me. "I'm Fran," she says. She is large and sturdy, with short-cropped hair. "Uh," she says, then laughs, and her eyes sweeten. "Well, I want to say 'Hi, I'm you're new neighbor.' But also, Lilly says she heard something strange under the duplex?"

"Plumber."

Harvey sticks his mud-caked head out of the trapdoor. "This is a goddamn mess down here!" Fran says goodbye with a wriggle of her fingers.

Harvey walks into the furniture-crammed living room, straightening his yellow bandanna as if that's the only thing off about his appearance. "I tell ya," he says, "with so many outsiders swarming into Durango, developers are just throwing up these garbage pails for buildings."

"Sorry," I say, opening the door for him.

"Hey, you didn't build it."

"No, I mean for moving here."

He holds a mud-caked hand up to his mouth. "Just get divorced?"

I nod.

He says, "Want to meet me at Farquahrt's for happy hour?" I breathe in but can't think of how to respond. There is a clump of rotted dirt on his bottom lip. He says, "Okay, maybe another time."

The other half of Jake's duplex is owned by a woman named Kat, a high school English teacher, but you wouldn't think it by the language she used against her flat tire the other morning. I often pass Kat as I'm going down to our mailboxes at the bottom of the road. She is a little gal with a determined walk and the focus of a baseball pitcher; she rarely sees anything but what's straight ahead of her.

One time I notice she's crying, so I touch her arm. "What's wrong?"

She says, "I lost the stupid key to my stupid mailbox." Then she laughs. "But it's not just that. My cat got into a fight, and I can't afford the vet bill. And my roof's leaking. It's just all the shit, you know? And having to deal with it alone."

"I can pick the lock," I offer, and she accepts. Kat's got huge blue eyes, slightly reddened. A messy ponytail of blond hair sticks out of the top of her head like a fountain. If the saying "cute as a bug's ear" ever applied to anyone, she'd be the girl.

Kat repays me with a bowl of homemade chicken soup. I've never had homemade chicken soup. We eat on her floor. She says, "My ex got the dining set." Then she looks over at me and laughs. "Isn't it all so strange? I mean, nobody wants to be alone. But here we are, two hot babes eating chicken soup on my floor."

I say, "We could visit Jake. I bet he has furniture."

Kat chokes on her soup.

At night, the temperature plummets as the autumn sun weakens and sets. I long for the warmth of a person; a real voice. Not the phone voices of my friends back East who think I'm crazy for moving here. Or of family, so questioning and concerned.

It's Friday. Happy hour at Farquahrt's is the place to go, people say — people like Kat, whom I've met but am not yet friendly enough with to be invited to join them. I'll go there alone. Yes, I will. It's a matter of survival.

At the mailboxes Saturday morning, Kat pokes my arm. "Saw you at happy hour. Those guys were all over you like stink on fish. I believe you're the catch of the day."

"Yuck."

Kat laughs. "There are so few women in Durango, the men go crazy competing with each other for the new ones. Try to enjoy it."

When the phone rings a few weeks later, I think it's my landlord calling for the December rent, but it's Todd. Who's Todd? He says, "I'm the guy who was standing by the rail at Farquahrt's. In the black tank top? Black cowboy hat. Sort of stank of horse manure."

"Oh, yeah." I laugh.

We go to the hot springs. He looks kind of funny wet. Big, tanned arms hanging off a pale, hairless chest. Water glistens on his red beard.

Todd's actually heard of James Joyce, and even, yes, remembers, yes, the Penelope chapter in *Ulysses*. I dip my head back into the hot water. Yes. The blackness around him steams.

Jake rings my doorbell the next morning. He's wearing a T-shirt cut just above his hairy navel. "I saw him," Jake says, ominously. He looks past me into the living room, then grabs my wrists. "Did I tell you I own my own business? I own Miami real estate. You could give up nursing!"

"I'm not a nurse!"

As he lets loose a high-pitched giggle, I close the door.

I'm on the porch drinking beer with Fran and her roommate, Lilly, when Todd comes to pick me up. We go to a seedy bar outside of town and play pool for shots of tequila. When Todd's drunk, he says, "You really shouldn't hang out with your neighbors."

"Why?"

"They're lesbos. This is the West. Traditional values. I mean, I'm pretty open-minded myself, but in a small town like this, you gotta worry about your reputation."

When we leave, it's snowing. My heart meets the lightness of it. It's my first winter outside a city and sooty, unnatural snow in about ten years. When Todd pulls into my driveway, I ask him in. He wants to see my office upstairs. My bedroom is also upstairs. I know where we're going.

As I lie with my head in the depression beneath his shoulder, someone pounds on the door. I sit up and look out the window. Jake stands in the fallen and falling snow, looking up at my bedroom. He takes in a deep breath, then rams my door.

"Shit," Todd says, putting on his pants. "It's my wife." Jake rams the door again.

"Your wife?"

Jake rams the door again. This time the door hinges give out, and the thud of wood and Jake reverberate up the staircase. When Jake runs into my bedroom, Todd ducks into the bathroom.

"Get out!" I scream, and grab my gun from under the mattress. Jake runs back down the stairs. Todd opens the bathroom door. I turn the gun on him. "That applies to you, too."

The next morning, I lean my unhinged door in the area of the doorway and slip out to get my mail. Fran and Lilly, a lithe girl, are shoveling the porch. "Thanks," I say, walking tentatively across the slick boards.

Fran leans on her shovel. "We don't know how to be tactful about this. But if you need help with your door . . ."

"Just ask," Lilly finishes. It's early morning, and already her eyeliner has smeared her pink cheeks. She sticks her snow shovel into the bank, barely impacting it, and tosses off about a teaspoon of snow.

I go back into my condo to grab my tool chest. As they help me rehinge my door, the snow keeps falling, thick. They glance back at it as if it were evil, but I think, *Bring it on. Coat me.*

In the morning, a light snowfall, like dust motes, pilfers the sunshine, but by noon it's snowing hard. After every two or three feet, I meet Fran and

Lilly on the porch for the shoveling ritual. Every now and then, the accumulation on our A-frame roof cascades onto the porch, and we shovel harder.

Across the road, Kat shovels her and Jake's porch. Our two duplex condos are built back into opposing hillsides, with a gully for a dirt road between. Our facing front porches rest precariously on tall two-by-fours. As each cascade from the roofs falls onto the porches, the snow packs against our windows, against the porch rails, weighing heavily on the two-by-fours.

Despite all our shoveling, the porch snowpack rises to our waists. The next roof slide puts the snowpack above us. Lilly gives up the fight.

I say I've got to quit, too. I've got a date with somebody I met in the ski pass office.

"A date? In this weather?"

I say, "You've got somebody to hibernate with."

Aaron shows up in shorts and Birkenstock sandals. He wipes the windshield. "No heater," he says.

We go to a pub. As soon as he says "dude," I know I want to go home. But he wants to talk about his rich, mean parents, in Vail, who caused him to turn to ski racing, which is a bummer because chicks want a man with a real job.

When we get back outside, snow has so filled Main Street we can't tell what's pavement and what's sidewalk. We tie my scarf to his wiper blade, and I pull on one end as he pulls on the other. I ask him to let me out at the bottom of the road. I don't want to spend the rest of the night pushing him out of a drift.

Headlights torch Kat's snow-packed porch as a truck pulls outs. A tousled Kat stands in the doorway. When the truck's headlights pass over me, slipping and slopping up the road, Kat waves and yells, "Wait!" then runs inside. She comes out in a puffy orange ski suit, the edge of her nightie sticking out of the top.

I help her drag out of her carport an old Finnish sled of her grandmother's. It's basically a straight-backed seat on two long runners. One person sits on the seat and one pushes, then jumps on the rails to coast. Kat is a little thing, so I push. And coast. The moon is full. We sail down Main Street.

And the snow keeps falling.

While we call for snowplows that can't come.

While we sleep.

In the morning, Aaron spins partly up the road, then honks his horn. I stand up from my permanently hunched shoveling stance and stretch backward. He yells, "Want to go skiing?"

"I can't!" I yell. "My porch is collapsing!"

He juts his head back, looking up at the snowpack. "Dude! That's serious!" He blinks. "Well, I'll catch ya later!"

And the snow keeps falling.

And, Jesus, it keeps falling.

And falling.

Lilly is sick, and Fran and I can't come close to keeping up with the cascades off the roof onto our precariously propped-up porch. Kat crawls up a ladder onto her roof.

"What the hell are you doing?" I yell.

"It's breaking in my roof!" She uses a broom to push the snowpack past the rain gutters.

I slog through the snow to Kat's condo and hoist my shovel up the ladder ahead of me. Kat, panting, says, "Thanks." Then, with a big smile, "So where are all our suitors now?"

On the roof, nothing surrounds us but stars. Stars, unobstructed, feel like a universe. Not necessarily warm, but touching warmth. I take in a deep breath, then slip and fall, taking much of the roof snow with me, hurtling onto the porch with an embedding crunch.

"Oh, my god! Are you okay?" Kat yells down. I wave one of my legs. She laughs and says, "Well, thanks for coming!"

The next night, I'm watching *The Fly*, the old version. The human-headed fly in the spider web is yelling, "Help me!" when a cascade off the roof buries the windows and the porch starts to crack. I shut off the TV and open my door. Fran is there. "I think we're in trouble," she says.

The snowpack is above our heads. We shovel through the night, sweat chilling when the wind blows. I can feel the porch swaying. Our efforts seem absurd. The porch is going to go. I collapse in the snow.

Fran looks down at me. "Okay, don't give up yet," she says, panting, and goes into her condo. She returns a few minutes later with steaming mugs of tea and sits beside me in the snow.

I say, "Tea? That's a big help."

She slurps. "It'll keep you going." And after a while, she says, "You know, I used to be real cynical. But now my take on the world is, good people recognize good people. And we help each other." She looks straight into my eyes.

I say, "You know I'm not gay, don't you?"

She laughs and nods. "Boy, did you just totally miss my entire point."

A truck, heading up our road, skids out on the wet snow, then backs up for another try. "They're here," Fran says.

I look at her questioningly.

"Our posse of lesbians."

The truck revs its engine and barrels up the drive, spinning up to our duplex. Five women pile out of the back, each with a snow shovel. Even-

tually, though it's still snowing, the porch stops creaking, and we move our efforts to Kat's porch.

Kat, in her orange ski suit, brings out a thermos of rum cider and a stack of plastic cups. She plugs in a tape player and starts wriggling and shoveling to the music. The "lesbos," at first so serious, now follow her lead, dancing and laughing—but most of all just good, old-fashioned shoveling snow.

B. J. BUCKLEY *Superior Laundry, Sheridan, Wyoming*

We could see it was bad when she stumbled in—
jeans covered in blood and that burnt-flesh smell, the wet red
clay to the hubs of her truck—
branding for three days running, she laughed,
and they weren't done yet, but if she didn't
wash these loads of clothes, tomorrow
they were doin' it buck-naked! And the
peach-fuzz ranch hand who held the door
blushed scarlet, said *Yes, ma'am,*
and ducked out quick. Her baby was asleep, thank God,
or thank the Devil, she didn't
care which—*Have you ever tried
to nurse on a horse?* And that did it
for the rest of the men, you never
saw cowboys ride out so fast.
We pulled our loads and left them wet, turned out her baskets
to sort on the floor—jeans here, shirts over there,
whites, *maybe*, pour in the bleach,
check all the pockets for pocketknives,
if it squishes don't look, just
throw it away—
Dee got her kid, and Jo took the truck
to the 4J Car Wash to hose off the mud,
and Connie came back
with the sequined dress she'd worn one time
to her high school prom. *Won't have to stuff
your top with socks!* And we stood that girl
in the laundry sink, washed her down
like a county fair horse. *Can't wear that gown
with boots! Ain't done! Gotta have them
strappy heels!* Shelley went home
and found her some, while the clothes
whirled around in every dryer,

while we sorted and folded and loaded
again, changed the baby, called out for food.
Nearly eleven we sent her home, sparkling like stars
in a party dress, and Jo said, *We ever see her again,*
we oughta ask her last name, I guess.

TAMARA E. ROGERS *Right Place, Wrong Time*

I pulled up alongside the huge, battered pickup, stalled in the gateway of the dry pasture, and rolled down my window.

"Need any help?" I called up to the young man in torn brown coveralls hunched over the engine under the raised hood.

"Nope. Just checking my timing."

Well, obviously his timing was way off, because he should have been doing repairs when he was in his ranch yard, where tools were at hand, not when he was out feeding cattle. But I didn't tell him that. I just returned his wave and stepped on the gas.

As I headed on up the highway, I thought about what I'd done. If I'd been in town or even on some other stretch of road, I wouldn't have stopped. Not only would I be hard-pressed to recognize a timing belt from a fan belt, but as a woman I no longer have the luxury of offering help to strangers. It's just too dangerous nowadays.

In this case, though, if the young man with poor timing had asked for a ride up the road, I would have welcomed him into my car without a qualm.

But I hadn't offered to help because I recognized him. I didn't. I had stopped because he'd been feeding cattle in my neighbor's pasture, and that was enough to vouch for him.

MARY FRANCES RENSTROM *Casserole Culture in Highlands Ranch*

The dead baby's photos lay in an album in my lap, and I was grappling with an appropriate response. I looked up to see Cassie's eyes, puffy with crying, her hand still clutching at a picture of the dead baby, Sierra. Her skinny husband, dressed in a mountaineering T-shirt and jeans, sat on the staircase with a vacant stare. Cassie's mom was in the kitchen, sniffing at my meager attempt at a casserole.

Finally, I found a few hoarse words and excused myself from the closet-like space the couple called home. Out on the street, I sucked in fresh air. I was really lousy at this visiting-the-sick-and-bereaved stuff. I wanted my mom. She would have known how to act and just what to say, and she would have made something edible for them, too.

In the car, I made up excuses for myself. Women aren't good at these things anymore. Nobody visits over the fence anymore, or hangs out at the laundry, or stops in for a spot of coffee. We are all too busy with our careers and our own lives to notice our neighbors. In my old Denver neighborhood, I knew all the neighbors' cars but wouldn't have recognized the drivers had I seen them out walking. Yet all I read about in the papers and women's magazines is that everyone is yearning for "community." Everyone wants it, I thought, but nobody is willing to make the effort to get it. That's not the way it used to be. My mom had community. So did her mom, and her mom's mom. Those old farmwomen had it without even thinking about it.

That fact hadn't concerned me as a young woman, but in my thirties I found myself with a house, a husband, and a newborn child. Suddenly, community mattered. I didn't know a single person besides my husband who would help me out in times of need. I could use a friend or two.

These thoughts crystallized when I returned to my hometown of Caldwell, Idaho, for my grandmother's funeral. For nearly a week, the doorbell of my parents' house rang incessantly.

Ding-dong. "Hi, Betty. I just have a little something for you." And in walked one of the most scrumptious cakes I'd seen in years.

Ding-dong. "Hi, Betty. I heard the news and just thought I'd bring by some dinner." Two savory-smelling dishes sailed past my nose, all cozily wrapped in their own custom-quilted carrying cases.

Soon Mom's kitchen was filled with cakes, pies, cookies, breads, sandwiches, and casseroles. Lots and lots of casseroles. Why people disparage them I do not understand. It was at that moment that the casserole was elevated in my mind to represent many things that are good: community, caring, love, empathy.

"Who are all these people, Mom?" I asked.

"Oh, just friends," Mom said. Hardly "just," I thought. These women were like blood sisters. My mom was enveloped in a lifetime's worth of friendships. And suddenly I was jealous—jealous of what my mother had and I didn't. I resolved then and there to become a casserole woman. Before I left, I asked Mom for a few recipes, and armed with a little stack of white file cards, I vowed to find community upon my return to the city.

I found it wasn't easy. When I left my job to stay home with my newborn, I left the only community I had known. But workplace community is a sham. As soon as you are gone, they forget about you, or worse, they talk about you. "Just too thin-skinned for the real world," I could hear them say. "Wants to stay home and play Mrs. Cleaver." I imagined them laughing. So I licked my wounds and began scouting the malls and parks for other "stay-at-homes," to no avail.

Finally, one day I read an ad in the paper for a new mothers' group that met monthly in a local church. They were all stay-at-homes looking for

some company. They were all from Highlands Ranch, which is not a ranch with steers or sheep, mind you, but a ranch made up of tens of thousands of nearly identical beige suburban tract houses. The "ranch" sprouted up out of the plains in less than a decade and features two- or three-car garages with attached homes. Cruising the ranch, all one notices is the mile upon mile of neat garages, jutting out in front of the houses, obscuring any windows or doors or other life as we might normally know it. I was surprised the ranch had any stay-at-homes at all, but I joined the group hoping that these new-style Western women had the same yearnings I did.

My prejudice against the Highlands Ranchers slowly diminished. The stay-at-homes donated a tree and an engraved brick to the local botanical gardens in little Sierra's name, and they joined the local fundraiser for sudden infant death syndrome (SIDS). That wasn't all. Time and again, this small group of young women visited nursing homes, cared for one another's children, delivered meals, and helped one another out in dozens of ways. Turns out many of them came from small Western towns, too. Some of them hailed from rural Alaska, Montana, and South Dakota. We gathered our little chicks in protective circles and hoped that, through our newly formed community, we could insulate our children from the brusqueness of the big city beyond. It was a small start, and we were certainly in the minority, but it gave me hope.

So that's how I ended up in Cassie's little house, hoping I was saying all the right things but knowing I wasn't. Even Mom's best casserole recipe wasn't enough to prepare me for that visit. But I had done it, and as the weeks passed, I felt all the better for it. Maybe if I practiced, I would get better at it. And I wasn't alone now. I had made new friends and new commitments.

Slowly, a new vision started forming in my mind. I imagined a new corps of young women marching toward a brighter future, remaking civilized society one recipe at a time. I imagined the quizzical "Gee, I didn't know anybody did that anymore" looks on our neighbors' faces when we delivered that banana bread or lasagna to their doorstep. And we would be proud: Proud we had overcome the barriers of loneliness and brusqueness in our modern world. Proud we had taken the time to show some kindness to someone else. Proud we'd proved them wrong—that there is good reason for some of us to stick around home. Proud we carried on the old traditions of our mothers and our grandmothers and all the pioneer women and small-town women and farm and ranch women who came before us. Proud to be casserole women in a sea of nameless, faceless, suburban tract houses called Highlands Ranch.

CELESTE HAVENER ✑ *Patchwork for Baby*

Having a baby is always a formidable experience. Having a son in a Rocky Mountain tourist town, nine hundred miles from home, was no exception. This child was the first to be born in many years, and the women of the community welcomed him with open arms. In truth, this was probably the first time I had truly experienced community in my twenty-eight years of living.

I waited tables at a restaurant that served as the focal point of the community, well attended by ranchers, tourists, and errant young adults.

The work was good, the wait staff and customers friendly and easygoing. It was Wyoming, though, so most of the residents kept you at arm's length, waiting to make sure you made it through a few winters before they made a place for you in their hearts. I was unaware of the importance of rituals such as baby showers to embroider a network of women—a network that was sincere and unquestioning. What was I to expect of a baby shower?

Instead of the ten people I expected, the ranch house was crammed with at least forty women—standoffish, close-mouthed ranch women rubbing elbows with crazy hippie types and chain-smoking cooks. In the center of the room was a playpen (itself a subtle safeguard for a young child coming home to a 150-year-old cabin) heaped with gifts. All of the women had been watching and monitoring my pregnancy, offering encouragement and advice. Opening the gifts, many handmade—quilts, sweaters, blankets—I was overwhelmed and amazed at the love emanating from the patchwork of women.

I knew my child was coming home to a community—a community that would be here for all of us.

MELINDA GREEN HARVEY ✑ *Wonderbra Soldiers*

Almost simultaneously
a score of SUVs arrive,
adorned with bumper stickers for Republican candidates.
Society girl drivers check their look in lit visor mirrors—
when mascaraed lashes, Lancômed lips, carefully careless hair
are perfect, they emerge
in the uniform of the season:
slouchy shoulder bags
white shirts tight across Wonderbra breasts
capri pants showing fake-tan legs
casually expensive shoes.

As though choreographed
they open passenger doors
and help small daughters climb down.
Juggling children, beach towels, birthday gifts
the entourage parades to the party room.
Inside
they discard gifts, towels, daughters
and stand in a clump, blocking the door.
Little girls,
all blond and dressed to echo their mothers,
strip down to their pink swimsuits
and march away, like a team of tiny synchronized swimmers.
Society girl perfume draped on the air
overpowers even the pool chemicals.
I start to leave, picking my way
past pink girls, gossipy moms.
Lacking their protective coloring
I am the one who becomes invisible.
Neither group moves aside:
they do not budge for one who is not
a soldier in their identical army.

DIANE MOLLESON *Picking Peaches*

The orchard stands just behind our house, more than sixty acres of small, carefully pruned apple, peach, and cherry trees. Living here, we now know that Bing and Rainier cherry trees produce fragrant white blossoms in April; peach trees turn pink. We also know the work never stops. Long after the last apples have been picked, crated, and hauled off to the store, workers are pruning trees, cleaning tractors, razing fields for new plantings. We know all this by watching these unfamiliar rituals—unfamiliar to my husband and me, who came from East Coast cities, but not to our son, who was only eighteen months old when we moved to our house in eastern Washington's shrub steppe country, near the Yakima River.

When I was growing up, home was a six-story brick apartment building between Roosevelt Avenue and Northern Boulevard in Jackson Heights, Queens, New York City. We were three blocks from the elevated subway line at Eighty-second Street, where train cars plastered with graffiti rumbled overhead. Two miles from LaGuardia Airport, we heard the steady drone of airplanes, a sound we learned to block out because it grew so familiar. Although our street was fairly quiet, tree-lined, and residential, a two-block walk north or south brought us to stores, movie theaters, ice-

cream parlors, diners, and restaurants. Walking east or west, we would pass churches, the synagogue, and the library, one of the biggest branches in the city system. Never quiet, the library could barely keep up with its thousands of users, many of them recent arrivals from Colombia, India, Korea, and Yugoslavia. Walking down one block, we could hear several different languages.

One rarely hears anything other than English in our neighborhood in Washington State. The "neighborhood" is really a subdivision of about eighty homes on the outskirts of a town called Richland. When we moved here six years ago, our house was bounded by orchards and undeveloped rangeland—short grasses, sagebrush, and tumbleweeds—and it felt as if we were living in the middle of nowhere.

By contrast, our neighbor Annette, who had been raised on a ranch in Oregon, found our suburban plots confining. She had the best garden in the neighborhood—shade trees, roses, poppies, hollyhocks, and alyssum spilling over her sidewalk. She alone managed to create a lush oasis in the desert. Free with gardening advice, she often brought over cuttings so even the city slickers could be coaxed into growing strawberries, lemon thyme, and creeping myrtle.

I soon met many of my female neighbors. One came to the door with freshly baked corn muffins. Others stopped me on the street when I was pushing my son in his stroller. Mary Ellen invited us to her neighborhood Christmas party, where, over homemade cookies, my son met a toddler who became his best friend.

The neighborhood was definitely the friendliest I had ever lived in. Perhaps it was because of its relative isolation. Perhaps it was because everyone had to band together to form a homeowners' association, since we all share an irrigation system for the outdoor sprinklers. Perhaps it was because much of the neighborhood was new; more than half the houses were built in the 1990s, and we were all newcomers in a sense. I was, and still am, one of the few Easterners and did not have that easy familiarity with people I barely knew.

Over the years, our neighborhood has come together to solve conflicts about the well and irrigation system. We've watched one another's children, many of them the same age, who play on the street or run in and out of one another's houses. When my son turned five, a neighbor, Sue, and her husband started a T-ball team. Practices were held on the neighborhood pump lot, near the well. Those not playing would climb the big willow tree to watch their friends and siblings.

Most of the children attend a local elementary school, now overcrowded. When there was talk of moving students from our neighborhood to another school a considerable distance away, more than 90 percent of the residents signed a petition opposing the idea. Many of the mothers at-

tended school board meetings, and we all spoke, planning what we would say to be sure we would mention different points. The school board ruled in our favor, and we like to think our neighborhood helped.

Because the town is fairly small, I see my neighbors everywhere: at the school, parks, library, grocery store, and T-ball games. I see them in the orchard picking cherries, peaches, or apples in season. Although the orchard and surrounding undeveloped land drew many to our neighborhood in the first place, sadly more and more of the orchard is disappearing under developers' bulldozers.

Still, we appreciate the forty or so acres of fruit trees that are left. In April, packing crates filled with bees line the dirt path alongside the budding trees. By June, the first crop—the cherries—are ready for picking, and people arrive in dusty pickups, boxes and buckets in hand, to choose the juiciest ones.

Ripening peaches mark the end of summer. By late August, the peaches fall so easily from their branches that some days it seems as if there is as much fruit on the ground as on the trees. When we step on the peaches, their skins fall off in one section. Our sandals make dust clouds as we walk home in the shade, carrying our bounty—peaches that still cost forty cents a pound because the eighty-two-year-old farmer who owns the orchard doesn't feel it would be right to charge more. It is often so hot and dry that a white haze hangs over the landscape, and in the distance we hear the tick of the irrigation nozzle as the water turns in slow arcs.

The last apples are harvested by special machinery in October, just as the trees are beginning to turn red and gold. A month later, the orchard looks almost plain—stark branches under a too-big sky. The eye is drawn to sudden movements—a pheasant flying to escape the farmer's dog, a hawk and its shadow.

We think of the orchard as we listen to the bulldozers and mixers razing the sagebrush and tall grasses of the undeveloped rangeland. We watch sidewalks, houses, and streetlights spring up out of the desert—an instant suburb built in a few months—and we wonder whether the orchard will face the same fate. Worrying about the orchard makes me realize that I've grown attached to this unfamiliar landscape and to this isolated town my son calls home.

ANITA TANNER ❧ Run Toward Suffering

For several years, I've walked two miles a day in my Colorado neighborhood. My neighbors have grown used to the sight of my diurnal blocks, no matter what the weather outside my home or inside myself. I dress accordingly and make my way.

Less than a month ago, my husband of thirty-five years died at home of colon and liver cancer, ten months after the diagnosis. During that year, every day, I kept walking—part of the regimen that still helps me deal with the reality I'm facing.

After the diagnosis, the shock of cancer became evident on the faces of people I met in stores, at church, at the public library. I grew used to that look: the frightened uneasiness over what to say, usually accompanied by a swift glance and then stony silence.

When hospice came to sign us up, the nurse questioned me about my religion and what kind of support my church was rendering. In abject honesty, I stated my disappointment. "Churches don't do well with terminal illness," she responded.

But some of my neighbors, none of whom belong to my church, ran out when they saw me on my daily walks—just to say they were sorry. One woman I hardly knew came around a corner in a rush toward me, saying, "I know you're suffering." That was all, four simple words, but I somehow felt lighter, as if my burden being recognized and validated made me slough off pounds right there in the street.

Six months after the cancer diagnosis, the first woman from my church visited my home. She came apologetically, saying she knew me to be a very private person. I voiced my thankfulness for her courage in coming and confided the lessons I'd been learning about how to comfort those who mourn, something I'd never been good at myself.

We talked about how going into pain is never easy, but it turns out to be the healthier approach. Healthy suffering and healthy dying are not contradictions in terms.

I've learned a lot the past year about spontaneous compassion, how some people are so full of it, not afraid to cry with someone. Others—like my previous self—are afraid to face the truth of some situations, not wanting to remind a person of his suffering, not knowing what to say. Even churches run away from what they imagine as undue suffering, not knowing where to put it, how to reconcile it with the God they believe in.

The hospice nurse, Shelley, and the massage therapist, Rose, though acquainted with my husband and me for only three months, cried with me when my husband died. They came to his funeral, invite me to lunch now, call and check on me.

They remind me of the poet and clergyman John Donne lying in his sickbed, thinking he is dying of the plague, listening to church bells for yet another and another funeral, and writing, "No man is an island, entire of itself; every man is a piece of the continent, a part of the main; . . . any man's death diminishes me, because I am involved in mankind; and therefore never send to know for whom the bell tolls; it tolls for thee."

That's what community means—feeling others' suffering and running

toward it, caring. That is what the world needs now. That is the person I want to be.

SUSAN MINYARD ✐ *Watch the Big House Burn*

My husband and his good friend, both about to leave this rural community near Gila Bend, Arizona, where they have lived so long, wish for me to write that no one can come into a rural community and ever really belong, no matter how long he or she lives there. He may lounge, Bud Light in hand, and hear all about old high school days and picture town leaders tearing up morality and desert, getting laid by you know who, and he may feel excluded, but still he grins, joshes, teases, acts. She contributes for twenty years, helps the community grow strong with meetings and respectful voices, brings new ideas for involving youth. He donates hundreds of hours of tractor work and electrical know-how; she coaches; he goes to more meetings; they both speak up, and every day show up for a long day's work alongside others. They may be fooled. Then "push comes to shove" or "the chips are down," and the old guard closes against the "outsider" or his children, the "newcomer" or his wife. Makes perfect sense. Plenty of true-life examples. We know now, nod our heads, sip our beer, give bear hugs at the end of the evening, and life goes on.

But once there was a fire at my house.

I lived in a huge farmhouse. Thirty-six hundred slump-block square feet, a basement and a main floor that sprawled across a handkerchief blocked out of a cotton field, a garage with automatic doors that opened when the jets trained overhead, and a swimming pool that had to be cleared of sidewinders on occasion before the children jumped in. The builder once told me he thought at first it would be the most magnificent of all his buildings; then something happened that sickened the project for him. I should have asked him about that.

Located outside of town, the house was built inside the memory span of every resident of Gila Bend when we arrived. It sat about a quarter mile north of Watermelon Road, through a bare, dirt parking lot that could hold thirty tractors, and down a driveway lined with stumped palm trees (no water; they grew as nature dictated, from slim spurts of downpour in December and August). The townspeople, all witnesses to the building of the huge house for a larger-than-life farm family planning to stay forever, clearly wanted only the worthy to be given the right to live there. Even in introductions, people would mention we had moved into "the big one." Faces were wreaths and eyes swept me up and down, and I could see the speculation. What would I do with all that house?

So we were questioned mightily when we arrived in a Ford Granada and one aging dump truck we babied along from the place of my husband's birth in northern Arizona down the Mogollon Rim and along the Agua Fria River to pick up the Gila River, and then down to the bend, where our new house waited. One lady banker asked me about the plantation we had left behind in Mississippi. We hadn't. One woman at the electric office said she heard about a relative that scrubbed tile for three days out there, and that was just the one shower in the master bathroom. I thought about never using that shower again. I guess I was shy, and ungrateful. The former owners were flamboyant, huge men with deep voices, and the house must have been where the conclave planned their day: wide doors, huge rooms. Plus that family was all soap opera, at least in story. Stardom and tragedy. Hubris, cause of all downfall according to the Greeks. Their lives were on display. We heard plenty when we moved to the farm, just like now—people probably talk about the Minyards that same way.

But the house was so special to people that when I tore out the flooring and took down the drapes and painted and wallpapered, the group took exception. Tut-tutted, asked about the old carpet, the old drapes, the old styles. When I painted the slump-block fireplace, I heard the outcry when the fact became public information. Usually, people mentioned the fire engine red kitchen countertops. With its deep brown cupboards, the stark drama of the place mocked my mottled Tupperware collection. Nevertheless, the kitchen is where the fire was.

It's complicated to explain, but life had caught up to us, and I thought a fancy meal would do us good. We had three children and were expanding our farm ground, and some of it was located twenty miles away; I had a part-time job at the medical center; I think the dog had run away and come home again as well. Also, we were housing a pregnant young mother of a preschooler; she had found herself in dire straits when her husband committed a murder. She had a wonderful way about her, loved Jesus, but her late-night hours had unsettled us as much as her sad life story.

The children napped that day, and I loaded the red counters with ingredients and went to work. I was cooking a special meal, shrimp. Then the phone rang, and I picked up in the bedroom, where I was checking on my sleeping baby. The caller was our houseguest's aunt, and when I finished with her and returned to the kitchen, the oil was on fire and searing the bottom of the cabinets above the stove. My oldest son, chubby legs bare below a sleep shirt, was staring in shock at the flames. I grabbed the lid, threw it on the pan, chased the children out of the house, planted them in the sand pile, went back in with a fire extinguisher, and finished off the fire with some automatic response I'd learned in elementary school. And yet I worried that sparks had made their way into the attic through the burnt cabinet or shorted out something. Perhaps the roof was gathering heat, about to

erupt in flames. On account of my vivid imagination and ignorance, I phoned town for help.

Gila Bend has a volunteer fire department, and after I explained the situation, the dispatcher warned me that we lived outside the city limits and she wasn't sure what would happen. The captain was a first-grade teacher, and she made the call. The telephone tree worked, and everyone in town must have received word, because everyone, not just the volunteers, came—in pickup trucks and cars and the rescue ambulance. Some people came on foot.

As individuals, and also in small groups, they searched every inch of the house—the patio, the garage, the courtyard, the backyard—for some useful, dangerous feat to perform. In and out, through every doorway. I was hustled outside and given oxygen because I was hacking and coughing from the chemical fumes in the fire extinguisher. I stood and watched in the boys' dump-truck dirt pile, and then the event took over, and I even lost track of the children. It became a parade: cars lined my drive; packed the big, empty machinery yard; parked single file along Watermelon Road. I am not sure, but it's possible that every family in Gila Bend donated a body to saving that house that evening.

My husband, coming back from a parts trip to Phoenix, arrived, saw the line of cars, was certain one of the boys had drowned in the swimming pool, and wasn't too upset to find the stove and cabinets burnt. He rushed up, and that's all I remember from that evening. Later, I wrote thank-yous, stark and pointed. One appeared in the local newspaper. I felt infamous, and yet the house still called to me. We moved to my in-laws' house while the repairmen worked to make ours like new, mostly dealing with chemical damage. Our houseguest had to move out.

Come December, when the ruckus had died down, I sent out invitations for a huge Christmas party. I cleaned for a week, cooked for three days, and almost three hundred Gila Benders came. We all hugged hello and goodbye because I am a hugger and insisted, and we drank a lot and ate a lot and laughed and told stories. Out of all those people, only one person acted disagreeably, and she spread her insults around so much no damage was done. To this day, I hear about what a wonderful party that was. The lady who cuts my hair, a friend now, came and admired my children's colorings hung all over the walls; the mayor's camp came; the citizens who would later cheer on my son as he played his heart out on the basketball court came; the school board members who would later turn down my application for work came; the women who loved to dance came; the art teacher who inspired my son's lifework came; the friend who talked me through every single medical emergency over the phone came; the wine connoisseurs came; the man who had helped himself to ancient relics in a hidden

ruin below our farm came; the parents of the teenager who would give my
son first aid when he cut his hand came; both sides of the law came. And if I
wanted to say that some of those people came before to watch that big
house burn down, well, that's the cynic in me.

These days, I get up every morning and do what I do, take care of two
dogs, and write. I feel inadequate to the task of saving the world. I don't
even know why I think it is my responsibility to save the world. If not the
world, my neighbor; if not my neighbor, my neighbor's dog. It has taken
me long years of many mistakes, *public* mistakes, to give up and just be. In
fact, all I may be capable of is taking care of myself. I joke to the squat, dark
woodstove that I am not even sure the doggies will make it through this
winter in my care.

RUBY R. WILSON *Room for a Small House*

Hollyhocks are just getting started
on the south side of my house,
like Granny used to have
outside her sewing window.
The morning glory seed came

from the vines that twine around
my mother-in-law's clothesline pole.
I moved the peonies and columbines
with me from my previous garden.
The flowering flax that crowds

the garden borders sprouted from seed
sent by a woman writer who showed me
how to draw pictures with words.
Volunteer chamomile grows
in the separator bowl planter

and, along the gravel driveway,
perfumes the path I walk after work.
My sister tried so hard to get it to grow
on top of the cistern at home.
I'm saving the seed this year

to give to my mother-in-law, Pearl,
who's never been able to get it to grow
in her garden. Maybe I'll start a large pot

and give the plants to her for Mother's Day
next spring. I'll say, "Just set the pot where

you want to grow some; it will seed itself."
Mom never cared much for flowers,
would chop down the hollyhocks that grew
next to the tiny basement windows.
I plant trees for her, amur maple and linden.

A half mile down the road,
two hulking lilac bushes stand in a sea of grass
with about enough room between them for a small house.
I see a woman pour her dishwater on them
when they are small twigs.

Purple rocket blooms every spring
south of the lilacs, near the soybean field.
They say that pioneer women brought the seed
with them and planted it on their homesteads.
I stop there for a visit again tonight,

pick seed from the garden phlox
that grows in the fence line,
and take it home with me.

SHAUNANNE TANGNEY *The Hippie Central Library Fest*

When I was five years old, my family moved to the small northern California town of Auburn. They wanted to live where community was important—in concept and in reality. There are a hundred stories I could tell about growing up in Auburn, but I want to tell one in particular.

When we lived there, the tiny library was in a small, cramped former store not designed for storing, reading, or circulating books. Resources beyond the terrible building and minuscule, overworked staff were nonexistent.

Still, the library was a favorite and important place for my family. My mother hated television; she called it "the plug-in drug" and refused to allow her children to become "junkies." We did not own a television. So my mother, father, my younger brother, and I were avid readers, game players, and athletes. We were not wealthy and did not own many books; our

weekly trips to the library were crucial. We devoured books the way wild-fire devours the tinder-dry California hills in autumn.

Then the unthinkable—for my family, anyway—happened. The county threatened to close the library. To my mother, this idea was unimaginable and unconscionable. She immediately organized the Friends of the Library, a loose cadre of concerned citizens. They pursued the usual channels, hacked away as best they could at the usual bureaucratic red tape and inaction, and raised the collective consciousness as much as they could (hey, it was northern California in the early 1970s), but without success. According to the authorities, there was no money for the library. My mother, organized and logical as she is, decided that the Friends of the Library would raise the money themselves and save the library.

My mother's idea was the Library Arts Fest. To really understand this event, you have to understand northern California in the 1970s and my mother: it was hippie central, and my mother was a hippie. Our house was full of macramé and tie-dye—tie-dyed napkins, tie-dyed place mats, tie-dyed curtains. Remember, we had no money and no TV, but we had free time and creative energy to make stuff. We also discovered and supported local artists who worked in various arts and crafts media—batik makers, potters, and beadworkers. Like these people, my mother was liberal, tolerant, freethinking, and open to experiment. With her we visited communes, organic farms, and art museums. We went to rallies and meetings and protests. So it was only natural for my mother to bring her love of handmade art together with her political sentiment. The Library Arts Fest was conceived as a gathering where artists and craftspeople could sell their wares, where children could produce their own handmade items—and all the proceeds would go toward saving the library.

Each fall, the Library Arts Fest was held in the giant library parking lot. Artisans rented space, the rent went to the library, and the artists kept the money from sales. We cordoned off a portion of the lot as the children's "Make and Do" area, where children practiced face painting, origami, and kite making. We organized a glue-in and a chalk-in. Parents purchased tickets; kids went wild with glue, chalk, paint, and paper; and all proceeds went to the library.

From the beginning, my mother made me a part of the Library Arts Fest. In the early years, we did all the publicity ourselves. I helped my mother hand-silk-screen posters and T-shirts, collected tons of scrap wood from local lumberyards for the glue-in, and spent hours painting ladybugs, rainbows, unicorns, and shooting stars on kids' faces. As the Library Arts Fest grew more popular, we added food booths and eventually a beer garden. When I was a teenager, my best friend and I rented a space and sold embroidered denim clothing and beadwork necklaces, earning money for school clothes.

By the time I was in high school, I was one of the coordinators of the event, handling publicity, money, and other duties. When we decided we needed a new name, I suggested Septemberfest.

Somewhere between Library Arts Fest and Septemberfest, we saved the library. More important, we actually did raise the consciousness of the powers that be, and government support of the library was reinstated. The need for a library and the support of the citizens of Auburn were so obvious that a new facility was built, spacious and gracious, inside and out. The children's section was larger than the entire previous library had been.

The library, nestled in rolling, oak-covered hills, was constructed with an inner courtyard featuring a Japanese garden and meditative water fountain. The architecture reflected its surroundings and the area's history and cultural diversity. That library became a haven and a refuge. I remember exactly where my favorite childhood books lay and how I spent hours of my teen years there, reading *The New Yorker*, scribbling juvenile poetry in notebooks, and pretending I was sophisticated and glamorous. I remember late-night sessions of counting money after Septemberfest, in a back office, my mother letting me sneak a leftover beer or two, fair reward for another successful festival.

When I left Auburn at eighteen for college and the rest of my life, Septemberfest was still going strong. When my mother realized that it had become an "event"—something to be attended and be seen at—and that the library's needs had changed, she graciously bowed out. Septemberfest continued with new organizers, following their new visions.

I do not want you to think I hold a grudge. We did that festival for more than ten years, and that's probably long enough for anyone to mastermind a happening. I know the value of that accomplishment. I wonder, though, if anyone remembers my hippie mom, her hair tied back in a tie-dyed scarf, and her little redheaded daughter saying we *need* this.

Community is a specific, namable place that is the beneficiary of the temperament, political bent, and practices of the people who live there. Many people moved to northern California in the 1960s and 1970s to preserve a way of life that included tolerance, liberty, experimentation, art, joy, and play. Auburn, California, and its Friends of the Library constitute an idea of community that is, I believe, particularly Western. The Library Arts Fest became an example of community that shouted with glee, grew with joy, provided for the common good, succeeded beyond our wildest dreams, and still sparkles and jingles in my memory with the good vibes of good people doing a very good thing.

JANIE TIPPETT ✑ *Rhino Rump, Chicken Palace,*
and Kindness

"Sharon, what's this rhinoceros rump stuck in your wall?" I asked my new friend.

"That's my desk," she said. "See, you open each side of the cheek, like this," and as she did, I was amazed to see a pull-out desk, complete with wooden cubbyholes for envelopes, pens, and pencils.

"Where did you come up with this idea?"

"Steve Arment. You know, our local artist who carves silly things out of wood?" Of course I knew Steve. He'd made my screen door, sporting a large sunflower, a row of corn ears, tomatoes, and crookneck squash. "Well, now he's making me the rhino's head, which I'll mount on the other side of the wall."

I'd met Sharon at our book club and liked her at once, even though she said things like, "If I put all my marriages together, I'd soon be celebrating my golden wedding anniversary." Well-read, she'd lived in California, Washington, and many other places, and judging from what she said, she'd been around.

Joseph, our rural community at the foot of the Wallowa Mountains in northeastern Oregon, is small, close-knit, and set in its ways, especially in winter's isolation. The highway ends right here. Most of the local women are quiet, especially the ranchers, whose characters reflect the hardness of living off the land. They sometimes resent newcomers moving in, retiring here with other means of support. Women like Sharon may come on too strong.

But Sharon says she's here for the duration. She embraces the cold and finds beauty in snowstorms. Her present husband, Jack (she chooses not to talk about the others), suffers from advanced Alzheimer's disease, making Sharon a full-time caregiver. Her love for this man is all that sustains him. They share a modest home with an old dog named Mooney.

Slowly, I began to learn more of Sharon's story and see her generous heart, her sense of fun. Once, when she came to our ranch, she grew nostalgic about chickens. "Jack and I used to have chickens on our small acreage, and I can still see Jack walking about in the morning, with all these chickens and ducks trailing behind. I miss them so," she said. So she persuaded a friend to build her a "chicken palace" right in town. City ordinances allow only four hens and no roosters, so Sharon had four nests built. The palace is painted gray to match the house, and driving past one would never know it was a chicken house. Sharon couldn't wait to gather her first egg.

Oftentimes, after Sharon tells me a story, she says, "That was before my brain blew up." I learned that she had nearly died and has a steel plate in her skull. Sometimes her right eye closes spontaneously.

"I've made a lot of money in real estate," she announced one day, "and when I die, I don't want to leave any to my kids. I'm going to spend it on things that give me joy." What gives Sharon joy is helping other folks: an anonymous donation to a friend's wife who had spinal meningitis, flowers delivered to doorsteps—bouquets for birthdays, anniversaries, and a Christmas wreath for Fishtrap House, our local literary meeting place. She gave me not only flowers but also red slip-on shoes, "for doing your chores," Sharon said.

She set up a charge account for the family of a struggling plumber at the grocery store. She took numerous young families out for Sunday breakfast. She became our community's fairy godmother.

Since Sharon feels that she and Jack are in their final days, she purchased their burial plot, on a high hill in a cemetery looking toward the Wallowa Mountains and the town below. Once the headstone was engraved with their names, a friend snapped a photo of them toasting each other with champagne. The photo was their Christmas greeting that year.

Now Sharon is having a bench installed near their graves, so her friends "can come sit a spell and visit."

Sharon's generosity has filtered into nearly every worthwhile charity and money-raising venture in our small community. She continues to donate anonymously to anyone in financial trouble, supports school activities, and has been generous to our Fishtrap organization. When one of her daughters, a professional chef, visited Joseph, Sharon bought ingredients and invited group members and their spouses to dine on roast duck, shrimp, and French onion soup.

Time is running out. Since Jack suffered a heart attack, he has resided in our nursing home. Sharon's memory is failing, but each day she takes the dog to visit Jack; both of them cuddle in bed with him. Sharon will be remembered for her rhino rump desk, her chicken palace, and all her random acts of kindness.

DIANE KESEY ✑ *Waiting to Dance*

For Pastor Kerry Grogan, who bought a watch when she was young and never missed a train

Women in waiting
Waiting in threes
Faceless on stoops
On steps, women waiting
Beside gates, beside the road
In anterooms, waiting rooms

Beside sickbeds, on beds of labor.
Waiting women, in windows
On kitchen chairs, waiting tables
Waiting by creeks, rivers, quays, queues.
Women waiting in line to see God
Waiting in line to speak to God.
Women waiting in line to laugh.
Standing on their knees to beg.

Faceless women waiting by wheelbarrows
Waiting on their backs, on one leg, two.
Waiting with nose to the wind.
Waiting in court, waiting on horses
Against walls, waiting like
Buds on tender branches.
Like flowers drooping with thirst.
Waiting under willows.
Women waiting in the sun for the garden
Waiting for spring . . . the red tulip
Waiting to laugh too loud
Waiting for the sweet, piping music
Waiting for the dance to begin.

Faceless women in the camps
Waiting for dried milk
Women waiting for the ax to fall.
For the wolf at the door
Waiting for praise, blame, credit.
Waiting for hell to freeze over
Waiting for ice skates.
Waiting for their milk to come down
For their blood to flow red.
Women waiting for the hard rain
Waiting to dance, to sing.
Women waiting for the right train
Waiting until they've all gone by.

MEGHAN NUTTALL SAYRES ⌇ **Where the River Bends**

What is community in a country still fenced according to homestead specs?
 Land, I suppose.
 When we moved to Valleyford, Washington, our family built a home on

twenty acres that adjoins my neighbor's hundreds. I had to look to the land for company when my husband left for work and my children boarded the bus for their hourlong ride to school.

There is no "town" of Valleyford. The post office, park, and general store are miles apart. The public school serves as a community center for the folks who live in this part of Spokane County, parents and students alike. But the lay of the land, the weather, and the distance most families live from the gleeful halls and grandstands play a role in how often the greater community comes together.

Thus my community is the river valley in which I live and the four-generation Paulicheck family with whom I share it. These neighbors gather on Friday evenings for pizza. They spend weekends roping, most of them being rodeo people. They motorboat or motorbike. They baby-sit for one another. I cannot say that my family is part of their blood community, nor do we necessarily share a common vision with them, as our aspirations and hobbies are dissimilar. We may share a conservation ethic, though I suspect for different reasons.

What bonds us, what makes us feel like a community here where the river bends ninety degrees, is mutual space. It is our appreciation of this land—and of the deer, blue herons, and elusive mountain lions; the sheep, horses, and cattle, that inhabit this river valley with us.

PHYLLIS DUGAN ❧ *Far-Flung Neighbors*

As newlyweds, my husband, Harold, and I lived and worked on ranches in the California mountains, and I loved riding horses and herding cattle. After our second son was born, we tried town life but were as miserable as our cowdogs, who stared at the horizon all day.

So Harold took a job on a ranch in eastern Oregon—country that I assumed would be mountainous and green. From the top of the last ridge, we looked down on barren desert and a volcanic plug of bare black rock towering over Fort Rock, our new home. The town, consisting of a small combination gas station, grocery store, and post office and a couple of houses, is 128 miles from Bend, which had doctors and shopping. As we drove into town, we passed a small red school and in the distance saw our house in a green field, an emerald square set among twisted gray junipers and sagebrush.

We settled on the ranch and made friends with another couple, the ranch mechanic and his wife, over dinners and evening walks. When they moved away, I was lonesome, but the desert intrigued me. The boys and I found arrowheads in the sand and little horned toads hidden in sagebrush shade. We saw coyotes hunting ground squirrels and watched jackrabbits zipping across the ground on long, springy legs.

In the fall, I took the boys to the little schoolhouse. Gene's first-grade teacher was Barbara Campbell, who taught first through fourth grades in one of the two classrooms. I was impressed by her composure as a dozen children ran amok around us. Small and dignified, she greeted us with warmth.

Dan's sixth-grade teacher, John Reck, stood almost seven feet tall. Dan took to him right away. John said that he and his wife, Pat, lived next door to the school and that Pat would love to meet me. Leaving the boys to their fate, I walked over to the Recks' house, where Pat welcomed me as she would an old friend. Her words poured over me like cool water on a hot, dry day.

Later, at a parent-teacher conference, Barbara mentioned that some folks were starting once-a-month dances at the Grange Hall. The evening of the first dance, Harold and I and the kids pulled into a full parking lot. I wondered where all the people had come from. Inside, the big room vibrated with chatter as Barbara introduced us to neighbors. It was exciting to learn that so many lived in the area. Barbara and her husband, Jack— a burly, friendly man—invited us to come over soon for dinner. Lights dimmed, local musicians played a Western tune, and the dancing began. I hoped I would get to know some of the women, but I couldn't imagine visiting often because of the distances between homes.

Dinners at Barbara and Jack's, as well as dances, became recurring events, and we were slowly drawn into the community. We attended several parent-teacher meetings, and at one Barbara commented that Harold would be a good Parent-Teacher Association (PTA) president. He laughed, but the seed had been planted. When elections came, Harold ended up as PTA president, and I was elected treasurer.

A few weeks before Christmas, Harold was laid off. We had three days to move from our ranch-owned house. We didn't have any money, and Christmas was coming. As I packed, I wondered what we would do, where we would go. Dan and Gene were happy and doing well at the little school—how could we take them away? How could I leave the friends I'd made and the desert I'd begun to love?

That afternoon, the phone rang. Hazel Ward, whom we had met at a dance, offered us a small house on their ranch, rent-free. It wasn't much, she said, but we could live there until we found a better place. I wondered how Hazel knew we needed somewhere to live. We followed her and her husband, Maurice, up eighteen miles of gravel road that wound around lava beds and rolling hills.

The old house had never been finished, but it felt friendly. Weathered boards covered the outside, while inside we faced unpainted wallboard and bare wood floors. There were two bedrooms, a tiny living room with a wood-burning stove, and a good-size kitchen that faced the morning sun. The house had indoor plumbing, electricity, and a telephone line. A huge

barn, surrounded by junipers and pines, stood a hundred yards behind the house. The dirt yard was full of deer tracks. We gratefully accepted the Wards' offer. Hazel told me that Barbara had called her to ask if the place was livable. I realized that quiet Barbara was the driving force in the community, the organizer who brought people together.

Morning brought us back to the house to start cleaning and fixing. I had barely filled a bucket with hot soapy water when I heard vehicles coming up the road. Pickups and cars pulled into the yard. Friends and acquaintances stepped out and rolled up their sleeves, some carrying rags and cleaning supplies, paint, brushes, hammers and nails, and food. I fought to hold back tears of gratitude.

Everyone scrubbed and painted, hammered and sawed, and by the end of the day, we not only knew everyone in the area, their children and parents, but we had a cozy, livable house.

At our old house the next morning, we woke to find Barbara, Jack, Pat, John, and several other families at the door to help us move. Before Fort Rock, Harold and I had always moved alone, lifting furniture, appliances, and boxes into and out of the truck ourselves. We were proud of being independent, able to do everything for ourselves, by ourselves. Now the kindness and helping hands were overwhelming. I didn't know what to say. Barbara took me aside and told me to let the men do the heavy work and to accept the help without guilt. She knew exactly what I was feeling.

The week before Christmas, the Campbells, Recks, and Wards brought another couple to visit. The men dragged Harold off to find a Christmas tree, and we women fixed lunch and talked. I thought about how the smaller the population is in an area, the stronger the community ties are. Ground rules in Fort Rock kept people friendly. Privacy was honored: no one asked who someone's dinner guests would be; no one gave advice unless asked. Personality conflicts were tolerated. The resulting peace was rarely broken by jealousy or arguments. Small populations get along because they have to.

The men came back with an enormous tree, which they trimmed until it would fit through the door. It filled most of the living room and brought the fresh smell of pine into the house. I wrapped it with colored lights and called everyone to eat. We gathered in the kitchen, shoulder to shoulder around the table. The children ate in the living room, watching the tree lights twinkle.

Before Pat left, she gave me a piece of an ancient sourdough starter that had been passed down to her. A year later, I gave some of it to Barbara after her house burned to the ground. I still have some of the starter in my freezer, to thaw and use for special occasions.

Because of Barbara's quiet insistence that we join in and Pat's enthusiastic encouragement, Harold and I became part of a community of far-flung

families. People opened their arms to us and gathered us in, and we enjoyed the hug. In Fort Rock, I had a taste of how pioneer women survived. Although vehicles and telephones make it so much easier to keep in contact now, I can imagine the heartbreaking loneliness of those frontier women, living hours or days away from female companionship. In Fort Rock, I learned that women hold a community together.

My kitchen is still the place where people gather, and no one leaves my house hungry. I try to return the feeling of belonging that I felt in Fort Rock. Friendships are sometimes forged by necessity, but they endure because of genuine caring and shared experiences. Thirty years later, although visits are rare, the Campbells and Dugans are still in touch.

PAT FROLANDER ❧ *I Suppose It Was the Food*

Branding . . .

I suppose it was the food
not acrid smoke, bruised limbs
rope-burned hands, bawling calves

no, it was Naomi's rhubarb pie,
Eva's biscuits, Ethel's angel food cake
Margie's tender ham

and it was fellowship
laughter as we heaped our plates
concern for rain between bites of corn

like woven saddle blankets
each year we plied
skeins of friendship over coffee

Funerals . . .

I suppose it was the food
that gave us strength
when laying friend and neighbor to rest

remembering
stories of his youth
his hand with a horse, his laughter

Haying . . .

It was talk of hoppers and weevil
as butter flowed like lava
down the mountain of potatoes

frustrations cooled over iced tea
sunburn healed with lemonade
fatigue melted with frosting on chocolate cake

sharing hay or grain
when crops were short as tempers
a handshake formed the merger.

Fall . . .

The gather, bawling cows and calves
anxious eyes scanned weights
at home and neighbors

shipping, sale day, sweat day
hamburgers at home or restaurant steak
depending on the buyer's wallet.

Weddings . . .

I suppose it was the food
spiked punch, nuts, and
too-sweet mints

shivaree, rice among the autumn leaves
and naughty humor
sealed the neighborhood blessing.

Winter . . .

Howling winds, frozen hands
spread hay to cows not all our own
fences snapped with weight of snow

a trip to town where coffee mingled
with a welcome visit to speak of spring
and calving.

I suppose it was the food
grown with our hands
watered with our sweat

that tied the fellowship
nurtured with humility, heartaches
and triumphs.

PATTY ZEIGLER ✐ *Bound*

The fence stretches into the distance, and I wonder what I got myself into, volunteering to fix last winter's damage to these fences that, like ribbons, tie the land into large blocks. No one in her right mind volunteers to fix fence. The pickup bounces to a halt. Dust and bugs cloud my vision as I check the corner post. I plant my feet and attempt to push the railroad tie into the four winds. It stands solid, like Carol.

This morning I went to visit Carol, one of our closest neighbors. We were sharing a pop and fresh-baked cookies when her phone rang. A death in the community, funeral in three days. It was a distant relative of hers, and she began calling other relatives, then churchwomen. In most small towns, when there is a funeral, the church ladies prepare the lunch that follows the service.

"Hi, this is Carol," she began. ". . . so I need you to bring a pan of bars. If you can't go to the funeral, you can drop them off here, and I'll take them."

". . . Could you bring something different? I've already got three Jell-O salads coming. How about a layer salad, cabbage, macaroni?"

"We'll start making sandwiches at ten on Thursday. Jane's out of town, so we're short of help and things could get crazy, so bring an apron. Would you check the supply of napkins and cups at the church, too?"

I sat and sipped my Mountain Dew as she spoke. I don't belong to the same church and felt left out. Carol knows all the phone numbers by heart, so she doesn't consult the phone book once. I'm new to the community, moved here when I married a year and a half ago, and though I've heard these names, many of the women are unknown to me.

I give the fence post one last tug, knowing that its strength is the foundation for the fence. Back in the pickup, I continue down the line of posts, wooden then steel, splintered, rusty, or freshly painted. Some are held up only by the wire. I pound most back into erectness and replace others, the new posts glaring with their galvanization and red tops.

♦ ♦ ♦

Jill told me her mom decided to stop coloring her hair, to let the red fade into a blend of grays and white. Jill is a social worker at a nursing home, and when she first started her job, she complained about how despairing it was to help those in their last years of life—the oxygen flowing through tubes into facemasks, rubber straps stretching wrinkled skin taut and back to youth. I know her mom's decision bothers her and wonder how both will manage the coming shifting of roles—the one relied on becoming the one that must now rely.

I recoat myself with bug spray and sunscreen, sweat dripping into my eyes. Two clips, the small metal wires that "tie" the barbed wire to the fence posts, are missing on the next post. Most of my stops have been to replace these small parts. I keep an eye on the clock so I don't miss the school bus.

Robin, the woman who drives the school bus my son rides, has cancer. Last week she wore a bandanna, so I guess the chemo isn't being kind to her. I enjoy going to the highway to meet the bus twice a day because Robin always greets me with a smile and a wave. I send up a quick prayer for her every time I see a school bus and try to smile and wave to the substitute drivers when Robin is sick. Most look straight ahead, focused on the highway and the next stop.

The clip I'm tightening drops into the tall grass, and I bend to search for it. Pushing aside a thick patch of buffalo grass, I find a bird's nest, the peeping young ugly in their transparent covering. The nest hugs the ground; the young are alone—small, sheltered, safe. The cows wander across the pasture on their way to the water tank. I pause for a moment, remembering to enjoy the small things.

Up ahead the bottom wire is down, probably a good forty-foot section. I hope both of our good fence stretchers are still in the pickup so I can pull the wires together until they can be bound. The wire is rusty; pieces flake off onto my gloves. I'll replace much of it with new. I stand to roll the rusty wire; the barbs poke into my side as I begin.

My sister, Teresa, used to do that, poke me in the side. Less than two years apart, we shared a room and trod heavily on each other. I was older, played hooky on my chores, and Teresa was there with constant reminders. To Mom it just sounded like a fight, subject matter and blame of no matter. We'd have to sit on the couch together, holding hands, until we could make peace with each other again. Sometimes it took hours.

I manage to splice one end of the new wire to the old but struggle with the other end. The wire slips through the catch on the stretchers with a zing,

and I jump back to avoid being snagged. Starting over, I reach for the old stretchers, paint gone, worn off by many years' use. The design is simple and straightforward. Pulling my gloves out of my pocket to continue my chore, I drop a slip of paper. Mom phoned to visit the other night and gave me Teresa's new phone number. I put it in my pocket so it wouldn't get lost in the junk drawer. Maybe I should call her tonight and see how her job is going.

Fences, like communities, are amazing inventions. The parts aren't much in themselves—wooden poles, metal rods, barbed wire, clips, nails, staples. Together, however, the order they give our lives is priceless. I usually take them for granted; they're just there, stretching endlessly around me. But they are landmarks, keep me on the right path, support me as I climb into another pasture. They are barbed and poke when I stray, standing solid through mostly air.

This isn't so bad. I'll have to complain a bit the next time I go out fencing. I wouldn't want anyone to steal this job away from me.

PAMELA RAMSEY ✑ *Soakers Unite*

We gather the first Monday evening of every month. Carrying our red wine, seltzer, and candles, we climb the flagstone stairs that lead to the upper terrace of my hillside backyard. At the top, we pause to gaze out at the scrub oak–covered foothills leading up to Pikes Peak. We hang our brightly colored robes—canary yellow, purple, pink, and blue—on hooks nailed into the privacy fence. Slowly, we ease into the 104-degree water of the hot tub—water so hot it almost hurts. Our skin tingles, burns, feels alive.

This meeting and soaking, laughing, and drinking, is a time for four women friends to talk and know that someone is really listening, understanding not just the words—often garbled, confused, inarticulate—but the meaning and emotions behind the words—sometimes hidden until finally shared out loud.

It's a time to look at the winter night sky and feel young and free and naked again. We discuss our bodies, which seem to be drooping no matter how much we walk, swim, or bike. We adamantly agree that we want to stay fit but refuse to let society's obsession with youth and beauty consume us.

This Monday evening gathering is a time to find our way back to our selves that often get left behind or ignored once we take on the responsibilities of marriage and children, careers, housework, church, and volunteer work; the fragile selves that never really die but sometimes become silent or shy, or maybe just too tired to make any noise.

Becky, Sukie, Laura, and Pam. We are old friends who knew one another when we were young, single, and free. We laugh about our youth, wild times that were full of dancing and questions, traveling and searching, looking for the right man and the right job, the right path.

We happily moved into marriage, and we reminisce about the plodding baby years—years of night feedings that left an exhaustion so deep we lived our days in a kind of dreamy, half-alert haze. Burping babies. Diaper rash and "binkies" poking out of purses and pockets. Lullabies, tantrums, and the always-present smell of baby puke and powder. We all loved that smell.

We survived Girl Scout cookie sales, science fair projects, and the turmoil of our children's middle school angst. Now we experience the sleepless nights of high school, when deep sleep will not visit until I hear the car door slam and, as required, my six-foot-three-inch son sticks his head in the bedroom and whispers, "Mom, I'm home. I'm not lying dead in a ditch on the side of the road somewhere." Smart-ass. Sweet, sweet smart-ass, who now smells of men's cologne—and is that smoke?

We bravely talk of our futures, once these precious children of ours are grown up and gone, and we're alone with ourselves again. We help one another keep our dreams alive and hold tight to the belief that there is still plenty of time to finish the book, live in France, build the straw-bale home, raft the Grand Canyon.

But mainly we talk about our present lives.

"Ed and I are starting to talk about getting married. What do you think?" Laura asks.

"You've only been dating for six years," I tease. "Don't you think you're rushing things a bit?"

"I know we've been together for a long time. Ed and Aaron get along really well, but being married, a family, that's an important step."

"And a complicated step. Blending a family can't be easy," says Sukie.

"I think you should go for it," says Becky. "It's obvious how much you two love each other. Life's too short to put off the important things."

Becky agonizes over whether to return to teaching after a long break to raise her children. "I know they're growing up, but sometimes I think they need me around now more than when they were little. I'm not ready to stop being a full-time mom."

I share my concerns about my health. For the first time, I say out loud that I'm considering the idea of leaving my job as a librarian. "John's business can support us, but the idea of quitting work makes me feel defeated, like the arthritis has won another round."

"Don't think of it as losing," says Becky. "Think of it as taking care of yourself."

"You have lots of interests. You can write and garden. You'll still have a full life," encourages Laura.

Sukie, the last of us to have young children, refills her wineglass, then stretches tired muscles that never seem to relax from the duties of raising three kids.

"Don't think of it as quitting. Think of it as taking early retirement, a blessing in disguise," she muses as she sips her wine and sinks deeper into the hot water.

The blue kitchen timer sitting on the edge of the hot tub finally rings, as loudly as a school bell. We set it for fifteen minutes more, but soon our evening comes to an end. We remind ourselves that taking time out of our busy lives, time to relax and talk, is crucial to our well-being. Leaving husbands and kids, dirty laundry and dishes, bills to pay and phone calls to return, to gather together as a small community of soakers helps save our sanity. This time together energizes us, enables us to go back into the "real" world and contribute. We quickly step out of the hot tub and into our robes in the cool night air. Gathering up our empty glasses and wine bottles, we take one last look at the inky sky that is now filled with stars and a rising half-moon. Slowly, we walk down the flagstone stairs and back into our lives.

SUREVA TOWLER ✍ *No One Baked Cookies*

What the obituary didn't say was that Agnes Peebles went
 into the garage
and blew her brains out. But that's exactly what she did on
 Thursday
morning. The local paper said she was seventy-four, widowed,
 mother of four, and
grandmother of nine. It said she had been born up
 Fortification Creek,
taught school at Mesa, and ranched west of town for fifty
 years before
moving to a new house on Oak Street last week.

It did not say how hard she had worked to buy that house.
 How much egg
money it takes to buy a dream. The little white doublewide was her
dream all those years. No one, not even Harry, had known about
 the dream
or the coffee can in the garage that would make it possible.
 The cash
in that can promised a new world, life without deer raiding
 the garden,
chickens crapping on the front porch, calves being pulled
 in the middle

of the night. The egg money promised freedom from milking, running
parts, slopping pigs. She could maybe read a book or join
 a bridge club.

The day the truck pulled the doublewide onto the little lot on Oak
Street that dream crashed. The neighbors lined the road to gawk,
standing as tall and immovable as the cottonwoods lining the city's
right of way. Mabel said it was too big for the lot. Lorraine said she
hated metal siding. Delores said it blocked her view of the
 mountain.
Liz said nothing, just harrumphed into her house to write a letter to
the editor reprimanding the Planning Department for failing
 to protect
the neighborhood from trailer trash. The paper came out
 Thursday morning.

BARBARA M. SMITH ✐ Boomtown, Babies, and Strawberry Pie

When people from other parts of Wyoming or the West ask me how I can
stand to live in a boom-and-bust place like Rock Springs, filled with wind
and light and not many trees, a town not loved by those who do not know
it, I think of the strange and wonderful people I have come to know here.
And I think of the first of June, 1977.

That day, I came home from the hospital after having twins by C-section
five days earlier. I knew I was in trouble. I wasn't moving too well, and I
had planned to let my mother, who had once had twins herself, show me
how this all worked. However, she was hospitalized in Montana with back
surgery.

In Boomtown, USA, I felt all alone. Coal was booming, as were the trona
plants and the new power plant. Hundreds of people were moving here,
living in tents if necessary; prices were high. The old-timers resented the
newcomers and the changes they brought. We had felt lucky to get a house
in one of the housing developments thrown up west of town.

My husband, Leonard, an electrician doing shift work at the coal mine
forty miles outside Rock Springs, was scheduled to go back to work that
night on the graveyard shift. He brought us home, settled Julie and Jason
into their bassinets and me in the rocker, and went to bed for a few hours'
sleep before work.

My three stepchildren—Bruce, ten; Todd, seven; and Scott, five—began

summer vacation that day. They looked at the newborns for a respectful wide-eyed minute or so, then resumed their celebration of total freedom, racing through the house and slamming doors with the neighborhood kids and dogs.

The nurses in OB had warned me that I had better get up and get moving while I was in the hospital, that it wouldn't hurt so much if I started walking the halls, but I didn't believe them. I had never had an operation before, it hurt like hell, and I moved as little as possible. So five days later, when they sent me home, I was still hunched over and hurting.

Of course, the first thing I did after Leonard went to bed was get the twins, one at a time, lay them out on a bed, and have a look at them. We had to get acquainted. They were perfect. Jason weighed more than seven pounds and Julie more than eight. The twins looked up at me expectantly, as though I knew what to do next, and I realized that we were all in trouble together. I turned around just as Jason slid off the bed. Not a good sign. But when I hobbled around the bed to find him, there he was, smiling up at me in the covers. Good. A survivor.

None of my friends knew anything about babies. Toni was still single, my schoolteacher friends were mostly gone for the summer, and none of the other couples we knew had children. Bruce, the ten-year-old, had more experience than I did with babies, having hauled Todd and Scott around when they were newborns, so he really helped. The day wore on. I fed the boys peanut butter sandwiches, shuffled around, and made formula. I leaned on the counter in the kitchen and tried to figure out how I was going to manage to get up all night by myself.

There was a knock, and my new neighbor, a young Afghan woman who had recently moved in next door, stood holding an enormous strawberry pie. We had smiled and waved to each other but never spoken. Her husband and other relatives had just bought Jay's Restaurant, where the pie came from. I knew that she had a busy life with a house full of elderly gentlemen.

In broken English, she introduced herself as Shari, congratulated me, and asked to see the baby. She was surprised and delighted at seeing two of them—one in the baby carrier on the table and the other asleep in the bassinet. She wanted to hold Julie. She didn't have children of her own yet, but she said she took care of her nieces and nephew while their mother worked in the restaurant.

Noticing that I was walking bent over and holding my side, Shari asked if I was okay. I said, "Well, this C-section hurts, but I'm starting to move around a little better, I guess. I'm worried about tonight, though. Leonard has to go to work graveyards this week, so I'm going to have to be up with the kids all day and get up in the night as well. I can hardly get in and out of bed as it is."

"Well," she said, "we'll have to see about that." I didn't know what she meant.

After she left, I had a piece of strawberry pie. I deserved it.

A little while later, another visitor arrived, a young Mormon woman from down the block named Connie. I didn't know her either. That wasn't unusual. Our subdivision was very new; people came and went quite often in the boomtown atmosphere. Connie came in to see the babies, and she wanted to hold Jason, the one who was awake. Connie said, "Shari talked to me and told me you had trouble here."

"I had a C-section, I just came home today, and Leonard has to go on graves tonight," I said.

Connie nodded. "Mike works shifts out at the trona plant, so I know how that goes. Listen, we're going to help. I'm going to come over to stay with you tonight and take care of the babies so you can get some rest."

"Oh, I couldn't ask you to do that," I said, hoping she would insist. She did. I didn't know angels looked like her.

"Don't worry about my family," she said. "Mike will be home with my little ones at night this week. I'll come over about ten o'clock. Shari and I can take turns staying this week until you are better. You have to get some sleep, or you'll get sick."

"You are a godsend. Here, have some pie," I said. Connie laughed, but she had a piece. I felt like a Relief Society project, but I really didn't care. These two young women, displaced from their own extended families, new to the community and the country, had come through for another woman, a total stranger in distress. We formed an unlikely alliance—a young Afghan, a Mormon, and me. They took care of the babies for four or five nights until I was almost back to normal. Although our friendship was brief and we went our separate ways before the twins' first birthday, I will never forget those women who cared for me.

When people from the beautiful parts of the West ask me why I live here, I tell them what everyone in Rock Springs tells them: "Oh, it's the people. The people are just great." I love Rock Springs; it's like no other place on earth.

GAIL RIXEN *No Treasure in Bismarck*

Mid-November 2001: Tokako Konishi found lying dead by Detroit Lakes, Minnesota.

There is no treasure in Bismarck.
Tokako's story blows out across the prairie
ghastly as black hair spilling across snow.

It falls on our table, front page.
A human interest piece,
something to keep up conversation at break.

She should have known.
Why Bismarck, why Detroit Lakes,
why us? Whaddo they say, fool me twice?
The lineman looks at his hands,
picks at a rough spot. *Everybody knows*
ain't nothin' here and in the winter no less.
The cashier twists her mother's ring.
Cops shouldda sent her home right away.

Didn't even get the right town.
It was a movie, for godsakes.
Made us look like fools and now this.
I don't care if those Coens are brothers—
look what they done.

The cashier looks up from the paper—
I wanna know who sold her that map.
She turns her fierce mother's eyes on the others.
Someone has the good sense to nod.

NANCY KILE ✍ *Grab Your Shawls, Girls!*

My grandmother's shawl hangs downstairs waiting for my attention. It is over twenty years old, made from durable cloth and bordered with satin string that is becoming frayed at the ends. I tell myself, "It will be a winter task, trimming and applying no-fray glue, one strand at a time."

It was made for an ample woman, true green in color, edging decorated with a tie that connects one fringe with the strand next to it. This pattern reminds me of the round dance I have seen at powwow and community gatherings: people in a circle, hands clasped, smiling at each other, laughing with the amateur at their clumsy steps. A temporary community goes round, sunwise, happy for a time.

I remember the first time I really paid attention to the Grand Entry. It must have been back in the mid-eighties. We hurried to get to the powwow on time, my mom saying, "I always like to see the Grand Entry, my girls." As I watched the Elders enter, I was surprised by the lump in my throat, and as the Honor Guard followed the Elders, I felt embarrassed that someone might see the tears running down my face.

To be so moved by the beauty of the People in full regalia doesn't surprise me today. The same feelings well up every time I watch the Grand Entry. Proud, wondering, awestruck by the visual realization that my grandmother's people understood much more than the ruling power could or would give them credit for. Today, as the tears run down my white face, I understand that they come directly from my Lakota heart—tears of gratitude for the Elders and the courageous people who keep these ways alive, who share the wisdom of centuries of living with creation rather than on top of it. I appreciate my mentors and guides who tell me, "Grab your shawls, girls! We're going to the powwow!" *Wopila.*

Mitakuye Oyasin!

KATHY HUNTER *Warm Hearts, Cold Reality*

"You will like the house," said little Linh, sitting between her parents in the back seat of my car. "It has lots of food and lots of clothes and lots of toys."

I was a journalist in Kodiak, Alaska, in 1979, and with my friends had spent months preparing for the arrival of a family of Vietnamese refugees. Linh, the eight-year-old, had flown in with the first contingent. Now, a few days later, we were returning from the airport with the second batch, which included her parents. My Vietnamese girlfriend in Kodiak had come along to translate, and we eavesdropped as Linh continued to babble in the back seat.

"You can turn something, and the water comes on. At the house, you put water in a container in the refrigerator, and it makes ice. When it's gone, you just do it again!"

She also gave her parents, belatedly, this advice for airline travel: "When you go up in the plane, your ears plug up and your nose plugs up. But you just yell a little, and it goes away."

Kodiak is a potpourri of Asian, European, and Native peoples. In the years I lived there, I relished the exposure to different worlds, both for the novelty and for the insights given to me about my own culture and, ultimately, myself.

In 1978 I volunteered to handle publicity for a community-wide sponsorship of Vietnamese refugees. Many Vietnamese had already been sponsored by the Lutherans, the Episcopalians, and the Church of God and had been absorbed by the city. A former airline pilot, for instance, did maintenance work at the high school, and one of my close friends was a former television journalist. Now she painted and ran an art gallery. Their terrible stories of suffering and heroism were woven into the fabric of our community.

Another of my women friends spoke at a meeting of the ministerial alliance that united Kodiak churches in this effort to bring a new family. We collected warm clothing, furniture, and canned food, as well as money to support the newcomers until they could become self-sufficient. We found a rental house and potential jobs. Kodiak's Vietnamese citizens offered to help with translation.

We were excited about a task that would alleviate the winter doldrums, the "rock fever" that affects Kodiak residents when the ice and wind and deaths at sea begin. "Give a New Life for Xmas" read one of my headlines, but as the campaign escalated, I found that I was filing stories that were never printed. Reporters at the town's newspapers were so intrigued by the happening that they researched and wrote stories of their own.

The process was a lot like the adoption of a baby. Our house was clean and furnished, with full cupboards, and we waited for a family. We requested a family with children and with two wage earners, so that they could live comfortably in Kodiak. We expected to receive, say, five people.

Finally, the long-awaited communication came, but it asked if we would take a family of eleven. An older couple would bring three children, ages eight, ten, and fourteen. Their older son had a pregnant wife and three children, ages four, seven, and eight. They would also bring a seventeen-year-old boy who had joined them in their escape. Our hearts were full. We said yes.

We had no advance knowledge when three of the group, including Linh and her married brother, flew into Kodiak. But days later, when the second group arrived, we were at the airport, eager and expectant, holding a giant sign in Vietnamese that read WELCOME, NEW FRIENDS. My ten-year-old daughter, Mindy, brought one of her dolls to give to the girl her age. She was Tuy (pronounced "Twee"), sister of the energetic Linh.

Eight exhausted strangers straggled into the building and squatted on the floor. Dressed in thin cotton, they had deplaned in the biting wind and walked across the blacktop to the building. When Mindy thrust her doll at Tuy, she didn't take it, seeming confused about what to do.

My Vietnamese friend translated the first comment made by the young father, Huy, to his parents: "It's cold." We learned that they had first been told of their destination en route and, in addition to the shock of the climate, were taken aback by our light skin and hair.

Days later, after the family had settled in, we held a food shower at the Catholic church. My friend translated as Huy spoke of their ordeal. They had been simple fishermen, he said, when the communists demanded that they relinquish all the fish they caught in exchange for food and oil to run their boat. Huy felt "like an ox" but knew that as long as the government needed fish, his family would be fed. But what if something happened to him?

Huy tried to escape and was caught. After the family fishing boat was confiscated as punishment, he ran away to Saigon. Returning in secret, he instructed his father to steal a boat from the government. On the stolen vessel, the family traveled down a river to the sea, where other refugees jumped aboard, until there were thirty-six on the small boat. One of them was the seventeen-year-old the family adopted.

After two days, they ran out of water. In desperation, they tried to ram a Japanese vessel to draw attention to their plight and in hopes that they would be picked up, but the Japanese ignored them. A chance rain saved their lives: they were able to catch water in the sail.

Five days and six nights later, they arrived in Malaysia and entered a refugee camp with a thousand other refugees. The camp was crowded, but compared with life under the communists, they thought it "the heaven of the earth."

Eight months later, the same camp held ten thousand refugees and lacked food and medicine. Their two-month-old baby died of starvation. In May, the family was told that they would be accepted in the United States when a sponsor was found. After what they had been through together, they were reluctant to break up into smaller units but despaired of finding anyone who would sponsor such a large family.

"Your country is cold," Huy told us, "but your hearts are warm." Their arrival in Kodiak may have been a terrible shock, but, he said, conditions were so bad in Vietnam that "if the people were all given one hour to depart, there would be no one left."

Huy's shy wife had enough to do with childcare, so the only dependable wage earners became Huy and the seventeen-year-old, who held low-paying jobs in Kodiak canneries. The old father was crippled and the mother very weak. Soon after they arrived, I visited the mother at an open warehouse where a job had been offered. I found her inches from the woodstove in the chilly space. We couldn't ask her to work in those conditions.

My friends and I, along with more than fifteen Kodiak families, made commitments to individual children, with a promise to remember birthdays, include them in activities, and ease integration in any way possible. The newcomers required trips to stores where discounts were offered, to doctors and dentists who volunteered free care, and to the health clinic, because all of them had been affected by tuberculosis (TB).

Everyone wanted to be a special friend to the gregarious Linh, but I asked for Tuy because she was the same age as my daughter. I remember her visits to our house—her darkness such a contrast to Mindy's pale skin and red hair. She was frightened of our big black dog.

At bedtime on the first visit, I pantomimed taking a bath, and Tuy said a very emphatic "No!" We gave her pajamas, and she put them on over her

day clothes. My grown-up daughter still recalls how Tuy hugged her all night long. In the morning, when I again suggested a bath, our guest climbed up on the kitchen sink, turned on the water, and threw it in her face. I later learned that although they had been a fishing family in Vietnam, the children didn't swim and didn't like water.

We had a full breakfast, but Tuy ate only pancakes. There had been no one to translate when I picked her up, so I didn't know when to take her home. As the day went by, I called my artist friend, placing the phone against Tuy's ear so that my friend could ask if Tuy needed to go home now. Tuy said, "No." I asked my friend to find out what Tuy liked to eat, as she had refused lunch, and her answer was that she wanted to eat pancakes.

At nearly dinnertime, the phone rang, and it was another bilingual go-between to ask about Tuy. Her mother was growing worried about her long absence.

About this time, I began to worry about the impact our generous impulse might have on my own community. By the time we had offered our sponsorship, the communists had ground their way through the upper classes to enslave the poor. This family was illiterate, and I now realized that they couldn't read the sign we had held up so proudly at the airport. We had furnished dining room furniture for them, but they didn't use the chairs, preferring to sit on the floor around a coffee table. Frequently, if food was placed on the dining table, a child would sit on the table next to it.

I was growing embarrassed about the wrong assumptions we had made about the family, about the charity that sometimes seemed self-serving. In my attempt to get to know them, I feared that they might believe I felt superior to them and resent me for it. None of these misgivings could be alleviated by a normal conversation, because the topic was too complicated for my Vietnamese friend to explain, as she was struggling with English herself.

Linh was learning English rapidly, but Tuy lagged behind, and soon my daughter tired of playing with her. By summer, although the old parents were weaving hammocks and bags and mending nets, the community was straining to provide financial support. Resistance developed when the family spent donated money on beer and cigarettes to accompany the card games they enjoyed playing for entertainment.

By fall, one Kodiak couple was so involved with the children it was easy to forget my commitment to Tuy. Huy appeared restless and dissatisfied, and one day when one of my friends went over to play cards with them, she found them packing. They were going to California, they said, to a Vietnamese community where the welfare was better.

Today I wonder if we did the right thing for our community and our nation by sponsoring this family. The months of preparation joined the Kodiak people in a common effort, but the sponsorship can be viewed as a

winter antidote with consequences we didn't foresee. I didn't anticipate the TB, the welfare, the family's isolation resulting from the language barrier. I wondered if these people would ever contribute to our society as the earlier Kodiak refugees did, gladly assuming jobs they were overqualified for.

For me the experience was humbling; the newcomers reminded me again and again of what I took for granted. I do believe that my daughter's perspective grew as a result of her exposure to a different culture. I also know that we did help the family: the contrast between the ragged individuals who arrived in January and the healthier ones of fall can't be denied.

Often I remember the industrious parents as they sat on the floor, mending nets. I remember the self-assured Tuy on my kitchen sink, the efficient way she splashed her face, and the chatter of her delightfully inquisitive sister. And despite my misgivings, I hold out great hope for them. Great hope.

MARY LOU SANELLI 🖎 *Standing in Line at Aldrich's Grocery*

In summer, when sun grips our days
without hesitation, we chat up possibilities of rain,
of tomatoes ripening, of leaving
windows wide-open and curtains
to billow and fan the muggy air. Aside from that
familiar nods and smiles
relayed through the line, the way we stand
cupping cups of coffee in silence
sometimes nothing to say.

Or, because we share so much . . . the same friend
whose marriage climbed, peaked, trailed off,
and severed, the same children
springing into the store at noon,
the same neighbor whose cancer rose
and spread like webs between her limbs . . . we talk
to air confusion, joy, amazement, fear
sweeping through the pits of our stomachs
like gusts of wind mounting outside
when fall is fully engaged, forcing us
to crouch and run to our cars, climb in
disheveled, angled
before righting ourselves, our bags

this blustery season, its dim light
lingering over those still inside
moving closer to revealing
some new remnant or candid glimpse
of our entangled lives.

MAUREEN HELMS BLAKE ✑ *A Light Shawl on a*
Cool Night

Nearly three decades ago, my husband introduced me to this western
South Dakota town on our honeymoon. I saw it through the eyes of his
grandmother, one of the first generation of his family born here in the late
1800s. His ancestors helped stretch and paint the canvas of the town, part-
ners in naming streets and laying out the golf course. They served the town
as bank workers, rural mail carriers, and postmaster, in a time when every-
one in town knew everyone else.

Grandma Blake, as the postmaster's widow, enjoyed the perks of small-
town notability, being recognized and remembered even after family mem-
bers had retired from their founding father duties. She took us into the
post office one summer morning on our honeymoon to mail a batch of
paper-wrapped jars of chokecherry jam she had taught this new bride to
make. She introduced herself to the clerk at the counter but received only
a generic response. Her clarification, "My husband, George D., was the
postmaster here," still yielded only courteous blankness. Watching the ex-
change from behind her in line, I saw her shrink, confusion wiping quiet
pride from worn features. Perhaps I'd witnessed her first encounter with
anonymity in a town where a few hundred inhabitants had swelled to a few
thousand, forcing the demise of an intimacy she'd once known.

We mailed our dozen packages to their destinations across the country
and turned to leave. Almost apologetically, Grandma Blake murmured
more to herself than to us, "That young girl didn't know me. Maybe she's
new in town."

Now, some thirty years later, this town is my home. Moving twenty
times in the first nineteen years of marriage kept my sense of community
largely confined to immediate and extended family, precluding any real
connection to a particular place. But after nine years here, being active in
church, community theater, Boy Scouts, and Girl Scouts, and now being a
freshman at the same college my three children attend less than a mile from
our house, I have developed a sense of knowing and being known. Is this
what it means to belong?

A few days ago, stretching at intermission during a performance at our

campus theater, I scanned the crowd, amazed at how many people I knew and how many more were familiar. Like rings in a crosscut section of a tree, these people sprinkled throughout the audience marked the passage of my life in this town. Down front were fellow church members and the lady who used to be our organist. Over to the right was my first professor when I dared to start college classes. In front of me was a classmate from watercolor class. In the back were neighbors. A few rows ahead were people with whom I'd shared a stage. The man over there drove us on a dinner and theater outing last week. When I turned to settle into my seat for the rest of the show, awareness of their presence wrapped around me like a light shawl on a cool night. I knew these people, and they knew me.

Leaving the theater to walk home, I headed toward the field house, where evacuees from a forest fire threatening a nearby town were moving in. I stopped to ask how I could be of service. The man in charge of food service at the college told me he'd call in the morning. Walking the rest of the way home in the gathering dark, I sensed compassion in action moving around me like an evening breeze. Though saddened by the difficulties being experienced by neighbors from the nearby town, I was animated by the joy of being part of the circle. I whispered into the night, "This is my community."

The next evening, in the college cafeteria, I dished out spaghetti and garlic bread for four hours, offering a smile to anyone who lifted his or her eyes. Some of the evacuees in line were perky and upbeat; others drooped with disheveled tiredness. One young couple held both hands of a bouncy little girl, dressed all in pink, who seemed to be having a grand adventure and asked for "please, no sauce" on her "pa-sghetti." Her mother came back later, able to voice only a tear-choked "thank you, thank you for all you're doing."

A man alone, grizzled in his senior years, was one of the last to come through the line. Holding his plate of spaghetti, he looked beyond me, then at my face, and began to speak. "When I left town this afternoon at four, I could see the flames. The chopper dropped a load of slurry and missed my chimney by this much." He looked down at his fingers spread to less than a couple of inches, then raised his tired face again. "Well, I don't guess I have much of a house left." I returned his gaze, murmuring, "Sir, I'm so sorry."

Today I wait by the phone to hear if I'll be needed to serve at dinner tonight. If so, I will again be among friends and strangers—people I know and people I don't know, connecting with a look, a touch, a word or two from the heart.

LOU DEAN ◢◣ *Echoes on the Wind*

The idea to ride across Colorado on my donkey, Jesse James, came to me on a moonlit night in March 2001. The shots from Columbine High School still rang in my ears, creating a storm of emotions.

I must do something more for the kids . . . , I wrote that night in my journal. *I'll ride my donkey across the state to promote nonviolence, give copies of my book to the schools and libraries, and establish a REINS Scholarship for kids who come up with ideas to stop school violence. REINS will stand for . . .*

It took several pages and the rest of that night to come up with words to fit the acronym, but I did: Responsibility, Empathy, Involvement, Nonviolence, and Spirituality.

The next morning, I drove into nearby Rangely to ask my friend Jean E. Smith if she'd make the pilgrimage with me.

"Sure," Jean E. replied, as nonchalantly as if I'd asked to borrow an egg.

We started making lists that morning, and within a week we'd set our route. We'd leave my home near the Utah-Colorado border on April 20, the anniversary of the Columbine shootings, and arrive in Holyoke near the Colorado-Nebraska border by early June. We'd get a sponsor for a new truck and a camper/horse trailer. Then we'd find a driver to follow along with the vehicles in case of an emergency.

The car dealer listened as I explained my plan, then he frowned. "Do you have any idea how much that would cost me?"

I felt my face flush from the neck up. I leaned closer to him over his plush desk and whispered, "What's the price of one kid?"

The rest of that day went much the same. When I returned home, Jean E. told me she'd struck out in her search for a driver. "No one has the time," she said.

As the days dwindled, neither of us could find one person willing to drive or sponsor a vehicle. No one offered money, even for gas or food.

"Okay, Lord," I prayed one night, "you know how hardheaded I am. If I'm not supposed to do this, help me accept that."

The next morning, Sarah, the local Episcopal priest, phoned. She had come into some unexpected money and wanted to cover our expenses for the trip.

Jean E. nodded when I told her, then an extended silence fell between us. It was certainly a start, but we were one week away from leaving and had no vehicles or driver.

"I've been thinking about buying a used four-horse trailer," Jean E. said. "We can take my truck and put the topper on back. My old truck is fairly dependable. The topper is just a shell, no beds, no heat, nothing."

"It's April," I said, without hesitating. "We should be warm enough."

"But how will we do it?" Jean E. asked.

"Well, I guess we'll just ride as far as we can each day, then one of us will stay with the horses while the other goes back for the rig."

Jean E.'s eyes sparkled with amusement. "But how?"

"I don't know. We'll hitchhike or something. Do you want every damn little detail worked out ahead of time?"

Both of us laughed. I pushed my hand toward my friend. "If we start this, there's no turning back."

Jean E.'s weathered face grew serious. She took my hand, and we shook on it. Neither of us knew how hard it would be.

On the morning of April 20, ominous clouds descended as we packed our food and supplies in the horse trailer and began to saddle up.

"Better tie our slickers on top," Jean E. said, as I felt the first sprinkle of rain. Reporters from local newspapers flashed pictures as we rode out of my driveway.

Thunder boomed and lightning cracked before we reached the end of the lane. Just as I untied my slicker from the back of the saddle, the wind gusted. The slicker popped Jesse James in the face, and he began to buck. My hat flew off and I lost one rein, hanging on for life while Jean E.'s infectious giggle echoed on the wind.

"Yee-haa," Jean E. yelled, and Tut, her twenty-four-year-old Arabian, pranced.

It rained, the wind blew, it sleeted, and then it snowed—and that was just the first day. "Springtime in the Rockies," I said five miles out. My feet were frozen, rain dripped from my hat, and a small mountain of ice piled behind the saddle.

"For the kids," Jean E. called out ahead.

I huddled deeper into my slicker and patted Jesse's wet neck. "For the kids," I repeated. That slogan would sustain us in the days ahead.

It rained and snowed most of the ninety miles between my place and Craig. Every evening after riding about fifteen miles, Jean E. and I would get "the boys," Jesse and Tut, groomed, fed, and settled inside a portable corral next to the horse trailer before we ate.

The first evening, soaked and exhausted, I luxuriated in the thought of a cup of coffee and some hot food. The charcoal was wet; it wouldn't light. Eating cold canned food wasn't appealing, so I slapped some pimiento cheese on a homemade bun.

"Give me that," Jean E. said, snatching the bun and smiling.

Those first three nights, we sat inside the topper, shivered, and watched it rain as we ate our cold cheese buns. We crawled into our sleeping bags too tired even to talk. Every morning we awoke to the sound of rain. I'd peek out and see Jesse and Tut dripping from head to tail, looking bewildered.

At our camp outside Maybell, cold rain turned to snow. I opened my

eyes to the howling wind, saw my breath, and had the first of many moments of weakness. I ached all over from hours in the saddle. I hadn't been dry or warm for days.

I can't do this another day, I thought, as I lay motionless, watching my breath.

Jean E. stirred in her sleeping bag but uncovered only part of her face. "Would you turn up the heat, please?" Her throat was sore, so she croaked the words.

I wanted to laugh, but my sense of humor was gone. I scraped frost off the inside of the topper window and stared out. Jesse and Tut had snow frozen to their backs; icicles hung from their ears as they huddled with rumps to the bitter wind, shivering. I couldn't force myself to face the day.

"For the kids," Jean E. whispered.

I crawled out of my sleeping bag and slipped jeans over the long-handled underwear I'd slept in.

When we rode into Maybell, a rancher offered a warm barn for Jesse and Tut. Others opened up their home, and we had our first hot meal, bath, and bed in three days. This was the beginning of the community of new friends that would renew our spirits along the way.

The next morning, we visited Maybell School, one of the last remaining one-room schools in Colorado. Twelve very enthusiastic little fans listened intently as we explained our journey and showed them our destination on the map.

Before we reached Craig, the boys began to tire. Jesse James would stop about every thirty minutes and put his head down so that his long donkey ears touched the ground. We referred to it as his "end of the trail" pose. At first I would swat him and get upset, but my hard head was no match for his. After a short rest, Jesse would look up, see Tut disappearing in the distance, and start off in a rough trot.

Tut kept up a steady pace day after day, stepping out with pride, leading the way. As the days mounted, we gave the boys longer rests at regular intervals.

Marie, our friend and the owner of JML Outfitters in Meeker, came to our rescue in Steamboat Springs. "It's not new," Marie said, as we switched all of our gear from Jean E.'s truck to hers, "but this truck will make it over Rabbit Ears Pass, and the camper has beds and a propane heater."

"You don't know how much a real bed and a heater mean to us at this point," I said. "You are hereby our official sponsor."

Marie handed over her cell phone, a heavier slicker, some tack, and miscellaneous gear. "Happy trails. Wish I could go with you."

Outside Steamboat Springs, the trailer brake lights quit working. A man at a mechanic's shop fixed them and donated his time. In a blizzard outside

Walden, I called the sheriff's office to get a weather report. "It's bad," the dispatcher said. "Don't travel if you can avoid it."

When I told her what we were doing, she didn't hesitate. "We've got a barn for your animals. You better rest at our house until this storm passes."

West of Fort Collins, when we were bedraggled and exhausted, Kit and Bill opened up their home to us and volunteered to pasture the boys while we took a rest.

In Sterling, the police department escorted us into town, and people rallied around us with encouragement and support. Near Fleming, tired from the day's ride, I stopped a man on his tractor to ask about a possible camping spot. He invited us to stay at his nearby farm. His wife cooked a wonderful dinner and insisted we have breakfast before we left.

Every day, we had the challenge of finding a ride back to our truck. The highway patrol and local law enforcement were good about helping us if we called them. But one night in between towns, when the cell phone wouldn't work, I stuck out my thumb to an approaching car. The man who stopped was one of Jean E.'s former students at the community college back home, more than two hundred miles away.

We had looked forward to the eastern plains, with warmer temperatures and less traffic. But when we began the last leg of our journey, we ran into constant truck traffic, and the trash in the ditches forced us to ride precariously along the side of the road. Extremely hot temperatures replaced blizzards, and places to water the boys became scarce.

On a narrow bridge, Tut shied when ducks flew up from the creek below. The boys veered to the middle of the bridge just as a semitrailer topped the hill behind us. The driver immediately hit his brakes, but he was driving too fast to stop. The truck came within inches of us. For the next hour, as I held the reins with trembling fingers and Jesse's legs quaked beneath me, I thought about the simple prayer I'd said every morning: "Lord, please be with us."

Two days before we reached Holyoke, our final destination, I called to see how much had been donated to the scholarship account at the bank: less than three hundred dollars. Not enough to organize a nonprofit organization, much less get a scholarship off the ground. That evening in camp, I couldn't hide my discouragement.

"Well, we've almost done what we set out to do," Jean E. said, with her usual optimistic attitude. "We've talked to lots of kids."

The next evening, about ten miles outside Holyoke, with Tut and Jesse stumbling tired and Jean E. and me nodding off as we rode, a young man ran out onto the road. "I read about you in the paper," he called. "Can I ride the rest of the way with you to Holyoke? I have a team of donkeys and a wagon."

The excited youth bolted up to me and threw out his hand. "Gade

Groshan," he said. "If you are tired, you can stay at our house. We could ride into Holyoke in the morning."

Jean E. looked back at me and grinned. "For the kids," she said.

I realized in that moment that the young man in front of me was the reason we'd taken the trip. The success of the scholarship took second priority to influencing even one young person. "You know," I said, "a rest sounds pretty good right now."

"You can camp at our place." Gade took off at a dead run toward his house.

That night, our last night on the trail, we added yet another family to our new community of friends. The Groshans and their three boys were perfect hosts and gave us shower privileges and a wonderful meal.

The next morning, we set off on those last nine miles—Jean E. on Tut, me atop Jesse James, and Gade and his brother Garet escorting us in their buggy pulled by donkeys. Jesse James perked up his long ears, and Tut seemed almost frisky. As we rode into Holyoke, a small group of kids jumped up and down and waved greetings from where they'd gathered at the library. Jean E. and I felt like celebrities in a rodeo parade, smiling and waving back. I said a silent prayer of thanks for all the help along the way.

"Welcome," a young man said as I stepped off of Jesse. "Wow, I feel like I should have baked you a cake or something."

Jean E. dismounted and stuck out her hand. "We did it," she said, then turned her attention to Tut. "Good job, buddy," she said, rubbing Tut's neck.

I gave Jesse James a kiss on the nose. "You're my hero, little man," I said.

"I wish the people who helped us could be here," Jean E. said. "Every single one of them."

I agreed with a solemn nod.

"Here's to the spirit of Colorado," Jean E. said, taking off her hat. "Colorado doesn't seem four hundred miles wide anymore. It seems like this small town of wonderful folks."

"Here's to our Colorado community," I said, jerking off my worn hat.

DIXIE PARTRIDGE *Cliff Dwellings: Mesa Verde*

Here rock has a soft face
and wind moves above like spirit.
I listen down the long slant
of switchback trails, steps carved
where red rock accordions through the canyon.

Lodgepole ladders reach the base of the dwelling:
three stories in places, a hundred stone rooms.
Noon heat wavers from fire pits
of the opened kivas. Brief shadows
at a window, footfall
on the terrace stone.

Far beneath the overhang, where full light
never touches, the dark cool
of heavy shade: cupped imprints along walls
collecting ghost water, sudden rivulets
filtered from the green table.
Grains stored in the cool caverns.

Despite the cords that keep us from all
but a sampling, my sister and I move in
and in. The quiet ripens
when the hikers leave.
Anasazi women felt
safe here, giving birth: a new cry
echoing off cascades of stone,
stilling the men
at worship below in the kiva.

Silence leans
from the rock as I place my palm:
a hollow, round from grinding,
the flushed pulse
from the sandstone walls.

DARCY LIPP-ACORD *Path to a Small World*

I don't feel I belong to many communities. Ever since college, I've moved around, changing addresses every two or three years, leaving little time to really become immersed in any one community. Because I am a stay-at-home mom and a writer, I don't have many colleagues and associates. And because I am somewhat solitary by nature, I don't belong to many social circles.

This morning, as usual, I drive my five-year-old daughter, Maria, to preschool, then cross town to the walking path by Clear Creek. I strap my son, Cody, into his stroller and head off down the path maintained by the city of Buffalo, Wyoming, where I have lived these past three years.

As I walk, I notice a couple, probably in their forties, walking ahead of

me. They don't stride off purposefully like the regulars who exercise on this path. They amble, pointing at the Big Horn Mountains rising ahead, and looking around at the creek and the cottonwoods. I slow my steps, not wanting to disturb them with my stroller and fussy baby, but as I climb one hill, I see that they have stopped and turned to wait for me.

"Where does this path go?" the woman asks as I near them. She wears jeans, a pink sweatshirt, and a scarf over her head, the way my mom used to wear hers.

"Oh, this main part of the trail goes on for a mile or so. Then there's a gate, and you can walk up past the veterans' home. Eventually, it connects with the highway."

We talk for a minute about the walking trail. Her husband points out another path he sees sketched into the side of the mountain, but I explain that it's not part of this one. "Good," he says with a smile. "I didn't want to walk that far."

"We're from South Dakota," the woman explains. "We just wanted to pass some time until the museum opens up."

"Oh, really." I say. "Where in South Dakota?" She tells me their hometown, up in the northeast corner of the state. I grew up in Timber Lake, I say, a tiny town in north-central South Dakota.

"Do you know Bill Bickel, then? He married a friend of ours," she says.

"Oh yeah—Lori. I don't really know them personally, but I know who they are. Bill went to school with my older sister—or maybe he was a couple years ahead of her."

The woman and I both laugh. "Small world," we say in unison.

Her husband says, "You don't by chance know the Garons, do you? I think they're from Timber Lake."

I laugh. "He was my high school biology teacher. And he's still there, I think." Instantly, my mind floods with memories of Mr. Garon's wire-rimmed glasses and thick black mustache, of late afternoons spent planning my project for the science fair my sophomore year.

"Well, we had a mechanical bull for a time, and they used to bring their boys over to ride it," the man says. For a moment, we all lapse into silence as we struggle to remember the names of the Garon boys.

They want to know where I live, what brought me to Wyoming, how many kids I have—the kind of information people seek when they make a stranger into a friend. In a few minutes, Cody cries. The woman says, knowingly, "Must be naptime."

"Yeah, I was hoping to walk him to sleep," I respond.

"We'll let you go, then," she says. "Nice meeting you."

And so we go our separate ways. I continue on up the path, and they turn back to Buffalo and the museum. As we part, I feel enlarged, a little richer for finding two more people with whom I have a small connection.

When I meet people from New York City, I never even consider asking

them if they know Chad, a boy I went to school with who works there now, or Annette, a friend I made at a conference I attended one fall. Likewise, I don't pepper acquaintances from Los Angeles with the names of all the relatives I have there, hoping for a mutual connection.

But when I meet someone from South Dakota, or from Montana, Wyoming, Idaho, Nebraska, or Colorado, I search my memory for anyone I know there, curious to see if we know the same people. I think we all do this in the West. Perhaps because of our sparse population and overwhelming amount of space, we are eager to make a connection with others. And I am comforted to think that all of us are part of the same community: the community of anyone who has ever lived in and loved this place we call the West.

COLETTE KNUTSON GJERMUNDSON
Simply, Soul Soup

"Soup to warm your bodies and heal your souls," read a three-inch-square note taped to a quart jar of beef vegetable soup in our refrigerator. Our closest neighbors had delivered it that morning when they came to feed our dog and cats in our absence.

The previous afternoon, my husband and I had spent two hours in a Minneapolis perinatal clinic enduring the most traumatic experience of our lives. Our unborn baby was diagnosed with Potter's Syndrome at twenty-two weeks gestation. Our first baby had renal agenesis: no kidneys.

The perinatologist explained that there were no medical options to save our baby's life. My obstetrician would monitor me and could assist us in deciding whether to continue or terminate the pregnancy. *Terminate the pregnancy?*

My husband, Casey, asked whether continuing the pregnancy would threaten my health or life. Hearing a firm no, he told my doctor, "If you're sure that's the case, we'll just go home to wait and see what happens."

We were relieved to arrive at our ranch home in western North Dakota, to sleep in our own bed. And a simple jar of soup in our refrigerator conveyed love and concern as I realized that people within our community were caring for us even before we arrived home. Still, inside I felt like a twin-engine plane forced into an uneasy holding pattern.

Later that evening, my mother-in-law delivered a hamburger noodle hot dish and potato soup. The following afternoon, two neighbor women, Deb and Linda, came to visit, bringing a jar of pickles, a jar of salsa, a Juneberry pie, and a tube of scented body cream I chose to use as a tummy rub in the hope that it would keep me from itching and help the baby we

had nicknamed "Jaz" feel loved. Two nights after we arrived home, our closest neighbors, Kelly and Kim, and their two children were back with supper. The next week, my mother brought donuts, and my aunt and uncle and mother-in-law brought complete meals. The people, and the food, just kept coming. Friends even did chores for us.

My friend Cheryl had purchased fabric, intending to sew a quilt for Baby Jaz. Shortly after the diagnosis, we received a navy blue quilt bedecked with two-inch squares of red, yellow, and green gingham. One red square bore a message in navy stitches: "Jazzbo with Love."

As the days turned into weeks, our community of support provided phone calls, cards, and prayers. While my husband and I hoped and prayed for a miracle, we opened ourselves to God's will, whatever that was. "Nothing more, nothing less, nothing else."

Some nights I slept well and continued my daily routine: working on agricultural stories that I'd promised to editors, preparing meals, straightening our home, and attempting to help with minor ranching duties. Other times I experienced cramping and spotting and spent days on the couch as my husband delivered meals to my lap.

But the diagnosis remained, and we began to prepare for the probable. Our neighbors Kent and Mona, local cemetery sextons, helped us choose a burial plot and placed straw bales over the spot to keep the ground from freezing so hard in case we needed to dig a grave. My godmother Peggy sewed a white, satin-striped gown. A baptismal gown or a burial dress? We didn't know. My husband's uncle Bob crafted an eighteen- by thirty-inch oak box and stained it honey gold. A box for treasured toys or a casket? We didn't know.

A Potter's Syndrome support group taught us to prepare ourselves, right down to taking a teddy bear to the hospital so we had something to carry home. These experienced parents also suggested that we purchase two of whatever we planned to bury with Jaz so we could put one in the casket and keep one.

Christmas drew near. We were eleven weeks into the Potter's Syndrome diagnosis, and I was thirty-three weeks pregnant. We celebrated Christmas with our families early. At 1:30 A.M. on December 24, I awoke with cramps. *Or was it contractions?* Since I'd experienced similar symptoms a month earlier, I figured the pains would probably subside if I rested. Wrong. Within four hours, we were en route to the hospital ninety miles away. With scared anticipation, I walked toward the nurses' station, explaining that I needed to get to labor and delivery.

In the delivery room—in the middle of another contraction—I became the centerpiece of organized chaos within a small, comfortable community: my husband and three or four nurses surrounded me as they pulled off my clothing and dressed me in a hospital gown. My obstetrician appeared,

pulling on blue rubber gloves, as a nurse explained what I should do when I had my next contraction. We were about to meet Baby Jaz.

Within fifteen minutes, Jaz was born. A neonatal nurse took the baby from my doctor's hands and announced, "It's a girl!" *A girl?* Our parents already had twelve granddaughters and only three grandsons between them. And Potter's Syndrome literature indicates that a high percentage of Potter's Syndrome babies are boys, so we'd convinced ourselves that our baby was a boy.

Casey stood staring at our daughter as the nurse asked, "Does our baby girl have a name?" He didn't answer. He later told me that he was shocked that she'd been born so quickly and was wondering if she was alive. I was proud to tell her, "Jasmine Leigh."

My husband and the nurse baptized Jaz; dressed her in a diaper, flannel baby gown, and pink cap; and wrapped her in a blanket. Our delivery room community shrank quickly to my husband, our daughter, and me. My husband and I took turns holding Jasmine Leigh throughout her life: seventy-two minutes.

In the four hours that followed, our community grew again as our families arrived at the hospital to hold Jasmine's body, hug us, and love and support one another. By midafternoon, our families headed home. That Christmas Eve, we sadly and tearfully—but oh so proudly—delivered her body to a local funeral home.

We arrived at our ranch home to find that our sister-in-law and two nieces had not only delivered our hospital bouquets but also had washed the dirty dishes, straightened the house, and left us a tray of meat, cheese, and crackers. Grammie Sharon was waiting for us, busying herself by ironing shirts.

On Christmas morning, our neighbor Kim brought us a roast beef dinner and Christmas cookies. Later, her sister-in-law brought more roast beef, more goodies. That evening, our friends Cheryl and Warren helped us upholster Jaz's casket.

On December 26, we planned a public visitation and a private family funeral. We dressed our three-pound girl in her burial gown and a Black Hills gold cross necklace; we stroked her forehead, combed her hair, held her. We tucked her into the casket with a baby blanket and her teddy bear. On December 27, Casey, a machinist, welded a vault. Relatives and neighbors dug the grave. Our local postmaster brought homemade sour cream twists. More than two hundred relatives and friends came to console us at the public visitation that evening. Sixty family members attended the private funeral the following afternoon in bitter cold. The congregation sang, "Have Thine own way, Lord, have Thine own way. You are the Potter. I am the clay." Among the Scripture readings was Psalm 62:5–6.

Our support community made it possible for us to celebrate Jasmine's

life in food and fellowship at our home that evening. Friends had cleaned, brought supper, helped serve it, and stayed until after the last dish was washed. Throughout our Baby Jaz adventure, we found support among not only family, neighbors, and old friends but also a wider group of new friends, churches from several states, missionaries, and mere acquaintances.

Always they brought food, prepared by the women in our community: Roast beef. Smoked chickens. Chili. Corn chowder and Christmas bread. Bars and cookies. Pies. And a simple jar of beef vegetable soup that warmed our bodies and healed our souls.

KATY PAYNICH 🌾 *After Moving Away from 610*

For Shelly and Carola

Looking out my kitchen window at 610,
I could see the lights on
in the house next door.
Sometimes, through the leafless aspens,
I could even glimpse
Gary at his kitchen sink,
taking a last gulp of water
just before bed.

I could observe the exact moment
their bedroom light blinked off.
And their house, sleeping
in darkness, was a great comfort at midnight,
like the warm back of my slumbering husband.

To be unconsciously attuned
to the rhythms of neighbors
To know the hour
by the sound of an ice scraper
or the revving of a truck's engine

To hear the familiar squeak of hinge
and click of lock,
the low barking of a dog,
and the cries of two cats—
To have distinguished love's sounds
from the yowls of defending boundaries crossed

To be buffered by the rhythms of daily chores,
the chugging spin of the washer upstairs,
the footfalls, heavy and light,
the far-off whining of a tired child before sleep

To be lulled by diapers lapping on the line

To know that the door sticks,
that the pounding of work boots echoing
in the hallway means someone
has come home

To have days wrapped
in guitar and piano, trickling
down to fill the cracks of silence

To gather like birds,
spontaneously, on a telephone line
then, just as naturally, to disperse
to attend to the pumping flow of routine
and the unexpected

To be there at the crevice
through which raw living
is shaped
To embrace a woman at the naked moment
of creation
before the edge has worn
and been dulled by retelling

To involve others in the intimacy
of my routine,
to be swaddled by human presence,
all sweetness and life,
gold of sunlight through honey,
the invisible cords of living
netting us all together

The Crows have a word for this, *Apsalooke*,
tribe, family.
And those who move from the Reservation,
more often than not,
move back

because of the profound loneliness
they feel in the gaping hollow of the world,
a mouth held open
in soundless wail.

B. LYNNE McCARTHY ✑ *Have Cattle, Will Travel*

I woke up terrified. The bed and sounds of my husband, Sean, sleeping next to me were familiar, but I could not remember what state of the Union we were living in. I thought of the post offices where we'd gotten mail; Buffalo, Missouri, seemed to be most recent.

Missouri! How did the cowgirl from the sage-covered flats of Montana find her way here? After my family's ranch corporation blew apart like a bad can of beans on a hot bed of coals, Sean and I bought a ranch on the Llano Estacado in New Mexico. I headed south to close on the paperwork and to ready the place so that Sean could begin shipping our livestock. In two weeks, we relocated our entire ranching operation, right down to the barn cats, and settled into learning the cow business Southwest style. Our new ranch covered forty-five square miles and was surrounded by five bigger operations. It didn't take us long to find out that the few people in this seven-hundred-square-mile area were all feuding. Naturally, being new, we were expected to take sides, but we refused to play that game. This set us apart from the beginning; maybe the never-ending heat makes the natives testy.

Before too long, we were invited to join some of the big gathers. I'm sure they were curious to see what we were made of, though perhaps they just wanted Sean to come. In eastern Montana, when you invite the husband, you'll most likely get the wife, too. She's just as involved in ranching as the husband and often knows the cattle better because she spends more time among them. Ranch wives are valuable working partners and most of them top hands.

I was a little dense at first; I should have gotten a clue when I was the only woman among fifteen men. I began to see the light when they always sent "the woman" off in some ambiguous direction away from the action to look for cattle that did not exist. My horses and I had an easier time if we stayed at home. Sean hated leaving me behind, but among the men, it was a poor reflection on him to have me along. Our ranch was in the very southeast corner of New Mexico, which put Texas a day's ride in two directions. God have mercy, we were truly in the South.

After that, I pretty much stayed at the ranch except for a few of the calf brandings. A wife of one of the ranchers told me that she'd asked her husband how I'd done at the job of heeling calves. He'd tersely replied, "She

had trouble." Then she asked their Mexican hand how my roping compared to the men's. With a big grin he said, "That Betty, sheez hot!" We laughed over that. Truth is, my ability lands somewhere in between, but it sure gave me insight into how the bosses felt about having me around.

That fall, I'd finished gathering the bulls, loaded the last bull and my saddle horse in the trailer, and was waiting to get onto the highway to return to headquarters. The group of cowboys whizzed by, headed home from a pasture down near Texas. They seemed to be having such fun. It hit me hard how alone I was to be a woman on horseback in that part of the world.

By the following fall, we knew we didn't want to stay, not so much because of the attitudes but because the oil companies were raping every inch of federal- and state-owned land. With all the oil wells, our ranch resembled a pincushion; roads appeared through our pastures overnight, built for oil tankers with no time to wait for a cow or calf to cross. Lights blinked at every well location, so darkness never came. The countless engines rattled empty hangers in the closet, keeping me awake at night. We had to drive forty-five miles one way to get our mail, but we certainly were not isolated.

So we put the ranch back on the market, and Sean took off to look for our perfect place. I was alone with my string of horses, gathering the cattle for shipping. No band of merry cowboys came to help. By the shipping date, Sean was back and asked for help from the surrounding hands. I spent two days of being ridden in front of, and ridden away from. I was starting to see red. I'd fed this group breakfast and lunch, kept the beer cooler full, just like a proper ranch wife should. I just hadn't stayed in the house in between.

But the offer on our ranch fell through. While we spent another year in New Mexico, Sean helped all of the neighbors whenever they asked; I stayed behind. One well-meaning ranch wife took me aside and said that what went on beyond the kitchen door was really none of her concern. I nodded my head and smiled, and kept right on doing what had to be done. It was in my blood, I was capable, and we couldn't afford to hire someone else to do it.

By later that summer, we'd had another profitable offer. Federal and state lease ground is so vulnerable to environmental whims, we wanted our next ranch to be fully deeded land. For that we had to look east, east to Missouri. Sean went on ahead to the new place while I stayed behind to gather and ship the cows to him. When the final load-out day came and the six semis were idling in the yard, two cowboys came to help me pen, sort, and load. They told me they were honored to work with our cattle because the cows were gentle and broke to handle. Proof, they said, that we knew something about stockmanship. They worked quietly and smoothly and

didn't give a damn that I was a woman. They redeemed the whole Southern male image in their soft-spoken, easy cowboy way. Once the trucks were gone and the dust settled in the pens, I jumped my four horses in the gooseneck trailer, loaded the cat crates, and called the dogs.

This new place had no buildings, so we set up camp and settled into learning the cow business Missouri style. It wasn't long before we realized that these oak-covered mountains require some pretty good hands, and better yet, their wives are out there with them.

I'm convinced we've found home, although the journey makes us appreciate what we have. Not too many people can say they've had their rope tangled in Montana sagebrush, New Mexico mesquite, and Missouri oak sprouts while chasing the same dad-gum cows. We've built a corral, a barn, and a house, and we're surrounded by an incredible group of riding, roping friends, men and women both.

KATHLEEN RUTLEDGE ✑ *Women of the* Journal Star

I work in a newsroom that used to be two.

The reporters and editors for the morning paper, the *Lincoln Star,* sat in one corner, a homey band that bonded over donuts and popcorn balls, a group that would have "days" — like Hawaiian Shirt Day. The women of the *Star* had their own tradition: an annual potluck party at which they exchanged Christmas ornaments by a blazing fire.

In the opposite corner sat the staff of the evening paper, the *Lincoln Journal,* in a grim hurry every day until that early-afternoon deadline. They wore rubber pig noses one day to send a pointed message to the "suit" who called the newsroom a pigsty. The women of the *Journal* stuck together but had no tradition, unless you count Thursday afternoons at The Underground to drink beer. But that was men and women, and the main event was trying to say something funny enough to make the environmental reporter launch into a laugh that sounded like the warning when a submarine begins to go down. "Dive! Dive!" we would cry as Mitchel honked away.

Then one day, this newsroom that had been two — year after year, ornament party after ornament party, submarine dive after submarine dive — became one: the *Lincoln Journal Star.*

Still, the women of the *Lincoln Star* assembled each Christmas season to exchange ornaments by the hearth. Their newspaper was gone, but their tradition was not.

I also work in a newsroom that used to be white.

All white, except for one African-American man with a master's degree

from the University of Missouri. He wrote court news and had a patient air about him.

Sometimes someone would ask him what black people thought about this, what they thought about that. He would be patient, but . . .

Then one day, this newsroom that had been predominantly white was no longer so white. We created a Native American beat, perhaps the only such beat in the country. We formed a council of readers of various races and ethnicities to advise us how to cover the community—all of it—more accurately. We joined a national internship program that brought college students of color to the newsroom.

We hired seven, eight, nine, ten journalists of color, including four Native American journalists, in a newsroom of about seventy-five full-time staffers.

One day, we had trouble. A clash in the newsroom over a special project—on cultural diversity—that a Native American woman was helping to lead. Roles poorly explained. Harsh notes. Angry words. Other clashes, other accusations. Who's disrespectful? Who's offended? Who's hurt? Who's afraid?

Heat and more heat, then cold—cold fear, cold stares, cold shoulders.

Turmoil that began in late winter stretched through the summer.

Three reporters formed a "welcome committee" to hear people out and recommend how to make this one newsroom into a welcoming place for all.

A psychologist was summoned from St. Louis to counsel us on getting to know our coworkers. A journalist from Florida was lined up to train us how to talk across differences and to tell the untold stories in our newspaper.

An uneasy peace, call it weariness, fell over the newsroom. But things were not right.

One of the white women of the *Lincoln Star*, the one with the glowing hearth, lined up for take-out one day in a tiny downtown shop. The Native American woman who had led the special project stood in the same line. For minute after minute, as these two *Journal Star* reporters waited for their orders, they did not exchange greetings.

December. Time for that woman of the *Lincoln Star* to haul in a bundle of firewood, unfurl the holiday tablecloth, and address invitations to her tightening circle of friends who had worked at the old newspaper, each old friend with a cache of ornaments from Christmases past swaddled in tissue paper and laid in bent boxes on top closet shelves.

She weighed the tradition. She decided to widen the circle.

The women of the *Journal Star*—those who had worked for the morning

paper, those who had worked for the evening paper, and those who had worked only for the consolidated paper—would gather to crunch baby carrots and exclaim over sugar cookies and chip dip.

The women of the *Journal Star* would draw numbers from a basket to claim their mystery ornaments from beneath the tree.

On a Sunday evening, by a popping fire, the women raised their wary but happy voices in a chorus of chatter. Two of the voices in the chorus were those of the two reporters who had been so silent that day in line: women of the *Journal Star*.

JEANNIE P. SMITH ✒ *Valley Essential: Gladys Smith*

A shrill phone rang in the living room. Gladys Smith quickly picked it up.

"Be right over," she announced.

She pulled on a jacket, grabbed her weigh books, and jumped into her pickup. Three minutes later, she arrived at the truck scales.

Gladys, in her late eighties, was until recently the weigh master of Fish Lake Valley, Nevada—a sprawling community of farms. Her hours were simple: 7:00 A.M. to 7:00 P.M. every day of the year, rain or shine.

This demanding routine was a piece of cake for Gladys. And this job was nothing new to her, as she had been at it for nearly thirty years. Each truck she weighed took twenty to thirty minutes. For this she received a grand total of two dollars.

"I used to only get a dollar a truck," she said with a chuckle, "but just recently, I got a raise."

Gladys and her late husband, Harry, who passed away in 1997, moved to the valley from Los Angeles. Both Gladys and Harry had been raised in Iowa—Harry in the country and Gladys in the city—and Harry dreamed of owning a ranch after retiring from the Navy. Gladys wasn't so sure about the move to rural Nevada.

But the move agreed with her. Gladys and Harry were the principal shareholders of an eighteen-farm co-op that owned the scales. For many years, Gladys did the weighing and Harry kept the books. After Harry died, she did both jobs.

Her main love, however, was the weighing. "Those drivers are like sons to me," Gladys observed. "They bring me corn, watermelon, tomatoes, or whatever is in season. I know all about their families, how many kids they have, and all that. We talk about all sorts of things."

One year, she weighed more than three thousand trucks, mainly loaded with alfalfa and carrots. "It's hard to remember a day when I haven't had at least one truck," Gladys said.

Weighing was not something new to Gladys. During World War II,

while Harry served in the Navy, Gladys weighed precision powder for detonators. She also worked long hours in that demanding position.

"I don't know what the valley would do without Gladys," said Carrie Hartman, a longtime neighbor and friend. "She is just someone we all depend on so much."

"Well, I don't intend to go anywhere!" Gladys exclaimed.

Today Gladys is still the full owner of the scales, although she has now hired someone to run them. If you are ever in Nevada, stop in and say hello to Gladys. She'll give you a smile and do all she can to help keep the valley's trucks rolling.

GRETCHEN RONNOW *Old Women's Domain*

Dad was seventy-seven when he died; Mother was seventy-five. They had been married and in love for fifty-three years. They were attending a party in Salt Lake City, three hundred miles from their home, when Dad unexpectedly had to enter the hospital. Mother had with her only the clothes she was wearing for the party and an overnight bag. She found a place to stay with friends in the city. I flew the 550 miles from Flagstaff, Arizona, as often as I could, taking a few days at a time away from teaching so that she could make some quick trips to her home in St. George, Utah.

As the weeks turned into months, I began to recognize the routine of the hospital and its effects on the families of patients. I was there only a few days at a time, but Mother was there day after day, week after week, month after month, as were a number of other elderly women. The hospital rented rooms to families of long-term patients. These rooms were near the hospital, but they were frigid, barren, anonymous, dormitory-style rooms. I'd see old women making their way along snowy sidewalks, going to the hospital to sit beside their husbands, then returning to the empty rooms after a long day. Mother decided to stay the whole time with her friends, but it weighed on her that she was "imposing on them" for so long. She had to drive back and forth across town over icy streets and through heavy snow in one of the coldest winters in Salt Lake City history.

The physicians, surgeons, and nurses were compassionate, dedicated, and skilled, but LDS Hospital is a huge institution with its own immense complexities. Dad was in a trauma unit more "intense" than intensive care. Those high-powered nurses—trained to make the instantaneous command decisions regarding the inevitable life-and-death crises that are common there—had very little time or inclination to accommodate the frail and elderly wives of their patients. Mother and the other wives were usually alone except for the community they formed among themselves. They sat long hours for long days and weeks in the foyers, waiting for a few words from the hurried doctors.

On one of my visits around Thanksgiving, Mother said that she'd grown tired of hospital cafeteria food. "Let's go sit in the car. I've got some fruit and crackers," she said. We made our way out into the icy weather of early afternoon, crossed the street, and entered the multistory parking garage. The sky was gray, the parking garage nearly dark in the wan light of the afternoon. Deep shadows stretched from the cement support columns and filled the corners of the parking platforms. As we ascended the ramps looking for my mother's car, I noticed that on every level, three or four of the cars were occupied. In each, an elderly lady sat alone, eating a snack as my mother intended to do, meditating or praying or just gathering her own internal strength in order to return to the hospital and re-enter the process of her husband's death.

We found Mother's Oldsmobile, a dependable late-model sedan like all the other family cars my father had chosen. We got in, and she quickly locked the doors. She told me several women had been assaulted in that parking garage, and each of these elderly women must have thought of that every time she hurried to her car. Mother did indeed have food: crackers, apples, cheese, milk, dried fruit, and some bread. I could see that she had often eaten in her car those past weeks. She also had a few books, a warm blanket, some of Dad's things, her Bible, her Book of Mormon.

I realized that each of these women had forged a place for herself—a small domestic space inside an automobile. Fortified by her own hands and the ache of memory and association, this tiny space enabled her as an old woman, who would prefer the safety of her own home, to enter the public world that so often intimidates even the youngest and strongest. The popular myth would have us believe that the car is a man's domain, signifying the open road, freedom, and power. A parallel reality is that the car is also an old woman's domain, a site of a static and domestic, yet public and perilous, "road" story.

I cannot shake that image of old women sitting solitary in their cars, gathering themselves inward to face the rest of life alone.

ROBIN BARKLEY ✑ *Mine Shack Memories*

I've never quite understood why I ran away from my home in Denver at fourteen. My parents weren't mean. I loved nature and was crazy about horses. Why was the urge toward adventure stronger than family ties and safety?

My boyfriend found work at a remote gold-mining operation. I was too far from a school to attend, with no transportation, so I learned from the outdoors, roaming among the piñon hills and swift creeks in the aspen-lined canyons. I caught trout by casting a pop can wrapped with fishing line into deep beaver ponds. In spring, I picked wild strawberries. In fall, I

gathered rose hips, picked out the seeds, and cooked them with sugar on my wood cookstove. I shot and cooked rabbits, found rhubarb at abandoned miners' cabins. In the white arms of an aspen grove, I felt hidden and safe. The fiery sunset on the Sangre de Cristo Mountains was awe-inspiring for a girl who had known only city streets. For a time, women were entirely absent from my life.

Then one day, a rapist found the perfect target. He invited my boyfriend to drink whiskey, then sent him to town for cigarettes. Inside the one-room cabin, playing with my kitten, I hadn't been paying attention to the men. When that doorway was blocked, my life changed.

When I told our boss at the mine I'd been raped, he took me to the local sheriff; I was too young to drive myself. And then I met the women of the town. They all seemed to attend the hearing. In the courtroom, the women heard testimony that the men had been drinking together and that I was living, unmarried, with my boyfriend. The memory of the cold-eyed looks those town ladies gave me hasn't left me yet. The charges were dropped, the man was set free. I returned to the cabin fearful and uncertain.

I still remember that place like no other, that abandoned miner's cabin where I came of age. Around the gold miners' headstock, ghosts forever haunt those hills. My pain and that of others who came before me are lost on the wind, except in my memory of the cold eyes of those women who did not know me.

A. J. HARNISH ✍ Well—*You Told Me To*

I had begun my practice as a family physician in Cheyenne, Wyoming, when I had my first child and was gathered in by the society of women. Pregnancy, childbirth, sore nipples, nights without sleep, overwhelming fear about a sick child, and discovering that rocks and dandelions are the best gifts all bonded me to other women. Suddenly, the mothers in my practice were giving *me* advice. They reassured me that eighteen-month-olds are emotionally deranged people and that blowing in a kid's nose gets her to swallow medication in her mouth. Neither of these pearls was mentioned in medical school.

Conversely, my own past experiences have helped me recognize women who are living with psychological abuse and the self-doubt it creates. I can identify with working all day and still being responsible for family meals, laundry, shopping, and other chores.

I am privileged to talk to women about their families and lives. My heart breaks with each of my new widows, and I pray that I'll never see in my own mirror the strength that I see in their eyes or the anguish that never seems to leave the eyes of parents who have lost a child. I've learned that

the best thing I can do for these grieving patients is put them in contact with others who have had the same experiences.

I had never considered my influence until a very healthy eighty-nine-year-old patient slipped on the ice. Due to osteoporosis, she sustained a compression fracture in her back and suffered excruciating pain until pneumonia claimed her three weeks later. Then I began my personal war on osteoporosis, telling patients to take twelve hundred milligrams of calcium each day with vitamin D. I was beginning to feel like a broken record, considering giving up, when the one-year anniversary of my patient's death arrived. By that time, women were coming back for annual exams. When I asked one patient about her calcium intake and she said she was taking what I'd recommended, I must have looked surprised. "Well," she said, "you told me to."

Suddenly, I realized I could change people's habits. Now I tirelessly try to motivate people to stop smoking, lose weight, exercise—and take their calcium!

I love my pediatric patients. I look for birds in their ears, frogs in their throats. Abby, a patient of mine since she was eighteen months old, came home from first grade one day and said, "Guess what, Mom! Did you know boys could be doctors, too?"

As women, I think we need to seize the opportunities we have to bond with those we encounter. A successful community respects and values all of its members. We start effecting change in those around us by changing our own lives. My patients continue to remind me how empowering respect can be.

DENISE BANKER ~ *Surviving at Great Cost*

For Tait, an exemplary student

> I only half heard the stories that night,
> listened slant, imagining a flat-nosed diesel
> school bus airborne off a bridge, spiraling
> into muddy waters below, the kids from my town
> tumbling as if clothes in a dryer.
>
> Linda's house was the gathering place. Her lights
> on all night as kids came and went, sat silently waiting,
> ate pizza, drank pop. We'd survived the principal's suicide,
> the Trade Center bombings, and now, more surviving to do.
> Linda, like a priestess, listened to the wounds
> without offering words, only her ears and food.

The funerals long over, four times standing somber,
offering our young to the earth, the air, the sky,
when Tait finally came home from the hospital,
victim, survivor, reminder. Joan organized the town
women to prepare dinner every night his rehab lasted.
I baked pork chops, boiled wild rice, frosted brownies.
Linda created her finest, too: homemade noodles,
chicken in broth, onion bread—
human transformation in kitchens, bread into body.

A year later, identified as a group at risk,
we listen in the high school gymnasium
as the crisis speaker talks of how to cope. She tells us how
to recognize the signs: lack of interest, unexplained anger,
crying, drug or alcohol abuse. *Our living are dying.*
On the edge of the bleachers one woman holds herself.
A man, the row ahead, hangs his head, his shoulders
shake inaudibly. We are the parents of the dead.

Our sacrifice never complete, we shuffle out of the gym,
silently walk east in a violet-blue dusk
under the ritual of full moon,
everything shimmering as if a reflection on a lake.

TRACY WANG *From Canton to Spearfish*

In 1997, I stepped into the land of the United States with a curious and long-
ing heart. America is the most prosperous and advanced country in the
world, and many Chinese people dream about coming here.

I came to live in Spearfish, South Dakota, where my husband has lived
for almost ten years. We met in 1995 in China. My husband's niece was my
colleague as well as my good friend. She introduced me to him. After a year
of phone calls and letters, we got married in China. Many people asked me
why I moved to Spearfish. There is a Chinese saying: "Marry a chicken, fol-
low the chicken; marry a dog, follow the dog." My husband was born in the
year of the rat; I had to follow the rat.

I had never thought I would settle in a small town like Spearfish, which
has only about ten thousand people. I grew up in Canton, which has a pop-
ulation of more than six million people. I worked there as a tour guide in a
five-star hotel for ten years. I took tourists from all over the world sightsee-
ing around China. Some of them became my good friends, and we still keep
in touch. I also worked in the American Trading Company as a secretary to

the general manager for five years, and I still write and talk with my boss and my colleagues often.

I didn't like Spearfish when I first came. Especially I didn't like the snow and cold weather. I had never seen snow before. And I couldn't find a job I liked. I stayed at home for a month alone. My husband was working all day long from 10:00 A.M. to 10:00 P.M. at his brother's restaurant, the Golden Dragon, as a chef. I felt very bored doing nothing but writing as many as fifty letters a day to my family and my friends.

A friend from Canton, living in Chicago, invited me to visit her. She had married a Chinese-American citizen, immigrated to the United States, and opened a travel agency in Chicago's Chinatown. She had a very good business. I flew to see her and lived in her house. She found a job for me the next day in an accounting office, but I worked there for only a month. My husband urged me to come home.

After I came back to Spearfish, I was very unhappy. The first friends I met here were Aunty Fang and her husband, Uncle Bin. They were also from Canton, but we hadn't known one another before. Whenever I was sad, Aunty Fang always gave me lots of warmth and comfort. Aunty Fang was just like my mother, taking care of me very well. We lived in the same building, and she always invited me to her apartment to eat her delicious food.

Aunty Fang and Uncle Bin both worked for the Golden Dragon. They were over sixty years old but still very strong and healthy. Since I couldn't find a job, I had to work at the Golden Dragon as a waitress. I had never done this job before, so this was a great challenge for me. When I held a big tray with three to four dishes of food, my hands trembled. My sister-in-law (the boss's wife) didn't like me at all. When I couldn't move the heavy table out to clean the floor, she said, "If you can't move the table, just go back home and let your husband feed you." After hearing this, I wanted to quit. When Aunty Fang noticed that I was crying, she said patiently, "Every new immigrant must experience some difficulties. You need to learn to overcome the difficulties and to balance what is more important in your life. If you want to work here, you don't need to care too much what the boss says. You just do what you should do." After hearing these words, I tried very hard to do my job well and let my sister-in-law be satisfied with me. Finally, I became a skillful waitress.

It was difficult for me to get used to the life and work in Spearfish. The first year, I often argued with my husband, and I cried a lot. When I was in a bad mood, I would leave home and walk along the street for a couple of hours or go to Aunty Fang's apartment. My husband would call and ask Aunty Fang whether I was at her home. If I wasn't, Aunty Fang and Uncle Bin would drive around looking for me. They were afraid I would get lost.

In return for their kindness, I was their interpreter, helping them fill out

necessary documents and going to the bank, the post office, and the immigration office in Rapid City to renew their green cards, as well as to the Social Security office to process their retirement. When they were sick, I took them to the hospital to see the doctor. They said they wouldn't be able to stay in Spearfish without me. I was just like their white cane for the blind.

During those five years, many good customers at the restaurant became my friends. I always show my best hospitality and friendly smile to the customers.

I have been back to China twice to see my mother, my brother and his wife, and many good friends. I send some money to them a few times a year. The world is unfair; this is destiny. The best way is to make money in the United States and spend money in Asia. This is why so many people are longing to come to America. I plan to go back and live in Canton when I am old.

The year 2001 was a big year for me. On June 1, I went to Sioux Falls and was sworn in as a citizen of the United States. This was a big change in my life.

On that same June 1, we also took over my husband's brother's restaurant, and we are working very hard to manage it well. From that day to the present, my husband and I have worked at least eleven hours a day without a day off. Unfortunately, another Chinese restaurant opened two months later. It's unbelievable that there are two Chinese restaurants in such a small town! Our business was down a lot at first, but now most of our old customers have come back.

Then my husband became very sick and seriously suffered from pain for three days. He was found to have a stone in his kidney and had laser surgery in Rapid City Regional Hospital. After the surgery, he went back to work too soon and came down with a bacterial infection. I took him to the hospital again and stayed with him there for two nights. I had a very hard time that month, since I had to take care of my husband as well as the restaurant. Fortunately, Aunty Fang and Uncle Bin helped. They worked hard to keep the restaurant open every day and didn't take a day off in a whole month. Without them, we would have had to close for a few days.

But soon after that, they retired and left for New York, where their children live. I couldn't help myself from crying when I saw them off at the airport. Now we talk on the phone often. They sometimes mail me very good Chinese snacks and dim sum (pastries), which are not available here.

We have been running our restaurant for several years. This is my first time to do business. To my own satisfaction, our business is good so far, and we have some profit. We hope that we are able to continue doing better and better.

A friend once asked me which was the biggest ship in the world. I an-

swered *Titanic*. He said, "No, it is *friendship*." I realize now that friendship is indeed very important for human beings. I have found that it does not matter if the place we live is big or small. No matter where we live, if we don't have friends, life has little meaning. Fortunately, I have found lifelong friends—both here and in many states and countries. I treasure this worldwide community of friendship.

CHERYL ANDERSON WRIGHT ❧ *The Brown Sofa*

Grandma had a brown horsehair sofa,
pristine, though very old.
If I was bad, I had to sit on that sofa,
bare legs
dangling over
the edge of the cushions.
When the Bible Thumpers came,
Grandma graciously seated them
on the brown horsehair sofa.
They never stayed long.

SHELLY WHITMAN COLONY ❧ *Feeding the Spirit*

Yesterday I went to a women's shelter in Portland, Oregon, ostensibly to teach food storage methods but mostly to feel useful.

I went because I know what it's like to be poor in spirit; because I believe eating food prepared by hand nourishes the spirit as well as the body; because I know that when you're down-and-out, your spirit is usually the last thing that gets any care. And because my spirit needed some care, too.

Beth, the volunteer coordinator, helped me carry in a dozen ears of organic corn grown by my friend Corrine. I explained that Corrine grows enough food for sixty families in addition to supplying gourmet restaurants and groceries and selling her produce at the Portland farmers' market. All that food grows on a little over two acres without chemical fertilizers or pesticides. I also had a grocery bag of apples from my orchard, five pounds of sugar, a jar of cinnamon, a pot, tongs, a sharp knife, and a box of quart-size freezer bags. Beth couldn't believe more gear wasn't necessary for preparing the corn and apples for freezing.

Inside, Beth showed me around the facility and explained that the ninety women who lived there came from a variety of circumstances. Some were just out of prison. Some were recovering from addictions. Some were

fleeing domestic violence. Some had simply become ill and lost all their resources, including their homes, and needed a place to stay until they got back on their feet. Some were mentally ill.

Seven women had signed up for the workshop. Two names had been crossed off the list. Beth went around trying to round up the others. It seemed everyone had appointments. She began to apologize, but I said, "It doesn't matter to me how many come." I could have added, "What matters to me is that I came."

I started a pot of water boiling and began washing apples, and women started appearing, asking what I was doing. So we eased into a workshop that was really just a bunch of women cooking and talking together. One of the women used to work in an apple-sorting facility and told me my apples were Galas and had bitter pit, a disease caused by calcium deficiency in the soil. Another woman came from the Crow Reservation in Montana, and we talked about how pretty the Bighorn Valley is this time of year. She liked me because I am from Montana, too. The woman next to me at the table was having difficulty shucking her ear of corn. She was trying to take too much of the husk off at once, but I didn't say anything. I've probably shucked a thousand ears of corn in my life, and I still remember how hard it was the first time, when my hands seemed too small and the husks too tough.

We blanched the corn and peeled the apples. Beth had to retrieve paring knives from the locked storeroom. Some of the women wouldn't touch the knives. I didn't ask why; I didn't need to.

The shelter had a small garden with three or four apple trees, so we all crowded under the branches picking apples, noting where birds had pecked the flesh. One quiet woman in a pink sweater murmured, "Solanaceae, European nightshade, I think." I commented on her knowledge of botanical Latin. "Oh, I just picked it up here and there," she said.

I watched their hands, clumsy with unfamiliarity as they tried to tong the slippery corncobs, or peel apples, or spoon the cut corn into bags and press out the air. I've considered these everyday tasks menial and unimportant, performed them with annoyance or resentment because they took me away from writing or other things I'd rather do. Here they formed a braid of hope and sanity. For some women, medication, the advocacy of a caseworker, or the support of a community is necessary to be able to hear the needs of body and soul. A simple, hand-prepared meal is one way back to oneself. I need to remember this.

TWYLA HANSEN ❧ *At the Greasy Spoon*

In a small town, in a dark-paneled café called Harold's,
at a plastic-topped table, I sit with my mother and her two sisters.

They debate roast beef or chicken, sandwich or dinner special,
coffee or just water. I scan the menu for anything of redemption,

keep my expectations low. They're getting up there in years.
I study lined faces, veined hands, clean-your-plate waistlines.

It's noon and the place overflows—feed salesmen, bankers,
retirees—folks who, my aunt says, like to eat what others cook.

I think of these sisters, their grins in the sepia portrait—
 bobbed hair,
best Sunday dresses—the handsome family gazing out at a world

before the Great Depression, before they lived an uncertain future,
no guarantee for that next meal. We would have starved to death

if not for our grandparents, my aunt says. Mother adds, They
gave us a chicken for the eggs, but we had to eat the chicken, too.

Now you might not guess: my mother's bent shoulders, one aunt's
unsteady hand, the other with excess pounds to lug around.

Their dinners arrive on oval platters: meat, potatoes, a layer
 of gravy,
rolls and overcooked vegetables. This is plenty, I insist, pointing

to my wedge of lettuce and watery soup. When they were young,
their options were limited; they kept their expectations low. Now

they relish each pleasant surprise fate happens to dish out.
We're all from a long line of the common, the ordinary, the land;

some lessons you never outgrow. On my mother's recent
 ocean cruise,
what she enjoyed most was the food: four complete dining rooms!

Woman who has lugged around her first electric range, since 1952,
from farm to city; it now resides in her basement. Never know

when you might need an extra oven. These sisters don't dwell
on the past. Our waitress stops by, my aunt winks. Pie, anyone?

RUTH HARPER ✑ *Vagina Dialogues on the Road Trip*

This poem recalls a trip to see The Vagina Monologues, *a play by Eve Ensler in which women's stories—both hilarious and provocative—are told from a unique perspective. The show is performed across the country as a fundraiser for women's shelters.*

The van is filled with layers of conversation,
an exotic torte made from what's in the cupboard,
as we drive to Sioux Falls.

Wine and dinner at Kristina's,
crisp Chablis and curried cod,
could last for hours,
but the show starts at 7:30
and we clamber up the slippery street,
arm in arm,
oblivious to ankle-deep slush.

Afterward, cradling coffee cups,
we clumsily review the script.
If your vagina could talk,
what would it say? I ask.
 I'm afraid of my own beauty.
 I hate being ignored!
 You work all the time. Can't we ever play?
 I need to be touched.

Okay . . . if you could dress your vagina,
what would it wear? I persist.
 Leaves. Flowers. A hint of an unfamiliar spice.
 A road map—with directions!
 A quilt of worn gingham dresses.
 Long prairie skirts. No underwear.

We share desserts and quiet conversation,
a warm blanket of colorful threads
carried effortlessly from month to month,
woven into tonight's talk therapy.

At the next table, younger women hoot,
raise their shirts like fearless sails in a breeze,
display tattoos to applause.

We smile and wonder
what their vaginas might say and wear.
　　Animal-print thongs. Bikini waxes.
　　Abstinence clad in Abercrombie indulgence.
　　Piercings? A close shave.
　　Gardenias. Pink lace. Shared secrets.

Driving home, we are subdued.
Talk is fragmented.
　Good night, vagina, vagina, vagina,
　I say as I get out of the car,
　feeling fond, smart, and somewhat daring.
　Oh, go sit on your husband's face,
　a friend snaps back.
　I gasp with laughter and run to the house.

KIM POTTS ❧ *Shelter for Each Other*

In the New West, two groups live uneasily and with occasional flare-ups,
not unlike the Native Americans and the new settlers of the Old West. I live
uncomfortably between the two groups, with enough sympathy for each to
leave me forever an outsider.

The natives now are the conservative members of the agricultural, min-
ing, and logging communities. Sometimes, listening to them, I think they
believed the promises of the films we saw in grade school that told how the
new technologies made American agriculture (or mining or lumber) the
most productive in the world. The films didn't mention that efficient tech-
nology meant fewer jobs.

They are a little bitter, this group, finding that the future is not what
they were assured it would be and that they have little control over it. They
blame the newcomers, "those damn environmentalists," who bring bag-
gage of regulation and zoning, who want to manage and channel the tides
of change. The natives hate these ideas the way the old-time cattlemen
hated fences. They think the newcomers are maliciously trying to take a
livelihood that was never easy and make it all but impossible. They have
hung on doggedly by their fingernails through hard times, only to have
their lives taken away by a bunch of granolas.

They think they are realists. You can't eat scenery, they say. But they are
not. The realists left the high country years ago. They went to the cities on
the coasts and are accountants or run heating and air-conditioning busi-
nesses. They come back to visit, to fish and hunt and admire the scenery

they can't eat. The stubborn romantics were left to be joined by the next set of stubborn romantics, the newcomers, the urban refugees.

This group came for the scenery, the sense of space, the wild lands, looking for a connection they couldn't find in the tamer, easier life in the urban or suburban places they left. Those who come with money have a harder time gaining acceptance than those of us who have to take the same low-paying jobs as the locals and scrape by any way we can. That rite of passage gives our lives here some legitimacy. But in many ways, we seem arrogant to the natives, telling people who have a lifetime relationship with this land and long memories of this place that they should preserve and protect their own and do it our way. And we are arrogant—as arrogant as the settlers who came and looked at the Indians and assumed that they had no relationship with the land because they didn't farm it.

We newcomers, in turn, are shocked and appalled at what we see as the carelessness of the natives with this precious place. We come from war zones where beautiful, or at least open, places have been overrun with industry and asphalt. We believe that avoiding environmental regulations is as insane as allowing someone to scatter gunnysacks full of knapweed and leafy spurge seed on your land. We feel that the natives are opening the gate to the Trojan horse. They see jobs and an end to the cyclical busts. We newcomers have seen the destruction that comes out of the horse to a place, to the community that lives there.

What each of these groups can't see is that at the core, they both love the same place and want the same thing. The natives blame the newcomers for trying to foist tiresome regulations on them, discourage industry, and make it harder to hang on through the next bust. The newcomers blame the natives for leaving the doors open to the forces that will destroy what they love. Each side reacts with such bitterness because they believe the other side is trying to take from them what they value so highly—a life in this high country.

Maybe if the new folks could look at the miner, the logger, the rancher and understand that it has always been hard to hang on here and that these people struggle to keep their roots in this dry ground . . . Maybe if the natives could understand that the new folks came here searching for the same things they hold dear—a life in this big, open country in a community where you are a person, not a cog in a machine—that they are trying hard to put down their roots in this dry ground . . . Maybe then we could begin to shelter each other from the harsh winds that threaten to wither us and blow the soil away from our clinging roots.

JEAN VERTEFEUILLE-CUTLER ✍ *Champagne Toast*
at Midnight

The sweating, exhausted mare lay in the bloody straw. At her side, a small wet body stirred to life, patches of brown and white coat barely visible through milk-colored membranes. The mare nickered and stretched her head around, ears pricked forward, to sniff the strange little creature. A tiny pink velvet nose returned the greeting; a powerful bond began.

Beside me, Carolyn put her hand on my shoulder. Christina hugged Mary, and Ann and I wiped tears from our eyes. We sat in the straw along the edge of the stall, arms wrapped around our knees for warmth. "Look, she's standing!" Ann exclaimed. We continued to whisper praise of the filly's perfect head, her long hip and sloping shoulder as she took her first wobbly steps toward the mare's flank. She discovered a nipple and began slurping and sucking hungrily.

For the five of us horsewomen, these midnight barn gatherings in a small Colorado mountain town were annual spring traditions: paints for Mary, Appaloosas for Carolyn, quarter horses for Ann and me, puppies for Christina. Our bonds of friendship deepened with every new life born.

Leaving the mare and filly to rest, we walked back to the house through the bitter March chill. Even though it was two in the morning, no one felt like heading home to bed, so Mary fed chunks of wood into the stove as we shed our coats and mud-covered boots and popped our traditional bottle of champagne. "To Mary's new filly!" Carolyn said, raising her glass.

Christina added, "To all of us for being crazy enough to be here to celebrate this event!" We all laughed.

"This is sure better than Christina's call last July." Ann said, setting her glass down.

"Lightning!" Christina had cried into the phone. "Three mares down."

That gray morning, we stared in disbelief at the still forms of Christina's old mares—not a mark on them—lying together beneath the lightning-struck pine. "We need to get them up to the boneyard." Christina's voice broke the numb silence.

With my tractor bucket, we loaded each mare as gently as possible into one of the three pickups, and they started the slow procession up to the end of our property. Mary and I rode our mares behind the sad parade. A dark layer of clouds hovered overhead, and we heard occasional thunder in the distance.

The ground in the boneyard was scattered with the bleached bones of Barrister, my beloved thoroughbred; Shareefa, Christina's Arabian mare; and the others who had passed before them. "So hard to let them go," Carolyn said in a quivering voice as we placed the last mare beside the others in a semicircle under a huge pine overlooking the mountains. We lit sage and

cedar smudge sticks, circling them over the bodies. The pungent smoke mixed with our tears, carrying our prayers up on the breeze.

Just as we turned to leave, the storm clouds burst into rumbling thunder. "It's Barrister and Shareefa," I said, "galloping across the heavens to welcome the new horses!" The five of us held hands, eyes turned toward the sky as the thunder faded away, and watched them go.

For most of the other women in this small ranching town, horses were something you rode to get a job done. The five of us loved to help these ranch women gather cattle, but we knew we were different. We were drawn together by a deep love for our horses, a craving for like-minded female companionship, and a need for belonging to something outside our constantly shifting day-to-day lives.

And how our lives have changed! We were all married when we first met. Since then, we've had kids and grandkids, divorced, been widowed, remarried, stayed single. We rarely get together anymore, yet the deep bonds that we shared through our equine experiences keep us connected. I miss the 3:00 A.M. calls and Mary's voice saying her mare is foaling at last. I miss the deep talks over hot coffee in Carolyn's barn while her stallion prances around his paddock. I miss Ann showing us a secret trail up the back side of our canyon. But we occasionally grab a quick lunch at the Lodge and try to catch up on recent events in our lives. And we know that if any one of us ever needs help or support, wild horses couldn't keep us away.

That cold March night at Mary's, when we finally bundled up to leave for our separate homes, we savored the warmth of parting hugs and the good-natured kidding, wondering who next would call us together for a midnight champagne toast.

NORMA THORSTAD KNAPP *The Logging Bee*

"This community has a special way about it, Ellie. And you're part of that," one woman said to our hostess. Ellie blushed with pleasure as she left the room to answer her phone—bad news, and one of the members had to rush home.

As a newcomer at the church circle meeting, I felt left out at first. We'd moved from a large city to this rural area just three weeks earlier. But by the time the group parted, I'd been welcomed into the neighborhood. Voices called to each other in the night: delicious cake . . . hope all is okay at Mary's . . . nice to meet you, Norma!

The following morning, I phoned Ellie. "Yep, pretty bad," she said. Mary's sixteen-year-old, Tracy, had been accidentally shot and was now in the intensive care unit. But Ellie's husband, Alvin, already had an idea how

the whole community could help. He and his logger friends could get a permit from the county to cut wood, and maybe equipment dealers would donate machinery. They could cut and sell wood to help pay Tracy's medical expenses.

Ellie told me with enthusiasm, "It's a grand idea! People will pitch in like nothing. We can do the organizing and the feeding." She and neighbors Lila and Edith became the steering committee. Other women agreed to work on subcommittees.

"Women in this community know you got to step out," Ellie told me. "Put yourself on the line; help the guy in trouble. People here really care and reach out to each other." They spread the word, and soon the Logging Bee was the major topic in the area. The men chose a forty-acre stand of hardwoods, mostly popple (Minnesota's quaking aspen), and set a date after two equipment dealers committed people and equipment. For three weeks, the women secured workers, painted signs, planned menus, decided working shifts, and divided tasks.

The night before the Logging Bee, the women made myriad trips hauling material to the logging site: tables, tablecloths, huge metal coffeepots, lawn chairs, coffee, dishtowels and bath towels, blankets, propane bottles, paper plates, silverware, napkins, dishpans, dish soap, and garbage cans and bags.

Early the next morning, it was like stepping back in time as the women made ready for the feast of potluck foods to come. Through the evergreens to the east, we saw the feller buncher and the skidder with its new-style grapple for grabbing logs. As the noise grew louder, it was like the finale of a triumphant war song. Two trucks pulling trailers with monstrous machinery came from one direction, and a parade of logging trucks, a shearer, and a hydraulic loader came from the opposite direction. The sights and sounds were more throat-tightening to me than any city parade of bugles, drums, or bagpipes could ever be.

The first truck driver leaned down to howl over the engine, "Where do you want her?"

With one hand, Alvin pointed across the "dining area" toward the stand of poplar trees where the men had begun gathering. "Set 'er up right in the middle over there," he shouted.

Under a gunmetal sky, women of all ages, colors, shapes, and sizes filled the makeshift tables with salads, sandwiches, produce, and sweets and placed hot dishes, wrapped in towels and blankets, in the camper we'd set up.

All day, while the men felled trees, skidded, measured, cut into eight-foot lengths, trimmed, hydraulically moved, sorted, and loaded onto trucks, people roamed back and forth to eat. As with the wedding at Cana, the food was secondary.

The air was cool and scented with sawdust and coffee. At any given hour, thirty or forty women worked and welcomed women like me, new to the neighborhood. This whole event was a job we women could do—a job to put our minds to, a job that quickly filled the stomachs of all who came to help. The intoxicating feeling of feeding all those people all day long made me want to throw my head back and sing, even with my throat full of sawdust dust and huge lumps forming in it.

As the day and the woodcutting progressed, smells of meats, coffee, breads, and sweets mingled with sweat, oil, sawdust, and gasoline. A steady stream of people took turns working and eating. Farther into the woods, children watched the loaders and cranes from a safe distance. Around the chain saws, streams of sawdust poured down to make cushiony golden mounds on the trampled grass.

When the sun fell and food ran low, we made sandwiches, pulled food from storage, and cut pies, cakes, bars, and sweet breads into smaller pieces. Laughter erupted, and conversations flowed: we got backup water in case of fire? . . . yep, the mighty Mississippi is only 'bout a mile east o' here . . . I forget how close she is . . . used to live in these parts . . . good to be back in the woods . . . we need to be encouragers, blessings to other people . . . good to be working outside . . . used to canoe the river here and stay at Coffee Pot Landing . . . those sure were the days . . . accident like this makes one stop and think . . . could've been my kid.

Soon a sphere of amber crept across the October sky.

"Harvest moon?" someone asked.

"Might be," someone answered. "This day was a harvest."

Men and women walked to their vehicles, tired but smiling: been a great day . . . don't be a stranger . . . good to spend time together . . . hope came out of nowhere, settled on me . . . heard we cut over two hundred cords of wood.

As Ellie propped her arms, overflowing with dirty tablecloths, against her goldenrod-colored pickup, a wide grin filled her face, and her contagious laughter drifted up to the clouds, decorating the night sky.

JANE MCGARRY ✍ *Wood Ash on the Wind*

The Wake Fire, July 4, 1994

We stand in Ella Mae's front yard
watching black smoke billow
and junipers explode in flame
around the home we built
with our plain hands

and the hands of many friends
who hold us now
as the world burns.
In a strike of lightning
we came adrift
untethered
unhindered by belongings
the voices of our neighbors
coming as if from far away
the sky orange
too strange for tears we
float free above our old lives
like wood ash on the wind.

CAROLYN DUFURRENA 🖎 *Nevada Firestorm*

At 2:30 P.M., lightning strikes the Horseshoe, on the road to our summer sheep camp. Shovels, water, radios; my husband, Tim, shakes the cowboys out of their afternoon naps—ranch days start at 3:00 A.M.

The fire is a wicked red smile at the base of the half circle of volcanic hills we call the Horseshoe. The little Denio, Nevada, fire truck is there when we arrive. Someone calls the Bureau of Land Management (BLM). Dispatch lady says, we can't tell you not to fight it, but we have no resources available right now. Thirty-two strikes have zapped the dry range and timber right around us.

We're on our own.

Only a few acres across, the fire moves east toward the canyon, then north. It swirls in a small circle in a fickle wind. "Denio Dan," our fire chief, takes the little community fire truck, loads up cowboys and shovels, and drives along the boulder-strewn flat. The truck will wet down the road; its ungraded shoulders are full of dry weeds, but the fire is not big yet, and we tell ourselves the road will probably stop the flames.

The wind changes; the fire backs south and west. Smoke rolls over us. Sam, our son, and I find a pipe wrench and drive to the windmill a quarter mile away downwind. We lift the heavy iron pipe and screw it in, shrieking, to the connection that will bring water to the two big round troughs. The fire truck holds only 250 gallons of water; it can refill here.

The fire eats a fence post, crosses into the main chute of the valley. Here convection currents make invisible Ferris wheels, cycling hot summer air high up into the atmosphere, bringing cool air down. Dust devils dance along the meeting line of the convection cells.

We watch, fascinated. In the convection of valley air circulation, the fire

grows into a flame-cored whirlwind, sixty feet tall. It sucks the smaller flames into itself, black smoke towering, turning in a slower column around it. The whirlwind roars like a live thing, blowing the heat south. The tongue of fire that has run west across the fence line turns full on us.

The pickups easily outdistance the flames, but the big vehicles, the water truck and the grader, are slower. I drive south with my thirteen-year-old niece, Magen. She came with her dad, now piloting the water truck. The red whirlwind is almost keeping up with us, cutting southwest across the flat. This is when I get nervous, and I tromp the accelerator of the quirky old truck that doesn't always start and sometimes dies. It will be good to be out of the way of this thing.

Jackrabbits dash back and forth in front of the pickup. The dust is bad; we roll up the windows. The sky darkens; we cannot see the sun.

We pass a woman on a three-wheeler with a shovel, looking at us over her shoulder. A man with a little Bobcat loader makes tiny circles around the power poles in the path of the wall of fire. Several carloads of tourists look startled. Cows and calves run down the shoulder of the road, all backed by the red tower of smoke and flames.

When it seems as if we are behind the fire line, I pull over to the shoulder. Then it jumps the highway, splits into four fires, and burns in all directions, unstoppable until the wind dies.

Another big cloud of smoke hangs to the north over the horizon. Someone says on the radio that there's a fire at Wilder, the summer buckaroo camp. We may need to open some gates, get the animals out of there.

Then I am in another pickup, driving north to the neighbors' to find saddles and horses. Teri, our postmistress, lives nearby. She is just finishing disking around her house with a little blue tractor. She loans her tractor to a man who takes off up the road to try to clean the weed-choked ditches before the fire meets the gravel. The wind is steady, from the north.

Teri grabs her shovel, and we follow. Mostly we sit in the pickup and wait; stand on the road, wait; lean on shovels, wait. There's no point getting in front of something you're not going to stop. Ranchers from the Oregon side of the line are building a firebreak along an old windmill road parallel to the fire line, hoping to stop the fire there.

The little tractor growls and clanks over rocks, back and forth along the firebreak, silhouetted by a smoky sunset. Volunteer firemen light a line of backfire; a water tender follows close behind. The wind holds steady, and the backfire does what it's supposed to, burning toward the main fire. The fires seem attracted to each other; when the two fire lines meet, the flames roar up, hissing; waves of fire crash on each other, then die, surrounded by the blackened landscape.

The community fights this fire, and the community wins. Neighbors save one another. One lone BLM fire engine lumbers up. "Well, you guys got this one," the redheaded kid driving says with a grin.

The huge red glow of the other fire lights the night sky over the summit, and we head back that way. As we crest Denio Summit, it is very much like driving into the gates of hell. Fire burns through 180 degrees of vision, all across the valley, up into the foothills on both mountainsides.

We sit by the road for a long time, watching the fire move north. It eats one power pole after another. Cows and calves are bawling for each other in the brush somewhere. There's not much we can do till daylight now.

Pickup headlights flash as the cowboys come around the far fence corner. Gradually, the lights come. Sam tells me later they cut the fence in four places, but there were still cattle running toward the flames, away into the dark, running everywhere.

Tim thinks we'll need the horses at sunrise to gather the animals. He stays the night on the hill, sends the rest of us home. Back in the house, too exhausted to sleep, I shower, wander around, get coffee ready for 3:30 breakfast. The house smells like smoke.

I wake well before the alarm; pull on my smoky jeans; make coffee, bacon, sausage, eggs. Nobody really ate yesterday, and probably nobody will eat today. Somehow men and horses converge with Tim at first light. It is an endless iteration this day: drive here, get horses, come back, meet the trailer, catch more horses, drive out, drop off cowboys, come back. The morning ripens as we begin to gather cattle, a job that would normally take the better part of a month. The wind starts early.

The cowboys are our teenage children and our neighbors. They bring the cattle down the highway fence line, to the seeding that burned yesterday, and trust that they'll head for home. "Don't hurry," Tim tells the kids. "Keep 'em mothered up." The kids nod, keep the bunch together.

Traffic is heavy — tourists, people with motor homes. The state highway people pilot them through the burning valley every so often. I watch through binoculars in the wavery heat. Fire whirlwinds are dancing again. Little bunches of cows keep boiling up out of the deep wash in the middle, where we can't see if a rider is driving them, or the fire, or both.

The fire jumps the highway behind the herd, even with two fire engines foaming and spraying water. It is midafternoon now. Some of the men have gone up the wash ahead of the fire, which has once more cut us off from each other. Tim and Sam are up there, ahead of the smoke, moving cows back to the north. The highway is closed; a state trooper shakes his head. "No, you can't take that horse trailer up there, not now."

I look back at the pillars of smoke rising from the fire line, where my husband and my son have gone. It is never a gentle country, and I am a bad churchgoer. Nothing in my safe childhood prepared me for this place. It is elemental: fire, flood, freezing cold, plagues of insects — young people and animals dying for no reason. I have prayed for things before, and they haven't worked out. I make a picture of my boys in my head and draw a circle of white light around my loved ones and their horses. I call my mother

on the cell phone and tell her what is happening. She'll be praying, too, she says, pass it around the prayer chain. "Let us know what happens." This is not jolt-of-adrenaline fear, but the heavy dread of watching the Apocalypse unfold.

The road is choked with gawkers with video cameras; king cab pickups full of kids, dogs, grandmas, beer coolers. Someone says there'll be four hundred firefighters here tomorrow. I wonder what will be left to burn by then.

I stand for hours on the highway with everyone else, all afternoon. And then, there they are, Tim and Sam and Bob and Clint and Josh, faces black with soot, horses wet, everything filthy. Safe. A north breeze lifts the hair plastered to my forehead. The smoke is clearing a little. Fires are still burning all around the country, but it's looking a little better here. I don't remember getting home.

The next morning, there are indeed four hundred firefighters on the scene, tankers of Jet A helicopter fuel, hotshot crews from Utah and the Arizona Strip, New Mexico and Wyoming. Choppers, portable potties, a caterer (Salisbury steak the first night, chicken-fried steak the next). A mushroom of little pop-up dome tents grows at the maintenance station, where they set up camp. The choppers fly, the hotshot crews head for the smoke, all up high now, and we turn to mopping up.

ASHLEY COATS ✐ *Women in Pickups*

Women in the West, who have different roles, budgets, and lifestyles, drive an amazing assortment of vehicles. Maybe we are what we drive. But when I spot another woman in a pickup, I smile and wave, no matter the age of the woman or the pickup.

Some days I miss the convenience of my old Suburban, but even when I'm hauling kids, dogs, groceries, bags of feed, and the odd piece of equipment, I find freedom in slinging sacks and equipment in the back of the flatbed, lashing them down with leftover baling twine I find stashed under the seat. Well, the dogs usually ride up front.

In our community, the majority of pickup drivers are male, but a fair number of women take to the roads in pickups—old or new, clean or filthy—and they always catch my attention. We nod at each other, and a surge of understanding flashes between us—a cord of camaraderie exists, no doubt about it. We live in the West, and we're proud of it. I feel privileged to be a member of this microcommunity. Long before we pass on the road, I recognize neighbors by the vehicles they drive. If a woman is at the wheel, all the better. And I admit I am partial to an older woman in an older truck. To me, she is the West.

DORIS BIRCHAM ⤔ **Gifts from Our Hands and Hearts**

We were gathered at a Piapot Lions Club dance in late November 1985, a tough year for our sparsely populated farming and ranching community in southwestern Saskatchewan. Not enough rain and too many people sick. We tried to be optimistic. "Next year" the grass will grow stirrup-deep. But what about the folks who were ill?

Two of my friends suggested we make Christmas hampers and deliver them. Word quickly spread among the women gathered together that evening. As individuals, we had often taken care packages to neighbors in crisis, but this would be a community response.

On a cold, snowy day in early December, women who drove several miles arrived at my home carrying boxes of home baking. Two tables stretching almost the full length of my kitchen were soon laden with gifts. Buns, breads, cinnamon rolls, mincemeat tarts, pies, kuchens, candy, and every kind of square and loaf imaginable, even sugar-free Christmas cake for diabetics, were among the offerings.

We made up fourteen hampers. Among them were one for the woman carrying on with the ranch chores while her husband battled cancer; two for the families of young mothers who were acutely ill; three for families who were making regular trips to Regina, 250 miles away, for treatments; one for the family who had just lost a wife and mother; three for elderly bachelors living alone. A volunteer delivered each hamper personally and received sincere appreciation expressed with smiles and words.

No committee, no meetings, no organization was required to create these gifts. They offered caring and comfort and cost very little, but they symbolized the way women nurture not only their families but also their communities. The seed was planted, watered, and harvested as gifts from our hands and our hearts.

JANE KIRKPATRICK ⤔ **To Dance with Grace**

The words that evening were woven inside women's ways of knowing.

At our small community's public school library event, the rancher wasn't the first to read, although I believe his poem defined the night. Field dust covered his pants; an effort to brush it off before he stood to speak left outlines of his fingertips on them. "It's nice to be where words aren't meant to manipulate or advertise," he said, "where they're just appreciated. I'm glad I came."

He read "On Rock Creek," a poem about a brother's death, an orphan girl, and a family's wish to heal. The place-names—Mikkalo, Wishram, the John Day River—were as familiar as the loss and grief that moved across the narrow room. It bound us together with a tender tie.

A high school sophomore, reading a poem she'd written about being different, had preceded him, and a former nun read after from her memoir. She'd been a nun for nineteen years, and her story breathed of the challenge of community and change, words that resonated with everyone in that room. A former Broadway actress read next, her stage presence capturing us all. She was followed by a playwright who lived out at windswept Klondike, in the shadow of that new wind farm with the massive silver windmills that look like fireflies at night. He read from Viktor Frankl's *Man's Search for Meaning* while the audience sat in stillness, the face of a loved one brought before us as Frankl once imagined his wife's face in that German death camp.

Then we had an intermission. People mingled beside home-baked cookies and plates of fruit. Words of weather, soil moisture levels, and the price of wheat were interspersed with graduation plans and gardens.

For six years now, since our small community formed the Sherman Public School Library, we've celebrated words and stories with a "read aloud." Once the library was a single room made up of donated titles. Volunteers checked books in and out twice a week and kept lists of overdues and borrowers, which were posted on the door. Neighbors could remind one another to return overdue books.

Finding it more cost-efficient to expand a high school library than create a new public library, the community voted to enlarge the school's collection and expand its hours to include evenings and weekends. Children's books abound, a newspaper rack invites senior readers, and at a bank of computers, dusty ranchers sit beside high school seniors, each helping the other learn to surf and sort.

Once a year, we celebrate community and stories with the read-aloud event. Each reader chooses a five-minute selection from a favorite author to share with his or her neighbors. Sometimes the readings are mixed with original works, if one's inclined to share. For two hours, we're inspired not by high-speed car chases or commercials blazed across a screen, but by the wings of words. Young adults listen to the local sheriff read a children's book or a county commissioner celebrate a biography. They watch these community leaders gain sustenance for the long winter nights through the power of words.

As I mentioned, the rancher wasn't the first to read that night. As the hostess, so to speak, I'd been asked to read first, from my own recently published work, *What Once We Loved*. "This story is about grief being a witness, meant not to hold us hostage but to transform," I read, thinking of the month before and the burial of my father.

The former school superintendent read from *Bridge to Terabithia*, a children's book by Katherine Paterson about finding special places. A poet from a neighboring town followed, and then a roving librarian—a woman who offers assistance to the many tiny libraries in the many tiny towns that

dot the wheatland, saving stories, tying us together despite our distance. A high school English teacher read about the price we pay for alienation and disconnection, the price we pay when a community shuts its eyes. The local pastor read, followed by two students, one of whom, blushing, shared a love poem of her own.

Then that rancher read. Rob Whitbeck. It was a narrative poem, and the narrator was an old man, remembering the orphan girl who left them, and how first his mother and then his father had died so quickly after she left, not able to bear another loss of a chosen child. The narrator couldn't find a way to go after that orphan, couldn't cross the chasm of grief, and so he stayed and ranched, never seeking her, even when she sent the horse back, the bridle carefully braided in its mane.

A feather fluttering to the floor would have seemed invasive in that moment, the words so bound us in our collective longing, our shared desire to get through grief together. We had found what T. S. Eliot wrote we must if we're to have a life with meaning: "a still place in a turning world."

We finished up with *Peace Like a River.* Being the local author, I got to end the read aloud, too, choosing this work by Leif Enger that I wanted the world to know—so rich the words, so meaningful the message about miracles. "We and the world, my children," the author writes, "will always be at war. Retreat is impossible. Arm yourselves."

Our community that night was armed with words, woven together because women know the value of collected stories. Connection lives inside the words. Healing lives there, too. Women must have known that years ago in towns across the land—that what we share, what weaves us all together into community, is our vulnerability, the uncertainties that find us all in wilderness places. With the help of others, we are somehow able to get through. Those women who began the little libraries, they knew that until we find the meaning in the stories of our lives, we're destined to wander in the wilderness, even though we're in a promised land. They found a way to save the stories so that a community could transform itself.

And then it was over, two hours having slipped by with barely a dry eye. People who nod at each other through the week, maybe lift a finger in a wave as their trucks meet on the treeless country roads or who chat over the clotheslines that still hang beside old homes, had joined with poets and readers from outlying regions, and we'd been transformed into a community. We'd remapped ourselves as individuals onto a new and richer surface.

"Where there is great love there are always miracles," wrote the novelist Willa Cather long ago. That night, the words formed miracles, and a community reaffirmed its formation. The poet W. H. Auden's words, not read that night, perhaps sum it up best: "If there when grace dances, I should dance."

On an April evening, the community of Moro, Oregon, danced together with grace.

JENNIFER GRAF GRONEBERG ✑ *Tupperware Therapy*

I live in the mountains of northwestern Montana, at the end of a tiny, winding gravel road. Before this home, my husband, son, and I lived on a dryland wheat and cattle ranch seven hundred miles east, still in Montana, on the broad, dry flats of the Powder River country. What these two different landscapes have in common is the attitude of my women neighbors. When anything important happens in our lives, we cook.

New babies, graduations, anniversaries; broken legs, breast cancer, a rib cage crushed by a wild heifer—all these events trigger the same time-tested response: make a hot dish. We pull out note cards with recipes handwritten in loopy scrawls, we gather ingredients, we clear a space in our overly busy lives, and we go to work in our kitchens.

Elk Steak with Tomatoes and Peppers from Michelle, Rae Ellen's Cabbage Salad, Sarah's Southwest Chicken, Phyllis's Beef Potpie with Thyme. I like to think I'm remembered for my Fresh Corn Chowder with Avocado, but I've also been known to send a spaghetti casserole made from my mother-in-law Joyce's recipe. Each of us has signature dishes, so predictable and unique that we can tell who's visited from the food lined up on the counter as plainly as if we'd all signed a guest book at the front door.

We chop and measure; we braise and roast; we assemble. Sometimes we have food wrecks and we must start all over again, because it wouldn't be right to share something that is less than stellar in our own eyes. Cooking is a way to release the nervous energy that comes in times of great joy or sorrow. Into our meals we pour our good wishes, our prayers, our hearts. We bake something for dessert: banana bread, huckleberry pie, pear butter, double-chocolate brownies. And at the end of the day, when the food is packed safely in plastic containers or casseroles or glass dishes, when we plop down in a chair for a moment's rest before we head out to deliver our culinary gifts, we all might wonder if it wouldn't be easier to get something from town: take-out from the Chinese place or something already frozen in tidy, disposable trays from the grocery. Of course not. To do so wouldn't be neighborly at all.

My first lesson in neighboring came from Helen, our white-haired landlady when Tom and I were newlyweds. She and her husband, Old Vic, owned a cherry orchard carved from the mountainside of Douglas fir and ponderosa pine that surrounded our little homesteads. In the summers, they sold sweet cherries "U-pick." Helen kept a giant weaving loom strung with parallel lines of white string in the front room of their house, on which she made rag rugs. Balls of recycled fabric strips dotted her floors. Next to the loom was a huge woodstove, which they kept fired round the clock, summer and winter. And although she'd never said so, I got the feeling that in addition to dropping off the rent check on time, I was supposed to pay her a neighborly visit now and then, which I gladly did.

My first tomato plants came from Helen. She showed me how to plant them, deep in the warm ground of summer. Then a quart jar of raw honey from the bees in the orchard appeared on the front porch, followed by buckets of pie cherries, then a bottle of homemade dandelion wine. These gifts were always unannounced and unexpected, like finding a forgotten five-dollar bill in your pocket. We tried to reciprocate with fish that Tom caught, or a day spent pruning the rosebushes. From her I learned that to live near each other meant more than just sharing an address. We also had a responsibility to each other. Our proximity in the sweeping landscape wove us together with ties almost as strong as family.

When I cook for my neighbors, I'm giving them a part of me, a part of my family. In return, inevitably, life's turns will cause me to need a part of them and theirs. This ritual is not taken lightly, this women's work of preparing meals that sustain us. Cheryl always brought store-bought, and it was held against her. She could ride and rope and brand, raise kids and dogs and chickens, but somehow that wasn't enough; she should have found time to throw a fruit crisp in the oven or make a dump cake like the rest of us. Not to do so was to diminish our offerings; not participating was a rejection of the help we wanted to give. One of the most disparaging things I've heard said about a woman particularly aloof to the healing powers of the hot dish was, "As you well know, she's not good about returning Tupperware."

The obligations we feel to each other, though strong, are not clearly defined and can cause confusion even among ourselves. What is the right thing to do?

Phyllis asked me to be with her for the birth of her fifth child. Her husband would be by her side, as would her sister and another old friend. The night before the long drive to the hospital, ever prepared, Phyllis baked cinnamon-raisin bread for all of us to share. We sat in a semicircle around her hospital bed and broke into the bread, soft and yeasty, filled with sweet, plump raisins and just a hint of cinnamon sugar, joking that it was just like Phyllis to bake for her own delivery. She couldn't help herself. It's what she does. It's what we all do.

MARGARET BENSHOOF-HOLLER

Banding Together in San Francisco

The early-morning fog, which makes me think of a journey along the river Styx, has lifted; light comes down through the clouds to touch the hills of San Francisco. A seagull flies into the eastward-blowing ocean wind whipping across the city. Caught by the force of the gale, the bird hovers against the current as I wait for the streetcar, part of San Francisco's MUNI pub-

lic transportation system. The N-Judah train, which I catch at Ninth and Irving, a block from Golden Gate Park, in the Inner Sunset neighborhood of San Francisco, will take me downtown to the peace march.

Yesterday, a workday, stressed people pushed and shoved to find a seat on the packed and crowded streetcar. I feel caught sometimes in this routine, taking the streetcar to work at City College of San Francisco and then back home.

Today, instead of the usual cursing and rushing, folks are festive on the congested train. Crowds of people carry peace signs bearing antiwar slogans. Babies and baby boomers, the white-haired and the frail, all banter in excitement as we head downtown to protest the dropping of bombs on Iraq. Hundreds of people carrying peace signs line the streets at every stop, waiting to get on.

Yesterday on the MUNI, a woman sat next to me, frantically shuffling papers while she simultaneously talked on her cell phone. A man yelled at everyone getting on and off, "Hey, don't just stand there! Move on and let the people in!" Everyone looked irritated or scared when they approached him.

Today in the streetcar throng, a woman turns to me and says, "It's great to see such a big crowd on the MUNI for a change. I'm thrilled to see such a turnout. We had one hundred thousand marchers in October. This looks much bigger."

Yesterday people on the streetcar sat half asleep, eyes closed or squinted. Today half the city's population, as well as people from throughout northern California—reports vary from 200,000 to 350,000 people—will march for peace without a trace of fatigue in their eyes or smiles.

Yesterday the driver announced, "We'll have a two-minute wait while we fix the door." And we waited and waited and waited. A man in blue jeans and a tweed jacket began to pace up and down the aisle looking at his watch every few seconds. Finally, he walked up to the driver and said, "Hell! Let me off this train. I'm reporting you to MUNI!" The man got off, followed by five or six others searching for alternative transportation.

Today the driver says, "Don't lean against the door bar. You're keeping the door open on car two. We're going to have to sit here and wait, and nobody's going to get to that peace march until we get that door closed." Not a single passenger twitches an eye or scowls.

"Hey, let's help the MUNI driver," someone yells from the back. Everyone smiles and laughs as the streetcar jerks forward.

In the city's workday hustle, I don't often have time to connect. Consciously, I force myself to slow down, smile when I meet someone on the street, stop to make light talk even when I'm in a hurry. I try not to lose touch with my humanity and neighborhood community.

We who live in San Francisco come from every part of the country, every corner of the world. Asians, Africans, South Americans, Hispanics,

gays and straights, singles and married couples—anyone can find a place here. Still, there are problems. People rushing to and fro get short-tempered. Road rage, fights, insults.

Today perhaps some of us here remember that the free speech movement began in Berkeley across the Bay in the 1960s. Some may even recall the union strikes at the docks in the 1930s, which helped label San Francisco a union town and created a different sense of community. Experts say that San Francisco is one of the most difficult towns in the country to break into. It's hard to find jobs, make friends, and develop community here. San Francisco's housing market is one of the most expensive in the country; more than 50 percent of the people rent. A wedge divides those "who have" and those "who have not." Men and women in business suits avoid those with their possessions in grocery carts. Homeless people beg on corners for money to eat or get a room to sleep. Yes, we have some problems. But the stimulation of the streets is what keeps many writers living here.

Today the sun shines on the homeless and the wealthy, the young and the old, the single and the married, the straights and the gays, marching together to let the world know that we don't want our money going toward another televised war. We don't want to watch the most powerful country in the world destroy another third-world country. We get off the streetcars, we hold hands, and we sing and march and cry as we walk westward against the wind.

JANIS RUSSELL-WILSON *Concert of Energy*

In physics, the law of conservation states that energy cannot be created or destroyed, only transferred.

> When I saw my first crop
> of wind turbines, in fields
> formerly remote and inhospitable,
> I compared them promptly
> to prayer.
>
> Like you Western women—
> whirling dervishes who combine
> career, family, ranch—
> they transform a harsh,
> windy clime into energy
> of liberating balance.
>
> Like you modern-day
> pioneers, toiling in tandem,

five thousand elegantly
simple turbines stoically
power over half a million homes.

Alone—each possesses
the wholesome,
inherent beauty
of a ballerina chastely
poised *en pointe*.

Ensembled—mysteriously
attuned, you embody
the symmetry and boldness
of formations of geese,
the echo of prayer.

II

*HALLELUJAH
AND A SHOW OF HANDS*

LUCY ADKINS ✍ *Writing into the Storm*

In this small city on the plains
we women are writing—
at our kitchen tables,
at the stoplights,
jolting out of bed at night
to rise and write.

We meet in groups of three or four
or eight or ten—
in living rooms, at coffee shops,
we women in our twenties or our eighties,
all of us equals,
the little groups opening and expanding,
flowing one into the other into the other
and back again.

And sometimes the wind rising
like it did that night at Nancy's house,
the wind chimes tinkling along
with the scratching of pens.
Marilyn writes the funnel cloud,
and when it is gone
the hen on a ledge where a kitchen wall used to be.
Janna writes the motorcycle going into
a dark cloud.
We drink tea and write the comfort
of a branch scratching on a bedroom window.
We write into the storm
together.

As our grandmothers did,
except that they would have been quilting, perhaps,
or shelling peas, or sharing extension club lessons
along with their lives.
We use our pens.
We write sickness and divorce, the darkness that comes to us all.
We write love and bodies touching and children,
and crocuses bursting through the snow.

ANNE FANTACI CLEMENT ✐ ***Too Busy to Be***
Church Ladies

When we were growing up, Sadie and I laughed at the church ladies. To be fair, two of the church ladies were our mothers, but that didn't make them any less amusing. Our mothers hauled us along to their meetings and sat us in a corner with books and quiet toys while their group drank coffee and ate cake and planned how to solve the latest problem that burdened our small community.

What amused us so much was how very serious the ladies were. Need a lunch served at a funeral? Call the church ladies. Need new library books for the elementary school? Call the church ladies. Those women were involved in everything that went on in our community. They took food to shut-ins, welcomed new families, cared for siblings when a baby was born, raised money for every worthwhile cause that came up, and manned the polling place when there was an election.

Sadie and I dismissed it all as "women's stuff." We were too modern and aware to want to do it. We'd both be too busy with important matters when we reached that age, accomplishing great things. We weren't going to spend our evenings knitting hats and scarves for needy children.

The summer we finished our junior year in high school, Sadie and I were working at the town swimming pool. We spent our free time cruising around in Sadie's VW convertible and eyeing every available male.

August came, the third year of drought. The area around our town was pine woods and tinder dry. The heat kept the swimming pool busy but didn't do much for the worried farmers and ranchers in the area.

Predictably, the church ladies were working on a drought project, raising money for a second pumper truck for the volunteer fire department. Sadie and I were pressed into duty baking cookies and pricing articles for the bake sales and yard sales that were held every weekend. It was unbelievable that such a small community could have so much excess stuff to sell. We priced thousands of ugly vases, hundreds of pieces of truly awful clothing. It all sold, for fifty cents or a dollar an article.

The second Saturday of August, Sadie and I were planning to go to the mall in the next town. Sadie came by to get me, but we never made it to her car. My mother came barreling out of the house and enlisted us to haul baked goods to the fire hall for the church ladies' latest bake sale. We filled the back seat with plates of cookies and boxes of cakes; at the last minute, my mother handed me a pie to hold.

Sadie eased on down the road because we knew that if one cake fell over during the trip, we'd never hear the end of it. We pulled up in front of the fire hall, and I extricated myself from the front seat while balancing the

pie and trying not to look too uncoordinated. Two church ladies came over to help us unload. We thought we might escape as soon as we unloaded, but Sadie's mother had other plans.

Word had come in of a small fire in the next canyon over; part of our volunteer firefighting team was going over to help. The church ladies put Sadie and me to work making sandwiches because "firemen can't fight fires on empty stomachs." I slathered on mayonnaise and margarine while Sadie layered on bologna and cheese slices. We thought we'd finish up in an hour at most and then we'd take off for the mall.

Two hours passed, and we were making iced tea and hauling ice up from the grocery store. As soon as we'd finish one job, one of the church ladies was there to put us to work on something else. We were sweating and thinking evil thoughts and rolling our eyes at each other. Were we ever going to be able to escape?

We had just loaded the fourth cooler of sandwiches into Mrs. Davies' pickup truck and were inching toward Sadie's car when Sadie's mother came around the side of the truck and fixed us with one of her "stop right there" looks. The local grocery store was out of sandwich makings, so she sent us to the next town for supplies. We didn't mind going so much as we minded our transportation—we had to take Mrs. Warren's station wagon because it would hold more than Sadie's car. I slid down in the front seat and hoped no one who mattered (meaning any boys) would see us. Sadie eased the big hulk out of the fire hall parking lot, and we rolled down the canyon watching oncoming traffic for cars that we recognized.

By the time we reached the next town's grocery store, I had a serious kink in my neck and Sadie was muttering words that had never before been said in Mrs. Warren's station wagon. The boxes were waiting for us, as were two football players from the local high school assigned to load the car. We were mortified to have to lead them out to the station wagon instead of Sadie's sexy convertible.

Just to be fair, I drove on the way back up the canyon. Since Sadie was four inches shorter, she could slide down farther in the seat and be much less visible than I had been. I muttered my share of unmentionable words. Why did our mothers have to be church ladies?

When we returned to the fire hall, we learned that the fire was spreading. More of our volunteers had gone to help. That meant more sandwiches, so the church ladies put us to work. We swore we would never eat another bologna and cheese sandwich.

By late afternoon, the fire was still spreading and the church ladies were worried. More firefighters had gone to the canyon. The ladies were discussing whether sandwiches were enough when the restaurant in the next canyon called and said they'd provide dinner for the fire crews if we would provide drivers to take it to the fire line. Sadie and I were ready to volun-

teer, but the church ladies wouldn't hear of it. They asked for help from the high school principal and our minister and put us in charge of caring for all the kids. The ladies called to check on neighbors who were closest to the fire.

Sadie and I set up games, groused to each other about enslavement, and bemoaned spending our Saturday afternoon watching children. Downstairs, trucks pulled out, and the church ladies rounded up more drink coolers and coffeepots for the fire line. A steady stream of ladies arrived and dropped off whatever they had. Then the church ladies' phone tree went into action. Every lady called two other ladies, who called two other ladies, and so on. In a community of three hundred, it didn't take long to contact everyone in town and on the neighboring farms and ranches.

By early evening, the fire was still spreading. All our volunteer firemen were on the line, and firefighters were arriving from other communities. Most of the children had been returned home, and Sadie and I were making iced tea. Then the church ladies told us to arrange cots upstairs in the fire hall so the volunteers would have a place to rest when someone came to relieve them. By then we were both so tired we didn't have the energy to complain.

Our mothers were telling us to go home when the phone in the fire hall rang. Mr. Matthews, who was manning the telephone because he had a broken foot, looked worried as he said they needed another pumper truck at the top of the canyon. Dry trees were crowning, and the fire would spread down our canyon if we couldn't get another tanker up there to wet them down.

With his broken foot, Mr. Matthews couldn't drive a manual transmission truck, and no other men were available. The church ladies sprang into action. Sadie's mother called Mrs. Reynolds, who lived on the first ranch out of town. Mrs. Reynolds was about five feet tall and weighed maybe one hundred pounds, but she drove loaded cattle trucks to market, and she said she thought she could handle a tanker.

When Mrs. Reynolds arrived, Mrs. Warren, who was in her sixties, volunteered to drive second seat. Sadie and I gawked as the two ladies got into the tanker and backed it out of the fire hall. Mrs. Reynolds's head was just visible over the hood of the truck; Mrs. Warren was leaning out the passenger window and directing. The tanker headed up the canyon while we just stared.

Sadie's mother smiled at us and shook her head. She'd been telling us for years that we should never underestimate a determined woman. The church ladies saw the need and met it.

Of course, all these years later, Sadie and I have turned into the one thing we thought we'd never become—church ladies.

MAURA T. CALLAHAN *How Do I Thank . . . ?*

How do I thank 45,382 people? The cost of postage alone would be prohibitive. But if not for them, I would not have my two youngest children, thriving, both in their early twenties.

The world would be minus a gifted photographer with special eyes—magic eyes—one sees in black and white and the other sees in color. With these eyes, Riain frames the world in an acute but sensual way, bringing to life her own perspective of beauty. Maybe every one of her cells remembers that she is here only because of some anonymous person who gave her life. To create a balance, her gift back to them is to make pictures from that vantage point. Even as she acknowledges the unspeakable harshness of the world, my Riain can see only unassailable loveliness through her lens.

We would also be missing a budding flautist. Ella has a special gift and is compelled by an unfaltering drive to create beautiful noise. She usually plays with a symphony orchestra or small ensemble. But when Ella brings her music, alone, to the forest where I live or stands on the rimrock of a Wyoming canyon, she imprints the world with her being. As Ella fills these wild elemental places with a supernal resonance, I feel as if she can do anything—summon birds to silence and wood nymphs to the edge of daylight. Songbirds could take lessons from her sweet melodies, saturating the air.

This music, these children, are a gift, and they wouldn't be here but for nine specific individuals unrevealed somewhere in that forty-five thousand plus.

Every city has folks just like my lifesavers. You may even be one: a community blood donor. In 1980, my baby Riain needed three blood transfusions while she was snuggled not-so-safely in my womb, and three complete exchange transfusions in those critical first forty-eight hours after birth. All of the blood volume in her delicate five-pound body was flushed out and replaced. In that year, fifty thousand patients in my western half of Washington State also needed donated blood. Today that number has doubled; we depend on even more donors to keep these patients alive: family members, friends, old people, babies, and even criminals. The sanctity of life dictates that no one is refused blood when it is needed.

As the Fates worked through my life, I came to work at the same blood center that was responsible for saving my two girls. In the fourteen years I have worked here, I've seen how difficult it is to connect the act of giving blood with the effect on the recipient's life. Sherwin Nuland, a noted surgeon and author, wrote of his euphoria after he saved a life that otherwise would have been lost. A moment of personal catastrophe, a moment that most can't even imagine, is met with skill, heroics, and compassion by those blessed with the ability and presence to save lives. It's a shame that our donors never get to feel that same euphoria. Even our staff members have great difficulty putting a face to the purpose of their daily grind as

they work the long hours and make the long drives collecting blood for more than seventy hospitals and clinics.

A good friend pointed out that 45,382 people is the size of a small city. Imagine a whole city of people with such a heightened sense of humanity that they are willing to let someone drain that fundamental life force out of their body every two months. My friend asked, "Why do people need donated blood? Can't their bodies manufacture enough in a crisis to save their own lives?" That is the mystery.

But it's no mystery why my body wanted to kill those two innocent babies. I know the physiological reason. I was a sensitized Rh-negative blood type trying to nurture Rh-positive beings; my body thought they were the enemy and tried to get rid of them. When both Riain and Ella were born, 98 percent of their blood volume was adult blood, blood from those donors who decided they would go in one day and give a pint of the red stuff. All they got in return was a couple of cookies and some orange juice. But my children were given a chance they otherwise wouldn't have had.

If I could, if Riain and Ella would let me, I would drag them around to every center we have—nine different donor centers in a 160-mile radius. I would take them to every blood drive we schedule in a week (about seventy-five). We would go from Vancouver on the northern side of the Columbia River to the small towns bordering British Columbia. We would go from the edge of the western Cascades to the Pacific Ocean, to small lumber towns and fishing villages, up to Neah Bay on the tip of the Olympic Peninsula, out to the little company town of Nehalem on the North Cascades Highway. We would go to churches and high schools and factories and into almost every office building in downtown Seattle, every government building in our state capital. We would go to every hamlet in the fourteen counties we serve. Everyone wants to touch humanity in a real way. Every community wants to give back what it can. In all of these places, I would introduce two of their successes. Our donors may not feel that euphoria, but sometimes I feel it for them.

So this is my belated acknowledgment of gratitude to all of those people in the small and large communities in western Washington who gave blood so that my lovely Riain and sweet Ella could live and love and create. I thank you from the core of my being.

CLAUDIA F. MANZ ✒ *We Four*

In late July, it is my house.

There is a space air conditioner and the grass outside is high and
dry-golden. Longs Peak sits beyond the mesa, a grandmother's
 shoulder

braced against the clouds. Nancy brings her special lemonade
 (not too
sweet with fresh mint floating on the surface like fragrant
 lily pads).
Steph is dressed in a new purple (her favorite) dress, all leg
 and limb, her
journal filled, prolific. Jo is effervescent, the native, her hair, wheat
deepening, her smile as bright as bleached glass. I put on
 Schubert and we
write steadily in the cool air, lingering, pulling the gauzy
 linen curtains
closed against the strength of the sun.

In October, the aspens' leaves glow.

The wind howls so loudly at night my house is a kazoo,
 responding to
the mountains' call. The four of us meet sporadically,
 desperately. Fall is the
busiest season. Nancy's boy needs homework help. Jo and
 Steph are in school.
I work too many hours. Still, we call, we persuade, two
 hours are found to
nourish each other. Not much writing is done, but the
 books are open, the
pens are poised, the intention is there. Nancy always
 brings a book to
inspire. She reads Carole Maso to us: "I love the beautiful
 surface of the
impenetrable afternoon." We leave kinder that night,
 gentler, edges
smoothed. I don't worry about making dinner. I invite
 my husband out onto
the porch to hold hands, look at the moon.

In January, we meet at the bookstore.

The snow is almost deeper than my truck's wheels, blowing
 in fast from
the west. I go anyway. Inside is the woodstove that has
 been there for
forty years, burning. The other women are already there, piles of
scarves, red down coats, and wool hats taking up a seat
 on the wooden

bench. There are hugs and voiced concerns about the drive
 through the
mountains to town, everyone's recent flu. Eyes gleam orange,
 warm in the
firelight; coffee steams heavily off four tall white cups. There
 is no place
to go but here. We write for four hours, puddles large at our
 feet. We write
separately; we write together, cutting and pasting our lines,
 a symphony, an
amazing, unprepared stew of everything left after a week's
 worth of meals.
The sky deepens, indigo; snow whispers. Parting, the
 sidewalks feel our
lightness, hold us, suspended.

In April, I miss the moment when the trees first bud.

The fairy pale green. The promise. Nancy, Jo, and Steph
 are calling me
nonstop. Nancy's cat is very sick. Jo's mom has been
 diagnosed with
ovarian cancer. My husband lost his job. It feels as if the earth is
moving in the wrong direction. I want to call a halt on
 spring, to back up,
hibernate a little longer. The crocuses have other ideas. We
 meet at Nancy's
house. The dirt in her yard is freshly turned and the air
palatable. Jo brings two dozen brown vials for our writing exercise.
There are oohs and ahs as we open the tops. I smell anise and
honeysuckle, the others lavender, sage, the ocean. Poems and
 laughter pour
out of us. We are ten again, twenty, thirty, remembering failed
 lemonade
stands, first kisses, friends we have lost. Under the cherry
 tree's branches
we form a circle of chairs. We lean in, our hands strong,
 reaching for each
other.

Here is where the ice begins to thaw. The water underneath
 runs fast,
determined, deep.

C. S. PEDERSON ✑ *A Haunting Experience*

That I am not from this place is very apparent to me, though you might not realize it on first acquaintance. But then, unless you count encounters with raccoons or salamander overnights, acquaintances here are hard to make. Having lived other places, I'm well aware that it takes some effort to fit in. But, like puzzle pieces, we can be flipped only so many ways. Maybe my edges won't let me be put into place here.

Yet it's the place itself I love. Daily I walk the fields and hedgerows, the creek, and a nearby patch of native prairie. Daily I return home to look up the life cycle of ant lions, the history of jewelweed, the reason for gnat swarms, or the hibernation habits of garter snakes. I do feel connected to the natural rhythms of life but not to the local culture, not to the people who inhabit this part of Missouri.

Despite my affinity for the rural nature of this place, more and more I've been wondering if it might be time to leave. I am haunted by an experience I had last spring. "Haunted," you will come to understand, is an odd choice of words. For who is doing the hunting and who the haunting? I should be the one, according to some, who goes abroad at night, haunting these hills and casting my spells.

Last spring, the principal of the grade school, bolstered by at least one complaining parent, accused me of intending to teach Devil worship to "her" children. Do I really appear to be a witch? Is it my interest in plants and their herbal uses? Maybe. I did notice that my elderberry blow muffins, the batch I made for the ladies' club when we participated in the cancer walkathon, had few takers. Then again, just ambling these hills on foot might be enough to label me. Walking is, in the country, a suspect mode of travel. I know this, so I always take the dogs. In truth, of course, they are not leashed or led; we are off adventuring together—sniffing, stopping, watching.

A couple of other demonic possibilities come to mind. Besides keeping a black cat, I adore frogs and toads. Whenever infrequent visitors ask about my many ornamental amphibians, I hasten to explain that I've been collecting these since childhood, that they're the legacy left from a nickname. My grandmother called me "Tadpole."

And let me explain about that black cat. When my husband and I bought this house, the young dog and middle-aged cat had been left behind to weather one of the worst winters in recent history. The previous owners said they'd come back for the cat. No one returned. Soon we were saddled with kittens. One of that litter is a feisty feline. And yes, her long fur is mottled, mostly black—the color of a woolly bear caterpillar—with hints of devilish red.

So these are my sins: I collect, identify, and sometimes even cook wild

plants. I walk. I welcome real Woodhouse's Toads, as well as gray tree frogs, with whom we share our acreage. I decorate with frog wallpaper. I keep a black cat with a mean streak. And one more thing, perhaps the most incriminating of all, I am a book person. I read a great deal. I have studied the history of books. I even own a small letterpress and do some printing. And it was this—this wizardish twist in my character—that landed me in trouble last spring.

Professionally, I work as a freelance storyteller and teacher. Four years ago, I performed, at the request of a neighbor (who is a member of a local ladies' club to which I try to belong), for her son's fourth-grade holiday party. Dressed as Babushka, I told the story of my life, trying to catch up with the Three Wise Men. Then I taught the kids to fold an origami ball. (Babushka carries various toys as she walks—forever in search of the Christ child.)

Two years later, I was asked to tell stories to kick off the school's latest literacy program—another freebie. I wrote and rehearsed an original story for the occasion, "The Wide-Eyed Tree Frog Who Loved Books." The program went well.

Last spring, a teacher (also in the ladies' club) asked me to tell stories to a hundred-some students, kindergarten to sixth grade, for two hours on Saturday morning while their parents attended a lecture. What a recipe for disaster! I agreed to start with a story, then design and manage multiple learning centers with alphabet and multicultural, book-related activities. All this educational fun (provided for a fraction of my usual fee) would lead up to a grand finale—the arrival of Johann Gutenberg (me in costume with a researched monologue). I would haul my clamshell printing press to the school so that each child could "take a pull" on the press and make a bookmark styled after an antique hornbook. I roped in my sister, who teaches educational programs for all ages at a university anthropology museum.

Calling this celebration "A Brief, Hands-On History of the Book," I typed up an outline and description of my program. The coordinating teacher wanted to use this in the school's bulletin, which is mailed periodically to parents. Two weeks later, the principal (a longtime member of the ladies' club) called to accuse me of witchcraft.

The principal was self-righteous and angry. She called me "a Harry Potter person," which, even in the midst of her screaming tirade, struck me as funny. The rest of what she said was not so funny. She accused me of being a follower of Satan and intending to teach Devil worship to "her" children.

Hoping to snare me into a confession, she asked, her voice like tightening screws, "Just *what* do you think you are planning to teach?"

"The history of the book."

"What book?" she shrieked, pleased with my immediate admission. "*What* book?"

What did she imagine? *The Wizard's Book of Spells*? Is there something called *The Book of the Devil*? I tried to clarify. "The history of the book—as in books, as in you open two covers and there are pages inside. But that's not what a book is in other cultures and ages." I started to explain about an ancient Mayan "book" called a codex, an accordion-folded affair, about scrolls in China, clay tablets in Babylonia and Indonesia . . .

She interrupted, saying something along the lines of "I won't have you teaching Devil worship to *my* students."

I tried again. Surely I could clear up this misunderstanding. Finally, it became clear that she would not, could not, listen. We hung up. I went for a walk. I talked to my cats. I drank a cup of homemade mint tea. I cried. And then I wrote down every stupid thing she'd said.

That evening, I called the teacher who'd invited me. She knew the scoop. The principal's end of our conversation had been made public; it had already made the rounds at school.

Needless to say, "A Brief, Hands-On History of the Book" was canceled—by mutual agreement. Since only an abridged description of my program had circulated in the school bulletin, I felt I should publicly deny these diabolical charges. Besides, I needed to write the hurt out of my system.

In April, two days before the Reading Fair (at which I would not be telling any dreaded creation myth, talking about Egyptian hieroglyphics, or appearing as Gutenberg to explain how "I" had printed my famous Bible), my editorial was printed in the weekly newspaper. The superintendent called to discuss the fact that he expected to get his butt chewed for such negative press. Then the whole thing blew over. It blew away like old ashes left from a pyre built to burn a witch.

Obviously, I lack local acquaintances, so I keep myself company. It's best, I think, to hang out with someone who has a sense of humor—so I try to cultivate mine. In that regard, let me tell you about my *happy haunting ground.*

Besides neglected pets, the previous owners left behind an antique cauldron. This summer, my husband helped me move it to the front yard. In it, I planted white wave petunias. All summer, bubbling up from that black cauldron, foamlike white petunias bloomed. I rested an old broom against the kettle's rim and, beside it, I propped an odd ceramic frog. If only I could train our black cat to patrol that spot.

The huntress, it seems, is not haunted by this incident. This fall, the regional principals' association honored my accuser as an exceptional administrator. I suspect it's all a matter of who seems to "fit" in this place—in this culture—and who doesn't. After all, if you've ever put together a jigsaw puzzle, you know you can't force a piece in when its notches and knobs aren't lined up right. I guess I must be a misfit who misses fitting in. Then again, perhaps this puzzle piece belongs in a different picture.

YVONNE HOLLENBECK ✑ **Rejuvenating the Clearfield Hall and Me**

A light snow had fallen, adding character to the photos I had shot for an assignment in an adult education class. As I sifted through photographs of the old country church east of our ranch in South Dakota and shots of a couple of abandoned rural schools, my eyes fell on the photo of the Clearfield Community Hall. Somehow I felt akin to this neglected old building. Unlike the hall, I had been a part of this community for only a short time. I was a divorced mother with two young daughters who had recently married a local rancher. I felt like an outsider.

And I pitied that old building. Before the age of paved roads, radio, or television, the hall had been vital to the community's entertainment. Now it sat alone in the snow in an awful state of disrepair, a neglected sentinel to the past.

My thoughts were disrupted when elderly Gen Fast stopped by for coffee. Gen was one of the few neighbors who had befriended me. As we visited, I showed her the picture and told her how I wished the old hall could somehow be renovated. I spent the rest of the afternoon hearing stories about the hall. Her parents had homesteaded in the area, and she recounted how her father and other men in the community had pooled their money so folks would have a place to gather. They'd hauled the lumber from Winner with teams and wagons and built that hall in 1916. Gen remembered watching her father lay all the beautiful hardwood flooring. For years, she said, that floor was known as the best dance floor in the country.

When Gen left, she hugged me and asked in her German accent if I would help her get things going so we could fix up the hall. I had no alternative but to say yes.

At first there was considerable opposition, especially from the men, who told us countless times that the old hall wasn't worth fixing. My husband was no exception. Regardless, a group of ladies joined me in organizing the Clearfield Hall Auxiliary, and, as word spread, more people joined. We held bake sales and card parties to raise money and soon collected enough donations to put a new roof on the old building. Then we replaced the windows and announced a dance. People were amazed at our progress, but we needed more money. We wrote and published a cookbook to sell, made and sold signs directing visitors to farms and ranches within the community, ran concession stands at rodeos and auction sales, made quilts to raffle off, held pie and soup suppers. Every project raised more money.

After a while, whenever we'd collected enough money to do more renovation, the area's men—including my husband and others who'd initially opposed the idea—came to donate labor and equipment. We repaired the

foundation, replaced the old siding, and installed a modern kitchen and even indoor bathrooms. We refinished that beautiful hardwood floor and gathered in the hall for dancing, family reunions, and school functions.

Today the Clearfield Community Hall is once again the hub of activities in this rural community. The ladies who make up the Clearfield Hall Auxiliary are the glue that holds it all together. To express their gratitude for the help they have received with this worthwhile project, the ladies host an annual community Christmas program each December. Folks come from a large area to hear the homespun talent. Each year, they enjoy the continuing "Saga of Ralph and Ethel," an original skit involving actresses from the auxiliary, the youngest in her seventies. After an afternoon filled with songs, poems, skits, and group caroling, we serve a lunch that would make Martha Stewart envious.

The Clearfield Hall Auxiliary meets the third Monday of every month. One month, when I was unable to attend, the ladies changed the meeting date to accommodate my schedule. Like that old hall, I feel as if I have truly become an important part of this fine community.

SHANNON DYER ✑ *The Wolf Pack in the School District*

The warm evening air of late August nestled gently against my skin. The sun wouldn't go down for another hour or more, leaving time for long strolls or leisurely bike rides. It didn't feel like lynching weather, but nothing about the situation had made sense from the beginning.

The entire school district consisted of slightly more than two hundred registered voters, and many of them wandered up the hill like cattle making their way to the windmill in the cool of the evening. Some people seemed festive; others felt growing doom. I've heard that's what folks were like at hangings in the Old West.

I watched as a trim, overdressed woman scooted around to the passenger side of her new SUV to help an ancient rancher slide out. She took him by the arm, gushing and fawning as she helped him up the steep hill to the schoolhouse. She was shuttling as many of the elderly as she could to the polls, filling their heads with her version of the story, which I felt was distortion and outright lies.

I won't pretend I'm impartial about this story. I liken what had been done to Tina the past few months to the way wolves hunt a weak animal, dashing close and running away, biting until the animal weakens and can be brought down. In any pack, there is an alpha wolf. In this pack, "Alpha" was the determined woman shuttling the old rancher to the polls.

I walked up the hill alone, seeing knots of people, mostly women, laughing and teasing. No secret whom they supported. A line had been drawn several months ago, and it had grown with each accusation and

item of gossip, until it now loomed as a black wall. We all knew where each person stood.

Inside the schoolhouse, a few folks lined up to vote. Bitterness, distrust, anger, bravado—all the faces of war—moved toward the small elementary school library. Even the election board members had taken sides. The polls would close in minutes.

I passed the child's desk that served as a polling booth. I'd voted earlier that day, a simple errand: Should Tina ____ be recalled from the District One Board of Education? Check the box yes or no.

Why should the fate of a school board member in this microscopic dot on the map cause such deep and bleeding wounds? Most elections for high school student body president involve more voters. But maybe because we are so few, the stabs we take at one another cut so deeply.

How did this mess start? Maybe it goes back to the battle over the last school superintendent. The newspaper editor loves to stir up controversy. Perhaps it stems from the frustration of the minority board member, out-voted two to one on most issues. Or it could be the superintendent, angry that Tina testified against him in a hearing and intent on getting even after he was fired.

My theory is that Alpha smelled weakness. She could destroy Tina and control the grade school. Maybe it would prove to the world, or at least this minuscule portion of it, how powerful she was.

Or maybe it is an old story of a group of people turning against an outsider. Tina and her husband had moved to town seven years before. She grew up on the East Coast, is well educated, and has traveled the world. She and her husband bought a ramshackle house facing Main Street. They remodeled it, replanted the front yard, and stayed busy raising four kids. She wears old khakis and bandannas instead of cowboy boots and Wranglers.

I walked into the library and took the nearest available seat. For all the civility and quiet conversations filling the room, I felt I'd landed in enemy territory. Nothing to do but smile at Tina, who sat at the board's table in the front. More seats filled up, and I saw a few friends.

Alpha waltzed in, made sure her video camera was trained on the board, and surveyed the room. She was in charge, even I admit that. She'd worked harder than we had, carried her petition door-to-door, told the disinterested people whatever made them angry enough to vote. She drove them to the polls, talked to them, made them feel important.

I'd kept busy with my own work, believing justice and clear thinking would prevail. I already knew I was wrong.

Alpha had mobilized her forces. They'd sent so many faxes, made so many screaming phone calls to the state attorney's office and home that he'd changed his home number and refused all calls from anyone in our town.

I hadn't made any calls. I assumed anyone with any sense would see

that a recall election held on the day Tina's term ended was silly and wasted tax dollars.

I suspected that Alpha manipulated the newspaper editor and made sure innuendoes and falsehoods were printed in the weekly paper. She hired a well-respected school attorney and, with five others, sued the board for not honoring her petition to recall Tina.

What had Tina done to warrant a costly recall election and subsequently an even costlier lawsuit? The accusations were that Tina had tampered with minutes and violated open-meeting laws.

Neither charge was ever proved, but no proof was needed. All Alpha had to put on the petition was that Tina hadn't acted in the best interests of the school district. To some who questioned, she said the petition was to reorganize the board, simply to allow Tina to be secretary rather than president. To others ready to see someone fall, she said Tina had broken laws and lied.

The signatures of more than seventy-five people appeared on the petition, people whom Tina saw almost every day: the postmistress, Tina's next-door neighbor, members of her church, the local sheriff. Tina couldn't get her mail or buy milk without seeing those faces, people who had signed their names to say that she had done something so vile she couldn't be tolerated.

The flip side of this hatred was that she also got flowers, cards, phone calls, and visits from people wanting only to lend her some strength, people who tried to fill her with encouragement and hope.

Tina called the meeting to order. Conversations ended, and the three board members read and approved the minutes. In her flustered state, Tina misread the agenda.

I heard the women behind me snicker. The one next to me shifted her weight and sighed. The woman in front of me corrected Tina.

During a break, when the antagonism toward Tina felt so palpable I wanted to wash it off me, I turned to the woman next to me. "Why is it you want Tina off the board so badly?" I asked.

The woman folded her arms and glared at me. "I don't approve of the way she handled the playground."

I shook my head, trying to keep in the anger. "The playground was finished four years ago. She's been re-elected since then. Why didn't you run against her?"

Now the woman sniffed in disgust. "I don't want the job. I just want her off."

The meeting resumed. Tina made more mistakes, and around me women laughed and stage-whispered about her unworthiness.

Finally, it was time to read the ballots. The election board members took their places—one at the chalkboard, one with paper and pencil, three at the ballot box to pull out the ballots, read them, and stack them neatly in piles.

At first it seemed there was hope. The no votes accumulated almost as fast as the yes votes. But soon the lead became two, then four, and then the trend was clear. We knew that Tina would be recalled by a substantial margin.

Angered by the callousness of the women surrounding me, I turned to a friend and stated loudly, "This is how the Nazis were able to carry out their atrocities. People enjoy cruelty; they love to be on top. And if it happens at another's expense, they love it even more."

No, it wasn't mature, and it didn't even make a lot of sense. But if I was that mad and hurt, how must Tina have felt?

Several years have passed since that night. Tina no longer lives here; she's found a new community that has welcomed her spirit of service. The wounds of that incident have scarred over, and we've moved on, working on church benefits, planning community celebrations, dancing at weddings, and crying at funerals—all side by side. But I suspect that there are others like me who have not forgotten the ugly face this normally friendly little town can wear.

WILLO BOE ✑ *The Non-Musicals Sing Their Last Song*

Nine life spans 'round the room.
Each unique, each precious.
Dressed and groomed carefully,
Regal women assemble.

There is formality here.
Robert's Rules. Flag Pledge. FCE Creed.
Three unaccompanied songs.
Everyone sings, Ida leads.

Beautiful Gladys, in a walker.
Dignified Ida, on TV ads.
Spry Wilma, cooks with love.
Accomplished Margaret, hip replaced.

Roll Call. Previous Meeting's Minutes.
Joan has been secretary forever.
Treasurer's Report. The money goes
To A Good Cause.

Lucille tells her "story"
with tears, again.

Esther doesn't drive, doesn't go to casinos.
Elegant Evelyn hates to read.

Committee Reports,
Old Business, New Business?
Wilma has the lesson.
"When a Loved One Dies."

Seven of the nine over eighty.
We've gone to funerals.
Hips wait to break, strokes happen.
The meeting is adjourned.
Time for the last dessert.
 Willo Boe, President

SARAH BYRN RICKMAN *Fifty Years of Potluck*

Nancy and I met in seventh grade because we both loved horses, the first of
many bonds between us. When we turned sixteen, we used to drive around
Saturday afternoons in her father's green Ford convertible, looking for
boys. She knew how to flirt. I wanted desperately to learn.

Our first year at East High School in Denver, Nancy and I gravitated
toward a group of girls with whom we both felt comfortable. "The rea-
son we all became friends? We're all so very different," she said to me
many years later. She believed we bonded together in our aloneness as a
defense against the cookie-cutter similarities of the other groups of girls we
knew.

We called our informal groupings potlucks because in the 1950s we
gathered on Friday night before the football or basketball game and ate
a potluck supper together—prepared, of course, by our mothers. Those
with dates were picked up at the house hosting the potluck. Those without
dates went to the game or to a movie as a group. We never left anyone out.

By senior year, our group numbered eighteen. Seventeen of us went to
college that fall. Just recently, the one who didn't confessed how much she
hurt that summer. The rest of us—youthfully insensitive and caught up
in ourselves, our plans, our impending adventure—never realized. That
summer, we did something we had not done before. We left someone out.

Nancy's parents, and mine, moved away from Denver after we gradu-
ated from high school. But the friendship we'd forged stretched to accom-
modate the moves, colleges at different ends of the country, and eventually
husbands, children, jobs, and years. Some of the potluck group drifted out
of contact, but most of us kept in touch. And most of the group eventually

came home to Denver. I am the only one of our current number who did not—by the mid-1980s—return to live on Colorado's eastern slope.

In 1980, when I visited Denver for the first time in seventeen years, eleven of us got together for a luncheon; we have continued to do so ever since. The bonds of friendship have been remade and strengthened over the years. The year we all turned sixty, we planned a slumber party like the ones we used to have in high school. We held it at Nancy's mountain cabin near Estes Park. Nancy and I shared yet another bond—a deep love of mountains and the spiritual essence that can be found only there.

We spent the August afternoon lazing on the deck, sipping wine, and gazing at Longs Peak and Mount Meeker—so close they looked as if we might touch them, yet so far away that the late-afternoon sun washed away all the crags and crannies, leaving instead a hazy aura of majestic unreality.

That was the night we learned of our friend's long-ago summer of discontent. And it was the night in which our real reconnection began. A magical night.

During the summer of 2001, ten of us held our second overnight gathering at a historic hotel in Empire, Colorado, to celebrate turning sixty-five. We did not talk about Nancy, who had died on Sunday, November 26, 2000. Her loss pervaded our thoughts but not our conversation. Time had not yet begun to heal us.

Using the Internet, we are now trying to locate our missing members. During the summer of 2002, eleven of the group met for dinner in Denver, including one who had been long lost to us, living back East. We don't dwell on the past, talking mostly about the present and future. But on that occasion, we began to talk about our high school days, collectively remembering people, places, happenings. Finally, we dared to talk about Nancy. Her loss remains painful to us, but we are learning to deal with it. We have our memories, and we have each other. I think she is bringing us closer together.

Now we have much more in common. We lost our fathers long ago and more recently have lived through the decline and loss of our mothers. Many of our husbands are in ill health. We suffer some infirmities, though as a group of women in our late sixties, we are generally hearty.

Our fiftieth high school reunion is approaching, and we are, if anything, better friends than we were in 1954. Back then, we could not even imagine being far older than our mothers were then. In some ways, I feel that we haven't aged at all. In our faces, I still see the seventeen-year-old girls I remember. But we are most aware of the inevitable tug of time.

We are not a community in the sense of calling people to action, of doing good works, of making a difference—other than to ourselves. But for more than fifty years, we women, all so very different, have been a community of support for one another.

In high school, we banded together as a youthful defense against the world. Now, in our senior years, we congregate to celebrate having survived; to revel in our enjoyment of, and love for, one another; and to reaffirm our strength in our differences.

CLEO CANTLON ✑ *The Woman Who Didn't Fit In*

Everyone knew Roberta wouldn't fit in. She was a cute, stylish woman whose skirts were as short as those of her teenage daughters. A divorced teacher who married a good German Catholic, she was a city woman, a golfer and tennis player, a terrific dancer who enjoyed a bloodthirsty game of Scrabble more than pinochle. An inspired teacher, she read weighty books and was rabid about politics. Her imaginative eye saw how to transform old farm castoffs cleverly, making her drafty old farmhouse a place of welcome.

Still, it was plain she would never become one of us, like us. And she didn't. Instead, she made her own place by teaching us. Where we saw obstacles, Roberta saw possibilities.

In our remote area, short on restaurants, she improvised. We started a cooking group, with monthly adventures into exotic cuisines, complete with wine or whatever beverage might best accompany the recipe we made from Germany or Greece, Ireland or the American colonies.

We explained why a fundraising style show she proposed was impossible because we had no women's clothing stores in the county. No problem! Roberta encouraged us to create and model our own designs, and we were both enriched and empowered.

She taught us playfulness we thought we had left behind in childhood. One Halloween, Roberta led our quartet, crawling on our bellies, into some friends' yard after the lights went off in the house. On their lawn, we set fire to cardboard boxes stuffed with paper, roasted marshmallows, and sang rowdy songs until our hastily dressed friends came out to join us. And then we dragged them along to repeat the process at another farm.

After dark the following Halloween, we hung signs at friends' homes and businesses: free coffee and donuts at the post office; bargains on repair parts at the farm machinery shop; and a huge rummage sale ("Come early for the best bargains!") at the home of a consistently late-rising friend.

In the years Roberta lived among us, some of us taught her, too—how to garden and to put up jams and vegetables, how to make sausage and to quilt, always with her own unique flair. She taught us inventiveness, pride in our daily work, and, most of all, joy. What a trade!

SANA AMOURA-PATTERSON

Wednesdays at Walgreens

Wednesday is senior citizen day
in Fremont, Nebraska, where the thick-soled women
and suspender-wearing men bring in coupons
for Friskies, Vaseline, and blue eye
shadow. I see them between
classes in the strip mall while I wait

for my next class to begin. I wait
for Helen to open the register and start the day
of niceties and inquiries between
prescription announcements on the intercom and women
with questions about Van Camp's beans and false eye
lashes. Helen quickly scans for coupons

in the Walgreens flyer—coupons
for Pepsi and pantyhose—while a mother waits
with her boy for someone at the photo counter to eye
them and begin the process, but Wednesdays
are hectic because the elderly men and women
get an additional five percent off and stand between

aisles looking for dates and prices between
the time they wait to be called and when they dig for coupons
in heavy card files or plastic purses the young women
are carrying again. The Coppertone girls impatiently wait
for the lady in a housedress to choose a day
for a makeover. The girls roll their eyes.

Why would anyone so old care about eye
shadow and lip liner? They spray perfume between
their breasts and laugh that someday
they will get implants. They will never cut coupons
or wear comfortable shoes. They can't wait
to graduate and leave the smell of old women

who remind them of their mothers. Women
who breastfed their children and bleach their mustaches. I
wonder how long I will have to wait
before my daughter recognizes that I am stuck between

loose powder and pressed. Will I carry coupons
in a plastic purse on Wednesdays?

I watch the women between
my classes. For now, I resist the coupons.
. I wait for my Coke and look forward to Thursday.

SISTER HILDEGARD DUBNICK, OSB
A Couple of Nights Before Christmas

The Abbey's choir director, Sister Cecilia, closed one book briskly and
reached for another one.

"Now the antiphons for Vespers of Christmas Day," she said, in her
businesslike tone.

Her air of efficient competence was a reproach to my fog of confusion,
down at the end of the long table, where the newcomers to the Abbey were
seated at the weekly choir practice. As a postulant of only a few weeks, I
still had only a vague idea as to what was coming next throughout the
nuns' daily routine. I had, at least, brought the right books to practice.
There were two of them, both thick, black, and written entirely in Latin.

Most of the pages contained music, with Latin words. The musical
notes weren't so bad—or shouldn't have been. But they were square, not
round, and had no stems or time indications, and the staff that held them
had too few lines, and no clef that I could recognize. I had played piano for
years, so I knew how to read music. But this notation was like hearing a fa-
miliar language spoken with a thick foreign accent. You caught scraps that
seemed intelligible, but even these often proved misleading.

Now, quite lost, I cast around desperately for a clue, soon finding it in
the encouraging smiles of the other younger sisters.

"Not that book, that's the Gradual, just for Mass," Sister Perpetua said
softly, gently removing one big black book from my grasp and replacing it
with another, indistinguishable to my inexperienced gaze. "For Vespers
you need the Antiphonal, with all the chants for the Divine Office."

I sighed, feeling like a greenhorn explorer who had fallen in with an un-
discovered tribe. Well, at least the natives were friendly. I let Sister Perpetua
open my Antiphonal for me and turn it to the right page, while I threw a
quick glance out the window of the community room.

It was a couple of nights before Christmas, and the late December sun
had long departed, leaving behind a green-blue sky free of city lights. The
Abbey of Saint Walburga is in far northern Larimer County, Colorado, a
short crow's flight south of Wyoming. The ponderosa pines near the top of
the granite cliffs stood out stark and black against the still-bright sky. The

evening star shone like a searchlight through the needles of "my" pine—the one I saw through the small square window from my choir stall in the Abbey church.

That very day, during morning prayer, I had watched the tree emerge from the formless darkness into the soft pink glow that heralded the rising sun. In the length of a Psalm verse, the light had dulled to yellow. A few more verses, and the tree stood bathed in mountain sunshine. Together, the tree and I had offered our praise to the Creator.

Now I drew my gaze back from Venus to the densely printed page before me. This time, our weekly choir practice included more Latin than usual. Usually, we just had the coming Sunday Mass to practice, but on big feasts like Christmas, we also sang Vespers, or evening prayer, in Latin. It heightened the solemnity of the occasion to use the ancient language of our Benedictine tradition.

We read over each text and its translation, then sang it through. For most of the nuns, it was merely review. Some sisters had been singing these pieces for fifty years; all had heard them before—except for us postulants, down in our fog at the end of the table. We scuffled along, panting to keep up, incredulous—and a little resentful—that these markings and sounds seemed to be old hat to our senior sisters. Would these strange melodies, these "tuneless wonders," ever seem familiar to us?

On the fourth antiphon of Vespers, Sister Cecilia began as usual, leading the rest of us: *"Apud Dominum misericordia, et copiosa apud eum redemptio"*—"With the Lord there is mercy, and plentiful redemption." But then, instead of continuing with *"De profundis clamavi ad te Domine"*—"Out of the depths I cry to you, O Lord"—she interrupted herself with, "And here Sister Richmundis died!" stabbing at the book with her forefinger to indicate the precise spot.

This startling departure from routine unleashed a flood of memories from all of our older sisters.

"Can you remember?"

"I'll never forget hearing the book fall behind me."

"I looked over and saw her collapsed in her choir stall."

All this was punctuated by a chorus of ignorance from us postulants: "What? Huh? What do you mean? Who? What happened?"

At length, Sister Cecilia addressed herself to our low-status corner of the room.

"Sister Richmundis died of a heart attack during Christmas Vespers in 1981! Right there in choir, right after the antiphon for the *De profundis*. Her heart just seized up and she died, immediately."

"Just think!" said Sister Perpetua enthusiastically. "One minute she was with us in choir, here at the Abbey, and the next minute there she was singing with the heavenly choir!"

She sounded really pleased at the prospect, which seemed strange to

me. I wasn't yet accustomed to the joyful anticipation of death that is typical of the monastic worldview.

"I'm sure she got in amongst the angels right away," Sister Cecilia agreed. "She was a very joyful and holy soul."

A few days later, after all the festivities of Christmas Eve and Christmas Day, we sang the liturgy we had rehearsed. When we got to the fourth antiphon, I thought of Sister Richmundis, singing with the angels. She had lived a simple and undramatic monastic life of prayer and service but had entered eternity in a truly unforgettable manner.

Throughout the following year, the rising sun reddened my ponderosa pine at different times up on the rocks and silhouetted it from different angles behind the cliff. By the time Christmas choir practice rolled around again, I had become much more comfortable with the daily routine of the community. There was even a new postulant, someone below me on the totem pole, lost in the fog that I remembered so well. The Latin antiphons still sounded strange and awkward to me, but I was now one of the friendly natives.

Sister Cecilia sang, *"Apud Dominum misericordia,"* then announced, "And here Sister Richmundis died!" The chorus of reminiscence resounded again: "I'll never forget hearing the book fall behind me."

My bewildered younger sister turned to me and said, "Who? What happened?"

"Right before the *De profundis*," I said, trying to sound warm and welcoming, but feeling pretty smug. "Sister Richmundis had a heart attack and died."

ROSEMERRY WAHTOLA TROMMER
Why We Still Sing When Other Choirs Dissolved

For Heartbeat

I once thought singing was the glue that kept
our group together. Every Thursday, three
to four, we seven women met to steep
ourselves in harmonies. Nothing except
the music mattered, and our voices leapt
through folksongs, twanged out bluegrass, jived to *bee
bop* tunes. No leader, just a coterie
with "zealous" sound, though some might say, "inept."

And no doubt, singing's still important, that
pursuit came first. But eight years later, it's

not scales that bind us. It's potlucks with five desserts.
Long hugs when Donna's mom died. Chats
about orgasms, being wives. What knits
us are the rhythms of our female lives.

JUDY ANN *Savoring the Circle*

How does a community originate? Some say it's fate, some call it a coinci-
dence, and others attribute it to synchronicity or divine intervention. How
long does it take for a community to form? Some take lifetimes, and others
happen in an instant.

Brenda had a dream of bringing together a Circle of seven women who
were each seeking spiritual insight. She considered the diversity and bal-
ance of the group and how the members could benefit one another, as well
as the wider community.

We would meet to explore together spiritual and life processes, using
Dancing the Dream by Jamie Sams as our springboard. Sams's book is based
on the sacred Web of Life, in which all parts of the universe are intercon-
nected in a Dream Weave. Every positive or negative thought, action, or
deed is a thread that affects all others in the web.

Each of the women responded eagerly to Brenda's invitation, but not
without some apprehension and wariness, as most of us were not previ-
ously acquainted. Our Circle began meeting every other week for an eve-
ning. We set ground rules, even though they had flexibility. We began by
speaking honestly. We agreed to disagree.

The beauty of this Circle is in the exchange of mementos, experiences,
and wisdom. We grow closer each time we meet. Our gifts come in all
forms: tangible items such as feathers, plants, stones, or handmade items,
and equally significant contributions of thoughts, ideas, dreams, and goals.
We use our intuition to sense the emotions of others. Through sharing fears,
burdens, joys, and gifts, we all grow. We feel acceptance and value within
our Circle. Our tears flow freely; there is no shame or embarrassment.

The balance of our Circle comes through our diversity. Our ages span
thirty years. We are mothers, some with grandchildren, and some with
young ones still at home. We cover all points on the spectrum of relation-
ships. Our careers range from student to retiree. Our recreational interests,
skills, talents, experiences, and spiritual walks are diverse. The thread we
have in common is a love of humanity and a desire to seek spiritual direc-
tion.

Some of the tools we use in our Circle are a burden basket, a giveaway
basket, and a talking stick. In the burden basket, at the beginning of each
meeting, we each place a burden, written on a piece of paper. We disclose

our burdens, if we wish, or they remain private. Then we symbolically release the burdens by burning them. We have not had many burdens to place in the basket since our third or fourth meeting. It may be that now we see them more as lessons than as burdens.

For the giveaway basket, we bring items we don't need anymore—books, jewelry, scarves, stones, candles. We may take an item we need from the basket, then donate the rest to a charitable organization.

The talking stick allows each sister to have time to share ideas, perceptions, and feelings. This tool empowers the more reluctant ones to accept that their thoughts are as important as any other's. When the speaker physically holds the talking stick in her hand, it reminds the rest of us that it is a time to listen.

Each time we meet is like savoring a chocolate kiss. For our birthday celebration meeting, I asked my sisters to bring a gift of self. Claudette displayed her watercolor painting of a flower. We were spellbound as Susan read an inspirational article with passion and eloquence. Christene read a symbolic story she wrote for her brother. Nancy brought her grandmother's hat collection, and we each chose one to wear for the evening. Brenda showed her sacred prayer Pipe and talked about the Native American path she follows. Randi brought the historical jewelry and costumes she wears when she portrays her Renaissance persona, Airmid. I played the piano and sang.

In this revelation of ourselves, we all grew in knowledge and experience. But I realized that at every meeting, we bring gifts of individuality. Through this we learn, and when we've returned to our separate lives, we continue learning by recalling the shared experiences.

We came together not knowing one another, but I feel I know each sister's spiritual essence now, without knowing all the details of her personal history. Claudette's watercolors reveal her gentleness and ability to see beauty in the natural world. Christene lights up with childlike wonder while describing a rainbow that encircled the sun in the sparkling hoarfrost of an icy morning. Nancy humbly offers wisdom with compassion for all people involved and brings "toys" to delight our inner children.

Randi's kindness is apparent when she tucks a blanket around one of her sisters who is chilly. As unselfishly as she loans her books, Susan shares wisdom gained through many experiences. Brenda's inner beauty captivates everyone she meets. Her loving and nurturing ways make all who know her feel indispensable.

Our Circle is not a self-help group, although our varied backgrounds help us provide solutions and ideas for each other. We're on singular paths, having similar and different experiences, but we all agree that we've been transformed—are being transformed—in some way. The group is our catalyst for realizing personal impeccability rather than an unattainable goal of

perfection. I find comfort in knowing I have a support group to help me be the best person I can be.

There is no power struggle here; we are all givers. We share responsibility and leadership. We help to clarify and develop each sister's ideas.

In sharing burdens, we receive support. While divulging fears, we gain courage. Through relating joys, we bring joy to our sisters and hope for similar joys for others. In confiding dreams for spiritual growth, we are given affirmation and direction. By bestowing gifts of self and of the heart, we feel appreciation and love. In acknowledging diversities, we find commonality. In admitting weakness, we gain strength. Through exposing pain, we encounter joy. By confessing uncertainty, we acquire confidence. Through revealing feelings of isolation, we become part of a community.

A bond has formed—a *need* to spend time together, for these are the moments that nourish. All of the threads that contribute to the rainbow colors of the Dream Weave are in this Circle of seven. These multicolored threads connect to and ultimately influence all other strands that form the Web of Life—the universal community.

LISA HELDKE *Perching*

I live, literally, on the edge of the Great Plains. In the morning when I leave our house, halfway up the side of the Minnesota River valley, I climb out of an oak and maple forest and arrive, in less than a quarter mile, at a great flatness. In the early-morning haze on a fall day after the corn and soybeans have been harvested, if I squint my eyes, I can see the tallgrass prairie out to the west. When I drive home in the evening, the car descends the twisting dirt road, and I am floating down a tributary of the Minnesota. Soon my canoe will enter that river and from there will float north into the Mississippi. Our very yard realizes it's on the edge of things. On the east side of the house, trillium, wild ginger, and trout lily flower thrive under huge oaks. On the west, prairie flowers and grasses flourish, despite the casual attention we give them.

The college where I work is similarly perched on the edge of things: it sits at the very top of the valley. A few years ago, you couldn't see the college from town, because of the trees. But the tornado took care of all those trees, along with hundreds of homes and nearly all the roofs and windows at the college. Now it looks like the little college on the prairie that it originally was a hundred and fifty years ago. Living on the edges of things has its risks.

Lots of the people I know here seem to live on the edges of things—on the edges of leaving, especially. Life here involves saying hello and goodbye a lot. There's a big round of hellos when the school year starts and I

greet new colleagues and new students. And then there's the always-pain-ful round of goodbyes as the students, with whom I've spent four years learning how to have a conversation, take off. Each year, they're followed down the hill by a sizable number of my colleagues. All communities are full of goodbyes, I suppose. People die and move away from everywhere, all the time. But most towns don't promise you that you'll undergo a mas-sive exodus every year. College towns do.

It isn't easy, living in a community of perchers. For me, it meant spend-ing the first several years being reluctant to make friends, "since I'm not go-ing to stay here anyway," and then the next several years afraid of making friends, "because they'll just leave anyway." Fifteen years into the story, I'm starting to realize that, in geologic time, perching is all any of us ever does. In a community of perchers, in a college perched on the edge of the prairie, making community is like making rag rugs: it requires a lot of stitching to-gether, a decision not to regard any one scrap of fabric as essential to the de-sign (for it will surely run out before your need for it has been exhausted), and an appreciation for the capacity of even the smallest scrap to pro-foundly affect the rug's design. If you can work within those limits and take the long view (geologic time again), you can be a part of something strong and sturdy and beautiful.

For fourteen of my fifteen years in this town, I've been part of one of these human rag rugs—a group of women who gather at the local café for breakfast every Wednesday morning. We occupy the long table in the no-smoking section, after the crew from the regional treatment center has va-cated it and before the retired guys have claimed it for their dice game. The waitress, our fourth or fifth "regular," has our orders memorized. The café changed hands about five years ago. The Cat's Away became Ooodles (with three *o*'s), rewrote its menu, stopped making homemade hash browns, and took down one plywood wall. Ooodles survived the tornado and served breakfast the morning of the Great Halloween Blizzard.

This group of women—well, *some* group of women—has been meeting at Ooodles née Cats for fifteen years. In the first year, the original group wrote a serial novel, passing the notebook from person to person on Wednesday mornings. Only two of those novelists are still at the table. The rest have scattered: to Rock Island, to Chicago, to Kansas City, to Boston. At fourteen years, I'm now one of the old-timers.

Other women have taken up the chairs they've vacated. Some have joined the table when they've arrived in town. A current member of the group invites the new arrival because, well, she just *seems* like the kind of person who . . . Still others, longtime residents of the town, have started coming when life circumstances changed: a divorce, a move, no more eight o'clock classes. Some of us go every week; some of us don't show for months at a time. Through a kind of human entropy, the group size always

hovers around six or eight. And by some completely unspoken but utterly understood policy, it has never included any men. (Perhaps we fear that if we spoke about their absence, we'd need to justify it. And once we started to justify it, we'd start to alienate or anger each other, as we realized that our reasons for enjoying this women-only space were utterly different, even at odds with each other.)

When I think of my life in this community, a life in which I spent many years perching, trying to escape, trying to get a job in the same town with my then-partner, trying to pretend I hadn't come back to the college I'd attended, and trying not to notice that other people kept leaving without me, this group of women stands in the middle of my thoughts like a strikingly bright, complexly braided rug. This set of relationships isn't the most important in my life, although many of the women are incredibly dear to me. More than anything, it's the continuity of Wednesday morning. It's the knowledge that if I show up at 7:30, there will be someone I can talk to over my hash browns and toast. And if today my mother is having open-heart surgery, or another woman's brother-in-law's cancer is back, or someone else's stepdaughter is being a shrew, we know we'll get listened to as we cry or worry or spit tacks.

But sometimes the comfort of the group comes precisely from the fact that no one will ask you too many questions, unless you really want them to. Seven years ago, I went through what felt like a spectacularly public breakup-and-takeup: I left my years-long relationship with a man to "take up" with a woman. Although I knew the news was being carried in the saddlebags of ponies all along the gossip trail, the breakfast crew didn't bat an eye, didn't ask a probing question, didn't do a thing—except welcome Peg warmly the first time she showed up at breakfast.

A few years ago, Peg and I pulled off the impossible: she got a tenure track job at the college, too. We looked at each other, said "This is for the long haul," and decided to "make some community." We worked alongside a small group of locals to start a community garden in town. We began volunteering at our local food co-op. We started hosting dinner at our house once a month for whoever shows up. We encouraged our students (notorious perchers) to involve themselves in community organizations by suggesting that, even if they're not here for the long haul, they need to start learning *now* how to make community where they live. Geologic time.

Although it sounds a bit overblown and symbolic to say it, I see my bisexual identity as reflecting and being reflected in my location: here on the edge of the prairie; here within striking distance of the Mississippi—that great symbolic and physical line dividing West and East. I lived on the other side of that divide for a long time—but not very far on the other side. Just about this far, in fact. I seem to like it here, in the interstice, in the in-

between place. Just as I like being in the in-between place in which I can love women, love this woman, while also honoring my history of loving men.

In some ways, I'd have to say it's a place of considerable ambiguity and no small discomfort, this place in between. For instance, I don't dare call myself a Westerner when I talk to Laura, from New Mexico, or Abby, from Texas; to them I live practically on the eastern seaboard. But to Peg's mother, from Massachusetts, I am the equivalent of Annie Oakley. Perching on the edge means someone is always trying to push you over to the other side.

HELEN M. WAYMAN ⤳ *Hallelujah! Faith Circle!*

O Fateful Day. Thirty Determined Lutheran Women
Have Convened Here to Chart a New Course.
And—You—All—Know—Luterns
And CHANGE.

Our church is growing, every week.
We all take great pride in that.
But our Church Women's Circle groups are dwindling.
In former years, many devout ladies
Banded together in dedicated Organizations with the names
Of Biblical heroines.
However, today modern moms are no longer content
With Christian Labor and Sacrifice.
No . . . They'd rather have
Another car in the driveway.

Now our Lutheran Octogenarians can no longer serve.
And there aren't enough sixty-year-olds to fill our ranks.
Ladies of fifty and forty? Forget it!

But . . . Abolish all our Circles?
"Too much of a CHANGE.
Instead,
Let's all combine into one!"

And what TITLE shall it be known by?
ETERNAL CIRCLE?
No . . . Nothing on earth is forever, you know.
JEHOVAH CIRCLE?
Too pompous.

FRIENDS CIRCLE?
Too common.
Well, we are all "saved by faith."
FAITH needs to be in the title.
Yes, yes. FAITH.

Then with admirable Christian tranquility
Our Convener listens to thirty suggestions.
Finally we are fighting over whether it should be
Circle of Faith—or Faith Circle.
Gracious! How can we possibly resolve such a
Devastating Dilemma?

For fifteen more minutes (I know—I count them)
We all discuss the ramifications.
(Always in a genteel manner, of course.)
Until finally a Show of Hands approves FAITH CIRCLE.

HALLELUJAH! FAITH CIRCLE IT SHALL BE!
And it took hardly any
CHANGE
at all.

HILLARY BARTON BILLMAN ✑ *Bingo Babes*

Bingo. Old women in large aluminum buildings play bingo. But, hey, it's something social to do in a small western Wyoming coal-mining town.

We started the club two years ago when Julie from New Jersey moved to town. The first rule was no men allowed. Pam's husband, Mick, tried to convince us he could be our caller. "B-64," he yelled. "There is no B-64," we yelled back. "No men either."

There aren't many opportunities for women-only get-togethers in this town that don't involve religion, quilt blocks, or breastfeeding classes. For some of the Bingo Babes, it's the only time we get together with other women.

Julie from New Jersey taught us the rules. Bring an appetizer or dessert, a ten-dollar gift, a two-dollar gift, and five dollars in cash. The drink, supplied by the hostess, started out as Bingo Punch, a concoction that changes at every house. My Bingo Punch is pineapple juice, rosé wine, and 7 UP. Punch with a punch. Now we drink whatever the hostess makes. At one house we had bloody marys, at another a vodka concoction.

We play the first round slowly, each winner choosing a ten-dollar gift and unwrapping it. After many *oohs* and *ahs* and *don't get too comfortable*

with that, the winner writes the gift with her name underneath it on a piece of paper. Bingo Virgins get really excited when they win in this round. The veterans shake their heads and say, "It's the next round that really counts." When all the gifts are gone, we eat. Appetizers only.

Bingo was supposed to be for *all* women. We didn't want to exclude anyone. But for a while, bingo filled with catty cliques. Some Babes elected themselves Bingo President and Vice President. The rest of us went along with their hierarchy because we were addicted to the prizes, the cash, the punch, and the monthly Friday night out.

"Don't eat dessert *now,*" the self-appointed Bingo President yelled one night when a Bingo Virgin grabbed a slice of cake with her mozzarella sticks during the appetizer break. It was her first night playing bingo; she never came back.

After eating appetizers, we play the timed one-hour speed round. In this round, we play as many games as possible, and each winner can steal a ten-dollar gift, scratching the former winner's name from the paper and replacing it with her own. There is always a favorite gift, varying from candles to dishware to lotion. Bringing the popular gift is like being crowned Bingo Queen. Sometimes a Babe likes her own ten-dollar gift so much she'll try to win it back.

"Time!" we yell, shifting nervously in our seats. Sometimes the callers don't call fast enough, or they laugh or talk. "*Time!*" We need to know how much time is left to steal. Once last year, a few women didn't like the tone of the caller's voice, and every time she called, they sighed dramatically. "Please," one woman said. "Somebody else call the next game before I scream."

As so many do, the self-elected Bingo President and Vice President moved away. The Vice President took the bingo set with her to a less windy, more populated state. Our new set is on bigger cards so some of our Babes don't have to use their reading glasses. The Babe who works at the library laminated the cards so they'll keep longer and we can wash them if we play with sticky fingers. For theme games, around various holidays, we get gifts at after-holiday sales to be ready for next year. We used to have theme markers, like jack-o'-lanterns and black cats for Halloween, but they left the state with the Vice President. Now we use pennies.

After the timed round, we have dessert and coffee and relax. Then it's Blackout Bingo, with the winner getting the pot of money. With each Babe throwing in five dollars, some nights the pot has been close to a hundred bucks. Across the street from my house, the men gather to play poker in the garage studio, which has a woodstove and paintings of nude females on the walls. They also take their game seriously, but poker is played for chump change: the winner for the night might go home with five dollars tops.

"We have Bingo Virgins here tonight." The Virgins are lucky, and they

usually go home with several gifts—so they'll get addicted and come back for more. In the speed round, I'm calling, watching my card, and reading a sheet of paper, trying to decide which gift to steal.

I'll miss the next bingo. I'm pregnant and due about the same time as that month's game. Last weekend, we had bingo in the basement of the library so nobody had to clean her house. We had one Virgin, and we were explaining the rules. When we got to the point where we explained the food and someone mentioned no dessert during appetizers, Vicky, an original Babe who never misses a game, said it was a stupid rule and we should drop it. Everyone agreed, no discussion. Eat your dessert whenever you want. The Virgin didn't win that night, and neither did I, but we'll both be back. The Babes want me to bring the baby to bingo sometime, even if it's a boy.

I see Bingo Babes in the grocery store, at the gas station, at town functions. We always say hello; bingo gives us something in common—something we were lacking before. It should be mandatory for small towns to have a bingo group. I've met women I never would have met because we run in different social or religious groups.

Why bingo? We could get together to do quilt blocking, or we could all meet at the gun club for target practice or at the walking trail for a morning walk, but we don't. Bingo doesn't take any particular talent or body type or motivation other than wanting to gather with women friends for a night of fun.

SUREVA TOWLER 🌿 *I'm Afraid I Can't Attend the Next Meeting*

Because I don't want to
hear any more bold, imaginative new ideas,
revisit the mission statement,
review another set of minutes
or
be empowered.

Because I'm tired of partnerships, coalitions and collaborations,
assessing resources,
strategic planning
and
checking the e-mail.

Because I don't need another
bigger-than-life item on my resumé,

a membership card,
newsletter
or
tax exemption.

Because I want to
effect change rather than discuss it,
have a bake sale instead of *doing lunch,*
do something, anything,
except
have another meeting.

Listen up sister.
It's time to toss the Day-Timer,
get off the Internet and into the streets.
Because meetings may be cool,
but
that ain't where it's at.

BERNIE KOLLER 🖋 *Concerning My Hutterite Cousins*

Carol's round face beams with welcome as she hugs me. Ten Hutterite
women and girls, chirping away in German, perch themselves on couches
and chairs.

I have been visiting this colony for ten years; we share friendly relations
and a common Anabaptist ancestry, from which the Amish and the Menno-
nites also emerge. My mother's people were all Mennonite Germans from
Russia, and my husband and I are members of a local Mennonite church. I
also work as a Step-On guide, "stepping on" to bus tours of tourists as part
of a local development corporation plan to bring visitors to the colonies.
(Church historians say the term "Hutterian" is correct, but most of their
neighbors call them "Hutterites.")

Carol has invited the women to her home so I can interview them about
how they work together. I figure they may have valuable insights, since the
Hutterian communal way of life has survived for half a millennium.

The women are wearing outfits sewn from one pattern—identical short
black jackets with long sleeves, white blouses and vests, and pleated skirts.
Hutterites dress differently from their worldly neighbors so as to focus at-
tention on God rather than themselves. I recognize many of the women in
the room, ranging in age from fifteen to fifty-nine, because they visit the lo-
cal library, where I am director. Although most of them wear traditional an-
klets with low-heeled shoes, teenage Jessica is making a statement by wear-
ing black hose, black open-toed wedges, and black polish on her toenails.

Explaining that I want to write about them for publication, I show them the biography of a German infantryman I published a few years ago. A visitor to the colony asks if she can take the book home. "Of course," I say, "and please share it with any others who might be interested." I mentally kiss the book goodbye because experience has taught me that members of a communal society simply forget that individual ownership exists in the outside world.

"Let's start by your telling me about some activities you girls do together."

"Everything!" say several voices. These women work together every day of their lives, taking swing shifts arranged by the head cook or head gardener, two of the few female positions of power.

"Eating!" Betty says, laughing.

Ruth explains in her calm and motherly voice, "The women are in charge of planting and harvesting the garden. We do most of the butchering, all of the canning, all of the sewing, the spring housecleaning, the cooking, and taking care of the kindergarten. We have plenty to do."

"Don't forget, we take care of the men, too." Stephanie jabs her finger at me, then continues. "Remember the day we did eight hundred jars of tomatoes? It was so hot. We worked all day picking them, washing them, and making tomato juice. At eleven that night, we were just finishing the cleanup, when all of a sudden a rotten tomato went flying across the room. Pretty soon, tomatoes were flying all over the place. After all our hard work, the canning basement was a mess. We went home tired, messy, wet, and feeling amazingly energized. Talk about a stress reliever!"

Everyone is smiling or laughing, except the fifteen-year-old, Heidi. Her birthday is today, which means she will leave the children's dining room, where the older girls serve food from the communal kitchen and do cleanup, to eat with the adults. More important, she will be expected to do the work of an adult woman. From now on, she will take her turn baking, cooking, and gardening, as scheduled by the woman in charge. Like the others, she's been doing minor chores since she was twelve—cleaning up or assisting with canning or butchering, or baby-sitting for an assigned family so the mother can work and go to church. Traditional ways of teaching women how to work with others at domestic labor have been passed down from generation to generation.

"What happens if someone is lazy or doesn't show up on time for her duties?"

"Oh, Rosa takes care of her!" Betty exclaims, and everyone nods. I know Rosa, the head cook, rules the kitchen, but this doesn't tell me how she deals with a lazybones or a no-show, and the question goes unanswered.

Curious about their private time, I inquire, "Okay, what do you do individually?"

"Showering!" says the shy Tilda. Her face turns bright red before she can get it covered with her hands. I realize that they are uncomfortable talking about personal matters, but I know that technology has influenced the gender-based division of labor dramatically for these women. No new work roles are replacing those taken away by technology, so the women have energy to invest in their homes. These girls enjoy rugmaking, crocheting, and knitting. Hobbies involving the collecting of "things" are not encouraged; however, I have seen a collection of toy tractors by the son of a boss and a display of Depression glass by a minister's wife. I decide to be patient and return to the community topic. "What is the best thing about doing a job together?"

After a moment's silence, Stephanie pipes up. "Laughing."

"Getting the job done." Linda's face is serious. She may be thinking ahead to her marriage, when she will go to her husband's colony to live; she cannot choose to divorce. "And talking with each other," she adds.

"You mean gossiping." Tilda raises her eyebrows and speaks softly as usual.

"No," Becky says, "it isn't gossiping . . . it's . . . it's . . ."

"Ya, it's more like arguing," Carol interjects. Carol and Becky do not want me to think that Hutterite women would sink to such a low level as gossiping.

"No, it's not arguing either . . . it's . . . ah, it's just being honest."

Um, yes, I think. The Hutterites are known for their candid remarks. "Honest?" I ask.

"No, *bossy!*" Stephanie shouts, and everyone laughs, although some cover their giggles with hands over their mouths or eyes.

"Well, then," I continue, "what is the worst thing about working together on a project?"

"Cleaning up after," Jessica remarks, twisting hair the color of brown sugar around her finger.

"But we don't mind," Ruth comments, heading off any disagreement in her motherly way. "Sometimes we have too many opinions, and then we get confused."

Carol folds her arms. "We like to settle our own problems. We don't go to the minister or the boss much. We never get loud like the men do." The ladies all nod.

"Besides the tomato episode, what else has happened when you were working?"

"Okay, there was the time we were canning—and we thought the pressure cooker . . ." Betty starts laughing. "Ya, and then . . ." She starts talking in German.

Linda explains in English, between giggles and corrections in German. "Well, see, we were canning one day, and there was this loud noise from the

direction of the pressure cooker. We thought it was about to explode, so everybody started running out of the basement. Stephanie's feet never touched the ground! It turned out to be a jar sealing with a little more noise than usual."

I ask the women, who live in a chauvinistic structure, how they feel about their lack of freedom. They reply that being born a Hutterite means accepting the security and traditions of communal living and what goes with it. They have no voting power and hold no positions of responsibility except for domestic duties, but they don't lose any sleep over it.

This topic leads to a candid discussion about Hutterites who leave the colonies. Becky surprises me by saying she thinks all young adults should spend some time on the outside to see for themselves how difficult it is— paying rent, paying for insurance, existing without the cloak of security provided by the colony, and, of course, coping with worldly sins. We ponder together the question of security versus freedom. It is rare to find a colony woman who will openly express dissatisfaction. Perhaps one must be born to community life to understand it. For them, it is not a matter of choice.

I ask whether the women try to change the traditions of the colony. They tell me that as far as they know, no woman has ever spoken in a rebellious way and remained in the colony. The Hutterian way is to present an unpopular request to the boss or minister in a group, and sometimes this works. The power to be heard comes through community, not individuality. There are no feminists here, at least not as defined by the outside world.

"Why," I ask at last, "do you think your way of life has lasted almost five hundred years?"

Silence. All eyes are on the floor. Becky ventures a reply. "Well, because the leaders were sometimes right."

"Sometimes right?" I echo.

Her courage stimulates the other women. "Because of prayer." Carol nods her head.

Stephanie says, "God's will. God's plan. Tradition."

I can feel the energy of these practical women, but I think this is all I will get from them today. As Carol and Stephanie disappear into the kitchen for coffee, my eyes meet Becky's. She says, "Well, Bernie, we enjoy talking to you, but we wish you could talk the German. By the time we listen to your question, translate to English, and get it out of the mouth, we forget the question!"

As we drink coffee, Carol asks, "Bernie, were you satisfied with us?" Of course I was. After a hearty hug, I depart with freshly baked buns, a pail of homemade noodle soup, and a warm heart.

WANDA ROSSELAND 🦚 *Straightforward and Unafraid*

It wasn't unusual for my "almost" mother-in-law to ask me to dinner. I had been out to the farm several times that spring, helping in any way I could while getting to know Milton's family before our wedding in June.

So when Dorothy called out the door, "Don't forget dinner on Tuesday!" as I got ready to go back to my folks' place near Wolf Point, Montana, I smiled, waved, and said, "I'll be here."

That weekend, I finished sorting through the things I wanted to take to our new home, a trailer house located twenty steps west of the house Milton grew up in. On Tuesday, I packed the back seat and trunk of the sports car he'd bought by saving up three years of Army pay, had a leisurely lunch with my mother, and headed south at two o'clock, sure I had plenty of time to drive to my sister Mary Ann's house in Circle, change clothes, and get out to Dorothy's before six.

"Wanda!" Mary Ann cried, bursting out the door as I drove into her yard. "Where have you been?"

"Home," I said, bewildered.

"You're supposed to be at Dorothy's!"

"I know," I remarked nonchalantly. "I'm going out for dinner."

"Dinner! It's lunch! You're supposed to be there now."

Now? What's going on here? Something's wrong, I thought.

"Do you know what they're doing?" she snapped.

"No," I said.

"It's a party. Your wedding shower. The Weldon Homemakers are having it at Marjory Twitchell's, and you're late."

Oh, no. I crumpled into the car seat. Dinner in the country meant lunch, at noon, and I'd thought it was supper. "Mary Ann," I said, "I gotta go."

I settled behind the steering wheel of that car like Mario Andretti. "Please, God," I prayed, "I have to get there without a wreck." I took those thirty miles of washboard gravel at eighty-five miles an hour, slowing down slightly for the curves.

Twenty minutes later, I walked through Marjory's door, wearing blue jeans and with straight hair, and those ladies rose out of their chairs like I was a queen. Women I didn't even know. Alma Thorgaard, first president of the club when it was incorporated in 1930. Dear God, forty years before that day in 1970 when the Homemakers held my wedding shower. Grandma Volla, ninety years old, whose parchment hands had butchered chickens, scrubbed on a washboard, and dropped dirt on her only son's grave. Marjory and her husband, flooded out by the building of Fort Peck Dam.

They pulled the casseroles out of the oven, took the lids off salads, and sat me down to a table full of dinner and presents. And love. It was my introduction to the Weldon Homemakers. Naturally, I joined.

Being in Homemakers put me in the community. Once a month, we met and did a project: sewing, cooking, or a popular craft. We visited the nursing home, taking pies and singing for the old folks. We set up a booth and entered exhibits at the county fair, served lunches at auction sales, held bake sales, made and gave away quilts.

In Homemakers, I met women from all over the county, visited with business people I might not have met otherwise, became friends with ranch women who lived miles on out in the country. I was elected president almost immediately, so I had to attend district meetings and learn to deal with the county agent on various state projects.

Years later, I realized that my association with Homemakers was like being thrown into a pond: the widening ripples were my acceptance into the community. At Effie Dreyer's, I rolled out Norwegian lefse. With Kay Jensen and others, I put together the Fall Fun Festival, a one-day workshop and luncheon for eastern Montana women. With Betsy Dunlap, I acted as secretary of the Christian Women's Club.

I assisted the judges at the fair, hosted baby showers, and grieved when our members started dying. Martha Arnston, whose husband had served in the *First* World War; Alma Thorgaard with her collection of painted plates and beautiful afghans, each crocheted by hand; Grandma Volla, sitting on her couch with arms out, asking, "Can I hold your baby? It's been so long since I've held a baby." Of course I let her hold my daughter Kristi, four weeks old, on her first outing—to Homemakers, of course.

Weldon Homemakers is gone now, disbanded after seventy years of women holding up women, but it lives in my heart. I can see all those ladies, standing in somebody's living room, holding up programs, and reciting the creed written by Mary Stewart.

Keep us O Lord from pettiness; let us be large in thought, in
 word and deed.

Let us be done with fault finding and leave off self seeking.

May we put away all pretence and meet each other face to face,
 without self pity and without prejudice.

May we never be hasty in judgment and always generous.

Let us take time for all things: make us grow calm, serene, gentle.

Teach us to put into action our better impulses straight forward
 and unafraid.

Grant that we may realize that it is the little things that create
differences; that in the big things of life we are one.

And may we strive to touch and know the great human heart
common to us all, and O Lord God let us not forget to be kind.

BARBARA JESSING ♪ *The Spite and Malice*
Sewing Circle

They have been gathering every Friday night since sometime in the forties.
Sometimes they sew—in fact, they call it a sewing circle—but lately they
are more likely to play cards, as they do tonight. They call the game Spite
and Malice but have a hard time playing it in the cutthroat manner that
gave the game its name. Any play that poses a disadvantage to another
player is prefaced with apologies, and the eventual winner is the humblest
of all.

Their names would tell you that these ladies were christened around
the turn of the century: Ethel, Hester, Ruth, Mary, Fannie Mae, and Evelyn.
I am the youngest player in tonight's game by at least two generations. I am
my grandmother's guest, having had a quick lesson in the rules of Spite
and Malice earlier in the afternoon so that I could be brought along tonight.
They are tolerant of my slow learning, though not to the point of giving
away an advantage.

They laugh and gossip and refer to one another as girls. They exchange
recipes, often featuring Cool Whip and Jell-O. Or make afghans for the vet-
erans' home and for new babies.

New to this city, they first met as neighbors during World War II. They
followed their husbands, and their husbands followed the jobs, away from
the dried-up farms and ranches and oil fields of Oklahoma and Colorado
and Kansas and Nebraska, and toward the California coast and its ship-
yards and industries tooling up for the war.

They raised children together, shared coffee in kitchens. Some even
moved in together, entire families, during times of joblessness and extreme
hardship. When, eventually, all left the crowded, working-class neighbor-
hood for better homes and more space, the Friday night sewing circle was
formalized. They have known my mother since her childhood, and they
have known me all of my life. I know that my grandmother kept vigil at the
hospital during the twenty-four hours prior to my birth, and I know that
they kept their own vigil for her, because now I have seen them do this for
one another on countless occasions of births and deaths.

Once it was women in the kitchen, sewing or playing cards, and men in

the garage or basement workshops, or later around the TV. As a child, I was aware of sometimes hearing the puzzling tail end of a dirty joke as the men came back into the kitchen for dessert. Now most of the ladies are widows, and only my grandfather sits in the living room with the TV tuned to a baseball game. But it seems that they might always have had a different, a more intimate, connection with one another than they did with their husbands. As my grandmother tells me, "We know each other so well; we know each other's families; we talk on the phone almost every day."

There is a code to it. The exchange of understanding seems never to consist of either explicit complaints or outright sympathy. But somehow all offer and accept comfort for the hardships of aging; of lonely widowhood or a failing, dependent spouse; of children or grandchildren in trouble with premarital pregnancies; of breakdowns and depressions, broken marriages and bitter divorces. But it does not have a somber tone at all. Tonight three among them have pictures of newborn great-grandchildren. And I notice the silent worried looks, spreading eye to eye, about my grandmother's cough that never went away after a bout of pneumonia last year.

When I lived in this house, just starting college, I remember being impatient with the ordinariness of these ladies. I could not wait to leave those Jell-O recipes behind in favor of tofu burgers and tabbouleh, which I brought—once—to a family potluck, where it served only to flush out a cousin I had previously not known to have health food tendencies. I would find friends to talk politics and philosophy with, who would change the world and not sit in the kitchen. What a young punk I was then.

But tonight, though its content is unchanged over these nearly fifty years, I see the process at work—the connections that I did not see and could not value before. I think of myself as being halfway to their ages, and I think about the friendships that have come along with every life stage, and the ones that have lasted. We may not play cards or knit booties, but we meet as book groups or writing groups or with no redeeming purpose at all beyond the social, like my Ladies Aid Society, whose main agenda is good food, a beer, conversation, and the occasional exchange of tofu recipes. A fifty-year network of friendships, though it may be ordinary, seems more rare and more precious to me now than it did then.

BETH PAULSON *A Square of Winter Light*

Aunt Addie, under a window
in a square of winter light,
your quilt clamps in a stand my husband built;
you pieced these twenty-five Dresden Plates
near as any family member knows

in the 1930s when women sewed patchwork
like their grandmothers had
a hundred years before.

I push my needle in and out,
its tail of white thread, and
think of you in the small rhythm of stitches,
picture you with your friends
in lawn chairs back in Hebron, Indiana;
you sewed together fragments of printed fabrics,
wore dresses of similar designs, traded recipes,
drank sugared lemonade, discussed children,
and wondered how you would last
through one more evening.

After you died in 1960,
your quilt top rested
in the Lane cedar chest of my husband's mother,
unfinished, but clean, neatly folded in tissue.
Some women are good at saving,
some at starting things.

For example, Betty Friedan
who was writing *The Feminine Mystique* that same year.
She put the pieces together about women,
saw what they had not, their need to grow,
go it alone, study for degrees, get paid for work
as I did at the university where I spent half a lifetime
before I picked up a needle, and you

in your later years played bridge,
gave birthday parties,
drove your own automobile,
and, to all reports,
were happier a widow than a wife.

GOOSE E. FEDDERS ～ *Speak, Throw Up, or Die*

After waiting for three years to be invited into the Santa Fe storytellers'
group, I thought I would throw up or die of heart palpitations the first time
I had to speak. I was warmly welcomed and introduced, but the inevitable
time came, after the rules had been explained, after some tea and fancy

bread and fruit, after the facilitator had tossed out a "prompt" and we had broken up into small groups to practice an impromptu story and then reassembled into the big group. Shiny, alert faces waited eagerly for the new gal to show her stuff. At that moment, I could not imagine why I was here.

Worse, for the first time in my life, I couldn't think of a story. I felt as if my imagination had been surgically removed. No DNA, no mitochondria, nothing. I stalled, listening to several women tell their stories. This nearly finished me off, because they were so good. They just opened their mouths and became a story, like singing canaries. They rolled into it.

But when each was done, a few sly, shy glances were cast in my direction: when was I going to speak up? But I wasn't thinking about speaking up or telling a story or ever opening my mouth again. I was thinking how embarrassed the good friend who finally invited me was going to be when I turned out to be mute.

At last everyone there, twelve or fifteen women, had told a story but me. The final prompt, or story idea, was announced. I drank another cup of tea and went to pee for the third time in two hours, and when the group recollected, I took a deep breath and told a story. I don't remember what it was and hope they don't either, but it was a true story because I was too paralyzed to make one up.

Perhaps it was about my aunt Nona Ree. In that era when vaginas were referred to as a sort of geographical location known as Down There and boys had an Outfit, Aunt Nona Ree was a legend. An innocent query, "How are you?" would bring this dreaded answer in her chain smoker's rattle: "Honey, my *vagina* hurts. It is as dry as a bone and driving me crazy. Listen, you keep your windows closed at night, you hear? Or else some old Outfit will crawl in there and get you." Once when Aunt Nona Ree had ridden with my family to a family reunion, she spent a long time in a gas station bathroom. When she came out, my father, her youngest brother, began to scold her. She explained that she'd lit a cigarette just after putting a lot of paper into the toilet, and when she dropped the lit match into the toilet bowl the paper flared up so fast she didn't have time to get her *vagina* out of the way, and she was scalded. My father said, "*I never want to hear another word about this, and you kids had better forget about it, too.*" But of course we didn't.

In desperation for a story, I always fell back on my eccentric family from Tornado Alley in the Red River country of Texas, and I shamelessly exploited them for the next year until I calmed down enough to start lying — or making up stories — altogether.

When my forgettable story was done, the storytellers kindly told me what they liked about it and invited me back. On the way home, I cruised through the arroyos in my car, flying low in a haze of fear and pride.

Over the next few months, I learned the simple ways of the group: we meet twice a month, and each time someone volunteers to be the facilitator

and bringer of food for the next time. The current facilitator announces her prompts, one at a time. The prompts are many and varied: verbal scenes, a guided meditation, a single word, a basket of oddities, photographs. Then smaller groups complete a short practice, two or three minutes for each person, before the group comes back together, and the facilitator invites everyone to retell her story if she wishes.

With time, we have become very interested in the differences between the first and second tellings of the story. When each story is finished, the teller is asked whether she would like to hear appreciations. Usually, she says yes, and we make supportive, constructive comments about the story and its delivery. We are not supposed to ask if it is a true story, but sometimes we do, and sometimes we don't have to ask. An undeniable high comes from having to create on the spot, again and again, and to try to tell a story well.

Originally, we all smiled and said hello to each other on entering meetings. But now, years later, we exchange heartfelt hugs and warm handshakes. One who has been absent is often greeted with applause. We meet in our homes, both grand haciendas and humble adobes. Since each member takes her turn as facilitator, feeding us both food and ideas to prompt us into stories, we have come to know each other well. We have cheered each other on through life's struggles on the outside: Miriam's mastectomy, the loss of Cindy's husband and mother, Harriet's retirement, Anna's legal battles, Susie's temporary homelessness. Yet all this "hard news" is exchanged during the first and last ten minutes of the meeting (except as sometimes revealed in our stories), because we stick to the guidelines.

Afterward, we find that the intense concentration and creation have completely rested us from everyday concerns. Some days the stories spill out and soar. Some meetings are so funny a certain member falls out of her chair laughing, and sometimes all of us cry. On a somber winter day, we agree that it feels as if we have been meeting this way for centuries, sharing our lives and becoming enriched in experiences and love together. Here is the coziness of a safe shelter, made up entirely of our hearts and our stories.

MARILYN DORF 🌿 *What It Took*

Not until later did I know what it took for those women to make dinner for threshers—farmwomen a couple of miles up and down the section leaving the kitchens they lived in, those kitchens of beans and flour and pork grease, kitchens where berries awaited canning, where toddlers toddled and babies teethed, kitchens with galvanized teakettles whistling and crocks full of yeast dough rising at the back of the range: those women leaving their own work for a day to go where they were needed more.

For me, threshing meant a day of excitement, going along with my

mother to shoo flies or sort silver, or to keep toddlers' fingers out of the pies. As we approached the place of the threshing, my spine tingled, for already the farmers were gathered with horses and hayracks around the great threshing rig, that unwieldy dinosaur puffing and belching at the edge of the wheat field, where a mixture of smoke and sweet straw dust mingled heavily in the air.

Other women were arriving, too, each wearing her newest wash dress and best feed-sack apron, some carrying pans of yeast buns or freshly baked pies. Our hostess, up to her elbows in flour, greeted us gratefully, and the women, with what looked like the ease of marbles settling into a groove, set to work peeling and slicing and stirring and mixing, pulling the table out long as a church pew, all the time talking of babies and gardens and setting hens, or complaining of rust on the green beans.

Excitement mounted as the morning progressed, the women's faces turning ruddy and moist what with potatoes boiling and chicken frying, heat pouring out of the oven and coffee steaming in pots as big as butter churns, for the day was hot and the kitchen hotter, and no one had invented air conditioning.

When noon came and the crew stopped for dinner, the intensity in the kitchen increased, the women carrying bowls of food to the table: hot mashed potatoes and gravy, green beans and corn, fried chicken and cole-slaw, cucumbers, radishes, sliced tomatoes, and homemade bread. Others poured coffee from the great urnlike pots, and still others were cutting pies—great slices of apple and raisin, gooseberry and mincemeat. And the men, a dozen or fifteen of them, crossed the yard, loud and rough in their banter, brushing dust off their overalls, stamping straw off their shoes. One of them opened the porch door wide and shooed flies away with his hat, while the rest filed inside looking for broom pegs to hang their hats on before stopping to splash cold water over their coarse, dusty faces.

They filled up the house like a storm and sat down at the table, faces red as the summer sun, shirts odorous and darkened with sweat, and they passed the potatoes and gravy, the bread and butter and beans, one to another down both sides of the table, until the soft sounds of mumbling and eating gradually took over, the women standing back watching and ready, refilling platters and bowls as needed, hoping there would be enough.

After the pie was served, and more coffee, they scooted their chairs back and stood up, lingering a few moments to stretch their arms, pat their bellies, or pop into the kitchen with a word of thanks before going back to their work. Then the women dished up plates for themselves and sank down to eat, scattered along the table, grateful for a chance to sit down. Still there was the cleanup to do, leftovers to put away, dishes and pots to scrub that would have filled up a lake, to say nothing of an afternoon lunch to prepare and carry to the field for the men.

Not until later, after my mother's feed-sack apron had been hung up forever, did I stop to think what it must have taken for those women to put on a meal for threshers. Even then, I could not really know, the era having passed, given over to combines and grain trucks, to microwave ovens, dishwashers, and central air.

KELLY MADIGAN ERLANDSON

You Always Start with a Baptism

For Tessie

You put your hands on our heads,
take the wasted strings of our history
in your fingers. You ask us what we want.

You always start with a baptism, acting
as though it is a simple thing, underplaying
your offering. The fine spray of holy water
is cool against our faces.

Your grasp, the skin of your wrist against our
necks or cheeks, changes us. We knew this
beforehand, it is what we came for. Some of us waited
too long, should have come before we did. Who
can say what small toils of the daily world
held us back? As you move in a circle around us,
we feel your body lean into us, and are comforted.

When we are in pain,
you tell us we might think that we
will fall away, tumble out of the world,
be lost. You throw light at our feet
saying *This darkness, I have seen*
this kind of darkness before.
It is sea deep, and you will feel
as though it closes in above you.
You touch our hair, our foreheads,
remind us *I can still see you;*
go as far as you must and I will
hold the gate for you. When we return,
we find our way by a ribbon you have loosely
tied about a lock of our own hair.

Sometimes, you do all this while being still
about troubles of your own. The fair skin
of your arms and hands keeps the secret.

After you do your work,
we rise up from the chair and toss back and forth,
new. What has been removed falls away into a dark
shape on the floor. We look down at it, disconnected,
as you move the bristles of the broom in short chops.

PAT OGLE, WITH BESS ARNOLD
The Brotherhood of Railroad Workers

During World War II, the railroad hired a lot of women, including me, to re-
place men who had gone into military service. We were aware that when
they returned, the men could have their jobs back.

Women worked as laborers in the roundhouse, the car shops, and the
store department—dirty work, requiring strength. Women washed en-
gines, wiped, swept, cleaned coaches, operated the turntables, and greased
the big steam locomotives. But in spite of the hard work, or maybe because
of it, we found time for fun and friendship.

I came from a farm in Nebraska where I'd worked for three dollars
each six-day week, cooking for threshers, taking care of kids, carrying wa-
ter. I arrived in Cheyenne, Wyoming, with seven dollars and a suitcase. I
worked first as a soda fountain clerk at Garlett's Drug Store and lived in a
one-room basement apartment with some other girls. We each paid seven
dollars a month rent. We had no place to cook; I kept food in a dresser
drawer. A girl I worked with told me about the railroad jobs, but if I quit
one job before I had another, I'd have to go back to the farm. So we talked to
a Union Pacific supervisor. He looked at my drugstore uniform and asked,
"Do you realize how cold these winters get down here?" An older lady
took me to Montgomery Ward to buy long-handled underwear and cover-
alls. Some of the girls wore bandannas, but I wore a regular hat with a bill. I
began as a laborer at sixty cents an hour in December 1942, sweeping snow
off the platform where they stacked materials at the scrap dock.

Each morning, I went to work in the dark, and I was scared of the trains
when I crossed the tracks. Someone read the safety rules to us, but it was a
long way from our work on the scrap dock around a train to turn in our
timecards. One time I was walking with two other girls, and one of them
ducked under the train, so I followed her. As I went under, the train jerked.
The brakeman saw us, but he didn't turn us in. We never did that again.

We hauled coal in wheelbarrows so the workers could build fires in bar-

rels and keep warm outside. Most of the men would come to get warm but wouldn't help push the wheelbarrows. The bosses didn't allow any bullying of the women. As far as I knew, there wasn't any discrimination against the women by the men.

I worked several jobs in the store department, moving up from laborer to scrap sorter. A crane dumped a big pile of scrap on the dock, and we worked with some Mexican men sorting the tin from the steel and other materials, using a long pole with a hook on the end. If we put the wrong piece in the pile, one man wouldn't say anything, just pull it out. He was a precious man, very good to us girls. We also stacked rail joints. They were heavy, and they had to be straight. When I got enough seniority, I got a job at the main store working inside putting materials away.

Our lunch breaks were short, so most of us packed our lunches. Men and women ate in separate boxcars equipped with tables and benches; the women had two cars. Sometimes in the wintertime, the fire went out in the old stove, and we ate our lunches fast. Some workers, called gandy dancers, lived in boxcars equipped with bunk beds. The parents of one young girl cooked for the crews in one of the cars. Sometimes we sneaked off to the Coffee Cup on Sixteenth Street for pie and coffee.

Some of the older women with more experience wouldn't invite two young Mexican girls to eat in their boxcar, so some of us decided if those girls weren't good enough, we weren't good enough either, so we wouldn't eat with those women.

When I sorted timecards, I got to come in a half-hour later, but that made me later getting home. After dark, I was the only woman there and had to lock all the buildings. I was so scared.

The store department supervisor, Mr. Rasmussen, rode a bicycle around the yards. We called him "Jitterbug" because he was nervous; if he saw someone loafing, he blew his whistle. We used an outdoor privy, and if you were in there longer than he thought you should be, he had someone knock on that door. Can you imagine in the wintertime staying in one of them places a minute longer than necessary?

We women came to one another's aid. One day when I was lifting tie plates, I got so sick I went home and the doctor came to the house—that's when they made house calls. One of the other girls came to visit and told me they would put me on an easier job when I came back. That never happened, but the girls were thinking of me.

In the evenings, we went to the USO, the Club Araby, or the Valencia, or we rode the bus to the military base to dance. We stayed home one night a week to clean the apartment.

Later, after I married, we enjoyed railroad-sponsored Christmas parties, where employees' children sang and danced; we played bingo; sometimes we brought back a big sack of groceries.

A lot of the girls married railroad men, and we kept in touch with one

another. Very nice people worked at the railroad. It was a brotherhood of women and men.

JO-ANN SWANSON ✐ Our Ladies of the Farm

Those times I travel the vistas of northern Montana and southern Saskatchewan, looking at miles of sagebrush, blistering crops, and swaybacked barn wood, I think of our Ladies of the Farm, who ironed my childhood with pressed linens and made it bloom with red geraniums. I watch the sides of the weed-infested roads to see how much their influence has waned. Any day now, I fear the sphere of our dear Ladies of the Farm will have vanished, and when Our Ladies fall, all will be gone. The roads of our backwoods communities will have grass growing down the middle of the ruts, as tall as "giraffe houses"—those grain elevators now going and gone. All will be lost except the violet seep of sunset on the ruts that led to the city.

Our small hamlet lay in north-central Saskatchewan, with lakes and jack pine to the north, tamarack to the east, and an increasing population to the west. Our own grid of community was defined by baseline roads five miles apart, north to south; this was the realm of our Ladies of the Farm. All of the women with the iron hands are alive, but many have moved to small towns; they still govern at a distance.

My childhood was run by the iron hands of these women, yet it took me years to see that women also managed the best-functioning family farms. Back then, I noticed only the lack of nail polish on those work-worn hands. Now I know that every community needs a "club" of hard-working women at its softest core. If these women had really formed a club, weekly minutes would have revealed a set agenda that grew over fifty years.

But the Ladies of the Farm would never create a report of their activities. They are private, after all. But for fifty years, the Ladies mapped our roads with invisible ink, and those fifty years took hard work.

The committee's enduring legacy will be childhoods filled with the aroma of baking, homespun clothing, and sweet evening stock floating through the windows. Generations of children know that the Ladies of the Farm were the healing balm that made what could have been a stark and poverty-stricken rural childhood into a cocoon of calm and rest and beauty. They didn't need a healer in their midst because theirs was a community that healed. Money was as incidental as it could get on this continent in that day and age.

We are the heirs of their beauty and bounty, destined to carry scraps of their "minutes" into our crazy quilt hours spent in other, larger communities wracked by the strong winds and tall weeds of increasing change.

DAWN SENIOR-TRASK 🖎 Convergence of Horse-Crazy Women

"My mother says, 'What do you need all those friends for, anyway?'"

Diane's spurs jingled as she stretched her long legs sheathed in fringed leather chinks. She glanced at her palomino, Tequila, to make sure he still stood hitched to a crooked pine next to Candy, my old sorrel mare.

Then she continued. "I said, 'Mom, don't you know how good all that love feels?'"

Her legs folded like an elk's, and she sat next to me on the lee side of a boulder out of the fierce mountain wind. We'd ridden up the foothills, where big black-bellied birds had burst from the brush, spooking our horses. Diane had squinted at them. "Pheasants?"

I shook my head. "Sage grouse."

Our horses' hooves had clattered on the rocks as we heaved up steep, winding deer trails, past budding serviceberry and bitterbrush, where horned larks skimmed just above the ground with their thin, plaintive peeping. Now we'd reached the edge of the timber, where four-foot snow-drifts blocked our passage and we could ride no farther.

Diane unwrapped the smooshed peanut butter sandwich she'd fetched from her saddlebags, while my cold-stiffened fingers peeled a boiled egg so clumsily that big chunks of egg white came off with the bits of brown shell.

Her eyes scanned the great timbered ravine below us on the mountain's southwest flank. It plunged with its meltwater creek into the foothills and the broad valley that stretched to other mountain ranges in all directions— the snowy Sierra Madre divide, the gentle Greens, and the Ferris Mountains, whose arched cliffs hump like a herd of fin-backed dinosaurs across the northwestern horizon a hundred miles away.

She licked peanut butter off her finger and said, "I have this strong feeling that it's about more, even, than the love. I feel like this convergence of women has some sort of deeper meaning, as if my whole life has been leading up to this. Think about it—we're all in our forties or early fifties, all married, or soon to be"—she winked at me—"some of us to men in their sixties. Most of us are childless, some of us artists, all horse lovers—and we all wind up here in the middle of nowhere, Wyoming!"

"Except for me," I objected. "I didn't wind up here."

"Yeah, you're the native. But it seems to me there has to be some reason behind it."

I nodded. "Maybe so."

Diane cocked her head with a faraway look. "Don't know what it is, exactly."

I said, "Maybe we'll find out."

As Diane unwrapped a granola bar and I munched on a carrot, I thought about all of us horsy pals and how it all started the previous spring with the first meeting of the Spurs of the Moment club. Since then, between five and eight of us, sometimes with husbands and boyfriends, sometimes just us women, had explored more country on horseback than I'd seen in my life. We wended silently through aspen forests, where sunlight set aglow the porcupines sleeping among quaking leaves, where the hermit thrush echoed his own haunting song and grasses grew thick among undergrowth hemlock, wild rose, and kinnikinnik. I rode lost in a tranquil trance. Sometimes we jumped deadfall across creek-side trails, or loped through summer meadows where larkspur, lupine, paintbrush, and prairie smoke all vied for sulphur butterflies, checkerspots, blues, and bumblebees.

The times we had! Horses bucked, reared, kicked, rolled in snowdrifts. We plunged cinch-deep in bogs, got chased by swarms of deer flies and angry half-wild stallions protecting their mares. We lost countless horseshoes, quirts, canteens, and assorted gear all over the county. But we found each other.

Now, atop the spring mountain, Diane and I stuffed plastic sacks of leftovers, napkins, and wrappers into our saddlebags; checked our cinches; and remounted Tequila and Candy. As we angled down the steep, rocky slope, the wind swept away any hope of conversation. I thought about what my life had been before this convergence of women had changed it forever. I'd been richly happy, with friends and family nearby, my horses and beloved land with all its creatures. Although I lived alone in the log cabin where I was raised, I seldom felt lonely, immersed as I was in the seasons of the sagebrush hills, where the coyote pair raised their pups along the trail of my morning walks, bluebirds and owls perched on the cabin to hunt insects and mice, and two antelope does hid their fawns on the ridge outside the window. A wild ermine followed me everywhere through the snow, and chickadees ate seeds from my hand. Yet sometimes a shadow of fear would swoop to touch me ever so lightly, like the wingtips of the prairie falcon that once mistook my head for a rabbit. Would loneliness haunt my future?

In those days, I never dreamed how much happier I could be. Now, riding down the mountain—Diane's spurs and our horses' bridles jingling, a fleece jacket wrapping me, and the earth spread in painted layers below us—I became conscious of my joy. I felt safe, warm, and secure in the future. I felt that whatever might happen in the lives of any of us horse-crazy women, we could count on each other. Whatever hardships, triumphs, or griefs any of us might go through, we'd never face a lonely old age.

LINDA ALDRICH ✍ *Hook and Turn*

Up at four A.M. to start the dough, Louise walks the path
from her turquoise trailer to the commune's kitchen.
This morning a February moon, and Orion stands
as he always does in winter: long legs, jeweled sword
hanging over the valley. "Walk. Walk," she says to him
with each step. Behind the building, frozen mops lean
with distorted hair as she lets herself into the kitchen
filled with moonlight and cold tidiness, wind blowing down
the stove vents, stiff arms and legs of utensils hanging
from hooks, and the two big Hobart mixers—
lions at the gate—holding her in.

She reaches for the Mason jar of yeast, decides
on white sugar instead of molasses for the first batch.
(A personal rebellion.) Molasses is messy stuff,
won't go anywhere until spring, until things warm up.
She wonders about her old Chevrolet and how far
it will take her. She wonders if she is too old.
She starts up the Hobart, watches the dough hook
turn and turn, hook and turn.

She can't remember his name, the one who wanted
to marry her, but they said no, she couldn't go
with him. He was not core substance. Uranda
did not like him, and that was proof enough.
She does remember how angry he was, backing his car
tail end into the ditch. His embarrassed face. How funny
it had seemed to them: a little piece of the anti-Christ
propelled out through the gates of heaven. Proof of Spirit
at work, sorting those who carried the tone from those
who didn't. But she had not been able to stop thinking
about him: of his kindness, of how he wanted to take
her away. Later, the radio fell into the bathtub
with her. Evidence of how wrong spirit comes back on you,
they said, more proof of how the Law works, and how
you need to come back in line with Spirit, they said.

She no longer remembers the song that was playing.
She knows she liked it, but cannot remember much
of the girl she was before her mind was changed

by electricity. She had lain in bed for many weeks.
No amount of healings could put her back together
or give her back the respect she'd lost.
There is no doubt: she can't tell them now
about the cancer growing inside her.

She stretches a bit of dough to check the gluten.
It needs to stretch but not break, leave a thin membrane
for light to show through. Pearlescent, no holes. Like an eye,
the eye of the needle, the big collective eye watching.
She tears the membrane with her finger. Now it is a window.
A window to crawl through. She turns off the Hobart,
lifts the hook, scrapes the dough into the bowl,
and covers its roundness with a white cloth. She will start
up the Chevrolet, take a long, hard right at the end
of the dirt road. Go all the way to California maybe.

She takes off her apron. Someone else can weigh the loaves.
Shape them. Someone else can watch them rise as the sun
comes up, let them cool on the stainless steel table
like Conestoga wagons without wheels, going nowhere.

JOANNE WILKE ✐ *Cindergals Never Looked Back*

The San Jose Cindergals Track Club began as a lark in 1968 when Julie Martin told her after-school recreation leader, Augie Argabright, that she'd like to be on a track team.

At first Augie coached both boys and girls, but then Little League baseball season began, and all the boys left. The girls had no other options; this was long before running shoes, carbo-loading, and Olympic distance races for women. Almost immediately, the Cindergals became national champions and a women's distance-running force, ultimately winning a total of forty-seven national age-group awards.

When Augie recently retired from his day job—driving trains—and asked the Cindergals if we'd like a reunion, I immediately replied yes. I wanted to see my old teammates. The reunion was held south of San Jose, California, at Vasona Park, one of our main off-track training locations. I remembered we always ran in groups there because of the flashers. Once, we were running through the neighborhoods in stifling summer heat, uphill on pavement, when a bunch of little boys sprayed us with a hose. To their surprise, we didn't scream and scatter; we ran toward them shouting, "Thank you!" The next week, they offered to spray us if we paid them a quarter.

Augie was one of the few coaches, maybe the first, who trained women hard, like men, running intervals and over-distance, and at least once daily. The Cindergals were most recognized for early member Francie Larrieu (Smith), who ultimately competed in five Olympic Games and during her career set thirty-six U.S. records and twelve world records in distances ranging from one thousand to ten thousand meters. But the key was the team. When you train at a high level every day against a group of national-caliber athletes, you become one.

I was a sprinter, but I joined the team with my best friend, a talented high school distance runner Augie had recruited. Cross-country season was approaching, and once, for Saturday morning training, we ran up Mount Hamilton. I'm not sure how far we ran or the change in elevation, but every step was uphill. I ran the whole way out of plain, pure stubbornness. It hurt; there was no runner's high. Augie gave me a funny look as I wobbled in, and at Monday's practice I was switched to the distance group.

We ran together as a team six or seven days a week during track and cross-country seasons, a bit less often from December to March, and mostly on our own during the summer. Augie scouted locations where we could run on grass or soft surfaces as much as possible, and he designed a cohesive training plan for each year. Every practice was important. Always we were building—building on previous training, building our base of strength and endurance, building our confidence, building toward new peaks.

The only thing that altered the training plan was rain. A regular California monsoon automatically meant a twenty-quarters day. We ran five miles of intervals in our cold, soaking, heavy sweats. Augie stood at the least windy corner of the sopping grass field, stopwatch in hand, wearing his black fur hat with the earflaps, and squawking that Bertha Butt and her enormous sister Louise were beating us. We cruised around the orange cones in a tight pack, strides and breathing synchronized, pacing one another at ninety, eighty, seventy-five seconds per loop. Sometimes Augie told us the pace, sometimes our legs chose it. Between laps, we bent over, hands on knees, water squishing from our shoes, blowing like horses before the next one.

At one state championship, the rain was pouring so hard I could see equally well with or without my thick glasses. The cross-country course was all mud, and Ronelle stepped in a hole two hundred meters from the finish. She heard everything in her ankle rip but finished that final uphill. She was our fifth runner; without her, we had no team score.

In the four years I ran for the Cindergals, I suffered from stress fractures, joint sprains, muscle strains, bone chips, tendinitis, high arches, plantar fascia, and blood blisters on my toes. I missed only two months of training. Others had surgeries and cortisone shots and kept running. Roxanne

wore a red ski hat pulled over her ears every winter day to prevent ear infections. She won that rainy state championship wearing it.

We had no trainer for the team, no one but Augie to advise us. We went to family doctors and treated our injuries ourselves, or tried to ignore them, while running every day. In the context of training, we walked sick teammates, counseled nervous and disappointed ones, and listened to one another. Janet's fiancé died in a motorcycle wreck; a drunk driver killed Cathy's father. My beloved grandfather died of cancer. It was cross-country season, and we ran long intervals over hills on rough trails in a September heat wave. I threw myself into practice, hoping for complete exhaustion. My legs burned, my lungs burned, my eyes burned. I found I couldn't run through this pain either, only with it, with my teammates. I warmed up for every race by telling myself, "Why are you so nervous? It's not like it's the Nationals or something." Then I gave myself the same advice at the Nationals and realized it was okay to be nervous.

Races were the rewards. Augie never gave a team talk, never said there is no "I" in team. Sometimes he'd offer a strategy, such as "Kick early" or "Be aggressive," but usually he just smiled and wagged his finger. "Watch out for Bertha," he said, and his confidence was all we needed. When I ran my best eight hundred meters, knocking six seconds off my time, he nearly fell from the announcer's booth in excitement. We were fresh off cross-country season, and eight hundred meters on the flat seemed like nothing. When Ann tried to pass me, I kicked early. I didn't win the race, but that wasn't the point. I stepped up to a new level, qualified for the Mount SAC race, and beat my old self by half a football field. I also beat Ann for the first and only time. On Monday, she joined the Cindergals and went on to the junior international team five months later.

Once a group of us took two cars and drove to Eugene, Oregon, for the 1976 Olympic Trials, our first road trip on our own. When we practiced in the stadium between events, Bruce Jenner recognized us, crying "Cindergals!" as we swept past. The energy was ecstatic. Then came the women's fifteen hundred meters final, a highlight among highlights, only the second time this distance was an Olympic event. All but two finalists were or had been Cindergals. Our teammate Cyndy Poor outkicked the field in the last hundred meters to win.

When I arrived at the reunion, seventeen years after Augie stepped down and the Cindergals era ended, it was hot. Of course. What a relief to find that nearly everyone had gained twenty pounds but was otherwise little changed—simply older versions of ourselves. Augie noted that we all still "loved to run quarters—ha-ha," but that we were a little more polished in our behavior. He most enjoyed the way we greeted each other—with bear hugs.

An enormous poster listed records held; a table carried silver trophies, plates, bowls, and plaques; another table displayed scrapbooks and photos; and a video showed serious little girls running: Ronelle taking the age-nine-and-under cross-country championships, Janet running second. But the conversation was about families, jobs, homes, current dreams—and where were Bertha and Louise?

Our children were surprised, incredulous, unexpectedly proud. "That's you?" they asked, pointing to photos of medal-draped teenagers. "Did anyone get to the Olympics?" One mother nodded toward Francie. "She went five times." Their eyes grew wide. This was their mom, their plain old mom. It was one thing for her to cheer on their sidelines or even go out for a jog, but another thing entirely to have a drawer full of medals and to know Olympians.

None of the children were runners. Many were swimmers or soccer players; they have so many options today. Would we still choose track and cross-country?

A few of the Cindergals continue to run. One, a former national champion, is now a grandmother training for marathons, another is fighting bone spurs, and a third uses a treadmill so she can watch her kids. I didn't meet one who was dissatisfied with her life.

When I left, I felt happy and sad together. What we had as teens, sweating and striving and laughing together for two hours every day, couldn't be re-created in an afternoon. During the intense teenage years, we competed intensely with and against one another. Not only did we survive the rigorous training regimen and related injuries, but we thrived on it. We were peed out and ready to puke at every starting line, but once the gun sounded, we never looked back.

VIRGINIA BIXLER CASSELLS *The Hobo Mark Swooshed*

During the Great Depression, a multitude of men rode the four freight trains that came through Harrison, Nebraska, every day. The hoboes were seeking work, struggling to survive, and when the trains stopped to take on water or unload freight, the men fanned out through the town looking for food and water.

Our small town had no soup kitchen, no Salvation Army, but individuals rose up to meet the need. Compassionate and caring women made sack lunches for the men—even though it was a hardship, since everyone was suffering from the Depression.

My maternal grandmother, Alice Davis, always shared food from her

table when the hoboes appeared at mealtime. Otherwise, she made sandwiches, cutting the homemade bread in thick slices so it wouldn't crumble, and adding to the sack an apple or cookies and something to drink. If I was there, I considered it an honor to carry the lunch to the hobo while my grandmother gave him a cup of coffee or water. Many times she gave the men clothing her three sons had left behind.

On the north side of her house, visible from the street, was a chalk mark placed there by some hobo who wanted his fellow travelers to find food. My grandmother would not let anyone remove the mark. My best friend's mother had the same mark on her house. I had forgotten the mark until I first saw the Nike shoe logo. Although the hobo mark was thinner, it *swooshed* in the same way.

In those days, it seemed people didn't need a central authority to tell them the right thing to do. I'd like to see a monument to these saintly women who helped the less fortunate in those dark days.

MARGARET EATON JOHNSON ✐ *Endurance in Harmony*

In 1955, the Harmony, Wyoming, Home and Community Club "adopted" five handicapped children who had been abandoned by their families in the Wyoming State Training School in Lander. The club still sends them birthday and Christmas gifts and cards and still keeps track of them—not easy now because they are over sixty years old and some of them have been moved from Lander.

GRACE E. REIMERS KYHN ✐ *The Caring Cleveland Club*

In Cleveland Precinct, Nebraska, where I lived in my youth, there was a unity of women who called themselves the Cleveland Social Club. Most of them were our neighbors. This group of rural women remained strong for years, in spite of personal differences, hard times, and drought.

Most rural homes in the 1930s had wood floors, cheap linoleum, and rag rugs. The men wore patch upon patch on their overalls, darned socks, and resoled shoes. Skirts from women's wash dresses became hand and tea towels. Money was very scarce, and everyone tried to make do with what they had on hand.

Within this community, living on a small farm, was an older, childless couple. They were told they were too old to adopt a baby. At club one day, Mrs. Jensen said that they had received the good news about a six- or seven-year-old girl whom they could take into their home. Little Jenny's

mother had died, and her father was too ill to care for her properly, so he had to place her in an orphanage.

Jenny arrived at the Jensens' home with very little more than the faded, washed-out clothes on her thin body. It was almost impossible for the Jensens to find money to buy all the clothes she would need for school. Their cream and egg money would not reach that far for weeks.

Word traveled fast on the rural party line about Jenny's arrival and the condition of her clothing. Everyone was so happy for the Jensens that they sprang into action. Most of the women were good seamstresses—they would sew for Jenny, using whatever they had on hand for material.

Meta, a tall woman with a long, badly worn coat, took the garment apart and reversed the material to make Jenny a coat. Hannah and Nora each made a cute dress. Florence got out her supply of bleached flour sacks and fashioned two petticoats with lace trim at the neck. Nell pieced together from scraps two cover-up aprons with pockets and two cotton handkerchiefs with Jenny's initials embroidered in the corner. Lizzie made bloomers. Emma donated a used set of hat and gloves that her daughters had outgrown. Mildred, the one lady who could hardly sew on a button, bought two pairs of long, tan cotton stockings from the general store with some of her egg money. Teresa pieced together a flannel nightgown with bias-tape trim.

In less than a week, Jenny had a simple school wardrobe. When she arrived at school, we children all thought she looked right in style. She was proud of the new shoes and overboots the Jensens had purchased.

Shortly after that, the Jensens moved closer to town, where Jenny was able to finish high school. Through all the years, they were a happy family. Jenny always helped the old couple with chores and the garden, and she loved to read. They adopted her when she was twelve.

Suddenly, Mrs. Jensen became ill and passed away. It was then that Mr. Jensen told old friends that Jenny had never been very well. Their doctor gave her only a few years to live. Mr. Jensen was already bent over and walked with a cane, but his wish was to have enough years in his own life to care for Jenny, who was now almost bedfast. His prayer was answered, as he lived a few years after Jenny's death.

This was only one of the many acts of kindness the Cleveland Social Club performed without hesitation. The club truly set a good example of "love thy neighbor as thyself."

BARBARA A. ENGLE ✍ *A Good Thing to Do*

It seemed like a good thing to do. My children were older, and after twenty-two years in Wheatland, Wyoming, I wanted to join an organization. Platte

County Search and Rescue is made up of volunteer men and women trained to find and rescue missing people. I wanted to join and to learn interesting rescue techniques. I wanted to contribute something to my community.

One year later: A cold October evening. I had delivered mail to my route, and thank God it was Friday. My teenage son, my husband, and I savored a good stew, warmed our feet by the woodstove, and decided on a movie to watch. The phone rang. Nancy's voice was urgent.

"Barb, we need you and Frank to grab your gear and come to Guernsey Lake." A teenage boy had been missing for a few hours. My husband had the flu, so I would have to go alone.

At the north entrance of Guernsey Lake, the sheriff, his deputies, and men and women from Search and Rescue huddled in a group, waiting for information. Thirty degrees, and already three inches of wet snow. We knew about how long the boy had been there—his car was there—and that he had been upset. We paired off with flashlights and began to search by the lake. I could hear muffled voices and footsteps in the snow. I kept feeling that we would come around a bend and see him sitting under a tree.

After midnight, we stopped for the night. We were cold but reluctant to leave. Sleep wasn't easy that night, and morning came too soon.

By 5:30 that morning, it had stopped snowing, but the blowing, bitter wind was miserable. I drank hot coffee, piled on layers of clothing, and drove to the lake. The reality of the situation was frightful. Our organization was called Search and *Rescue*—not recovery. I had an aching pain in my chest, not from the cold, but from noticing a woman in a nearby pickup— the mother of the missing boy. She was hoping beyond all hope that these total strangers—men and women from the sheriff's department, volunteers from Platte County Search and Rescue, a rescue dog from Goshen County, and the fire department's divers—would bring her son back alive.

We searched again in pairs, looking for any sign. By 8:30, someone found a tennis shoe and a baseball cap along the shore. In a moment's time, the whole focus of the search changed. I watched in a daze as crews launched boats and divers began to comb the depths.

Long day. Twice my close friend Joanne and I returned to the base camp to warm up. The wives of state park personnel brought donuts, sandwiches, pop, and hot coffee. These warmed our grateful bodies, but a cold sense of foreboding filled me. On the lake, in the lake, and on the shore, men and women worked together for hours with a determination that matched the fierceness of the weather.

At 6:30 P.M., we found him.

All of our lives had changed. As I drove home, I felt horror, shock, exhaustion, and emptiness. Later, we had our debriefing, and then we took time to heal.

Two years have passed, and I see things more clearly. My family still doesn't go to Guernsey Lake, and I worry for my own son. But what these men and women do to find and return members to worried families takes a dogged commitment and goes way deeper than learning rescue techniques. Now when the phone rings, I feel the urgency and am ready to drop everything and go.

MARY K. STILLWELL ✑ *The Circle Dance*

The great circle dance at the September powwow
is about to begin, but
this family has lost a child
over the summer, and the grief must be combed
from their hair before they can enter
the circle. The mother walks the grasses
to the west side of the circle. The father
walks the grasses, then the other children,
then the aunts and uncles of this family
that has lost one of its children to accident
over the summer. They stand just outside
the circle, and the old people come with

finger combs and begin running them through
the hair of the family, combing the grief
from the mother, the father, each sister and brother,
aunts and uncles, combing out the grief
like snarls, casting out grief
in tangles. On the north side of the circle,
my scalp tingles. It is grief caught
in my own hair, and I must comb it out
if I am to join the circle. I, too, use my fingers
as a comb, pushing the hair up from the head
and away so the grief can loosen.
This combing takes some time,

and the family begins to cry and the old people,
too, begin to cry, and I on my side of the circle
begin to cry. Tears and grief spill
over my shoulders and run down my legs.
Tears and grief spill over their shoulders
and run down their legs.
The earth receives it as rain, takes it in

as if it were her own because it is her own.
From it she has already begun to fashion
new children to send to us. We
bow to the wisdom of the old people,
enter the circle that we may dance.

DOROTHY BLACKCROW MACK ✑ *"I Bring You the Gift of My Dying"*

I'd been working with death for many years before a friend taught me the difference between curing and healing.

When I was married to Selo Black Crow, a Lakota spiritual leader, death had been among my duties. I'd learned how to feed the mourners at a wake, how to "keep the body" (keep watch all night, out of respect), and how to "keep the soul" (keep the memory alive by feeding the soul and making gifts for the memorial dinner one year later). During the twelve years I lived in Wanblee, South Dakota, I attended more than two hundred wakes and funerals: Catholic, Episcopalian, Native American Church, American Legion, and traditional pipe ceremonies.

I also attended many traditional healing ceremonies, always waiting for the miracle of a cure. There were so few cures, I lost faith. Because I was focused on curing, not healing, I was doomed to disappointment and despair. I knew how to honor the dead, but not how to honor the dying.

I met Leslie when I moved to Corvallis, Oregon, to be caretaker of a Quaker meetinghouse three blocks away from my elderly father, who'd had a heart attack. I also realized I missed native healing ceremonies and joined the Red Cedar Circle of Johnny Moses, a Nootka memorizer and storyteller. In this Sisiwis, or Sacred Breath, tradition, unlike the Lakota tradition, women drum and sing, and soon I knew many songs.

Leslie and I, both lovers of books and ideas, became immediate friends. Like me, she'd raised her children and was now raising plants. Gardening, nurturing life, was her passion. Our difference was that I had survived cancer, but Leslie was dying of leukemia.

The whole Quaker meeting was worried about Leslie. Sundays we prayed for her. She stopped coming to meeting for worship. We worried more. Lay ministers were sent to visit her. She sent them away. Her husband said she wanted to be left alone.

Then one day, Leslie came to me and changed my life. Sitting on the couch, she spoke remarkable words in an ordinary voice. "I bring you the gift of my dying."

That's a helluva gift, I thought, but I kept quiet and nodded, remember-

ing how my sister-in-law, Sylvia Black Crow, had died in agony of breast cancer, despite many Indian doctoring ceremonies. We did everything we could, but she left behind six kids.

Leslie continued, "Please don't try to cure me, like the doctors, who are afraid to let me die."

"Oh," I said. *Good*, I thought, *no praying for a cure*, because I had lost my faith in cures. How hard we'd tried to cure Sylvia's ten-year-old daughter, Carla, who'd gotten leukemia after her mother's death.

Leslie gave me a searching look, as if she realized I was lost in sad memories, and spoke slowly and clearly. "Dorothy, I *want* to die."

I stared at her round face, chipmunk-cheeked, like Carla's, by prednisone. She didn't want to be cured, and she wasn't afraid to die. With Sylvia and Carla, I hadn't known what to say or do, and I still didn't know. "Okay," I said, "but tell me what to do."

Leslie sighed. "Dying well is such hard work, I can't do it alone. But you don't have to *do* anything, Dorothy, just *be* with me."

But could I do nothing? Could I be nonjudgmental? Could I let her die in peace, even help her to die well? Could I believe what Johnny Moses taught, that death is but a change of worlds, a crossing over, separated by a veil?

As I listened to Leslie, I forgot my doubts, remembered the ancient Sisiwis healing songs, and began to sing to her. But it was not *me* singing. The power of the ancestors flowed through me that day. The Spirit of God singing through me touched and transformed us both.

Thus I came to sit with Leslie, and over the months she took to die, she taught me the difference between curing and healing. Curing the body prolongs life, but healing restores and renews faith. Healing connects heart and soul with God. My miracle was that in receiving the gift of Leslie's dying, I received the gift of healing love. My fear of death vanished, and my shriveled, doubting heart grew twice its size, filled with faith.

I began leading Sisiwis healing circles, for I needed the power of more than one gathered in prayer and song. One day, I asked Leslie, "Do you want to come to the Red Cedar Circle?"

"As long as they won't make me feel ashamed," she replied. "As long as they'll just accept me."

I gave the traditional Sisiwis response. "Whoever gets to the Circle is supposed to be there."

But would the others accept Leslie's gift of dying? I remembered how angry I'd once been when Sylvia and Carla had let themselves die. I'd considered them failures, weak in willpower and ultimately selfish. Now I thought differently, but it had taken me a long time to change.

The other Circle members did understand the difference between curing and healing. When Leslie came to the Red Cedar Circle, she sat in the

center in a straight chair while the rest of us formed a circle around her, drumming and singing the ancient Sisiwis healing songs. As we ceremonially "brushed her off" with fresh ferns and "lit her up" with a candle, I could feel the room itself and all of us in it lighten.

"I feel surrounded by the healing love," Leslie said afterward, "flowing through all of us. It's enough"—she paused, not searching for words, but for the breath in which to utter them—"to just sit and be accepted for what I am—dying."

Near the end, I fed Leslie raspberries from my garden—red raspberries, traditionally called "the blood of Mother Earth." And I sang her the blood of Mother Earth song and told her the ancient story of how the berries came to be. For Leslie was going peacefully to Mother Earth, and the taste of Mother Earth's red blood sweetened her life and gave her strength.

Because of Leslie, I knew what to do a year later when my father had another massive heart attack. Although the EMTs revived his body, his brain was lost. For a whole week, I "kept the body" as I had learned from my Lakota relatives, sitting by him day and night to help him die. My father had wanted "no undue measures" taken to keep his body alive, but he wore no metal tag that said so. Fortunately, his doctor and I agreed not to prolong his vegetative state.

It was not easy for my father to die; he had worked all his life, and his body was strong. I remembered Leslie saying, with her gently ironic smile, "Whoever said dying was easy?" As I watched my father enter his final labor, I sat by his side, held his hand, talked to him, and sang the Sisiwis healing songs to ease his journey. The week he spent in limbo in the ICU, his soul neither here nor gone on, was the hardest for us both. My father had given me the gift of life, had named me Dorothy, "Gift of God." Now I was receiving the gift of his dying. It was not easy to stay by his side and watch his labor. It was not easy to see his body shrink and shrivel, his cheeks sink, his tongue thicken, his muscles contract into a fetal position. But at last he was ready to be reborn, and I was there to hold his hand for the journey.

Then came rosy-cheeked, fair-haired Valerie. Because her eight-year-old daughter wanted her mom to live, Valerie had fought her breast cancer valiantly, trying many cures, and had been in remission for a while. But eventually the pain of her metastasized cancer became too much, and she chose to let go, calling in hospice and me during her final days. She chose to die, but peacefully and well. She said her farewells, finished her emotional work, and sank into a meditative state. As her body wasted, her face became more alive. It glowed. Her honey hair became a halo about her.

Valerie asked me to come and sing to her every afternoon. Only then could she slough off the fear creeping in around her and sink into a deep, relaxing slumber. I placed a miniature cedar canoe on a blue altar cloth; in Sisiwis tradition, a canoe without paddles is used for burial. Then I lit a

candle, set it in the canoe, and sang Sisiwis ocean-healing songs, softly, so that she could drift off on an ocean of rest.

When Valerie neared the end, she called for her best friend, Ruby, and me. We sat on each side of her, holding her hands, and sang what she called "those healing lullabies." She wanted all three of us to have garlands of forget-me-nots in our hair. We picked the delicate blue flowers blooming outside her window, bound them into three wreaths, and placed them on our heads. We became beautiful in our tears, a magic circle of linked hands and wreaths. When Valerie died a few hours later, the flowers were still fresh in our hair.

I still have my dried forget-me-not wreath. When I planted old-fashioned blue forget-me-nots in my garden, I cried tears of remembrance, tears of joy.

Because of Leslie, my father, and Valerie, I have become a spiritual midwife, one who eases the labor of dying. Healing, not curing, has become my work. Curing the body is important, but so is healing the heart and soul. Dying is as much work as birthing, and healing songs can ease the dying labor. We can choose to die well, finish our lives and pick our own time of rebirth, our union with the Divine.

The dying are grateful to have someone just sit with them—no sermons, no tears, no false cheer or hyper energy—just peaceful lullabies, a listening ear, a praying heart. They are afraid, lost, and weary—seeking the healing love. I feel blessed, and humbled, for they share the greatest gift of all. They bring me the gift of their dying. And I am ready. When it is my time, I will bring you the gift of my dying. I will ask for red raspberries and garlands of forget-me-nots in our hair.

ELIZABETH KEOUGH McDONALD

The Ramah Farmers' Market

lured me an hour south of Gallup, New Mexico,
every Saturday morning from late summer through
early autumn. With my friend Sherry I
watched the Zuni Mountains yawn through sunrise.
Each bit of conversation shared was charged with
Daylight lifting herself from the east.

Today, market vendors sit under cottonwood cover.
I purchase Flora's "Garden Silk" homemade soap.
Vicky's organic produce reaches from two long tables.
I pluck lettuce, beets, and tomatoes quickly before

they sell. Monica's "Swiss Bakery" treats, raspberry
chocolate cake and apple torte, accompanied by coffee
made by a woman with helper-kids, lull me into more
conversation with passing women—Kate. Lucia. Milagra.

Globe mallows, purple asters, and the touch of *chamisas'*
yellow etch a path to the outhouse. The flip hand of
a passing wind cautions a cold nip. Across the road,
prairie dogs race and three horses do the same. The last
Saturday of Farmer's Market, today dawned in twenty-degree
temperatures. Goodbyes bustled, I already miss the
way this morning began—women's hands giving, my hands
receiving.

JANIS RUSSELL-WILSON ✍ Forecasting the Future of Food

On a cold, bright January morning, a baker's dozen of us arrive early at the
church for the monthly reunion of the Warrensburg Natural Food Buying
Cooperative. An unusually large order of food and supplies may take
forty-five minutes to unload from the truck and three hours to divide and
load into our cars.

As usual, I have other things to disperse to members. As Gina and I sort
frozen items, I encourage her to try her hand at writing a children's nature
book like the one I brought from the local library. She and her husband run
a bed and breakfast they proudly tout as the only one in Missouri certified
as a National Wildlife Federation Habitat.

My order is small, since my family is just my husband and me. After it's
loaded, I help others. Three members have huge orders. As I begin gather-
ing Renee's nonfood items, I realize that I'm stopping to play with her
daughter, Ashley, more than usual.

One of the members startles everyone by dropping a bottle of olive oil,
which shatters. Almost immediately, Renee says, "Here's a sack, Kathy, to
put the broken glass shards into, and there's the solvent under the sink,
which will probably cut through that grease, and . . ." That's Renee. Once
again, she acts fast and efficiently, something I'm still aspiring to in my
fifties. Renee's actions energize three other women to help.

With a jolt, I realize why I'm focused on Ashley. Two weeks ago, a four-
year-old in town became ill and died within twenty-four hours, a terrible
shock to our campus community. I ask Kathy if she knows the family, real-
izing I, who almost never cry, have tears in my eyes as we discuss this

death. I don't know why it took me two weeks to understand, but suddenly I am truly, totally cognizant of how bereft this family must be. I needed this conversation. What tough skins we develop without realizing!

Kathy, a scientist, also has insider's knowledge of the contagious respiratory illnesses that might have caused this sudden death. She promises to report to the group's mothers when she learns the autopsy results.

As Beth is ready to go, I quickly retrieve the booklet I've brought, hoping to persuade her to volunteer for the Children's Literature Festival held annually on our campus for sixty-five hundred children and a thousand adult guests and authors. This year, we need two hundred volunteers. Not only does Beth volunteer, but her enthusiastic recollection of previous festivals encourages other women to consider volunteering.

Kathy is cleaning up, so I begin gathering the order for her best friend, out of town today. Her order is the biggest because last summer she and her husband adopted two children: a newborn and a two-year-old. Like Ashley, they are being raised on the healthiest foods their mother can find and prepare.

The second book I brought with me is on adoption for a friend who is adopting a Cambodian child. Taking a break, I decide to try out the book on Ashley, and we curl up in one of the large windows to read.

Finally, Kathy gathers six or seven remaining members and encourages us to contact one of our senators this afternoon about an important environmental bill.

As we turn toward our cars, Melody updates us on information about the co-op distributors and promotes another local activity. Her sister-in-law has cooked up a project to introduce the community to local "alternative" businesses.

During the summer, with extension office help, nine of us "adopted" a farmer who knows she can sustain her small farm because we buy her produce. We hope to double her "eaters" by next year and to add three more farmwomen to this program. Our food is harvested the day we collect it, and unlike grocery store vegetables, it's free of harsh pesticides and chemical fertilizers. Nor has it been grown from genetically altered seed or ripened with gases.

The co-op is particularly concerned about these issues, since the community is home to an inordinate number of women with immune system disorders. We think the ground water contains dangerous substances, and a member is researching the problem now that her daughter has started kindergarten. Several mothers are also trying to influence our school district to buy more local food under the Farm-to-School Initiative, a program gaining popularity in many states.

A few years ago, I became so ill I had to quit my full-time job. Diagnosed with rheumatoid arthritis and fibromyalgia, I became more inter-

ested in eating nutritiously. Similar immune system disorders have caused four others in my co-op to change their eating habits and the way we rely on one another. With less energy than other people, we want to stay involved in our communities, so we stay attuned and informed through our co-op. Many co-op members, including me, live in the country, so we are responsible for numerous outside chores besides caring for our families and working at jobs in town. Several of us take an occasional class at our local college. To stay active politically, many of us are involved with state and national forums and conferences, as well as with various local committees. We're busy but keep up a lively e-mail correspondence, even though we might see one another only once a month on co-op pickup Friday.

All of these connections between a dozen women and a few husbands define the Warrensburg Natural Food Buying Cooperative and affect our community in various ways. My Western women role models include Molly Ivins, Ann Richards, Diane Feinstein, and Barbara Boxer—women who are articulate and authoritative, with innate leadership abilities. None of these qualities comes naturally to me, but the co-op uses the diverse talents of many women. As a *group*, we are leaders. My friends who live in more populous places envy the co-op. Maybe it's a portent of a better future.

CHRISTINE VALENTINE ✍ *Down Gravel Roads*

> *I remember how it was to drive in gravel . . .*
> —THEODORE ROETHKE, "Journey to the Interior"

Roads in England where I was raised were either paved or muddy; very few were surfaced with gravel. While I was being interviewed in England for the job I applied for in Birney, Montana, the interviewer told me that all the roads around Birney were gravel roads—no paved roads for miles—and that I would be living sixty-five miles from the nearest town.

I wasn't worried; I desired an "experience," an adventure I would remember for the rest of my life. Unpaved roads sounded romantic, and I thought I could always catch the bus to somewhere else on my day off.

In July, I flew to Denver and then took a bumpy flight north in an old propeller plane along the Rocky Mountains. My stomach was still reeling when I arrived in Sheridan, Wyoming, and met my new employers. After I tasted my first American ice-cream cone, we set off in their new Buick Electra. I marveled at the scenery: the cloudless blue sky, the Big Horn Mountains, and the green irrigated pastures. But slowly the landscape flattened, and the only features breaking the wide horizon were brown, flat-topped hills—buttes, they told me—capped with red rocks.

Suddenly, the car rocked and dipped, and I heard a roaring underneath us—the sound of rocks hitting the underside of the car. We'd entered Montana and were buzzing along on great hunks of red scoria—one of those gravel roads I had been warned about. The romance of gravel roads became part of my daily life. I did not return to England. A few years later, I married a man from Birney and got my own car. As an Avon lady, I drove miles into the countryside with my bag of cosmetics samples—a perfect opportunity to meet local women and form friendships.

Women on ranches rarely had visitors during the day, so they usually poured a cup of coffee and sat down to chat when I arrived. I am sure many a husband was surprised when he came home for lunch and was served pot roast by his wife, wearing her usual blue jeans but made up to the nines with Avon foundation, lipstick, and eye shadow.

Each family in my Avon territory became special to me. I got to know the children, heard reports on how the cows were doing, learned the name of each dog that greeted me as I drove up, and found out firsthand about forest fires. Since the men ranchers grouped together to fight fires, the women supplied the fire crew with food and often drove many miles to purchase fire rations. In the spring, we talked about the ice going out in the Tongue River and bridges that were threatened by ice jams—huge blocks of ice ramming into their pilings.

As I got to know the countryside better, I ventured farther afield. I discovered the old post office at Quietus, abandoned after homesteaders gradually sold out. Years later, second-class mail still lay in the slots waiting to be collected. The Quietus women related stories about these homesteaders, many of whom were their forebears.

Eventually, Avon decided to reduce the commission paid to its representatives. The new rate was not enough to cover the expenses of driving such long distances. I wrote to the company president and sent photographs of the lonely gravel roads I traveled and some of the families in my little Avon community. He wrote back apologetically and said he could do nothing about the new policy.

And so my voyages down gravel roads came to a regrettable end. But the friends I made during those years became my friends for life.

CAROLYN DUFURRENA *Woman Sculpted of Stones*

On Linda Fleming's sculpture Gramma Seed

A human form outlined in steel:
Grandmother, filled with stones,
held back by structure from the angle of repose.

White quartz cobbles, pieces of the earth,
tumbling down a canyon river,
gathered fragments of our mother.

So feminine to remain,
to permit abrasion beneath the running water's surface,
be made smooth.
Not soft.

They are individuals at first glance,
but closer scrutiny reveals another truth
within each stone:
quartz is nearly as hard as diamond,
yet beneath the weight of mountains, flows.

Bonded rows of atoms,
as though locking arms, shift as one:
"translation," it's called,
those boundaries between grains pressed inexorably together
so tightly we name them sutures.

And so we are sutured
by the weight of mountains, the press of experience,
metamorphosed into each other,
into another, harder version of ourselves:
welded, smoothed, female.
Sustained heavy pressure: in the end it makes us stronger.

As with quartz pebbles
only the sudden sharp strike causes us to shatter,
fall into a handful of unrecognizable fragments from
the speed of the blow, an accumulation of blows.
Each shard will be smoothed in its turn: the seeds of our daughters.

BONNIE ANDERSEN ❧ *Making Room for Jesus*
and Buddha

Even on such a cold November day, the drive was beautiful. As the little
blue sedan took the roller coaster hills and curves with grace, if not power, I
drank in the intense blue sky and medley of green, gold, and brown fields.

Passing occasional homesteads, I wondered whether they housed any

lonely women. I had my own vivid memories of intermittent deep depression in my twenties, living in a rambling former parsonage seven miles from town, seeing no one outside my husband and two children for weeks, having to count every penny to pay for fuel oil that heated only the first floor of the uninsulated frame house. Feeling at times utterly trapped and friendless in winters that seemed never to end. How far I'd come in the intervening years: the freedom of this car, the time to visit friends ninety miles away now that the kids were off at college.

Yet loneliness is a persistent son of a bitch that can cling for life no matter what one's circumstances or environment. Empathy was driving me to Teruko in her ranch house on the hill outside Verdigre. Teruko had come to Nebraska as the wife of a serviceman and had lived here for thirty years. Their three children attended college only ninety miles away, so they frequently came home, but Teruko still felt very isolated. She eagerly made full-course Japanese meals to lure me and the other members of our small, scattered Buddhist group to her home. The nearest community center is in Omaha, so we met monthly among ourselves, each time at a different member's home. Teruko was the farthest out and especially hard to get to via steep, icy roads. Since she'd never learned to drive, she practically begged to host the meetings whenever possible.

Teruko had tried to make friends in the village, even inviting some women for homemade rice balls and green tea to teach them a little about the religion she'd practiced since childhood. They were polite enough, but she could tell they didn't understand, trying instead to talk her into joining their church. Their unspoken message: "You'll never be a real member of this community until you're a Christian." Knowing that tolerance can be such a cold, long distance from acceptance, Teruko didn't insist on her children being raised Buddhist.

Our scattered Buddhist group was the Sioux District, under the larger lay organization, Soka Gakkai International, centered in Omaha. At the time, it contained only five members, living in Columbus, Wayne, and Brainard, Nebraska. We all managed to make it to Teruko's the following spring. After doing *gongyo,* reciting parts of the *Lotus Sutra,* and chanting *Nam Myo Ho Renge Kyo,* the invocation of the Mystic Law, we shared, as usual, our individual experiences in faith.

Yuko, an art history graduate and mother of a six-year-old boy, asked, "Do any one of you struggle with being the only Buddhist in town?"

Sunne, one of our two Korean members, responded without hesitation: "Absolutely. If someone asks me my religion at work, I am reluctant to answer. When I did once, the person looked at me like I was a weirdo or something. They're always trying to convert me to their faith without listening to what mine is." Sunne's eyes flashed angrily, disproving the stereotype of the shy and passive Asian female.

Her friend, Kumok, also from Korea, nodded agreement. Kyong, from Korea but living in Hastings, Nebraska, added, "I tell them how chanting these syllables with faith in the Mystic Law has helped me overcome many obstacles in my life."

Then Teruko mentioned her health problems for the first time. "I have diabetes and heart problems, which I've been chanting about for many years. But sometimes I get discouraged about anything really helping." Yuko encouraged her to keep chanting, and we ended the meeting chanting together, focusing on Teruko's health. The next time I saw Teruko was in an open casket in a low-ceilinged Verdigre mortuary.

During the three years before Teruko's death, I had stopped attending any group meetings, having decided after much soul-searching that this particular Buddhism was too doctrinaire for me. I took refuge in Thich Nhat Hanh's philosophy, in which there is ample room for both Jesus and Buddha in the simple mindfulness each taught in his own way. There being no such Zen community in Nebraska or adjoining states, I fell back on my life-long solution of meditating and praying at home. I practice my hybrid form of religion, an amalgam of East and West, no longer fearing that I'll be struck down by some angry, jealous god of either side.

I still write to Yuko and Kyong a couple of times a year. Kyong keeps trying to convince me to return to the fold, not understanding my view any more than the Christians visiting Teruko had. The only "meeting" I've attended since my decision to go my own way was Teruko's funeral, attended by both Christian and Buddhist friends and family members. I sat with the Buddhist group on one side, chanting among them. I was drawn by Teruko's spirit, which I felt now was in a kind of Every Soul's Land, where there is no place for foolish, divisive distinctions between religions.

I spontaneously got up to light a candle for her, one of several of our group to do so after we had recited the *Lotus Sutra* liturgy and chanted. I hadn't intended to say anything, but the words tumbled out: "I will miss Teruko deeply. I remember a saying she had propped on her altar: 'Misfortune comes from the mouth.' Teruko always spoke the truth, but she did not complain or slander others. She lived her faith and let others be and do the same, no matter what their beliefs." I knew that Teruko, lying in her pearl gray casket under embossed pink roses, would understand and accept my tearful tribute. We were both alone yet never so much in community as now.

The drive home alone was anything but lonely. Another circle in my life had been completed.

ANONYMOUS ✍ *What I Hate Most About You*

Dear New Neighbors,

I've never met any of you. If I did, I would be perfectly polite. Probably I'd even think you're nice folks. But here's what I hate about you.

For a hundred years and more, this was remote ranch country with widely scattered houses out of sight of one another. All it took to change that was one land sale: a developer looking to make a buck and some people who wanted to live in the country. Within a few days, a new road was bulldozed, some flat places were scraped out, and your new houses were hauled in and plopped down. You do realize you have destroyed the very thing you paid so much for, don't you? This isn't ranch country anymore. Now it's a subdivision.

I hate how you've chosen to place your houses right along the crest of a hill. You have a great view up there, but have you considered winter's blizzards? Summer's lightning? Have you thought of how you dominate the landscape? I doubt I'm the only one annoyed, because your houses are visible for miles in all directions. But I take it personally. No matter that you're some distance away, you peer down into my ranch yard like a peeping Tom.

I hate to think of how much water you'll be pumping for your newly laid sod and your non-native trees. I hate to think of all those septic systems scattered above the water table being filled by people used to a city sewer system where you flush it and forget it. How can that many new households not affect our ground water?

And I'm really beginning to hate having to pick up your trash from the road ditches and unsnag it from the barbed wire fences. Oh, sure, I know you're not actually throwing all that garbage out your car windows. Some of it has obviously blown down from your houses. Maybe in town no one can track your carelessness, but out here we know.

Besides the trash, I hate the other changes you've brought to the gravel road that goes past my place. It used to have little traffic. The county had to grade it only two or three times a year. But all the big machinery necessary to make your new driveways and install your new houses has turned the road into a washboard. And all you new people with your many trips to town have kept it that way. Now the county has to have the grader out here every month. It used to be a safe road, too. Now your cars whip down the center, over hills and around curves, as if you've never heard of loose gravel or deer or livestock in the road.

While we're on the topic of livestock, I'd like you to remember that you're the ones who wanted to move to the country. You do realize that ranchers make their living by running livestock out here? So don't complain about the noise and the smell. Fences keep livestock from wandering

onto your manicured lawns, so don't tear out sections of fence and then whine about animals in your yard. Learn who owns the adjacent pasture and do your fair share of the upkeep on the fence.

I'm still holding out hope that you'll keep up the fence on your place, because fences are good things when you have dogs. You do still have dogs, don't you? A ranch neighbor told me he's given up trying to track down the owners anymore. "Shoot, shovel, and shut up" is his new motto. Now, I'm not going to shoot your dog. I don't even shoot the coyotes around here. But I'm really starting to hate that tomcat who oh-so-coincidentally has appeared and is attacking my chickens.

And what's with all the lights? It's starting to look like a Wal-Mart parking lot over there at night. Why did you move away from town if you're afraid of the dark? I'll tell you what I'm afraid of. I'm afraid that pretty soon all your house lights and porch lights and garage lights and yard lights will prevent me from being able to see the Milky Way stretching down to the horizon or blot out the rare displays of the northern lights.

I'm afraid that I'll never be able to forget you're over there, day or night.

I'll never send this letter to you. What's the point? You're here, all settled in and happy with your new homes in what used to be the country. No doubt more will follow you.

I think that's the thing I hate most about you.

DONNA APPLEGARTH MENTINK ✒ Pickin' Chickens

Silence.
Up before dawn,
They begin to arrive,

The beautician, the teacher,
The housewife, the ranchwife,
At the old bunkhouse.

Water boiling on the two-burner stove.
A system developed through the years.
The chopper, the plucker, the gutter, the cutter.

They giggle, they talk, share secrets, make memories.
End of the day, clean the mess,
Clorox the table, the washtubs.

Ready for tomorrow, and tomorrow.
Five days, two hundred ten-piece meals.
Finished at last.

Exhausted, they drop around the table,
Kinship forged in the old bunkhouse.
Job complete, loath to go.

Giddy and silly, a glass of tea.
Raise the glasses, chink together.
"Women who pick together, stick together."

Laughter.

DIANE JOSEPHY PEAVEY ✏ Watch Where You Step

This story of the consequences of animals and people sharing the same space began in the fall of 1990 with a phone call about sheep droppings.

"Are those your sheep on the bike path?" the caller asked. "They are making a mess, and their droppings are getting in my Rollerblades."

I sighed, I hoped inaudibly. This was not the first such phone greeting we'd received that day from recreational users in the community. "Golly, I don't know if they are ours," I responded in my most neighborly, thoughtful fashion.

And in fact I was unsure. Three other sheep outfits also trailed their animals down the back roads near the Sun Valley/Ketchum, Idaho, resort community, then south thirteen miles on the sheep easement, behind the town of Hailey and through Bellevue. We moved our sheep north each spring to high mountain meadows, then south each fall to desert pastures, using this familiar route.

This migration had taken place for a hundred years. At one time, more than two hundred thousand sheep moved through this valley during the summer and fall. But as lamb and wool prices slumped to historic lows, many families were forced to leave the land. Soon only four outfits and twenty thousand sheep were left. Our family was one of the four, and we held on for dear life, pleased when old-timers told us that seeing the sheep move through the valley was a kind of harbinger of changing seasons.

But the area's rural character was rapidly disappearing as year-round construction filled the landscape with new subdivisions, multimillion-dollar estates, condominiums, and golf courses. This development spilled across the valley floor, consuming open space and blocking traditional sheep paths. We were forced to find ways for the animals to circumnavigate the tumult.

As if this were not enough, the county decided to put in a bike path along the route for recreational use. Sheepmen, displaying their usual neighborliness, agreed to share their roadside easement with the community, and soon a paved black stripe cut through wild grasses and sagebrush.

The bikers, joggers, and Rollerbladers who used our easement did not seem inclined to reciprocate our neighborliness.

At first the phone complaints seemed a bit ridiculous to us ranchers, familiar with the ordinary habits of animals. But as the complaints became more numerous, we paid attention.

After all, my husband was running for re-election to the Idaho state senate, and we were in a tough race. He was one of the leading environmental proponents in the legislature, representing as he did one of the most environmentally vociferous counties in the state. He spoke out against nuclear waste and on behalf of recycling, land-use planning, and saving Idaho's water from development pressures.

But in 1990, hard-line environmentalists were espousing the public lands grazing philosophy "Cattle-free by '93." As a ranching family with both cattle and sheep, we knew that "cattle" meant all livestock, including sheep. The opposing sides were digging in, shouting at each other in the press and over fences. Often I wondered if my environmental friends shared this anger against us.

Then John hatched a plan, based on his conviction that the best way to make friends of skeptics or adversaries is to share our lives with them. We often invited newcomers and friends unfamiliar with ranch life into our landscape for a cattle drive, a lamb shipping, or a Sunday barbecue. They saw our work, listened to our stories, and understood better how we used and cared for the land. True to this style, he proposed that we invite the community to help us herd sheep through the valley. It just might work, I thought.

The following week, I ran an ad in the newspaper. In response, thirty residents showed up at six o'clock at a local café on a chill fall morning. Over coffee, John explained the history of sheep in Idaho and the nomadic life of moving animals every few days to fresh feed. He talked about today's sheep business, then answered questions.

Buttoning jackets and pulling on gloves, the group joined the herder at first light several miles south of town to help move the sheep through the tall grasses along the highway and, at the same time, keep them off the bike path. After school, children and their parents took up the parade. As we walked and talked, the community became involved in the landscape.

We continued this event for several years. Teachers brought their classes out to walk with us, and John told the kids the history of sheepherding in the West. But to my surprise, there was a growing interest in the event among local organizations in the community. Led by the Sun Valley/Ketchum Chamber of Commerce, several groups gathered to discuss an event to celebrate this sheep migration. Ideas filled the room, especially when we learned that, at one time, the area had been second only to Sydney, Australia, as a sheep center.

The first sheep ranchers of southern Idaho were Scots and Basques. Both of these groups came to this country as herders and eventually started their own sheep operations. Basque and Scottish names fill the phone books in our small towns, though today most of our herders are Peruvian.

We reasoned that we could provide the music, dance, food, and traditions of these people in a cultural potpourri. We could demonstrate the work of sheepherding—shearing, herding animals with dogs, spinning, weaving, and even camp cooking—with displays of sheep camps. This was the stuff of an impressive sheep folklife fair.

The discussion soon took on a sense of urgency. We were losing sheep families in Idaho—those who couldn't survive plummeting lamb and wool prices. With them, we were losing our heritage. What better use of a weekend than to share and record the stories of this community? So we added a second component to the weekend festival: a storytelling gathering.

Finally, we planned the centerpiece: the sheep trailing—not a re-enactment but the actual sheep drive that we would hold with or without the public. We proposed a parade to the Ketchum City Council. Instead of taking the back streets as usual, fifteen hundred sheep would parade down Main Street on Sunday in honor of the town's history. The council loved the idea, and the Trailing of the Sheep Festival was set for the second weekend in October.

The first year, perhaps a thousand people attended the events. The next year, the crowd grew. Major publications wrote about the festival. We had sparked something in the national imagination, a combination of the Old West and the New West.

Our fourth year was 2001. *CBS News Sunday Morning* sent out a camera crew with Bill Geist to capture the story of a community saving its heritage and honoring its past in the wake of national turmoil. That same year, the Trailing of the Sheep Festival won the Governor's Award for Cultural Tourism.

By 2002, the crowd numbered more than eight thousand. "Be careful what you wish for," a friend called out to me at the Saturday Folklife Fair. At that moment, the months—no, the years—of work seemed a startling accomplishment. The community was no longer just a glitzy ski resort but also a place aware of its traditions.

In our community, we are all making new friends. The ski businesses, after struggling through several light snow years, now have October sales to rival those at Christmas. Old-time residents who grew up watching the sheep move through the valley every year and dining at Basque boarding houses (now long gone) relive the old days. Newcomers, shocked at first to hear the hooves of sheep clicking on pavement outside their newly constructed second homes, now suggest that this is why they moved here. And the community of sheep families look around with a new sense of pride

and purpose, amazed that "all these people would come out to watch a bunch of sheep go down the road."

But the weekend is also about our stories, hinting at the mysteries of our landscape and the struggles and triumphs of living on the land. Seventy-five years ago, sheepherders etched dates and drawings into the aspen trees north of town. Like those records, the stories are the weekend's lasting legacy, whispering, "I was here."

Now the droppings on the bike path (instantly swept away by county workers) seem less significant than the echoes of living history in a community that sometimes moves too fast to listen to itself.

JANE WELLS ✑ *Comments from the Crow's-Nest*

I belong to a place of believers. I am part of the brotherhood of sisterhood. I am fluent in horse and dog, and understand enough to get by in cow and donkey.

The community I am proudest to be a part of is the Johnson County Cowgirls. And when I die, I expect to read that in my obituary.

Every Tuesday night during the summer months, the Cowgirls put on a rodeo in either Buffalo or Kaycee, Wyoming. I don't ride competitively, but members of my family do, so I volunteer my services up in the crow's-nest. Over the years, I've taken entries, figured earnings, balanced checkbooks, announced times, kept records, and wielded one of the fastest stopwatches in the West. I've been yelled at, rained on, dust choked, sunburned, windburned, and froze out. At the end of every season, I say I'm not going to do this again. But come next year, I'll probably be back. It's just too much fun to miss.

"Do you have the checks ready?" asks the little cowgirl with eyes the color of spring runoff and wearing her older sister's outgrown boots.

"What did you win, honey?"

"Peewee barrels."

"We don't have the checks made out yet because the event just now finished. Is your family in a hurry to leave?"

"No, we're hungry."

Her grandma told me later, "That one's always been the type to tell it like it is."

One time, a proud daddy brought his miniature shadow minus the sideburns up to the pay window.

"What did you win, honey?" I asked the solemn little guy as I stooped down to his level.

Without changing expression, he looked at me from under his cowboy hat and said, "I don't know. You haven't given it to me yet."

I think if God could compete in a sport, he'd probably pick rodeo. I know for a fact he watches it. And I know of no other sport where the golden rule is the code of conduct handed down from generation to generation.

Competitors, including the horses, are treated like family. Human nature being what it is, sometimes it's tough being all that friendly with your rivals. But rodeo is a way of life involving people who expect the best from others and demand the best from themselves. Wyoming is the Cowboy State, and rodeo is the cowboys' sport. But it's the cowgirls' state of mind keeping the traditions alive.

Rodeo depends on cowgirls. They instinctively recognize they have to pay entry fees all their lives. They don't put a price on heartache. Cowgirls learn to put all they've got into every ride and aren't ashamed to admit they need a good pickup man now and then. They know to spit out dust instead of swallowing it after a fall, because choking can suffocate the best of us. Look beyond where you're headed, says a cowgirl, because you might be riding in circles. Cowgirls who say a prayer before a ride and give thanks afterward never look foolish. They know that competing only for money limits a girl's winnings.

Most of all, a good cowgirl knows to give life her best shot, because nobody gets a refund or an exchange for making a bad run.

KATHLEEN GOTSCHALL ✎ *Rodeo Moms*

"Do you know the difference between a rodeo mom and
 a pit bull?"
It was Jokin' Junior,
and this joke sounded familiar.
"Lipstick." The punch line, *pow,* smack between the eyes.
Yep, it was last year at this very same rodeo,
Jokin' Junior tellin' the same sorry joke.

I don't mind it so much being a rodeo mom, I think
as I check to see
if I am wearing lipstick.
I know he's just jokin',
which is what he does best.
He sure doesn't know rodeo moms like I do.

Maybe he thinks that we ride the range every day,
barkin' orders, chewin' tobacco, eatin' jerky, drinkin' whiskey,
and then howlin' at the moon all night long.

Maybe he thinks we would sooner
chew a man up and spit him out
than look at him.

I suppose he's never shared an umbrella on a scorching day
or shivered under a quilt in the wind and rain with a rodeo mom.
For then he would have heard her words of support
for every kid, not just her own.
It's likely he would have heard her hearty cheers
for every good effort, not just the buckle winners.

He might have seen her grieving
with the mom who lost her daughter
in the accident last spring.
Or all the rodeo moms
collectively holding their breath and whispering prayers
when the ambulance takes one away.

He probably doesn't realize that besides being tough cookies,
 rodeo moms are
artists and nurses and teachers and poets and massage therapists
 and coaches and marketing specialists and hotel managers and
 musicians and med techs and accountants and receptionists
 and caterers and daycare providers and secretaries and vet
 assistants and delivery drivers and bank personnel and press
 operators and business managers and household engineers and
 volunteers and yep . . . ranchers.

Maybe he never followed a rodeo mom home
to see all the plates she keeps a-spinnin'
and her ducks in a row, mostly.
He might really be amazed when he sees her roll up her sleeves
for whatever task is at hand.
Likely as not he would admire her pluck.

I suppose his ole jaw would just drop in awe
if he sensed the friendship and camaraderie
that rodeo moms share all over the land.
You know, I'm not the gamblin' type,
but I'd almost wager Jokin' Junior
a whole saddlebag full of lipstick on this one.

Say I were to drive east to west across the state,
and supposin' my rig were to break down

every hundred miles along the way.
Each time I could call a different rodeo mom nearby,
and I'm bettin' she'd be there to help
before you could even say "pit bull."

NORMA NELSON DUPPLER ✐ When the World Split

Many evenings, I sit on a hill on our family ranch where a 4,000-year-old Indian calendar is laid out in stone. The sunsets and scenery are gorgeous, peaceful.

On September 10, 2001, I watched the sunset, as goldenrod, wild rose, and bluebell faded to lavender. Then a figure appeared in the clouds, hovering horizontally, just above the crescent of fire slipping behind the hills. At first it looked like an angel, with sweeping wings and a trailing robe. But instead of a face, it developed a huge hood with a blank purple spot inside—like the Grim Reaper.

My, that looks apocalyptic, I thought. I never put any store in cloud faces or figures, but this one persisted a long time, and I regretted not having a camera to capture the odd phenomenon. After the sunset dissolved to a tangerine smear on the horizon, I careened down the face of the hill on the four-wheeler, tore through the pasture, and bumped over the ruts on my way home.

The next day, in my job as an emergency manager, I was hosting the North Dakota Emergency Management Conference in Valley City, so my mind was filled with myriad conference details. As I watched morning television, the most stressful thing on my mind was the group's response to the one-person art show I'd hung on the conference room walls.

Sitting on the edge of my bed, I saw Diane Sawyer mention an accident at the World Trade Center—a plane had crashed into the building. Smoke streamed from the tower. I couldn't move, staring at the television. Then the second plane sliced into the other tower like a knife into a stick of warm butter. The wings didn't even fall off.

"God, protect those people," I said under my breath. I grew momentarily dizzy recalling my stay on the towering top floor of a hotel at the World Trade Center complex.

I scurried to my office and called 911 dispatch. "Hi, this is Norma. Did you hear about the World Trade Center? Call me if anything weird happens." I gave them the conference hotel phone number. Then I called all the medical facilities in the county and asked them to let me know if any unexplained illnesses turned up. My fear was that the plane attack was just a diversion for the real attack—with a bioweapon.

After calling the sheriff and police, I called the National Guard, where I received chilling information: "The Happy Hooligans are patrolling Wash-

ington. There is an errant airliner. They might have to shoot it down." The Happy Hooligans are North Dakota's Air National Guard out of Fargo. They had planes and personnel stationed near Washington, D.C., as part of our national security plan.

In the hotel lobby, emergency managers from various parts of the state stood silently transfixed in front of the television screen. We usually greet one another with back slaps, hugs, or huge handshakes, but now we stood pinch-faced and sick, staring at one another, speaking in hushed tones if at all. We envied distracting conference jobs.

When I stepped outside, I saw no contrails.

Some of us were watching when the south tower crumbled. "They had to have a bomb in there, too," I said. "Those things were constructed to take a plane hit." Not until later did I understand how the fire warped the steel girders. Once one floor went, the floors underneath couldn't stand the stress, and they pancaked.

The second tower crumbled. The Pentagon was hit. The heroes on board the errant airliner fought the monsters who took it over and crashed it in Pennsylvania.

When the conference started, I looked around at my friends who were trying to swallow the lumps in their throats.

For an old emergency manager, finding new information is like mining. Sure, there are gold nuggets, but we have to mine through dirt, rock, and clay for hours for one of those nuggets. While I was mining, I studied the handful of other women.

These women routinely leave children and husbands to come to conferences, attend to emergencies, stay in the office for sixteen-hour days when all hell breaks loose in their various jurisdictions. Now we were trapped together in a narrow conference room, helpless, knowing there was nothing we could do to change the situation in the outside world. They could have gone home, but they had handled their work by phone as I had. Just glancing at their faces made me feel better. Competence, warmth, exuberance, sincerity, and professionalism looked back at me.

The strength of these women doesn't come from rippling muscles. Rather, it is evident in the quiet smile, the humor, the sterling character, the shoring up of one another when we are together, because we work alone when we are in our own counties. We face old boys' attitudes, ignorance, and sexual harassment, yet we go on and do our jobs well.

For instance, while doing my job, I have been told: "We make women cry." "You sound just like my wife." "How do you make love, and do you use handcuffs?" "I'll screw you on a hill for your birthday" (only the perpetrator didn't say "screw").

And these remarks were not made by criminals or drunks; they came from my bosses—during meetings. I am not little, young, sexy, or cute. If I

catch this much harassment, I can't imagine what some of the other women have endured.

Once I worked sixteen-hour days, seven days a week for six straight weeks. I don't even know how I got my laundry done; my husband must have done it. He took care of the kids. These women have done similar things. In addition, we have suffered through floods, fires, tornadoes, droughts, state demands, a bad economy, crop failures, and the stresses of trying to do three or four full-time jobs in a twenty-four-hour day. We have the honor of working with dedicated volunteers who work even harder than we do.

When the September 11 conference was over, I felt better than I would have if I had been alone. Normally, I would have stayed and socialized with everyone late into the evening. But on September 11, and for the following two days, I went home to stay with my daughter, to consider what these women gave me, hoping that my daughter would gain strength from me, from them.

The 9-11 attack gave me perspective on what is important. It didn't matter that the conference had to be rearranged because the speakers couldn't fly there. It didn't matter what the others thought of my art show. And the lectures to improve our job performance didn't matter either. But sharing the impossible situation of 9-11 with these women did matter. Sharing made us all stronger and made it easier for us to endure the realization that the world broke into two communities that day. One camp grieved for us. One camp rejoiced.

A painting of one of the Happy Hooligan fighters now hangs in the repaired Pentagon. Ground Zero has been cleaned up. By a true miracle, fewer than three thousand died in the collapse of the twin towers. Widows, widowers, children, parents, siblings, friends, and survivors are trying to get on with lives devastated by the death and destruction. There is a hole in the heart of America. But we go on.

Now I look for cloud pictures when dusk descends on North Dakota like an old cluck hen settling on her eggs. The amber light softens to pink and then fades to supple purple.

I still don't interpret cloud pictures as omens. But I vividly remember the angel of death I saw before the Pearl Harbor of my generation. I am reassured that all the sunsets since then have been normal ones.

BETTY DOWNS ✎ *Tuesday Tea*

Sometimes Margaret doesn't come.
She likes to cook, you see, and go
to soccer games and such.

Elaine had a stroke a while back,
and she just plumb forgets to come.
Unless she marks it on her calendar.
Maurine moved into the retirement home
clear across town, so we never know about her.
Sometimes she brings Jane, if they don't go to Deadwood instead.
Pearl always has a joke to share.
Or cute pictures of her grandkids.
Leona comes with bells on. Her gentle smile and sprightly step
reflect the wisdom of her eighty-five years.
She swears she doesn't dye her hair.
Vivian comes to Tuesday Tea
every week, rain or shine. Unless she's in Florida,
or Seattle. Last week she drove to Minnesota.
Tuesday Tea, it started at Hardee's when tea was thirty-six
 cents a cup.
What would I do without my friends and Tuesday Tea?
Go crazy, I suppose. Those girls have kept me smiling
for years now. I'd go alone rather than miss it.
I bless the day we started Tuesday Tea.
Yes sir, I bless the day.

SUE HARTMAN ✑ *Choir Practice at the Bongo Lounge*

The phone rang at 1:16 A.M. I sucked in a breath. "Salt Lake Rape Crisis Center, this is Sue. How can I help you?"

"Wake up, bitch." Heavy breathing. "I know where you are."

No, he didn't. Not likely, anyway. The calls were forwarded to volunteers' homes. No one but the other crisis workers, the district attorney, and the cops knew that.

"Honey," I said to my nonexistent husband, "it's for you." The line went dead, then rang again.

"Your friend with the funny name, DeLynn? She tried that, but she didn't fool me either. What color panties are you wearing?" He lisped on "panties."

Not the Snake. We all knew his hiss. I took the police whistle that I kept on the bedside stand and blew—murder on the eardrum. Now I'd have something to joke about that night. It was already Thursday, which meant it was oldies night at the Bongo Lounge. Time for Choir Practice.

In the late 1970s, calls to the Rape Crisis Center (RCC) hotline clustered around holidays and early Saturday mornings during the full moon. Often there was little activity for a week, then three violent cases might occur in

one shift. More likely, a caller whispered filth. A founding member of the RCC, I'd graduated with the first class of twelve women and one man to take up a controversial mission. Conservative citizens feared we were "feminists" and claimed "these incidents" were "private." Others said women "asked for" assaults. Victims reported only one in seven assaults, denied the crime, avoided medical and psychological help. But we were committed, empowering ourselves as well as the community. By day we joked about idiots who threatened to stab us, who called us whores, dykes, and baby killers.

When the phone rang again at 2:45, I was annoyed until I heard a woman sobbing. She cried for thirty minutes before she was coherent. She was curled up on the floor in the dark so no one could see in.

Her rapist, a guy she recognized from campus, might have followed her home, might be in the parking lot. She didn't want the police; she could be pregnant. Could we come? I told her I would be there within a half-hour with a male escort. We would identify ourselves using a code word. She felt filthy; maybe she would take a shower. I asked her not to; evidence would be destroyed. But if she pressed charges, her boyfriend would find out. She could decide that later, I assured her, but the choice would be gone if she washed evidence away. First she needed medical treatment. She agreed to wait for us to escort her to the hospital.

I checked the schedule to see who of eight male backups, from fifty volunteers, was on call: Chas Eckenrode, six foot three and imposing. His presence should deter the perpetrator if he was lurking, and he specialized in consoling brothers, lovers, and fathers. Then I called the ER for a private examination room and paged Core 10, an elite rape crisis team trained by the county attorney in exam procedures. Team members accompanied victims first into the examination room and then into the courtroom, providing continuing support and advocacy. Core 10 also monitored evidence collection, but since treatment itself could be excruciating, its most important service was providing comfort while preventing further trauma.

When Core 10's Terry Smith arrived at the hospital, I introduced her to our client, who trusted her immediately, so I didn't need to stay. The client thanked me but snapped at Chas. She didn't need crisis support for her boyfriend; she wasn't going to tell him.

As I left the hospital, I assured Terry that I would see her at Choir Practice that night and invited Chas to join us. I wasn't offended when he declined. The RCC had its cliques, and our Choir was one. University of Utah social work students and a church women's group were others. Chas was a loner. Within a month, he committed suicide. We stopped sleeping, debated blame and causes, and ultimately, saddened, decided that Chas alone was responsible. But next time, we would notice the signs sooner and intervene.

Grieving Choir members sympathized at the Bongo Lounge. We were

rowdy, mostly twenty-somethings, cavorting, downing pitchers of beer, singing and swaying to the music. But these sessions weren't all goofiness. We developed policies, learned to know and trust one another, building our own community. In any city but Salt Lake, after-work socializing in a bar might not have raised an eyebrow, but we were playing in the shadow of the Mormon Church. In defiance, we called this gathering Choir Practice, after the carousing of off-duty rookies in Joseph Wambaugh's novel *The Choirboys*.

At one Choir Practice, Sergeant Charlie Alexander picked up a chair with Patrolman Frank Hatton-Ward already seated in it. Charlie hoisted it above the table and planted it, with Frank still aboard, at another table so he could sit next to Mary Jo Jackson. Another time, a rookie dropped his off-duty weapon on the pool room floor, and DeLynn Anderson smirked and planted her platform boot squarely on it. Replacing her rhinestone-studded cigarette holder between her lips, she lifted the hem of her maxi-skirt and dipped down to retrieve the weapon. "I believe you lost some-thing," she whispered to the embarrassed kid. "I trust we're not loaded." DeLynn was as adept at intimidating state legislators as she was at kidding cops.

Sometimes an assistant district attorney joined us, or newspaper reporters and cameramen, neighborhood organizers and others who were as concerned as we were. Sometimes one of us overindulged, but that was seldom the objective. Besides, by Utah law, the beer was only 3.2 percent alcohol, and not everyone drank it. Just in case, we designated drivers. The purpose of Choir Practice was to let off steam after a tough case, a rough shift, an awful week. We cheered each other on, and we slapped—and watched—each other's backs.

We learned to love and respect one another in ever-changing ways—a strange and tender coalition, a bond that compelled us to meet twice a week for more than three years. Three hundred Choir Practices, give or take a few.

Several events combined to cause my midlife crisis: a difficult relationship, reduced funding, and, the most crucial, my last rape crisis case. A preschooler was asleep in her bedroom while her parents watched television. An adult male from the block climbed through a window, covered her mouth with his hand, raped her—causing horrific injuries—and sneaked away. The mother discovered her bloodied daughter and called police. Responding officers sped the child, surprisingly still alive, to the hospital, sirens screaming. Six police units followed. Some officers vomited; some howled in outrage.

The neighborhood pedophile was cheerful when he was arrested and told officers he was a pillar of the community, well connected in the church. Although she would never have children, the girl survived. Her parents'

marriage did not. In court, the rapist pleaded no contest to a lesser charge. He had a previously unblemished record. Prominent church and community leaders rallied to his defense and recommended a light sentence. He served no prison time and was off probation before the child's parents' divorce was final.

I quit everything and fled to Colorado. A year later, returning for Charlie and Mary Jo's wedding, I saw most of my RCC and police buddies and lost my guilt feelings about leaving; my friends were also ready to move on. Choir Practice was canceled. The RCC grew stronger, with a stream of volunteers and secure funding; the paid staff tripled in size.

Over time, I heard from my RCC friends less frequently, perhaps at Christmas or when I visited family in Salt Lake. I never went back to the Bongo Lounge. The RCC moved to a central location and become the Rape *Recovery* Center, shifting its focus from crisis to healing.

On occasion, I contemplated the Choir, how my friends had scattered, settled down, and drifted apart. Then, in June 2000, my father died unexpectedly. On the morning of his funeral—which was also my birthday—the phone rang at my mother's house. It was Mary Jo; she'd read my father's obituary and contacted Terry, from Core 10. Did I need them?

My Choir Practice women friends came to offer welcome support; Terry even brought a cake. Six months later, when Charlie died, it was my turn. I hadn't spoken to Frank in ten years, but I called to inform him. We reminisced, and then I drove. Over long stretches of empty road, memories flooded back: of Frank's good-natured enthusiasm; of how it was Charlie who had initiated sensitivity-training programs for officers and had set policy, trusting me as the first RCC representative to ride along on patrol. After twenty-five years, I realized that I recalled nothing about most cases and only a few names of former colleagues. But I remembered the Choir.

In Mary Jo's Salt Lake City home, I noticed a framed snapshot among the family portraits on her bedroom wall: Mary Jo, Terry, DeLynn, and me. Choir Practice! Physically older and unquestionably wiser, we had changed, yet our deepest memories would not fade.

Since its inception in 1974, the Salt Lake City Rape Crisis/Recovery Center has provided services to more than fifty-six thousand sexual assault victims and their loved ones. It remains a twenty-four-hour, nonprofit organization, operating on memberships, donations, and grants, charging no fees to its clients for services.

MARIANNE HOFFMANN WOEPPEL ✏ *Popcorn in the ER*

Finding a few free minutes amid the chaos of the emergency room, we grabbed handfuls of popcorn from a newly sterilized bedpan and sat around the desk charting and discussing various body fluids between bites

from our tuna fish sandwiches. We had just finished delivering a baby in the back seat of a Volkswagen. The parents had thirty-six miles of dirt roads to travel to get to the hospital, and that baby was not about to wait.

We are a team. We rely on and trust one another when quick decisions need to be made. When a tangled body from a farm accident is wheeled in, we see a teenager who could have belonged to any one of us. We treat more than just his wounds, while reassuring his family or calmly breaking the news, holding back our own tears. We are family. For this eight- or twelve-hour shift, this is our home.

RUTH DANIELS ✺ Old Woman with a Mind

At loose ends with family gone,
alone all day struggling
with crippling arthritis

I joined some clubs thinking
to find companionship
and enrich my life.

While sitting in a group
of farmwomen
listening intently to speakers
telling me how

to can tomatoes,
to make a dress out of burlap,
to cook hamburger meat
five dozen ways,

I wondered silently,
"What in the hell am I doing here?"

Now don't get me wrong,
I can can tomatoes
though freezing is easier,
make a dress
though I prefer a softer material,

and I can cook a country dinner
that will melt in your mouth.
Cornbread, pinto beans, fried okra,

mashed potatoes,
and a good thick slice of ham.

I'm not interested in much more
and so ended my days
as a club woman.

I came home and sharpened
my pencils,
found some scrap paper,
rolled up my sleeves,
pulled up my socks,

and wrote my first poem.
Now it did not win a Pushcart;
in fact it has not even been published,
but it started a quarter-century quest

to see things with new eyes,
delve deep into my head and heart,
scan my thoughts,
to fill my mailbox with submissions,

my wastebasket with rejections,
and earn the title
in this small Bible belt hidebound
place not even on the map as
"The crazy old lady holed up
in the back room with a computer."

No one has ever disputed
my right to the sobriquet.

GERALDINE CONNOLLY 🖎 *Electric Avenue Books*

After our children had grown, I moved with my husband to Woods Bay,
a few miles south of Bigfork, Montana, population three thousand. We
left suburban Washington, D.C., for the Flathead Valley of northwestern
Montana, on the east shore of Flathead Lake. The buzz of freeways and
glare of streetlights gave way to a landscape of wide sky and rugged moun-
tains along the shore of the glacial lake. A frantic schedule of readings,
classes, workshops, and meetings turned into an expanse of quiet, unstruc-

tured days. Both of my grandmothers and many of my aunts and uncles had lived on farms in Pennsylvania, and since I grew up spending time in the country, I thought I knew how to be alone. I looked forward to writing more, savoring my solitude, relishing the sunrises and sunsets, taking hikes where I would encounter new plants and animals, enjoying a deeper knowledge of nature.

After our first glorious summer in Montana passed, I was not prepared for the dense sadness of blue, late-autumn evenings when four o'clock brought the setting sun. Tall ponderosas like cloaked monks at Vespers cascaded down the hillsides, and dark wings of unknown birds fluttered past our windows. The distant mountains at morning, the fog-enshrouded gray lake, offered no comfort. Most of our neighbors left for the winter, and as the cold deepened, lights from houses around the lake grew thin and scattered. What I missed most were social evenings with poet friends, gathered in a circle in someone's living room with hot tea, poring over new work, the currents of gossip and poetry buzz lighting the room.

After living a few months in Bigfork, I joined an aerobic dance class, where I met a woman named Aurora. She had been a teacher, too. She introduced me to a woman named Regina, who invited me to the women's book club at Electric Avenue Books.

Electric Avenue—how appropriate. Books had always provided me a jolt and a current. Reading enthralled me, lit me with ideas and inspiration. Talking about books with other women brightened my life. Since I had written two books of poems, the book group graciously discussed my poems and asked me to talk about them at one meeting. The bookshop became a haven. Soon my social life ignited, with friends to meet for lunches, for hikes, for birthday parties and dinners.

In a fluster of forgetfulness one busy afternoon, I locked my keys and purse inside my car. Somehow it seemed natural to stop at Electric Avenue for help. The alternative was a five-mile walk, half of it along two-lane Highway 35, the only route to our house. I asked to use the phone at the bookshop. We tried the number at my house first, hoping to reach my husband. No answer. He must have been out in the yard working. The contractor was there, too, finishing a project, but his cell phone number was unlisted. The proprietor of the bookshop, Katie Callan, then hit upon the idea of calling the contractor's mother, who owned a small gift shop on the hill above town. She called Vikki, who called her son Peter, who reached my husband, who drove over with an extra set of keys and rescued me. Over the two-hour stretch while this drama unfolded, I sat in a stuffed chair in the front room talking with the owner, browsing through books about the West, and reading a local newspaper. I helped myself to some lemon drops from the crystal candy jar.

I've always loved libraries. I grew up in a small town where each Saturday, my father drove us to the Main Street Library and my sister and I each

checked out six books for the week. Electric Avenue reminds me of those pleasant mornings among the books. The front room faces the street, with a seasonal display in a bow window near the proprietor's desk. A middle room holds children's books and small painted child-size wooden chairs reminiscent of my childhood public library. The back room, where the book group meets the first Wednesday evening of each month, contains a window looking over the lake; a wooden piano set against the back wall; an antique cupboard filled with poetry books; an assortment of couches and wing-backed chairs, crocheted afghans and pillows; and a table to hold coffee, tea, and cookies.

This community bookstore is more than just a place of business. It's the heart of my community. When I drive on a winter night down a dim road and across a narrow bridge over an icy river, past the dark closed stores, I see a lit window shining. The rooms spread beyond with shelves of novels, framed posters, a community bulletin board. A group of women who love books gathers to talk about them, to confer, empathize, make connections and friendships.

The selections we make as a group for each month's reading reflect varying points of view and differing literary tastes. Some of the women are native Montanans. Some have lived in Bigfork for decades, while some visit for only the summer. There are newcomers like me, some from California and the Midwest, pharmacists and housewives, teachers and insurance agents. The owner of the shop loves testimonies of pioneer women, memoirs by Western women writers. A founding member loves humorous books. The dichotomy between those who love more popular and those who love more literary books seems to mirror my dichotomy of a peaceful versus a difficult life.

My turn comes to lead a book discussion. Even though I have taught classes and led workshops for almost thirty years, I am so nervous that I leave my notes at home and find that I must try to recall my points of discussion from memory. One woman asks if I would give a brief summary of the book's plot and characters before I begin. After half an hour, the talk becomes lively and animated. Everyone else seems to have read the book and is willing to share an opinion. We're having a good discussion, honest and frank and lively. I like the way the evening is progressing. There's laughter, animated exchanges, polite disagreement, thoughtful comparison to other novels, until the end of the meeting when a feisty older woman chimes in, announcing how much she dislikes the book we've chosen. I announce that the *New York Times Book Review* gave it an excellent review, then immediately regret my comment. On the way out, I am so dispirited about her remark that Katie takes me aside and says, "That's too bad. The group chose the book together. If she didn't like it, she shouldn't have come to the meeting. I think the evening went well."

Our book group continues. Different kinds of women are getting to

know one another. It's a balancing act, like my new life in the West. One afternoon, a book group woman I meet at the grocery store comments that she's enjoying our discussions. This year we're mixing up the selections, reading some history, some memoirs, and some novels. We're a community, in which the lives of different kinds of women, like the different women we read about, cross:

Once when I visited Electric Avenue Books, I noticed a framed scroll with a poem by Hai Gaon from the eleventh century on a wall near the entrance. Its calligraphy inscription still holds true: "To three possessions / Thou shouldst look. / Acquire a field / a friend / a book."

KATHRYN E. KELLEY ✑ *September 12, 2001*

Our lives are a song of communities. A list of our communities is a litany of our lives. To name them is folly; those accidentally omitted would fret. At birth, we are endowed with immediate and extended family. Webs of their connections to others are our first community. Peers and mentors weave threads and fibers, creating warp and weft of our characters, foundation fabric, a canvas for our portrait of life.

Education opens our eyes to wider communities, fresh ideas, growth. Communities of scientists, writers, historians, and futurists lift us. Music, politics, travel, languages, and causes great and small carve intaglio on our characters.

Every breathing moment immerses us in community. In life's holiest moments, our emotions are woven into our souls: babies are born, baptized; we share union and communion, health and illness, death and a litany of life with the human community.

We are paean singers, chanting jump-rope verses on the playground, erupting into burbling giggles at a slumber party, cackling at a cocktail party. We murmur confidences, sing lyrical hymns; our voices grow husky with passion.

We are pain singers, mourners, keeping vigil, holding hands, raging when we are wounded by betrayal or in the anguish of loss, a keening widow, a bereaved parent. We have howled with pain, been mute with shock. Our hearts are ragged, our faces haunted, our nightmares tortured.

We are standard-bearers for the shadow women who came before us. Individually and collectively, we are a sorority of quilters, gardeners, caregivers, teachers, and learners. From humble fleece we have woven courage, faith, integrity, and a ferocious determination. We are the American woman. We are the victorious survivors.

B. J. BUCKLEY 〰 *Funeral Meats*

It's an old, old thing, to cook for the dead.
Eva Dabney was making pronouncements
to everyone who came in the door,
and directing a traffic of covered dishes.
And they can't eat it, so fill your plates!
Half of Arvada would feast for a week
on the favorite dinners we hadn't made
for two or six or twenty years, not
since we washed and buried and waked
our mother, our neighbor, our great-aunt Anne,
or in this case, Biddy. Eighty-six,
and gone to glory with nine of her hens,
roasting slow in the old school oven,
Some of them older than Biddy! we laughed.
So desserts to the right, salads left,
hot dish, covered dish, straight ahead.
And you've never cooked, really, until the dead
reach out through flour and salt and milk,
stand next to you watching water boil,
a little of this, a little of that,
when I was pregnant I wanted scones
every meal for three whole weeks!
When little tricks you never knew
come into your hands from hands so cold
the pie crust puffs like never before,
and when anyone asks for more,
there's more.

III

COWGIRL UP, CUPCAKES

LORA K. REITER ~ *Weeders, All*

To pull and pile weeds well
Is woman's work.

We rear back with old thistles,
Bend them hard,
Break them if we can—
Across our knees, we can—
Watch their juices glisten
On the shards of stalk,
Then twist the bunch
To make its weight a balance
We can throw precisely
On the pile.

We bend over foxtail,
Pull it up,
Then fold it twice,
Careful of the head,
Twist it hard,
And toss it on the pile.

The twist—
The lock
To form a bundle
That won't sprawl
To trip
Or scatter seed
Beyond the fire—
The twist's our secret,
The wringing tight
To shoo back chaos,
Clarify a place,
To justify a corner
Of our own.

I see my mother's hands,
My aunts',
Their mothers' hands before.

We're weeders, all.
We've always done it,
All the same.

The motion is our mark
In a garden by the creek,
Beside a pasture house,
On the horizon of my days,
This twist of women,
Bonded by our hands,
Our hearts,
The weeds.

SHEILA VOSEN-SHORTEN — *The Communion of Saints*

"Prayer cloths?" Rose Marie Black Hawk questioned, her liminal voice still stitched into my dream. "Go in the living room. Take what you want. We have lots."

The golden light of dawn had wrapped the family dwelling in promise. Its ivory paint-chipped screen door sucked in and out softly as I knocked. No one answered. "Still sleeping," I whispered. My fingers pinched the old wooden spool, and I pulled the screen door open without a hitch. The room held the brown arms and legs of Crow children sprawled out in half-covered sleep on floor mats and couches. I stepped over the threshold of my shadow and slipped from my dream into theirs.

An undulating linoleum floor of blue and gray flowers rolled beneath the balls of my feet. Dawn's ghostly light revealed a large sitting room. A bedroom held the close-comfort smell of shared bedclothes and old feather pillows. I padded along a fuzzy red path worn through the floral print, erased by the comings and goings of five Black Hawk generations.

Rose Marie lay sleeping on a gray-and-white-striped cotton mattress supported by a scarred metal bed frame. I stood waiting at the threshold of her bedroom, adjusting my breathing to hers. When our breathing became synchronized, she turned her ample body, stretching the groan of springs and metal slats beneath her. Her eyes opened, and she raised her chin from the pillow cradling her black and silver braids. The corners of her eyes creased and her cheekbones raised in a welcoming smile.

"I'm sorry to come so early. I need cloths for prayer. I feel so lost and empty," I said.

"It is good of you to come. Help yourself," Rose Marie replied, in a voice humbly secured by its wisdom and age.

Rose Marie's daughter, Anda, looked up from a bed adjacent to her mother's. She greeted me with large, unconcerned eyes, not questioning why I had entered while they slept. She pointed to the living room and a large pile of bright and darkly colored fabric remnants. "Just dig through that pile of cloth and take what you need," she urged before settling back into the slow rhythm of sleep.

Tiptoeing away from their bedroom, I set my feet down in a cautious fox pattern, which propelled me toward a mound of paisley and calico. I stood before the possibilities of prayer, sucked in deeply and held my breath. Every color imaginable had been accumulated into this pile of material swatches on Rose Marie's floor. And as I picked up and unfolded the silky soft attributes of each cloth, the sighing of child-slumber and the slight rustling of quilts and blankets on the couches and floor of the living room invited me to breathe.

I considered which would be best for my prayer need, which would help me find myself, fill the emptiness, invite openness. And then I touched yellow, felt the surge of life and healing energy pulse through its taffeta weave. There were four yellow scarves. They would cover the four directions, would center me, and would hold me in the sunlight of new life.

I gathered up my scarves and backed away from the sleeping, taking the power of rest with me as I moved without sound toward the door. Strength and resolve tickled my awareness as I eased the screen door into its casing and walked back out into the rose of dawn.

This dream surfaced again and again in the daylight of fall's routine. My motions were prescribed by time, which had moved on from the flowers of summer's bounty into autumn's fleshy stalks, roots, and bulbs that needed to be dried, blanched, or bathed in a rolling boil for winter's keep.

Ping—ping. Ice cubes crackled and hit the sides of the metal bowl as they popped out of the tray and into the water. I suspended the wire basket, hot with steaming chard, above the icy slurry that waited to stop these vegetables cold in their enzymatic tracks. I was forty-six years old, waiting to miscarry the baby that my husband and I had long tried to conceive.

I moved from stove to sink, from hot to cold, draining and stuffing dark green chard into plastic freezer bags, sucking out the air before I zipped them closed. I began to bleed.

Rose Marie had come to me in dreams several times after her death. And before I miscarried—the last chance I would ever have to join the community of women who call themselves mothers—Rose Marie offered me prayer cloths.

In the Crow tradition, a person presents a gift before asking for God's pity on himself or herself and family. A square of new cloth or tobacco might be left in gratitude for Ah-pah-tah-de'ah's blessings.

I have seen prayer cloths of many colors tied to trees and bushes, marking the sacred places in which people talk with their Maker. Out of respect, such offerings are often purified with prayers of thanksgiving, which rise up with the smoke from aromatic sage, flat cedar, and sweetgrass. This pungent, sweet scent clings to the threads of these prayer reminders.

It was a powerful medicine that this matriarch of the Black Hawks urged me to take as I reached through the veil that hangs between life and death, past and present, sleeping and waking. Yellow represents the sun's energy and healing. Yellow is the pollen of fruitfulness carried on the whirlwinds of possibility.

Ever since my midwife had told me she couldn't hear the baby's heartbeat, my body had been waiting to catch up with my mind. Out of its own memory, my body struggled in disbelief. It needed to be pregnant. It wanted to feel full, and I wanted to feel that I had something to give. Morning sickness still rose up inside of me. The familiar thickening around my waist weighed in solidly. How could it be that the baby my body had prepared to nourish and fashion from its own tissue would not be manifest in the form of a child?

While my body acted as if it were still supporting a live physical entity, my soul reached into the spirit of my womb, seeking ways to turn the possibility of my baby's life so that it could be delivered into reality. Delores Porez, a Zapotec Indian from Mexico, brought rich black clay for this transformation. I would experience birthing in a new way, but through a very old art.

Several days before the prognosis of my impending miscarriage, I'd begun attending a series of pottery demonstrations by Delores and Alfredo Porez. Pottery was a family business for them. Nearly every family in their small village in the Oaxaca Valley had its own backyard kiln. They dug their own clay from the sides of hills near their village. This clay breathes through microorganisms and live bacteria, which gives it its black color.

Each day that I observed Delores, she wore a wreath of red cloth, which accented her silvery white and black braids, twisted into a spiral at the back of her head. Festive turquoise, yellow, and red embroidery designs stood out against a white apron covering the front of her calf-length, floral-print dresses. I loved the irreconcilable irony with which she confidently scooped up the sticky black clay in her hands, showing no concern at all for the beautiful clothing of her culture.

Delores's soft, supple skin belied the birth of many children and the reality that she was now beyond the age of childbearing. She stood barefoot on the cement floor. Adjusting her skirts, she knelt in one graceful movement, tucked her legs beneath her, and settled her weight. Her every movement was wolflike in its husbandry—nothing wasted, always centered, like her clay.

Delores made building pots without a wheel look so easy. Even though she had already worked six hours, she presided with dignity and grace. In the morning, she had demonstrated how to fashion pots using soft coils. By late afternoon, and with the stamina of an artist who considers herself part of the clay, she'd completed leather-hard vessels by adding lifelike images of plants and animals from her native land. Finally, Delores helped us struggle to transform our lumps of clay into recognizable shapes. An ever-present smile suggested that she was grateful for this labor-intensive process.

I'd experienced this same quality of gratitude in Rose Marie while camped with her family during a Sun Dance, in the Wolf Mountains. Rose Marie's daughter, Jacqueline, was participating in the Sun Dance. Jackie sat, knelt, and slept on the ground behind a circular blind of drying cotton-wood branches. She had been singing and fasting for two days and nights. We'd stayed up with her on this last night, praying to the rhythm of the eagle whistles' high-pitched petitions, as we sat around the perimeter of the Sun Dance arbor in the rain.

But now, in the cooling air, I just wanted to go to sleep, so I curled up in my dry Hollofil sleeping bag inside my small, watertight tent. A soured smell of wet wool mixed with the fresh earthy smell of rain seeped through an air vent above me. As I lay there, I recalled that on our way back from the arbor, I had noticed water collecting inside Rose Marie's tent. I'd watched her shake out sodden blankets. I'd wanted to dry them for her, to make her comfortable, but I'd said nothing.

The smell of Rose Marie's wet bedding dampened my own comfort. I soon crawled back out of my bright green cocoon-style tent with a bundle and stumbled over to Rose Marie's soggy brown walk-in tent. "You don't have to sleep in wet blankets. Here, my other sleeping bag is dry."

"Maybe we'll give your bag to Jacqueline," she suggested. "This last night will be a long one, and hers is wet. I'll be all right with my blankets."

"I don't mind at all letting her use it. I have two," I said.

Rose Marie responded to my offer in a clear and careful voice. "One thing you'll learn about Indians: we really know how to pray. We're not afraid to take a long time, and we pray the hard way."

Rose Marie was so patient with life, so willing to live in the environment that nature provided. Sacrificing her own comfort for that of her daughter made Rose Marie seem full and content, like a grandmother who had already lived her own life and was now living to serve others.

Delores sat on the floor of the pottery studio, just as Rose Marie might have done. A mound of black clay rested nearby. She drew a small lump into the crotch space between her knees and began kneading. Delores patted and pulled its elastic mass into limber rolls, which she coiled into layers and blended with her fingers. Round and round a small pancake of clay,

her supple bronze fingers worked to mold a vessel with walls so uniform in thickness and strength that it could become a bowl, a platter, or even a woman holding calla lilies, doves, and iguanas.

I worked to create a bowl as I watched Delores form hers. The intensity of her love for the clay animated the feeling in me that I, who had come to learn, also had something to give. As I hollowed out the inside of my vessel, my breathing eased into the smooth, slipping rhythm of clay beneath the outward pressure of my fingers, and I stroked the emptiness that I felt as I wondered when my miscarriage would begin.

Delores watched me work the clay for a few moments, then left her bowl and padded silently in my direction. Speaking no English, needing no words, she knelt beside me. I felt the warmth of her body as she reached across my arms and slipped her hands through the small opening of my vessel. When Delores placed her fingers over mine, smoothing clay ropes into the wall of the bowl I was making, I felt the red slip of my earthenware dribble between us, like blood. I let her guide my hands, pulling the walls of my vessel up and opening outward, until I felt something other than air fill the vessel we molded together. We had made room for the spirit of the child that had died inside me.

The next day, I sculpted four angels. Using a fork, I scored the damp outer wall of the bowl's leather-hard surface. My fingers smoothed the red clay slip, like salve, into the scratch marks. Pressing angel torsos and wings into those softened places, I welded them to the outside of the bowl. As the seam between their bodies and the body of the bowl disappeared, I smiled at the oneness I had created.

It was some time after my miscarriage that I fired my bowl in our kiln at home. It rested in the center of our dining room table. I sat next to it. My gaze focused on the glazed white surface of the inside. Even though I'd dedicated this vessel to hold the spirit of my child, my sense of loss perceived a hard hollow reflecting emptiness, like my womb that had been scraped clean.

The angels held out their arms to the four directions, but their hands were empty. I ran the tips of my fingers along the glassy lip of the bowl, feeling the caressing drag of each unglazed angel's head. An image of Delores turning and sculpting the clay like an extension of herself, her Saint Francis medal swinging back and forth against her chest, comforted me. I felt her creative energy flowing out from her faith that she had something to give.

And then I remembered the dream I'd had about Rose Marie and the prayer cloths she'd given to me. Like pollen whirling within me, yellow suddenly filled up my insides, awakening the need to bring life back into myself.

My feet sprinted to the stairwell at the end of our drafty hallway. The

scent of winter's coming and the smell of moist earth rising from our dirt basement filled my nostrils. My hands grabbed the grooved handrail on the wall, and I pulled myself up the steep stairs leading to the second floor of our home. Straining stomach muscles reminded me of the healing I still needed.

Reaching the attic door, I lifted its hooks from their eyes, pushed the door open, and ducked under its low frame. I flipped on the overhead bulb and rummaged through boxes. I found yellow fabric.

Several quick, swishing cuts with scissors gave me four prayer cloths for the angels to hold, four yellow lifelines thrown to me from beyond the grave.

Inside my head, a woman's low, patient voice enunciated, "God can walk across time." That's what Jackie had told me years before, over tea, as we laid out for each other our loneliness and losses like negative space. The truth of Jackie's words renewed me with the efficacy of prayer. God can walk across time. My moon time is drying up, but I still feel the urgency to be fruitful. "God can walk across time," I repeated to myself as I folded each of the four small cloths and inserted them into my angels' hands.

I stepped back from the angels, their arms like conduits channeling golden energy from a body of red earth. It was an energy that pushed to be let out. I realized that I had to become the vessel through which that energy could find form.

A bridge exists now between the subliminal community of people who have crossed over into the spirit world and those who cross my path and leave healing footprints in this temporal and earthly life. I am a part of this continuity of souls. We believe in the Communion of Saints; we dance with them at powwows. They assisted me with clay and yellow prayer cloths.

My bowl was complete. I had joined the Communion of Saints.

JACKIE PUGH KOGAN ✑ *Desert Filament*

From brown alfalfa stubble, from autumn fields, quail spill
 onto roads,
one behind the other: staccato measures of hen and new chicks.
A thousand quail ribbons curve, furl on macadam, stretch,
 then vanish
into Oregon bunch grass, desert sage, and bristly rabbit brush.

Each staccato measure of new chicks and hen, one behind the other,
linked like a chain of newborn algae cells in spring's desert marsh,
thread effortlessly through trackless desert sage and bunch grass;
one behind the other, they run in an indiscernible stream.

Linked as a chain of newborn algae cells in spring's desert marsh,
the yellowed winter wedding pearls my father gave my mother
circle on an indiscernible thread, rest one beside the other.
As for fifty years, each pearl is mirrored in the curve of its
 companion.

I circle, clasp the string of yellowed winter wedding pearls
 at my neck
for Mother's summer funeral. I turn to reflection, and expect
 my face
of fifty years, but only hers is mirrored in the curve of cheekbone
 and jaw.
My car follows the road to the cemetery with barely a touch
 from my fingers.

At Mother's graveside, beside me, neighbors. Our eyes, our faces,
 reflect each other's
presence as stoic hope, as did our families', in this place, a century
 before my knowing.
The road home gleams in the rose of desert dusk; I stop and lift
 fingers to wave
at the line of shining headlights, one behind the other, that thread
 from Mother's drive.

As my family's women did for theirs, those neighbors a century
 before my knowing,
I wave thanks for food women carried through unlocked doors to
 fill her silent kitchen.
Ribbons of light serpentine from her drive; they connect and
 merge, beginnings blurred, endings melded, into the invisible
 seam between all that defines us.

SOPHIE DOMINIK ECHEVERRIA
The Far Side of Maple Street

Don't even get me started about living in this town. I could write a book
about the births, weddings, and funerals; the divorces, cheatings, and beat-
ings; the comedies, disasters, and triumphs—in short, the drama. The only
thing that is holding me back is that people keep driving around, so I get
their names and stories mixed up. I think it's best if we stay right here on
Maple Street just so that I don't get lost. But first I have to tell you some-
thing.

In this town, you will be held accountable. When you flip the high school principal off, or when he has an affair with one of the teachers, word gets around. Gossip is the great ancestor of the media, but much more interesting. Why settle for "just the facts" when you can get the inside scoop? If you should fall from grace, and you will, the proper response is to look people in the eye and bide your time. Some people never learn this. They move from spot to spot trying to get out of the spotlight, but let me ask you this: if the universe is infinite, isn't every point the center?

One day, I walked across the street to the Center of the Universe (COU) to invite my neighbors to a pre-Christmas dinner. I rang the doorbell, and they welcomed me into the middle of a huge fight. Bill had been out all night drinking, and Celeste was sitting on the couch crying, nursing her six-week-old baby. After a few tense minutes, I decided to invite their two other children to bake sugar cookies. Five-year-old Carrie and two-year-old James were both delighted. They stayed for a couple of hours until Bill stormed in to "check on *his* kids." He told me his side of the story, which I have since forgotten. I gave him a hug on his way out the door. A few minutes later, Celeste showed up to get the kids. She told me her side of the story, which I also have forgotten. I hugged her, too. They left without taking any of the cookies.

That night, Bill called at eleven to tell me I was a beautiful woman. "No, I mean really, really beautiful." I've always prided my ability to pick up drunken sailors off the street, but I prefer men who are madly in love with their own wives, especially my husband. A few months later, Bill and Celeste moved three blocks away to the new COU. Their dog, Jack, still comes over now and then to visit my dog, Sally.

Next door to Bill lives Claire. Claire is my daughter-in-law's aunt. Claire and I used to be closet smokers. Two summers ago, we came up with this plan. Every time one of us smoked, we had to pay the other a dollar. We were running back and forth like crazy, swapping dollar bills and bumming cigarettes. I eventually kicked the habit. I think Claire still smokes, but I haven't seen her since my son's wedding seven months ago.

Walt lives four houses to the north of Steve and Claire, and he loves sugar. Walt is ninety-two. Don't park in front of Walt's house; he will come out and jump in your car. And don't bother to wave either.

One day I asked Hank (Hank is Albert's son; Albert lives next door to Walt; Hank offered to kill my husband if I should ever need that sort of thing), "What's up with old Walt? Is he some kind of snob? Every time I wave, he ignores me."

"He's blind," said Hank. I was relieved. I thought it had something to do with letting my dogs snoop around his house. But it is curious; whenever I take sugar to Walt, his eyes unfailingly go to my cookies, cakes, and pies. He licks his lips and says things like, "I sure do like chocolate."

Another curious thing about Walt is his son, Mick. Three times a day,

Mick pulls up in front of Walt's house in a maroon 1987 Lincoln Continental. He cusses and yells and kicks up such a fuss that you would think Walt was dealing drugs instead of just wearing his jacket on a hot day. I talked to Albert, and he brought up a good point. Who else is going to take Walt to the football and basketball games, or out to eat, or to the funerals of his good buddies? Mick has the unpleasant task of informing his father each time a friend passes away.

I remember when Mick told me about the death of my neighbor Kay. Kay lived in the white house on the northeast corner until she was ninety-six. I met her while we were both walking in the cornfield across the street. I was holding a fistful of dirt when she stretched out her hand to shake mine. I confessed I was practicing hoogie-boogie as I wiped my hands on my jeans. She said that she understood completely, that she, too, believed in Jesus. Then she sang me a Jesus song right there under the big blue sky.

I didn't visit her often because she told me right up front, "Good neighbors are friendly, but they don't camp out in your house." I asked my husband what he thought of that. "Well, she sounds sensible," he said. "I think Hank's offer to murder me is a little too friendly, and if Bill calls the house one more time, I'm going to beat the living hell out of him." I didn't share any of that with Kay. We were more about singing. I would go over to her house, and she would bang on her piano, warbling about the good Lord. Once, as she was banging and singing, she leaned in such a way that I could see her black and white polka dot bra.

Another time, she came to my house and mistook the plumber in the driveway for me.

"And he walks with me and he talks with me. . . ."

"Over here, Kay dear. I'm up here on the porch."

I lost touch with her in the end because I was away from home. I had just gotten back to town when I ran into Mick. "How is Kay?" I asked. Mick never said a word. He didn't have to. He took his finger and drew a ghastly line across his neck that went from ear to ear, accompanied by a gurgling, gasping sound. I knew right then that Kay had been hung from the nearest elm tree. Albert said she died peacefully in her sleep after a rough bout of pneumonia. I didn't have the heart to tell him otherwise.

Albert's house is on the other side of Walt's house. Albert is retired. His wife, Colleen, was very ill with cancer when I moved here. I spent a good deal of time with her and became close to the family before she died. Not so close, however, as to prevent us from fighting over parking spaces.

One night I came in late. There were five cars parked in front of my house because it was my birthday and my family and friends were waiting inside to throw me a party. So I parked my yellow Cadillac in front of Albert's girlfriend's house. (Dulce lives next door to me and started dating Albert after her husband, Kenneth, died.) I accidentally overshot her drive-

way by two feet. The next morning, the police were banging on my door. Dulce and Albert had called the cops!

A few weeks later, I had an African dance troupe over for lunch. They parked in front of Dulce's house. The next day, a stake was driven into her front yard. Attached was a sign that read: PARKING FOR NORWEGIANS ONLY. *I* called the cops!

Apparently, if a sign doesn't specifically contain the *N* word, it isn't against the law. We fought back and forth. Dulce always claimed she had no part in it, that it was all Albert's idea, but I saw her dragging a large tree limb to the empty space next to our driveway. A week later, I ran into Albert and Dulce at the grocery store and decided to handle it face-to-face.

"How you like I throw eggs at your house?" I said in my best Russian KGB accent. Dulce ran off to the frozen food section. Albert stood his ground and chewed me out about horse trailers and teenagers' cars. After a couple of years, it ended with a wave and a "How are you?" although the sign still stands.

We also have an ogre living on the block. Patty and her two daughters, fourteen-year-old Camille and eleven-year-old Glassy, live with the ogre in Steve and Claire's rental.

The other night, I was walking home from the park with my three-year-old grandson. Glassy wanted to walk with us because it was getting dark. We were all holding hands, talking about hot chocolate verses warm chocolate, when the ogre appeared.

"What are you doing down here so late? It's time for you to get home." Glassy walked very slowly. "I mean now and I mean alone!" said the ogre. He grabbed her by the back of the neck, shook her, and then pushed her. She stumbled, regained her balance, and slowly walked the rest of the way home five feet in front of him.

"You better watch how you touch her, mister," I said. "If I see something I don't like, I'm calling the cops." (I like to call the cops.) I watched the house for a while because her mother was out of town for the weekend. Finally, I called my son, who is a firefighter. He told me to be careful. Then I called my daughter. And then I called all my friends, my sisters and my mother, my daughters-in-law, and the fire chief. When Patty got home, I called her, too.

Glassy came over a few days later to walk my dogs. I paid her fifty cents and offered to let her use my phone anytime or stay at my house if she ever needed.

"I've got my eye on him," I said.

"I know," she said. "I told him that."

"So many gods, so many creeds, / So many paths that wind and wind, / While just the art of being kind, / Is all the sad world needs." I don't know if Ella Wheeler Wilcox was referring to my neighborhood when she wrote

that, but I do know this: she better be careful if she comes around here. We may offer her a cigarette or some sugar. We may sing her a song or call the cops. We live on the far side here on Maple Street, even if it is in the center.

BETTE-B BAUER ✑ *Quilting a Dissertation*

In midlife, I decided to return to graduate school at the University of Oregon to prepare for a new career as a teacher. I soon began attending the Eugene Friends Meeting. An important part of that first winter for me was being part of the women's weekly reading group, which met for discussion and lunch. The warmth and caring nourished and replenished me after the cerebral rigors of the academic world.

I was passionate about my subject, exploring the narrative strategies of women's spiritual journeys in literature, but the isolating nature of the work undermined my motivation and confidence. At the halfway point, with the work moving more slowly, I began to see why so many people never finish Ph.D. research projects.

Because of my teaching schedule, I often had to miss the women's meeting. Over lunch one day, Ruth and Sue asked me if there was anything they could do to help support me in writing the dissertation. I couldn't think of anything to say except to go on supporting me as they had so far. They exchanged a look, brought out some tissue, and told me that for six months the Quaker women's group had been working on a quilt for me in support of my dissertation. They had finally decided to tell me about it so that they wouldn't have to keep hiding the squares and lying to me, very un-Quakerly actions. I was amazed by this news, too numb even to cry.

The next morning, when I sat down at the computer, I felt that I was taking my place in the circle of women working on the quilt. The debilitating feeling of isolation was gone. I e-mailed Ruth: "I feel so strong." The images of the completed squares I had seen floated through my imagination as I worked. Knowing about the quilt transformed me inside, but I soon began to realize that this gift wasn't only about me. Quaker practice is based on love, and I was just grist for their mill.

When Muriel, who was doing the embroidery work on the quilt centerpiece, asked if I wanted anything special, I told her a turtle, a special talisman for me since my days as a cordon bleu cook on a small island in the Caribbean. I once met a giant sea turtle as I swam in the middle of a school of baitfish. We hung suspended for a moment in the refracted light of the water. I carry the memory of the turtle's gaze with me as I move through life on land.

Muriel said she would look for a pattern and invited me to her house to see a columbine plant I'd given her. I drove over on a hot afternoon, thinking, *I don't have time for this.* Later, as we sat in her living room, I noticed a

pillow of embroidered flowers—the work of her grandmother, Muriel said. She'd had it for years. As I turned it in my hands, I found on the lower edge, not visible from the front, a small turtle. Muriel had never noticed it, but she knew those knots, and that afternoon the turtle became a part of the quilt. That was why I had to go to her house: to find the turtle handed down to us by her grandmother.

When Ruth invited me to go with her to choose background and border material, I was again uncomfortable about interrupting my work. (Now I treasure the experience of working on the quilt with my friends.) They had picked cloth in which lavender, turquoise, and black predominated. I had always thought that my colors were red-orange and bright blue, but I decided they had chosen colors for the next stage of my life.

As I was revising the final chapter of my dissertation, Ruth was finishing the quilt. Her hope was to bring the completed quilt with her to the dissertation defense, which was open to family and friends. When I looked at, or thought about, the quilt, I felt borne along on a wave of love.

The quilt was presented to me at the meeting house the day before I was scheduled to defend my dissertation project. Friends and family came, and each woman who had made a square spoke about the experience for a video of the event. Ruth commented that women working together "reminds me that none of us is alone and that women have worked together always." Then she added, "One of the best things I've learned is that each one has an idea that seems crucial for the whole . . . a gift essential for the creation . . . a nice comment on how life works as a whole." Lynn reminded me that our lives are "really just patchwork, that we come from many places and we end up in the same place." Several of the women had never worked on a quilt before. Mary said, "When the quilt project was brought up, I didn't know Bette. At first I wondered, *You mean I have to do some hard work sewing for somebody I don't even know?* A very un-Quakerly thought."

That night, I nestled under my quilt, feeling love infuse me with courage for the oral exam. The following day, some of the quilters and I took the quilt to my defense, and my committee signed it. Five days later, I left for a teaching position in Baton Rouge, Louisiana. I turned on the air conditioning so I could sleep under the quilt. Now I live in Omaha, Nebraska. As I wrote this story, an early blizzard produced a foot of wet snow, knocking down trees and power lines: perfect weather for what one friend has dubbed the Power Quilt.

MARJORIE SAISER ✑ *The Living, the Warm*

Aunt Wilma touches the corpse, touches
her aunt Clara, lays her hands on top of the hands
in the casket, looks into her dead aunt's face and says:

Doesn't she look pretty? So pretty, isn't she?
And it's true, Great-Aunt Clara, 99, looks sharp
and Sunday-best in her turquoise suit,
ruffles at her wrists and throat, her eyes closed,
her hair that certain shade of blue-white she wanted,
a capsule of bluing in the rinse water
to keep a shade of yellow from stealing in.
Yes, she is pretty, and Aunt Wilma lays her hands on,
and keeps them there, and looks into her aunt's face
as if they had the afternoon to talk about plums
or pies or the need for rain. Perhaps it was
customary to lay your hand on the hands of the dead
as my father did
when my grandmother lay in the mortuary.
He encouraged me, saying: *See, she doesn't mind,*
but I shook my head and wiped my wet face
with a Kleenex, not wanting to know
if the body is hard, if it is cold, how cold,
the body more or less empty. Perhaps my father
touched his father's hand, that same gesture,
when the body lay in the casket in the farmhouse
north of the point where the Niobrara
and the Keya Paha flowed—still flow—together.

I wish I had asked. He would have told me,
if I had sat near his hospital bed,
put my hand on his arm and said:
Would you tell me of your father's death?

When my father's body lay in the church,
I came early with my mother; the time was there,
I could have laid my hand on the wrist, maybe his cuff
or his fingers, one cold nail, or his shoulder.
I could have straightened his already straight tie,
but I hung back, as he did in family photographs,
the shy child beside his big sister. My mother
laid her hand on his. My hand on her back,
on the ridges of her spine, the curve of her thin shoulders:
the living, the warm.

After the funeral, my aunts sit on metal chairs
in the church basement, taking turns talking to blind
Aunt Hattie. They laugh about that time

Anna and Louie started off to the Black Hills in the Ford.
They laugh about somebody in a bear suit trying to
keep the kids away from the still. My turn next,
so Hattie's hands take mine, clasp them; I'm what's
left, what's here today of my golden-haired father,
Hattie's laugh that same little waterfall he heard,
her hands small quick birds fluttering and resting.
I wonder how it feels to touch the dead

but I don't want to find out. Chicken, as my aunts
would say, though I've been amazed at myself
lately, driving in a hailstorm like it was nothing,
the leaves beaten off the trees, sticking to the windows,
hail smashing on the windshield and pounding on the roof,
smeared images all around me through the glass.
Trees and the road and the trucks. I'm
trapped in my car on the road in a hailstorm,
thunder very close, lightning a quick yellow
knife. But I breathe in the smell of the storm
and go right ahead. Not quite scared to pieces,
as my aunts would say. A chain of hands
coming on down, funeral by funeral. Soon
I'll be laughing, raucous
in a car full of women. I'll move to the back

and let my daughter drive. After the funeral,
I'll take my sister's hand in the church basement.
On the table, our food will be waiting:
cup of coffee, sandwich, Jell-O, cake—
a plate of cake as necessary downstairs
as the sermon was upstairs. That will be after. But first,
at the casket, when my turn comes, maybe
I'll lift my old small useful hands and lay them—
unpolished fingers, cool dry palms—
onto the hands of the others.

LESLIE I. BROWN ✍ *The Elegance of White Things*

Before I knew her, people told me she was very private, practically a recluse. When I first became aware of Susan, after her husband had left and it was all the talk, I caught only glimpses of her. Susan and Bob had remod-

eled their old house, installing floor-to-ceiling windows or glass doors so that even inside felt like a garden sanctuary. She secluded herself in the acreage of her gardens, tending them into perfect, peaceful havens.

I got to know Susan near the end of her year of living in town, after she rented out her country house to a young married couple, to get a break from the memories, she said. Her apartment in town was in an old house on a large lot that extended far back of the house, filled with trees and paths through rock and flower gardens, so Susan still had the kind of private outdoor place that seemed to sustain her.

Her medical saga began shortly after she moved back to her house from the apartment. We were riding in my truck, dogs in the back, on a late-summer wildflower drive. We stopped for a picnic and talked about her recent annual exam; doctors had found a grapefruit-size tumor on her ovary. She was scheduled to see a cancer specialist in Salt Lake City, but she believed the tumor was a lump of sadness, and those of us watching could not dispute it.

The Salt Lake doctor rushed Susan into surgery. In her hospital room a few days later, I sat with her. She asked the nurses to give most of the flowers away, not wanting to clutter up the space. Her waiting ended when the doctor came with the results. I held her hand while he explained that she had stage three (of four) ovarian cancer. He was understandably vague and recommended chemotherapy; she had her first round before leaving the hospital.

Meanwhile, the hive was buzzing up north, preparing for Susan's return home. Many friends who admitted to feeling closer to Bob had reached out to Susan through the divorce, and she had taken hold. These same people, mostly women, now organized themselves for her postsurgical care. Susan was not close to her Mormon family, having left the church as a young woman. Her parents were elderly and ill, her siblings scattered. One sister, Sharon, stayed with Susan until her friends could step in, rotating days and nights of making meals, dispensing medication, screening phone calls, and keeping her company.

I spent an afternoon with Susan. She rested by a south wall of windows looking out into a sheltered garden decorated with white columbine, tiny white lily of the valley, white lilac. She loved the simple elegance of white things, preferring vanilla ice cream, sleeping on white cotton sheets. I washed the array of small panes in the windows and French doors, glancing at her through the glass as I sprayed, wiped, swiped, and squeaked those windows clean to let in the sunlight that was her salvation. She told me later that she only dozed and was secretly peeking at me, feeling delicious lying there while a busy little person puttered at her tidy task. It was a small gesture of my love for her, to ease her discomfort and my helplessness, busywork to keep me from drowning in the truth of her illness.

Susan's recovery was speedy, although she sometimes grew tired and she lost her hair. Her illness drew people closer. I often arrived at her house for a visit to find someone there, so I became acquainted with her fruit basket of friends. Susan was an artist and a landscape architect. Her friends included those from the bookstore/café, the baker and her family, a nurse and her inventor husband, schoolteachers, musicians, a Tai Chi Chuan teacher. The geologist and the woodworker, who also would succumb to divorce. The bearded, ponytailed contractor. The white-clad, shaven-headed spiritual seeker. The retired English professor and his equally delightful wife. The book buyer. The horse breeders. The Southern sister shopkeepers. Susan's long blond hair grew back in tricolor curls.

In less than a year, though, a tumor was found on her lung, up against her liver. Another in her abdomen. More chemotherapy was not recommended. All that was left were alternative or experimental treatments. Susan decided on a stem cell rescue, similar to a bone marrow transplant, the treatment most recommended by her doctor. Because it was experimental, her insurance would not cover the ninety-three-thousand-dollar cost.

But the hive took to buzzing again. Susan's eighty-year-old father took a second mortgage on his home so Susan's treatment could proceed. But it didn't seem right that he should be so saddled with debt, and the fundraising effort moved ahead in parallel.

I don't know which was harder for Susan, the thought of this difficult and risky medical procedure or the fundraising threat to her pride and privacy. In order for us to raise money for her cause, people had to be made aware of her physical and financial circumstances. She didn't want her picture on change jars in the grocery stores. She didn't want her story printed in the newspaper. She didn't want people to go to a lot of trouble on her behalf. But she allowed all of these things to take place, and the money started trickling in.

Our big push, though, was organizing an art and antique auction. Donations were collected in the bookstore, closed for remodeling. Our little committee was absolutely bowled over by the response. Everyone from well-known professional painters to knitting grandmothers to ceramics students to bead and fabric artists to art teachers to antique dealers to woodworkers to Jane and Joe Schmo who had something lying around that they'd been meaning to sell or give away came through the door with their items. Everyone had something—or three things or five things—to give for a stranger in need. The auction was magical. Four inches of fresh snow couldn't keep people from cramming into the country club to throw money at us, at Susan. The revelry went on for hours. Susan was hospitalized, preparing for treatment, but her friend Catherine called her from the auction and held up the phone so Susan could hear the laughter, the bidding, the cheering. Catherine described everything and let Susan hear for herself the

energy of the crowd, unified toward a goal that looked like money but was actually hope.

In a final surprise move, Susan's gynecologist offered up two mammograms, Pap smears, and annual exams, and a local businessman (yes, a man) who'd already spent thousands of dollars that evening bought them. When our cashiers counted, the auction had raised more than forty thousand dollars for Susan.

Once again, Susan flew through her recovery, came home to sisters and friends who cared for her, and once more her bald head slowly sprouted baby-soft peach fuzz that became marvelous curls.

In spite of everything, all that money bought her only a little time. The lump of sadness was gone, but its seeds lingered on, taking root in her lungs. Susan knew what she had been given, something far beyond money and even hope. Before her cancer, Susan had considered moving away. Later, she said, "How could I ever leave now? After everything people have done?" I'm pretty sure she never realized what she'd done for us—for our committee of helpless and desperate strangers who grew into a company of friends.

In a small-town coincidence, another friend, Cindy, had bought the big old house with Susan's apartment in town, the one with the rambling gardens out back. After Susan's death, Cindy gathered a few of us together to mark Susan's life and her passing. With candles and a bottle of wine, we congregated in the rock garden where Susan surely sat many times, and we reminisced. We all brought perennials to plant in the spot that Cindy had cleared for a Susan memorial garden. We planted white columbine, snapdragon, phlox, and whirling butterfly, reverent and playful in our earthy task. Watering them in, we shared a meal and more wine and thanked Susan privately for bringing us together once again.

DANNY BERGIN ✍ *Celebrating Mass in a Nightgown*

At times in my life, I was the only community I had. But the strongest and most constant, enduring, and invigorating community for almost seventy years of my life has been Catholic. I often say prayers of thanksgiving for my dad, a Catholic man who adopted me and enrolled me in the best community I've ever found.

I was an only, lonely, adopted child in 1932, carrying memories of rejection that I wasn't able to analyze until later. We always lived near the church, and most days I stayed after classes to help the sisters—who were the janitors in those days—clean their classrooms. As I helped empty wastebaskets, wash blackboards, and pound erasers, we talked about Jesus, the Mass, vocations, and being kind to kids I might not like. Dur-

ing eight years of grade school, four years of high school, and nearly two years of nurse's training, I was accepted, befriended, loved, schooled, and molded. My teachers were the Sisters of Charity of Leavenworth in Grand Junction, Colorado; the Benedictine Sisters of Chicago in Cañon City, Colorado; and the Dominican Sisters in Great Bend, Kansas. To this day, I can put names and faces together for more than three dozen women who showed me courage, compassion, patience, humor, sympathy, how to pray, and, best of all, love and acceptance, along with love for Jesus and Mary.

Sister Rosine, my teacher for the last four years of grade school, was my all-time favorite. When others in my class went to public high school, I spent four years at a Catholic girls' boarding school three hundred miles from home. Later, Sister Rosine, who transferred to an orphanage in Denver, wrote me regularly. Each year, when it was time to begin school, she gently suggested I might enter a convent. I never did, because I dreamed of being a mother, but I visited her at the orphanage. After my marriage and first baby, she sent me two beautiful hand-crocheted bonnets. When her convent sent me her death notice, I felt as if I had lost the most important person in my life.

I laughed at the good sisters when they tried to teach us in high school why we should marry a man of our own faith, but I found out firsthand what the problems were when I married a non-Catholic. I found myself stranded at 7,500 feet on a mountaintop in Utah raising eight kids on a cattle ranch with no running water and the outhouse down a hill. If time passes quickly when you are having fun, I must have had fun, as time passed quickly while my first husband worked there. I went to town once a month, a two-hour drive, for necessities; canned six hundred quarts of vegetables from my garden; canned more fruit we bought in town because we were too high to grow it; fed the hay crew; and produced a new baby about every fifteen months. Each year, I made a new temporary friend when the teacher came to our one-room mountain school.

No Catholic community existed on the mountain, only a thousand head of cattle. But each time I had another baby, I went to a Catholic hospital in town for a few days. Going to Mass in my nightgown and bathrobe was a different experience, but it helped my mental state, and I knew God understood.

When my youngest child was twelve, my twenty-year marriage failed, and I became a single, working mother, hating the implication that I hadn't worked all those years I spent as "just a housewife." I listed my job as domestic engineer. I joined several Catholic organizations of women—Sodality, Altar Society, Women of Faith, women's Bible study groups—to build a connection wherever I lived. My Catholic community has been primarily women, although I also formed connections with women of other faiths who are still my friends.

Five years after my divorce, thirty years since I had dated within my faith, I met an engineer, and love blossomed again. All the years of hardship were necessary for the unity I found; we celebrated twenty years of a sacramental marriage in 2003. Since my marriage, I have been a Benedictine oblate, a Christian individual associated with a Benedictine community for enrichment.

CHRISTINA HUTCHINS *In a Time of War*

In a time of war the canticles we make
matter more: your hands
on your guitar one at the neck
the other at the black hole of an open
mouth Your fingers work the strings until
wood sings in its curves and still air
quivers This evocation occurs in Kentucky while in California
at the edge of a grieving and brutal continent

in the silence between cataclysmic
waves I am listening hard
as I can the black hole of me grabbing
vibrations warped by gravity Some forces
change everything though still free space hovers
under a raindrop under a turning Pacific wave still
the immense space abides under the fallen towers
just before the collapse There are stairwells

lobbies and concert halls tunnels and ancient caves there are
storm surges footsteps down and footsteps up resonant
chords enjoined of strings and echoes Like Annie Sullivan
 spelled
water into the hollow of Helen's hand spell into air
the necessary gestures Amplify the damp
breath of the buried Their last exhalations—*Life so quickly
passes, and moments of suffering are years—*
seek no retribution only love

KAREN M. BERRY *Stitching My Life Project*

In three years, I have moved from one state to a second and now to a third. I am not someone who makes friends and creates relationships easily. I'd

never expected to leave where I had lived, first as a child, then a wife and mother, and finally a divorced other. I was comfortable.

When I was a child in Sheridan, Wyoming, supportive women in my church, bridge group, and various organizations had made a difference to me as well as to the community. When I wanted to learn to play bridge, for example, a woman in Altar Guild orchestrated a new bridge group of women who were willing to include novice players.

For a new job, I moved to Denver, Colorado, but despite the positive benefits, I soon realized I didn't have to keep my apartment clean because I didn't know anyone who would visit. I am shy and reticent about inviting people to share my life, but I expected to be in Denver for the rest of forever, so I carefully formed deliberate relationships.

I met a woman who had lived in northern Wyoming and could recall many of the same geographical landmarks I knew, if not the same people. I met women enthusiastic about their pieces of the Denver community who taught me about city neighborhoods—small communities that are remarkably like small towns.

In another organization, I came to know a woman so committed to the success of the organization's projects that she always said yes to work. When she finally said at a meeting that she just couldn't do it alone anymore, I learned something about community-building. Silent at first, group members volunteered to take specific tasks from her: I'll send out the notices, yes, I'll make the calls.

Then I found a superb bridge studio with an excellent bridge teacher. A few of us, singles and couples, created a weekly bridge group with an approximately thirty-year age range. Each Saturday night, we exhibited our culinary personalities as we began to learn about each other. The food we ate was personal; sharing it with people helped us to learn about each other.

I had a handful of solid acquaintances and steps toward some good friendships. But I had yet to find someone who lived near me whom I could call at two in the morning if I needed something—or who could pick me up from the hospital when I'd had outpatient surgery and wasn't able to drive. Calling someone at two exposes vulnerability! When was an acquaintanceship ready to embrace the neediness that an emergency would bring? What is the magic measure by which I could feel that my acquaintance was ready to become my friend?

I'd been in Denver less than two years when I was selected for a job in Tucson, Arizona. Mingled with the excitement of a new job in a new city was the reality that I'd have to start over, making a place for myself and creating a new, personal community. Was it worth it? I might never see my friends in Sheridan again; I'd be leaving new relationships, uncertain if they were resilient enough to last.

Still, I'd learned that big cities consist of small communities whose peo-

ple are connected by mutual interests and interdependence. In Sheridan, my interests were few, shared by many of the same women. In Denver, my circle, my community, was larger. As I weighed a move to Tucson, I remembered nights in Denver when loneliness had wrenched me from sleep. I'd sit at my computer writing messages to Sheridan friends but never send them.

My success at making new friends in Tucson has been directly related to my own efforts. I have connected with groups and am starting to develop personal relationships. I want more than a Christmas card community of Sheridan friends, the women who were there when I moved through so many important steps in my life. I don't want to lose the Denver relationships either.

Each person in my life is unique as a skein of yarn. I want to keep each color in the work, making my own pattern, stitching them together, creating my life project. My family and friends are vivid reds, blues, purples; I am the neutral shades of white, black, and gray. I yearn to make my life rich with hues and textures, but only I may bring each skein into the pattern.

When I lived in Sheridan, I didn't dwell on thoughts of family and friends. They were there, so we could easily set times to meet and talk. Yet without the friend I met every Saturday morning for exercise and coffee and to work through marriage and family entanglements, I would not be here. Another friend called from her home 140 miles away to say the words she needed to utter about her life. Now I realize that she had lived in Sheridan, moved away, and was struggling to maintain a relationship with me.

Now I see her efforts from a different valley. I've been less supportive than I could have been. So I wonder, have I done my part to build community?

By moving to Tucson, I understand that I have allowed my community to unravel; I have not purposefully stitched my project every week. If I want my relationships to work in this new, distant way, I must hold the yarn in my hands. It's time to gather my yarn from the worn wicker basket and wax my needles—to nurture my community and meet new people.

MARCIA HENSLEY *I Like It That Way*

When I first moved to the Eden Valley, a community with a population of about five hundred people scattered over twenty square miles, I was an outsider, and I liked it that way. A city girl, I left my hometown of five hundred thousand to move to Wyoming, a state with about that same population, in my own personal version of downsizing. My first Wyoming home was in a town of twenty thousand, which seemed small until we moved to

a few acres of land located on the edge of the Eden Valley, five miles from the tiny town of Farson, with its post office, school, café, Texaco station, and historic mercantile known for its excellent ice cream.

The isolation of this place was a gift, offering respite from a life too busy, too complicated, too filled with noise. Our nearest neighbors were a mile away. It didn't bother me that I knew few people in the community, since I commuted fifty miles daily to my teaching job in a small city, where I was surrounded by people making demands on me. In the winter, my husband and I cocooned on weekends in our little house away from it all. In the summer, we puttered in the garden, rode the horses down the dirt roads, read books in the shade of cottonwood trees, soaked up the quiet. We went weeks without having contact with anyone but the strangers we saw when we picked up the mail at the Farson post office. We smiled and said hello, and they nodded and said hello back in the way that friendly strangers do. Tanned and fit, dressed in their lived-in-looking jeans and flannel shirts, they made me curious and a little envious as I imagined the men working with livestock and big farm machines and the women cooking for haying crews and doing ranch chores. From my outsider's perspective, I saw a sepia-toned stereotype of a ranch community, set about fifty years in the past.

With our isolationist attitude, getting acquainted with our neighbors took place over a period of years. One of my earliest community interactions was when I taught a night class in Western literature at the little local school. I began to develop a more realistic view of my neighbors. I learned that most families had to have some kind of job to support the ranch, and some commuted to town as I did. We generally agreed on our appreciation of the Western landscape, history, and lifestyle.

Another time, a cow helped me get to know the neighbor who pastured his cattle around our house. We'd seemed more like adversaries than neighbors when we'd called him to complain that his cows had broken down our fences or his irrigation water had flooded our barn. But once while I was out walking our dog during frigid weather, I noticed one of his cows had fallen into a ditch and couldn't get out. We called the rancher, and my husband helped him get the cow up and moving. A few days later, the rancher's mother, a longtime resident of the valley, drove up in our yard and honked the horn. When I went out, she presented me with a homemade angel food cake as thanks for our help. I felt proud that we greenhorns had actually done something to help out our ranch neighbors.

I made another connection when a young former student living nearby invited me to join a newly formed quilting club. Once a month, we shared our enthusiasm for our hobby, and as I listened to the quilters talk, I realized how much was happening in our community.

Then my daughter decided she wanted to be married in the Eden Valley Episcopal Church. Since it didn't seem right to use the church without be-

ing a part of it, my husband and I began to attend services. When rain threatened the outdoor reception for the wedding, an acquaintance offered to clean her barn so that we could hold the party there. Long after the wedding, we continued to meet with the tiny church congregation every other week when the minister came, and we found that another small community within the community had become a part of our lives.

Then one day I received a call from a woman asking me to bring a cake, casserole, or salad to a funeral dinner for one of the valley residents. Someone had put my name on "the list." That day I knew for sure that I belonged.

Although I am still handicapped by not always knowing who is related to whom and where everyone lives, I am beginning to get the hang of living here. I have heard the stories of settlers who came in the early 1900s when irrigation made it possible to farm this high desert area. I have learned the pros and cons of flood versus pivot irrigation. I know that giant white top is a noxious weed, not a pretty wildflower. I've learned how to use pans of soapy water to attract and kill the miller moths that invade us in the summer. I can ask neighbors to feed our horses when we're out of town and know that they will willingly agree, and that I will reciprocate when they are gone.

I now believe the people who settle in this sparsely populated area are like me; they choose land and space over convenience and closeness. We compare temperatures. "Our thermometer read thirty below last night; what was it at your place?" We commiserate about frozen pipes. We worry about the rain or—more often—the lack of it. We swap wildlife stories. "Did you hear someone shot a mountain lion down by Eden?" We tell of the deer eating from our haystacks, eagles spotted in certain parts of the valley, an errant moose that wandered down from the mountains. At the post office, I no longer see strangers but instead linger to visit with friends.

Maybe it's the space between us that makes us appreciate one another more. After eleven years of living here, I realize that being part of a community is much more than owning property within its boundaries. People sometimes wrongly assume that a small community is a gossipy, uninteresting, stagnant place. Instead, it is a microcosm of the larger world, with drama, dangers, and delights on a smaller, more manageable scale. I no longer feel like an outsider—and I like it that way.

LAURA HAWKINS GREVEL 〜 *Leaving Sad Town*

I will call the place Sad Town, Texas, so I do not betray this broken-down collection of buildings and memories on sunburned, bristly ground. In this prickly environment of scrub mesquite, stunted cedar, and cactus, thorny people propagate.

Its history is haunted by rattling bones and hardships: Indians, and settlers pushing them out. Comanche raids. After the Civil War, two gangs of white men fought over land, money, and power. From the 1920s to the 1940s, the town boomed: two grocery stores, two movie theaters, a train station, a school. Ranchers raised sheep and goats. But the young left for bigger cities, ranching income declined, and an itinerant hunting population came and went. As the 1990s approached, families escaping the problems of the big cities, fleeing suburbs but trying to re-establish suburban ideals, transplanted themselves among the old ones.

Women and religion held them together, and women and religion kept them divided. In this Sad Town of 214 souls stood the crumbling stone Methodist Church; the newer, boxlike Church of Christ; and the newest, the Baptist Church, under the welcome shade of three or four oak trees. Somewhere in private, the Primitive Baptists met. Twenty miles in one direction stood the Lutheran Church in Germantown; twenty miles in the other direction, in Anglo-Saxon Town, was the Big First Baptist Church, whose members surrounded a tiny colony of mostly Hispanic Catholics, who kept very quiet and just survived.

Today in Sad Town, there is not much other than churches. Some once-fine houses have surrendered to dilapidation, poverty, and apathy. The domino parlor is an unpainted shack with holes cut for windows and doors; the mayor, bless him, mows the lawn regularly. The shack faces a collapsing train station. A relic of the merchant district, late-1800s limestone, is half torn down, the portion still standing labeled DOWNTOWN GROCERY and AUTO PARTS. The latter is always closed; the former has rotting floors, and milk, eggs, and candy bars for sale. The customers appear tipsy on cigarettes and Cokes in this "dry" Texas county. A hardware store labeled with a GUNS sign is seedy-looking, fenced-in, and guarded by goats.

The new main business in this town and county is foster kids, shipped in from big cities and reflecting their ethnic mix. Foster kids outnumber local kids, so the little school has become overwhelmed by these children with problems. The county newspaper reports each week how many times the sheriff assisted Child Protective Services or made a drug raid.

The newspaper also reports how many persons who didn't look white and American enough were escorted to the county line. That's what Sad County wants. I am not from Sad County; I am part Comanche but also a sixth-generation Texas whiteblood. My husband is a foreigner, from Germany. Together, we tried to tame our beloved little ranch for eight years. We planned to stay forever. But it wasn't the scratchy land or the increasing heat and drought that eventually broke us; it was the people. Friends died; friends turned against us.

Our friends: Shall I begin with Josepha or Sevra Lee or LeeRoy Ann or Cheri or Beth? Sevra Lee had been here the longest—fifty years. "We're new

here," she said, "not from here. The locals never let you forget that." Which is why she and her family had built a newer, independent Baptist Church in Anglo-Saxon Town to end their oppression within the Big First Baptist Church. Sevra Lee and her house-builder-turned-unconventional-buggy-builder husband welcomed us. We enjoyed her bubbly laugh and practical know-how. Four kids raised, no alcohol drunk, lunch on the table at noon. She was diagnosed with stomach cancer not six months after they'd become our closest local friends. We visited frequently, learned to keep company the old way, felt her pain, and attended the funeral with the rest of the county.

Josepha was German, Catholic, and a refugee from what is now Poland. During World War II, at age sixteen, she married a nineteen-year-old American soldier. She was shocked at the ugliness of her new Texas world—many buildings cheap and impermanent, her husband's childhood home a shack with the wind blowing through the holes. They settled in Sad Town after retirement, and Josepha tortured them both for seventeen years with her constant urge to move away. She told us about knife fights after the bingo games, drugs and rapes in the school. She and her husband became hermits. But she liked us, nicknamed us the "Health Apostles" because of our healthy homegrown food. She enjoyed speaking her native tongue with my husband; she liked that we were Catholic and Lutheran. She called intermittently, even after the brain tumor was found and she began to bloat with water and not speak lucidly. Her husband had to lift her everywhere; her pretty face was no longer identifiable. But she was kind to the last. We attended the rosary with a few family and friends.

The devout and bewildered LeeRoy Ann and her adolescent children were sent to us because they were interested in fresh milk and food grown without pesticides and chemical fertilizers. They were escapees from urban sin and on welfare—the government's and the local Church of Christ's. She and the three unruly kids lived in their newly purchased A-frame without air conditioning through that last summer of 100 to 113 degrees. They needed help and looked up to us, though we had no standing. But we did have food. So we gave them extra vegetables and eggs and milk and advice. They gave us respect. Just before we moved away, we attended the fifteen-year-old daughter's wedding to a seventeen-year-old boy; the pastor made them and everybody present promise never to let them divorce. We gave LeeRoy Ann our flock of fine Buff Orpington laying hens: our last view was of a pickup truck loaded with our portable chicken house and chickens sailing down the road with feathers, dust, and straw flying.

And then there was Cheri. She and her family were business people, following her husband's dream of escaping the city. They kept quiet about their old urban habits of parties and dancing and drinking, wanting to fit in. They lived in Sad Town, worked in Anglo-Saxon Town, and attended

Big First Baptist Church. She was from a wealthy family; he was a cow-boy. She wanted to re-create suburbia, except they believed in nonsubur-ban breastfeeding and midwives and homeschooling; the town considered such beliefs dangerous, witchcraft. They seemed extremely friendly to us, as we were also advocates of midwives and all. But, like the old locals who would tell a flathead joke and wouldn't admit that their grandfather was German, Cheri and her husband looked askance at my husband's foreign-ness, at our goal of a self-sustaining farm and our Amish-style farming with horses. Perhaps to ambitious, suburban want-to-fit-ins, it was all too unfamiliar: our string of college degrees, our walls of books, our giving up lucrative professional careers, our lack of pursuit of the holy dollar, not car-ing how we fit in. Our big mouths. And then our baby son, born so healthy and whole at home with a midwife, began to lose weight. And through my neurosis and arrogance about how to nurse a baby, and by ignoring my husband's advice, I got us into trouble.

Cheri came one day to visit. (To snoop?) And here came my husband, sweat-drenched from a 108-degree day's fence-building work. Cheri said, "Speak of the devil now." I humored her. She said, "Take that skinny baby to the doctor." I told her I had. She said, "Take him again. Something is wrong." And I did. But it wasn't enough. She reported us to the doctor and to Child Protective Services (CPS), who came, with support from the local sheriff. We were part of the sheriff's main business, oversight of childcare both foster and local. Our nightmare had just begun.

We spent a year having everyone watch our every fart, a year of praying constantly, a year I listened carefully, desperately, and gratefully to my hus-band's sound advice. A year of fear. Of wondering whether without our white skins, our five college degrees and middle-class status, we might lose our kids. We lost our independence and our sense of humor.

We heard from others in Sad County who'd had similar CPS experi-ences. The butcher's mother: "Corky's daughter told the school he had spanked her. For years, CPS was in their hair. The kids are wild now—the parents have no rights and no control." The lay preacher: "Yeah, we had our trouble with those people, too. It took a long time and a lot of lawyers for them to leave us in peace." The county judge: "There aren't a lot of free-doms left in this country."

And then there was Beth, also a recent transplant. She grew up on her family's ranch. She knew there was something good and basic in rural peo-ple and lifestyles. She gave us friendship, support, and privacy. She home-schooled her three kids. Her family didn't have much stake in the com-munity: her husband commuted far away to a job in the Big City. They attended the small Baptist Church in Sad Town. Beth was with us the eve-ning the heavyset, six-foot-four CPS man marched in and threatened to take our son: "I have a report you're only feeding that kid breast milk and

cow's milk. The boy looks pale. He could die any minute. I'm taking that kid to the hospital."

Beth said, "No, he's darker than his sister. See, she's very fair." And she calmed my angry husband and the big, wild-eyed CPS man. She said, "These are good people. They really care about their kids. They've been to the doctor; he said to feed the baby cow's milk and breast milk. The baby's only three months old." Finally, we were allowed to escort our son to the hospital with the CPS man. Beth baby-sat our two-year-old daughter while we waited all that terrifying night for the doctor to come and tests to be performed.

Beth said that the CPS experience upset her, too. She always feared a neighbor would report her if they saw one of her homeschooled kids outside on a school day. She was very supportive. However, a year later, Beth's husband, a former military man, seemed to be keeping his family away from us. When we asked him why, he said, "As long as you aren't building bombs or something." Beth seemed embarrassed and apologetic. I wrote them a letter saying we were sorry our friendship was dying.

It became increasingly clear to us that we were living in the wrong place. We sold our ranch and moved away. Now, four thousand miles distant, we're still farming with horses and trying to be gentle on the land, and we're grateful for our beautiful family. Beth brought us back into friendship with her family and writes faithfully.

I cry when I see pictures from that life where we were so hopeful, so idealistic, where we worked and dreamed. But I see now that we were providentially kicked out of Sad Town and given a peaceful home place in Europe before September 11, 2001. What happened in Sad Town now seems to me a premonition. I have lost my innocence; so has my country.

JANET E. GRAEBNER ✑ *Silent Renewal*

Our mountain community has a yoga studio, where I attend weekly classes. This respite was imperative after the terrorist attacks of September 11, 2001. Our minds, bodies, and spirits were quietly refreshed and energized as we flowed silently from posture to posture, our focus centered on calming the nervous tremors of our emotions that had been wounded by the heretofore unthinkable: a foreign terrorist attack on U.S. soil.

There was a sense of unity at the studio—like a choreography or a meditation—that I privately began to call the community of silence.

Unity. Comm*unity*. Of course! With the practice of yoga comes mental clarity.

Unity: the quality or state of not being multiple: *oneness;* a condition of harmony: *accord;* a combination or ordering of parts in a literary or artistic

production that constitutes a whole or prompts an undivided effect, according to my dictionary.

I like Rabbi Jonathan Sacks's image "that we are sentences in the story of our people, but that there are other stories, each written by God out of the letters of lives bound in community."

Which brings me to today, the one-year anniversary of September 11. As I write this, I'm reminded of Hartley Burr Alexander's words in *The World's Rim:* "What *must* men think in order to be human at all, and what in the constitution of nature and the world can inspire or validate this human thinking?"

This is, perhaps, the most important question that one anywhere can consider, and it includes, I think, a universal concept of community that reveals its ambiguity.

September 11 forced us to recognize that *community*—a word with a positive connotation, usually—has a dual nature and can also refer to an organization or group of individuals whose mutual purpose is directed toward a negative end.

Now when I'm at the yoga studio, surrounded by others in a community of silence, I think of those sentences that we all are, everywhere, and how the letters of lives bound together in community write such different stories.

FAYE EGGERT 🌿 *More Alike Than Different*

When I became involved with United Church Women in Casper, Wyoming, I got acquainted with several ladies from Grace African Methodist Episcopal Church. The year I was president, I went to Rawlins for the state convention, and our treasurer, Mildred Ewing, went with me. Mildred and her husband were live-in servants of a wealthy family. She was the housekeeper, and her husband took care of the grounds. In everything except education, I expect Mildred was my superior. She was more of a born leader, was friendlier and more outspoken. She was prettier and for sure, even in her employer's wife's castoff clothes, better dressed than I was.

The custom in those days was for churchwomen to stay in local homes as guests instead of going to motels. When Mildred and I showed up on the doorstep of the assigned home, the woman looked at us askance and was visibly embarrassed. She stammered, "I'm sorry. I didn't know—I couldn't have known from your names—I'm awfully sorry, but we just have the one guest room."

We assured her that we would be glad to share the same room. "But there aren't even twin beds . . . just the one double bed." We told her that was fine.

When we were unpacking and hanging up our dresses, Mildred said, "You know, Faye, this will be the first time in my life I ever slept with Whitey."

"Me, too," I replied. "The first time in my life I ever slept with Blackie." And we both laughed.

That night, when we were ready for bed, Mildred knelt on her side of the bed to say her prayers. I was of the persuasion that a person could pray at any time in any position and was in the habit of hopping into bed and saying my prayers in comfort—often, I must admit, drifting off to sleep in the middle of them. But in deference to Mildred, I knelt down on my side of the bed.

It should have been a beautiful and dramatic moment: black and white kneeling on either side of a shared bed, praying to the same God who loved them equally. But the fact was that I felt constricted and uncomfortable. When I finished my prayers, I peeked through my clasped fingers and saw Mildred still bowed low. I closed my eyes again and added a lengthy P.S. When I looked again, she was still at it.

I wouldn't have interrupted Mildred for the world; I was too polite for that. But I thought, *"Heavenly days! Black people are sure long-winded pray-ers!"*

The minutes dragged on and seemed like hours. I felt as though I ought to *do* something. But what? I was getting more and more uncomfortable. My knees ached, and I was getting chilly in my fancy best nightgown.

After what seemed like ages, Mildred finally took the situation sensibly in hand and with a firm "Amen" got into bed. When I turned out the light and followed suit, she said, "What under the sun were you *doing* all that time? I waited and waited. I thought, *White folks sure have a lot more to settle with the Lord than we do!*"

"I finished long since," I answered. "I was waiting for *you* to get through."

We both burst out laughing at our own foolishness. And I realized then that we were more alike than we were different.

LOREE PEERY ✑ *Ongoing Sustenance*

The women came that April of 1975. They straggled into the house one at a time or arrived in a parade of twos or threes. Compassionate smiles and condolences ushered in their offerings of casseroles, sandwiches, desserts, and even cans of coffee.

Most of them were strangers to me but friends of the family. I greeted them at my mother's door. "Please come in," I welcomed, and then I would move my pregnant body back a step or two.

"I'm so sorry about the loss of your father."

"Our hearts go out to your family."

"If there's anything I can do . . ."

"It's all in God's hands."

"Oh, my dear. I'll take that. How close are you?"

I acknowledged their comments with thank-yous and responded to questions about how soon the baby was due. Present in my barrel-shaped body, I stood in my mother's kitchen. But my mind? I didn't know where it was, other than somewhere else.

A baby boy nestled in my womb—I was sure of it. He rode low and heavy and protruded straight out in front. Those were the days before ultrasounds, but I knew. And his middle name would be William, the same as my husband's name and my father's middle name.

My father, whose crooked smile I could see only in my mind's eye, no longer lived. I often stopped mid-task, imagining his body dumped in the ditch a couple of hundred feet from the country driveway. The words "murder" and "unsolved homicide" came later.

For now, the small Orchard, Nebraska, community was in shock. The town had its share of men who closed out the tavern, but none before Dad had been killed on his way home.

Women flowed through the kitchen to give of themselves to my mother and brothers and sister and me, just as the lifeblood flowed through my body to my babe. And the women kept coming: from St. Peter's Lutheran Church, from farms in the Orchard area, and from the farms of my Neligh childhood. Those women I knew—like Marcella Hughes and Lucile Back-huus—whom Mom had supported after they lost their sons.

Later, during a quiet moment in my mother's kitchen, I reflected that I hadn't spent much time there. Mom and Dad had moved from the Neligh farm the year after I graduated and left home. Now I felt as though I was a totally different person from the teen I had been eleven years before. In 1964, neighbors had come, rumbling in from east and west, bringing trucks, tractors, and cutters, to chop Dad's corn into silage while he recuperated from back surgery. Those men brought in the bounty from the fields; the women provided sustenance, feeding their husbands and sons and neighbors, just as the chopped grain would sustain our milk cows through the upcoming winter months. On that day, I had been somewhere else, doing what teenagers do.

The women came yet a third time, following my mother's death in August 1978. Through my mother's kitchen they streamed again. I tried to appear present, but still my mind was preoccupied, tuned in for the cry of my three-week-old daughter, Chantell.

My sister, Renée, and I had grown closer during the three years between the deaths of our parents. We were growing stronger as women and in the bond we both have with the One who gives us strength.

Our closeness was cemented when I became one of the women who reached out. I arrived at Renée's home after a concrete truck ran over her only son, Stanley, while he was riding his bike. I could see right away that my sister was somewhere else, as I had been back in the seventies. I received her friends and neighbors as they brought outpourings of love through her front door.

MARY ALICE HAUG ✑ *Tapestry Woven of Stories*

"Look at this. Just look at this," my mother demanded, waving a newspaper clipping under my nose. "Read it," she said.

It was an obituary for a woman named Ethel. "Who is she, Mother? Am I supposed to know her?" I asked.

My mother shot me the look, and I was five years old again and shrinking. Meanwhile, my frail mother, eighty-four and five feet tall, seemed to tower over me, impatient and imposing.

"That's Ethel, and you *do* know her," she said. "You ate lunch with her one day. Surely you remember her; she pounded the table when she wanted her food."

Oh, Patty the Pounder, I thought, remembering how I had laughed when I described her to my husband at supper that evening. I had lunched with Ethel one May afternoon at the assisted living facility, my mother's new home following a string of serious health problems. Although Ethel's name had escaped me, I remembered how she had sat across the table, a small woman whose spine had settled so deeply into her hips that her face was level with the tabletop, her pinched nose at the table's edge. Her hair was permed in pencil-thin curls and tinted that curious shade many elderly women favor, not quite beige or pink, like the last leaf clinging to the branch of a November cottonwood. Ethel stared for several minutes at her coffee cup before she raised a gnarled, speckled hand and reached across the polka dot oilcloth for her coffee. She brought the cup to her lips in a precise motion, more like a salute really, placed the cup back on its saucer, and then began to pound the table, still staring straight ahead.

As Ethel pounded, I looked around the room, hating the attention this crazy old woman was attracting. My mother, undisturbed, leaned over and murmured, "Do you want your roll, Ethel?" She continued to whisper while she buttered the roll and put it on Ethel's plate. Ethel stopped pounding, picked up the roll, bit and chewed, still staring across the room.

The obituary I read described a woman I wouldn't have recognized from that day's lunch. Ethel had studied nursing in the 1930s, earned her stripes, and gone to work at a regional hospital. During World War II, she had enlisted as a WAC, serving in military hospitals in England and the

States, rising through the ranks during a long career in the Army. In her final years, she had worked at a private hospital, where she had become the head of the cardiac unit.

"Why did she move here, Mother?" I asked. "Where is her family?"

Irritated at herself for her ignorance, Mother shook her head. "I don't know. But she was more than just a silly old woman pounding the table. Just look at what she did during her life, and nobody around here knew it. We need to know these things about each other."

Later that night, I thought of the difficult adjustment my mother had made in moving to the assisted living facility two hundred miles east of the county where she had lived for more than eighty years.

I recalled our conversation shortly after she moved in. "You know," she said, "as hard as it was to leave my house and to have to give away so many of my things, that's not the hardest part about living here. The hardest thing is that nobody here knows anything about Lyman County, where I grew up, where your dad and I farmed, who my children and my family are. They don't know any of the important things about me."

What they didn't know, she meant, was her story.

Story is important in small, rural communities like my hometown. Where I grew up, we came to know one another by knowing the particulars of others' lives. As an insecure, self-absorbed adolescent, I resented living where people knew so much about me and imagined their gossip on Saturday afternoons as I walked down Main Street to the Ben Franklin Five and Dime. I could see the faces of several women sitting at the front window of the Rainbow Café drinking coffee and supposed they were saying, "There goes the youngest Woster girl, the chunky one. Do you remember when she and that Smith kid shot out all the streetlights on Main Street? I hope her parents made her pay for the damage because she needs to learn a lesson."

Even in my own home, I couldn't escape gossip. I'd come home from school with my friends to find our mothers gathered around our shiny chrome kitchen table, hands folded around yellow coffee mugs, shoulders touching as they leaned across the table to whisper their news. My friends and I were irritated with their chatter but shared a healthy respect for their uncanny knowledge. Before the last school bell rang, our mothers already knew we'd been caught passing notes in math class. We'd stand before the kitchen table to face the united front of their disapproval, aware that our crimes would become instructive little parables for other teenagers at supper tables all over town.

On most days, the women talked about their children's grades and minor scrapes with the law. Sometimes, however, I would hear a woman say, "Wait until you hear this," and it seemed to me the conversation became more malicious, more focused on some sad or sordid tale about men who

drank or couples who played parlor games in the bedroom. I'd detect a sense of urgency, which I believed came from a perverse satisfaction in being the first to know and to tell the unfortunate story.

My epiphany came the spring a tragedy touched our lives, a story so sad that it haunted us all for years.

The story went like this: One quiet, lazy Saturday morning, the second son of one of my parents' close friends, a small, dark-haired, teenage boy with intense brown eyes and a quick, rebellious mind, walked through his parents' new house, room by room, floor by floor, dousing the furniture, the carpet, and the curtains with gasoline. He struck a match and ignited the living room sofa, then fled like a wounded animal to the bluffs of the Missouri River, the flames glowing behind him as he ran.

That afternoon, I listened as my mother and her friends gathered around our kitchen table to discuss the event. They spoke in low, urgent voices, recounting how the searchers found the troubled boy shivering and babbling in a grove of cedar trees above the river, how the father wept uncontrollably as he watched the flames, and how the mother stood apart from the crowd, arms clutched around her stomach, refusing the blankets and coffee offered her. As I listened to them tell the story, I sensed that the urgency in their voices was somehow different from that I heard when I suspected the women of harboring a secret, guilty pleasure in recounting someone else's troubles. That day, their storytelling seemed to be filled with compassion, understanding, and empathy, and I puzzled over the change in tone.

As I consider it now, I think these women needed to retell the particulars of this story, as if somehow in the retelling, they might comprehend a tragedy otherwise incomprehensible. In the same way, our entire community needed to tell and to hear this story in order to absorb its horrific impact. We needed to draw the suffering of our neighbors into our lives and to claim their pain before we could begin to heal as individuals and as community, before we could help our neighbors rebuild their home and their lives. For it is story that enables us to immerse ourselves in other people's lives and experiences; to participate fully as a member of a community; and to communicate, to teach, to learn, and to heal.

No wonder, then, that my mother felt so keenly the loss of story in her new home. All her life, she had lived in a community where others knew her intimately because they knew her story. She had felt the security and the connectedness of being part of a small, familiar circle of storytellers. One of the most tragic circumstances for the elderly may be that in their final years, when they desperately need to maintain their personal dignity, to be identified through their individual stories, and to be comforted by known stories and storytellers, they are denied this basic life-affirming need. Instead, they are moved into dormitory-like facilities that a friend calls "warehouses for the elderly," where they are surrounded by strangers.

And then they are chastised for failing to make a successful transition into this new and final community.

My mother felt disconnected as she walked down the corridor of the care facility, but I was not. I knew the women looking out the café window as well as the women gathered around my mother's kitchen table; they gave me identity because they knew my story. By sharing the most mundane details of my life, they drew me into their own lives and thus secured my place in the community. And so I have come to consider their presence in my life a blessing. I treasure the connections created by story, the loom on which we weave our lives in a rich and deeply textured tapestry we call community.

PHYLLIS M. LETELLIER ✐ *Your Sister's Keeper*

One day, I visited a friend in a nearby town to deliver pieces of plastic foam I thought might solve her problem. At the time, "Jane" was a fifty-ish single lady with no family near at hand. She was used to taking care of herself until she suffered a badly broken leg in a fall at work a few weeks before. She couldn't put any weight on the leg for at least five more weeks. The doctor had put a different kind of splint on it, and now it was hurting. She thought that she could buffer the bad spot if she had the right material.

I found that she was allowing herself to be helped by friends and neighbors with much more grace than I expected, all the while worrying about a little old lady with no family for whom she held power of attorney. From her recliner, Jane had dealt with doctors, nurses, the state social work bureaucracy, and the little old lady herself—let's call her Miss M.—by phone, all to sort out the finances of a recent move to a nursing home, made necessary by failing mental and physical health.

Jane was planning, crutches and all, to tackle boxing up Miss M.'s remaining possessions the next day.

I came away with a thought: The system works when you let it. If you're willing to be your sister's keeper, to accept aid when you need it, and to offer help when it is your responsibility—woman to woman—small-town life goes on with hardly a ripple.

EDITH RYLANDER ✐ *Ghost Dance II*

Tucson to Albuquerque. Beehive ovens at Isleta Pueblo.
Quick flash of antelope running New Mexico grassland.

Beginning to hunger
For homegrown vegetables;

For leafless basswoods,
For round glacial hills.

Flat Oklahoma panhandle, field after plowed field;
Kansas plains, mile on mile of stockyards, beef cattle
Knee-deep in their own dung. Waves of stench
Gag us as we drive.

Beginning to hunger
For the steely blue
Of small lakes
Rimmed with russet cattails,
For the place
Where we dug in to stay.
For the woodstove talking,
For the first snow.

In the parking lot of The Land Institute, Salina, Kansas,
A bumper sticker: "Dance back the buffalo,
Sing back the swan."
Earnest interns. Eighty-five acres of remnant prairie,
Serving as a site for ecological research
Experiments in large-scale perennial polyculture.

Meaning, many beings all growing together,
None dominating, none claiming God as its warrant,
None demanding all the sun,
None wearing out the soil, growing in beauty
Till the next ice age and then adapting—
(Dance back the big bluestem grass, dance
The dams down, the toxic dumps away—)

It is not easy.
Wovoka and Black Elk
Did that dance long ago.
What good did it do them?
How shall we dance that dance,
Knowing the things we know,
Paying the debts we pay?

Two people, half of two lives, trying to go
In a good way. To find at least
The beginnings of a better way. To turn

From rape and ruin, snatch and bank it, fuck and flee,
To dance the two-step, swapping leads; to dance
All the green world together, holding
The Great Mother's hands—

It is not easy.

Take the road for home.

MICHELLE M. SAUER ✑ **Feeling North Dakota
and Looking California**

I'm a native North Dakotan, and I love my home state. Yep—barren plains, windswept prairies, treeless expanses, snowy fields—love 'em.

But as much as I love my home state, I've often felt like an outsider here. I've been too smart, too young, too short, too dark, too plump, too mouthy, too aware. More recently, I've been too alternative, too radical, and too aggressive. As an example, the title of this essay was inspired by lyrics from the Soundgarden song "Outshined" on the album *Badmotorfinger*, produced by A&M Records in 1991: "I'm looking California / And feeling Minnesota." Let's face it: I stick out among tall, strapping, blond Scandinavians.

You see, I'm an invisible minority in my home state. And I'm not just talking about racial or ethnic identity, although I have that issue, too. I'm Asian in a state without any Asians. I happen to be half Pakistani, although most people assume I'm Hispanic. But I'm just as much of a minority because of who I am. I question authority. I welcome and celebrate difference. I enjoy Industrial Goth bands. I'm not the average Fargo product.

But I digress. Of all the communities I belong to, the one that has shaped me the most, whether I want to admit it or not, is my family, which just happens to be all female. They've been described by a [male] colleague as "hard smokin' Dakota women." Perhaps. Dakota women, though, can pick up a bale and chuck it. They work with crops and cattle. They work with the hurt and the hungry. They are bankers, lawyers, farmers, doctors, nurses, teachers, dentists.

None of the women in my family married. This was by choice, you understand. From them, I learned self-reliance, independence, strength, and assertiveness. Anything that needs to be done, I can do, or arrange to get done. I speak when I need to. From them, I learned about my faith, about my culture, about my talents. I pray when I need to. I don't require people's approval, assistance, or advice.

From them I learned to be me. They'd be shocked. I'm a radical, they

think, teetering on the edge. They don't see that I took their examples and became who I am today: fiercely committed to gender equality and social tolerance; happily married to a supportive egalitarian; tenacious and assertive (maybe sometimes aggressive) in the face of ignorance and opposition; doggedly North Dakotan. I wonder, when they see the person I am today—eclectic, intelligent, ambitious—do they see themselves in me?

EMILIE HOPPE ✒ *Things I Would Not Miss*

In 1855, my great-great-grandparents were among the fifteen hundred German Christians to build what they called the Amana Society along the Iowa River in Iowa. They pooled their resources and purchased more than twenty-six thousand acres of farm and timber land. Holding all property in common, they made textile weaving and farming their chief means of support, living communally until 1932. Today the original tract of land is protected by the 1932 compact. Although we no longer live in a formal communal setting, we have joint ownership of the land and the other Amana Society businesses. Descendants of the original settlers, and those who came to own stock through purchase or inheritance, are members of this joint-stock corporation. A board of directors, elected by their stock-owning relatives, neighbors, and friends, oversees the corporation. The original Amana Church still thrives; there members meet to pray, read the Bible, sing hymns, and listen to the words of men and women inspired by the Holy Spirit to speak, just as they did when the church was founded in 1714.

The non-community-owned property—the private homes and small businesses that come up for sale here—are bought by folks who generally wish to commute to Iowa City or Cedar Rapids, or to open a tourist-oriented business. Some become discouraged after a year or two because this small place of ours, seven tiny villages, is no city. It's no theme park. Amana would be "perfect," I was told by a new resident, if only it had a Starbucks; a supermarket; well, maybe a mall; and a water park, too. I wondered what she meant by "perfect."

Those who stay and prosper are the ones who come to cherish Amana for what it is. They join in, take part, and help out. I am grateful to them for saving our old homes and our traditions; sometimes they are more likely to fight for preservation than the people who have lived here all their lives.

Those who come to love it here do so not because Amana can provide them with a livelihood, but because Amana can help them build a life. Other than the few years I was away at school, I have lived in Amana always. Here are some things I have come to feel and to know about community.

Community means you are there when the neighbor kid spills a bike on the gravel at the end of your driveway, and you are there when they bury

your neighbor in the cemetery at the edge of town. On one occasion you offer Band-Aids, and on the other occasion you offer prayers; in both situations you are glad to help but very sorry to have to stand by and witness the suffering.

So many people I know have left the little towns where they were born because they could not stand to watch the suffering. They could not stand to watch their parents grow old, to cart their folks' laundry and junk mail to the nursing home, to visit their elderly aunts and uncles, to watch their high school friends divorce or lose jobs, their sweethearts grow old, their town wear down. So they come back only for the funerals.

Yes, they have good reason to leave. Better wages. Better jobs. I do not blame them. And there are moments when I blame myself for staying, although the truth is, I cannot leave. There is too much that I would miss, including the exquisite pain and the blooming joy of staying in one place so long you feel rooted to the earth like a morning glory.

When you stay, you get to meet and get to know the babies born and given names you thought were long gone. Here now again is one Harry Zuber, in sixth grade, celebrated in the newspaper for having hit a home run for his Little League team. Harry Zuber, great-grandson of my grandfather Harry Zuber, who died in 1982. Another Harry. Another Edgar. Another Anna, John, or Katie to carry on.

Staying, you get to watch all the miracles unfold. The lilac twig you planted in 1987 grows so lush that its scent drifts heavenward each spring. The house on the corner that no one loved is suddenly reborn with an owner who restores its stone foundation and clapboard siding. The garden your grandmother planted is now someone's backyard, with two swing sets and a sandbox. The old town park, which used to be little more than a meadow really, now has three soccer fields and a bandstand, bustling most weekends with ball games and parties.

You get to sit in the auditorium at the high school graduation and congratulate the graduates, happy that they are going to colleges you know by reputation or the university you attended. I have been delighted to see them at my doorstep selling popcorn for Cub Scouts or raffle tickets for the band, or at the drive-in selling ice-cream cones. I have been delighted to see them all their lives, and now I am thrilled to see them handed diplomas. I wouldn't miss that for anything.

Nor would I miss mornings at the horse barn, when my daughters and I are feeding our quarter horses and my neighbor leans across the fence (ours is such a little town that our horse pasture is just beyond my neighbor's backyard) and calls to me about the rainfall or his dog's latest escapade. When my daughters do well at the fair or my son does well in soccer, my neighbors congratulate them and me, and we adults share a smile because here before our eyes is another miracle: kids growing up.

I wouldn't miss those chats in the HandiMart (our one convenience

store) or on the sidewalk in front of the church or in the library at school—any of those places where people meet by chance or by appointment. I wouldn't miss the good talks or even the times we argue. I have argued with so many of my neighbors about things such as school bond issues, local politics, the fate of an old building gone to seed, the future path of a bike trail, a dog who slipped his collar and ran through the garden, a misspoken word, a sore point, that I would not want to make a list of all those who have heard me yell. But the fact that I am occasionally allowed to yell and am still called a neighbor, or even a friend, says something, I think. For I can stand in a dark room and speak, and even if they don't see me, those of my community will recognize my voice. To be known so well means that no matter how my physical body changes through time, my friends will always know me by my voice, or even by the memory of my voice.

The history of my community *is* community. My grandparents and great-grandparents were members of the Amana Society, one of the largest, longest-lived communal groups active in nineteenth- and twentieth-century America. From 1855 until 1932 here in Iowa, the Amana people lived communally, sharing the land, sharing the housing and food. In 1932, in the face of America's worst economic disaster, the community, sixteen hundred people, dismantled nearly a hundred years of communal tradition and started again. Spang in the middle of an economic depression, they started over, reinventing themselves as a different kind of community. They got rid of some customs, adopted new ones, changed their hairstyles and dress, learned to drive cars, talked more English and less German, sent their kids to high school and college, started businesses, and founded a corporation. They kept their church and changed the rest. And they stayed.

When they came here and started this place in 1854, the land was an attraction. The wooded hills that rolled down to broad bottomland, the winding brown mud river, and the rich prairie soil proved an inducement to leave the settled East and move west. But unlike all those pioneers who wanted space to be apart, my forebears wanted space to be together: to worship together in a church of their own; to live and work together. Their definition of freedom involved the complexity of creating a community where more than a thousand men, women, and children could live and work at peace with the world around them. Today much has changed about Amana, but one thing is the same as it was in 1854: there are people here who define personal freedom not by what they are able to buy or to say, but by the simple fact that they are free to make a life for themselves here, among others who have made the same choice.

Each person is a member of this community by virtue of his or her presence in this space. There is some regard for those who once called this place home and for those who were born to sons and daughters who once called this place home. But blessed be all those who stay or move in and take up the work with zeal. One of the great myths of our age is that community is

something you belong to, not something you work for. It's your community if you are willing to work for it: to man the polls, bake the pies, visit the sick, shovel the walk, sit on the committee, or, best of all, encourage those who do. I have earned the privilege to call this place my community not because I grew up here or because I am raising my children here, but because I work when I am asked to work and speak when I am called upon to speak; because I have prayed, sweated, cried, laughed, and mourned with my neighbors; and because I have dreamed. I have never felt more a part of this place than when standing in the school lunchroom serving chocolate pudding by the spoonful to noisy second graders, flipping pancakes at the annual firemen's breakfast, or filling sandbags at Price Creek levee when the water is rising.

The community membership you value most is the one you earn by serenely accepting or blustering through countless day-to-day situations made holy by the presence of love. The community membership you treasure is the one you exercise when you meet your neighbor at his gate and rejoice with him at the perfect gift of a spring morning, or when you stand with him at the foot of a friend's grave singing an old hymn you both know by heart. You could have left, but you did not want to miss a thing, or to miss being known so well and being loved despite all the community knows about you. So you stayed.

KATHERINE MANN GALEY ✑ *Stretching Friendship*

My husband, Bud Galey, and I always worked on ranches in the Nebraska Sandhills and usually lived about sixty miles from the nearest town. When Bud wanted to move to the lake district close to Gordon, I thought, *Finally, I'll live near a town.* I spread open the map, placing my finger over the biggest concentration of lakes. The small town of Merriman was nearest my finger. Total population: seventy-two.

We accepted a ranch job between Hyannis and Merriman. Leaving Hyannis, we occasionally saw a ranch house, but more often only a sand road gave a clue that humans might be in the area. We saw few trees, fewer antelope, and met three cars in forty miles. In the middle of miles and miles of nowhere, we found a sign proclaiming DEER CREEK RANCH, TWELVE MILES.

I was impressed with the one-car-wide blacktopped road and overlooked the deep chuckholes every twenty feet. We crossed a small stream and passed several lakes and huge hay meadows, just the kind of ranch country we craved. Cows grazed the low, rough bluffs to the sides of the long valley. Deer Creek Ranch, which happened to be the historic U-Cross Ranch we'd read about in Western books, became our home.

Three families lived at the main ranch, two single men in the bunk-

house, and a Japanese cook, Keiko, in an apartment above the cookhouse. Four family homes stood along the blacktop, with three more situated miles apart on wheel-track roads, so each family had the impression of living on its own place. We were happy to find the stock work was done with horses.

Mail was delivered three days a week. We went to town once a month whether we needed groceries or not. Usually, we planned a meal out and attended a movie.

The rest of our socializing was with the ranch families. We might not have become friends in other circumstances. Some of the couples had come from Iowa, some from Wyoming, and several were Nebraskans. Four of the women were young mothers. Two had school-age children who attended a country school with eleven students. Three of us were older, our children in high school, married, or on their own. Our connection was a telephone line.

I talked to one lady by telephone for months before I actually met her. Marie lived at C-Bar on the east side of the ranch. Our husbands seldom worked together, so we met only briefly at the main ranch when our husbands were loading feed or fence posts. We became accustomed to visiting by phone, but I'd have been hard-pressed to describe her.

Quiet Delores lived on the far west ranch and was not particularly well. She was the mother of Lisa, who lived with her husband on the middle place. Delores said little about her family, but we discussed ranch happenings. Her road was impassable in winter because of snow and in summer because of dry sand. Delores and I seldom met, but her husband and mine worked together several times a week, riding horseback over the hills or taking horse teams to feed cattle or check windmills.

I saw more of the younger families, since I lived in the middle of the ranch on a passable road and could baby-sit for the children. Still, most of our conversations took place by phone. Once in a while, we'd all meet for a birthday supper or a card party.

A cowboy minister suggested we form a family Bible study group, and all the wives agreed. Most of the husbands attended, and even the young single guys living in the bunkhouse enjoyed our milestone Bible study of the Book of John.

After a few months, our cowboy minister left for the Bible rodeos in South Dakota, and we found no one to replace him. Besides, it was calving time on the ranch, which left our husbands hardly time to shave, let alone study the Bible.

The women decided to conduct our own Bible study, beginning with Genesis. Each of us would lead, taking turns. When our study books came, we started with, "In the beginning. . . ." We studied all fifty chapters, one chapter a week, with everyone enthusiastically bringing material she found studying before the meeting. We gained in Christian understanding,

learning a great deal from the study guide linking the Old and New Testaments.

Today, twelve years later, whenever I meet one of those women, we still talk of the study group. We might have wasted our time in bickering and jealousy, miles from the nearest mall, but instead we stretched ourselves, creating trust and friendship. The families joined Bud and me to celebrate our thirty-fifth wedding anniversary, a day made more special because my husband was losing his battle with cancer. Bringing old friends together was a satisfying milestone, an ending to our ranch years.

MARY LODE *Alone, Not Lonely*

I am part of a community in the sense that I help produce the food these people eat and do business in town to help keep it rolling financially. I cannot say that I've never wanted to be a bigger part, but it was just too awkward. One of my best friends is much like me and isn't involved in the social scene. I know a few others as well. We are not lonely; we just live as part of a community without belonging.

On the first warm, bright day after two solid weeks of freezing sleet and slush, I took advantage of the break for a quick trip to town to pay bills and such. I was born and spent a greater part of my life in the area of this small Montana town. The sidewalks were busy with folks in spring fashions and high spirits, having a word or two at every encounter. I wondered what they talked about.

I pulled up to the post office, where two familiar-looking women were visiting. I could not remember their names. As I approached, I overheard Pink and Green Floral Dress finish with, "And she was wearing the smartest shoes!" Crimson Blazer with Matching Accessories was ready for an equally enthusiastic reply when they caught sight of me. I smiled tentatively. Pink and Green's eyes slid away, and Crimson's returned smile looked more like a grimace as I passed by. The glass doors of the post office reflected my image back at me—faded T-shirt, worn baggy jeans tucked into the tops of rubber barn boots. The boots still held traces of the morning's chores. I shrugged and went about my business, thinking my boots were the smartest.

I stopped at the grocery store for some staples and exchanged a friendly "hi" or two with people too caught up in the beauty of the day to realize they didn't know my name or me theirs. It felt so odd when everyone else seemed to know each other.

When I returned home, two black and white Border collies greeted me. I laughed out loud at their exuberance. I felt my muscles relax and wondered when the tension began. Looking around at the uncluttered miles mostly free of people, I felt content.

CONSUELO N. SMITH ✌️ *Tortilla Round*

1950: Consuelo at age eight, three brothers, mother Lola.

Mmmm! Mmmm! Mmmm!

Mama! They're doing it again!

Boys, don't ape your sister.

I can roll my tortilla smaller than any of you!

Cannot! Cannot!

Consuelo, don't tease your brothers. Tommy, your butter is dripping; bend the tortilla like this. Jimmy, don't butter your brother's hand, just the tortilla. Here, let me.

Mama, when you were my age, did Grama Consuelo make tortillas for you and your brothers when it was cold outside?

Let's see, no. When I was eight, I made the tortillas—when it was too cold for us to work the sugar beets.

Sugar beets? Are they like pickled beets?

No, sweetheart, not the beets we pickle, the beets people make sugar out of. It's time to go play in the snow! Let's help the boys get into snow-suits.

1958: Consuelo at sixteen, her grandmother Consuelo.

Mmmm! Grama Consuelo, your tortillas are the best! I think they just might be better than Mama's.

Well, your mama must go to work now, so it's time you learn. Watch. Make the little ball; pat it out with your hands a little. Dip it in the flour, that's right! Now take the *palote* and start in the center; roll forward. Turn and repeat.

But mine isn't round like yours!

It takes time and practice.

I better comb my hair. The girls will be here any minute, and we are going to buzz the Owl.

Buzz . . . ?

Yeah, we drive through the drive-in so the guys can get a good look at us and then follow us around town. Later, Grama. Love you, bye!

But the tortillas . . .

1968: Consuelo at twenty-six, her husband.

I wish this recipe was in English. *Taza* is cup, *manteca* is fat, and *espauda* is baking powder. I should have paid attention. I wish Grama and Mama were here!

Well, they're not, and I'm off. Those cows must be halfway to Kimball in this blizzard. Don't know how we'll find 'em in this. Now don't stand too long. Remember, Junior won't be needing those tortillas until about a year after he is born.

She will be a little Consuelo, and don't forget your gloves! Pat it out. Dip it in the flour. Center, roll forward. Center, roll back.

1978: Consuelo at thirty-six, her children, including little Consuelo.

Mama, can I make tortillas, too?

Sure, Consuelo. Call your brother and sisters, and we'll have a tortilla-making party!

Yeah! Yeah! Guys! Let's make tortillas! Johnny! Stephy! Leigh! Let's have a tortilla-making party!

Boys don't make tortillas!

Now, Johnny, you love to eat tortillas, right?

Yeah.

Then don't you think it would be a good idea to learn how to make tortillas?

Come on, it'll be fun, Johnny. I bet I can do it better than you!

Can not!

Can too!

Consuelo, don't tease your brother! Okay, take a ball, pat it out, like so, and dip it in the flour. Johnny, just the tortilla, not Leigh's braid! Center, roll forward. Turn. Stephy, don't eat the dough, it'll give you a tummy ache.

Mama, look! Mine looks like a cloud! Just like yours!

Very nice, Leigh! Consuelo, always remember, center first.

1999: Consuelo at fifty-seven, her grandson.

Grama Consuelo, why do you like to make tortillas?

Because your great-great-grama Consuelo and your great-grama Lola made tortillas. The tortilla is our family bread. You like to eat tortillas, right?

Yes, but Mama buys them in the store. Why do you make them?

Well, let's see. I like to make tortillas because it reminds me of when I was your age and my brothers and I would eat tortillas as fast as Mama could make them. I like to make tortillas because my grama Consuelo taught me how, and I want to always remember her standing in the kitchen making perfectly round tortillas. And making tortillas reminds me that when your mama was your age, we used to have tortilla-making parties, and your mama, aunts, and uncle called the tortillas "clouds" and would say, "This one looks like a buffalo!" I like to make tortillas because you like to eat tortillas. Look, this one looks like a turkey! Now it's your turn. Take a ball and pat it out like this. Okay, now dip it in the flour, like so. Good! Time to roll! This little rolling pin is called a *palote*. Start in the center and roll forward, then return to the center and roll backward. Very good! Turn the tortilla over and do it all again. Again. Again. Very good!

Look, Grama! My tortilla is round!

MARY SOJOURNER ✌ *Slot Mamas*

We four women are not in a cozy kitchen or around the embers of a late-night campfire. There is no fresh-brewed coffee, no home-baked cookies, no softly glowing crazy-quilt patches in our hands. No Orion shining overhead. And still, we are ancient. Telling stories. Keeping faith.

Each of us has worked all day. It is 7:00 P.M. We are tired, hungry, eager for home and respite. Still, there is almost no place we would rather be than here—sitting on institutional chairs around a battered table, under the chill flicker of fluorescent lights, breathing air a little greasy, a little sweet with the scent of whatever the senior citizens had for their free lunch seven hours ago.

We are here, in the arts and crafts room of the Adult Center, on an icy Flagstaff, Arizona, night, by choice. By bad luck and good. We've been shoved, jolted, dropped, and lifted here by grace we most often did not welcome. And we are telling stories.

A silver-haired woman, elegant and slender as an egret, begins to speak. "I'm Donna," she says, "and I'm a compulsive gambler." We know her story—a good girl from a bad family, ten years of taking care of her drunken dad, her broken mom; ten years of being mom to her four younger brothers and sisters, beginning when she was eight; twenty-five years of taking care of a boy-man husband; a year of knowing exactly where he was while dinner went cold, the weekends alone dragged by, and the hotel at which he was hypothetically attending a trade show had no record of his registration.

We know her story, and we listen as though each word is a revelation. "So," she says, "when I walk into a casino and see there's no one at my favorite machine, I know I'm safe in my own world. For me. Nobody wants anything from me but my money." She grins. "That's a hell of a lot more honest deal than marriage."

Shelly nods. She's an abundant young woman, the divorced mom of three kids since they were six, five, and four. "That being in my own world," she says, "that's what hooked me." She laughs. "It hooked twenty thousand dollars of my hard-earned cash, and a hundred and fifteen thousand bucks from the company I worked for." She laughs again and shoves her probation paper across for somebody to sign. It's a requirement of her probation. Meetings. And checking in every day. And never, ever going back into her "own world" again.

We don't find her laughter odd. We've all laughed the same way. Gallows humor. The sound of the fellowship of those who got caught and are serving time. Hard time. And there is something more. When we laugh about our gambling losses, about five hundred dollars, one hundred thirty-five thousand, and, in my case, thirty thousand, our tired faces come alive. Our eyes sparkle. Our tense jaws relax.

Always, when the laughter dies, we shake our heads ruefully, and the sparkle in our eyes does not fade. If you look closely, you can see the delighted eyes of a little girl, a naughty girl, a girl whose favorite words are, "You're not the boss of me."

All of us—Gloria, whose husband has no idea half their retirement is gone, because "he's such a baby I have to handle the money"; me, who has essentially embezzled exclusively from myself, my time, my future—all of us are "good" girls grown inexorably into "good" women.

We are the women you can count on to take in the lost teenage soul nobody else can stand; bake cookies at five in the morning for the VFW fundraiser; stand in the sleet in a peace demonstration when a president we don't want visits our mountain town. We—Donna, Shelly, Gloria, and I—are the last women in the world you would expect to find on a slot machine seat at 3:00 A.M., happily breathing secondhand smoke, ignoring our neighbors, and, should you interrupt us, snapping, "Hey, I'm not here to talk. And yes, there's nowhere else I'd rather be."

Now it's my turn to tell my story. "I'm Mary," I say, "and I'm a compulsive gambler." I take a deep breath. I hate saying those words, because every time I do, I know my smoky 3:00 A.M.'s drift farther and farther away. The other women wait quietly.

"What hurts the most," I say, "is remembering how it feels to walk across a scorching Nevada casino parking lot, push open the smoked glass doors into the Belle, and walk into a cool neon rainbow. I look at the slot machines, and I see an infinity of possibilities. It's just like Xmas morning."

I stop. I feel tears starting to form, not so much in my eyes, but deeper within. My throat. My belly. "And Xmas morning," I say, "was the only guaranteed four hours of safety in my childhood."

I hold back the tears. Every other woman nods. And then I say the hardest words, the ones that open out into a slow, quiet stream of tears. "I can't stand to give that up. And I can't do it without you."

DOROTHY BLACKCROW MACK
Crone Circle: Grandmothers Giving Wisdom

I love being a Crone. I even give speeches titled "Please Call Me an Old Hag." *Crone,* according to Barbara Walker's *The Crone,* means "crowned one," and *hag* in Greek means "sacred." Knowing this, who wouldn't want to be a Crone?

When I fill out forms, I don't mark single (though I am), married (though I have been, twice), divorced (though I have been, twice), or head of household (though I am, since I live with a cat). I make and mark another box: free Crone.

So what if our youth-worshiping society has written us off as decrepit and powerless. Because we're invisible, we can do anything, and no one will notice. Not only can we wear purple, we can wear orange stripes with polka dots, or nothing at all. We don't have to blue our hair; we can wear it long or shave it off. We can be outrageous, go places alone, do what we've always wanted to do.

But often we don't. For it's hard to believe the opposite of what we've been spoon-fed for years. It helps to be surrounded by others who have chucked off such narrow notions. Crone Circles can strengthen us, help us reclaim our rightful roles in society. Crones were once midwives of birth and death, and leaders of puberty, marriage, and other ceremonies honoring fecundity and life. We are the anchors, watchers, guardians, healers, storytellers. We are roots, tree, mountain. We are the web of the world.

But how can we find one another? We're not likely to find companions in bars, churches, bridge clubs, or senior centers, or inside the covers of the AARP magazine. I found my Crone Circle, *Si Taeweksin*—Grandmothers Giving Wisdom—by belonging to the Red Cedar Circle, which practices the Sisiwis, or Sacred Breath, tradition of the Pacific Northwest Coast. Native women have always been leaders and healers, whose songs and ceremonies have survived for thousands of years.

We began Si Taeweksin with several different purposes: to find role models for menopause, and support and renewal in other forms. And for fun. We meet quarterly, sharing leadership, each bringing insights from our talents and gifts. We wear loose caftans for comfort, cook and eat luscious meals, talk and pray and sing together. After a lifetime of being ordered around by parents, husbands, children, and bosses, it's relaxing to have no set leader. The hostess usually convenes the circle and may set a topic.

In the Crone Circle, each person contributes ideas and gifts. We've made our own crowns and worn them in a Croning Ceremony, anointed one another with Crone Oil, and fashioned Crone images from clay. We've painted our dreams and visions and shared stories. We've tried cradling—wrapping a woman in a blanket so that many hands can gently rock her—to find security and love. We've played a hilarious game called Midlife Crisis, like Monopoly without a Boardwalk. We've done Tai Chi, Qui Jong, and Sisiwis spring dancing circles. We've bathed in the ocean, in hot springs, and in mountain streams. We've taken sweat together and held healing circles, brushing off and lighting up one another with ferns and candles.

We've also explored ancient sites on weekend trips. We visited Oregon's Hug Point to honor the return of the salmon and become connected with the ocean, the earth, the red cave, the red paint, and the spiral. In Washington, on the cliffs above the Columbia Gorge, we saw the petroglyph *Tsagaglalal*—She Who Watches—and understand that we, too, are guardians.

On our third trip, near Depoe Bay, Oregon, we honored a Crone in a re-naming and rebirthing ceremony. On a secluded point above the ocean, near a sea cave and spouting horn, we covered her and mourned her passing with memories. Then we called her forth by her new name, passing her between our legs and bathing her new body at a nearby secluded beach. In honor of her rebirth, she sponsored a feast and giveaway.

Crones are often called upon to do such honoring work, the natural work of our grandmothers. Others are called to blessing work: house, office, or store blessings, or housecleanings and exorcisms; we even bless hot springs and tubs.

We have so many things to reclaim, so many stories and ideas to share, so little time—yet all the time in the world, six thousand years' worth. We act locally yet think globally. As our world becomes more and more ravaged, we remember that we are the roots, the trees, the mountains, the Rock Grandmas who hold the world together.

STACY GILLETT COYLE ⌇ *United Methodist Fellowship*

In Lost Springs, Council Bluffs, and Marion, echoes
of Almire, Allshire, Herefordshire or Rosenheim, Volga
and Saratov: Blue collects beer cans in the migrant wheat
and spotted rose along the Catholic stretch of the Pilsner
highway, Alberta dries bridge cards in the oven—they will plump
like nervous hens—and Virgie waits with a spade
and her last granddaughter for the moles who only move
in the minutes after sunset.

After everyone has eaten sandwiches of ham and butter
or ham and no butter, Neva confesses praying three Christmases
for a doll or brother, how they kept on coming. The fine-lined
widow filling iced teas bends to say Great-Aunt Mildred
killed herself at thirty-three, heartbroken over a Baptist doctor,
that cousin Lloyd burned to death, playing with matches
in the chicken house. And a woman with lips shaded
like an elephant heart plum recalls my father, black-eyed
and over-mustached, who came in Navy white to eat
dumplings, dense as drywall mud, three pieces of seeping
cherry pie, then begged to sleep on her floor.

Their stories grow incestuous in the fellowship hall
like dateless photos with pinked edges in an inlaid box
or white peonies plopping heavy heads on the granite spires

and keys of the Woodbine cemetery or lines inscribed
then re-inscribed on the flyleaf of a German Bible or a nest wall
or nomadic army ants created by their own sticky legs and bodies.

KAY MARIE PORTERFIELD 🖎 *Beadwork*

I pull the blue plastic chair close to Dad's bed so that when he searches for me with his eyes, I can touch his arm and read to him from his Bible. Only his eyes respond. When their near-transparent lids close again, I pick up my needle and dip it into the plastic container balanced on my lap. I spear the hole of a red cut bead and affix it to the hatband I am making. In time, a pattern emerges beneath my fingers.

This task is tedious, requiring great patience, but not as much as my father's work. Breath by faint breath, he waits for death. As I bead, I think that time must be a thin length of filament like the one in my hands, capable of holding only so many bright and dark moments before it is too full for even one more.

For the most part, the nursing home staff lets us be. Nothing can be done for him except to turn him every few hours to prevent pressure sores and check his vitals. He hasn't eaten for two days and sleeps more than he is awake. "Your father has a strong heart," the nurse's aide, a Lakota woman, tells me as she takes his pulse. His arm is so fragile, it appears weightless, as though the bones are hollow—like bird bones, like beads. When she leaves, head bowed, I continue to slide the beads down the thread, sustaining myself in this dim room with their brilliant color.

As a child, I was bedridden with chronic bronchitis when my father gave me the Genuine Indian Beading Kit. "I thought it would take your mind off your troubles," he said. I did not want a beading kit. How would I know what to do with a genuine Indian beading kit? The closest I had ever been to a genuine Indian was on the cover of my Big Chief tablet or watching Tonto and Princess Summer-Fall-Winter-Spring trapped behind the thick glass of the television set we had purchased the year before. I wanted him to remove the burden of sickness that had kept me confined to my bed for most of two years. He was my father; he owed me that much.

Every night for a week when he came home from his day job, he stopped in my room to ask me if I'd made a belt yet on the bead loom. Each time, I shook my head, knowing I had failed him. My mother finally stored the kit in the back of a closet.

I spent most of my life avoiding beading, until many years later when an Indian friend, desperate to finish a traditional dance outfit in time for a Veterans Day powwow, asked me to help finish it. Out of curiosity, I agreed to give it a try. I hated it.

The beads skittered across the table with a life of their own. They mysteriously changed places on my needle and threw the intricate pattern off. Or the thread broke. Or I tripped over my tray of beads. As I had done when I was an invalid child, I gave up, hiding the loom in the back of my closet.

Months afterward, my widowed father suffered a stroke that destroyed his short-term memory and much of his capacity for logic. I begged him to allow me to move him to South Dakota to live with me, but he refused, insisting on remaining four states away. We couldn't find a live-in caretaker, so he began living in a nursing home, where he frequently forgot not only where he was but also who he was.

I pulled out my beads, and finding a hat like the caps he had worn every working day of his life, I began to decorate it. With each clumsy stitch, I did penance, praying for the return of his mind. When I finished the edging, I wrote his first name across the front, tracing it with white beads. My bargaining was futile. He did not get better.

The hat did become his most prized possession. The nursing home charge nurse called complaining that he insisted on wearing it to bed each night and refused to remove it when they bathed him. A few weeks later, he began wandering the hallways wearing only the hat. There were more calls. He had fallen. He was oppositional. "We can't do anything with him," the nurse said. "We'll have to use restraints."

After fierce, long-distance fighting, I brought him to the prairie to live with me. Through it all, I kept beading. My hands took on a rhythm I did not will. The beadwork seemed to shape itself, demanding its own form and design. I did not know why I made bracelets and necklaces, key chains and earrings, only that I must.

Agitated by his dementia, Dad paced for hours both day and night. Only when I began to bead would he stop to sit at the kitchen table and watch me, mesmerized by the rhythm of my work. "Those beads are very small," he would repeat every few minutes. "You do good work." Soon he began referring to it as *his* beadwork and told everyone who would listen how he had made the key chains. "Those are very small beads," he told visitors. "I do good work."

One morning, I awoke to a commotion coming from the kitchen, only to find him bent over the sink spitting into the basin. Afraid he was sick or having another stroke, I hurried to his side. He held aloft the cake of beeswax I used to keep my thread from tangling. A chunk was missing. "You aren't very good at baking." He picked wax from his teeth. "These cookies taste like crap if you ask me."

The cookies weren't the worst of it. He wandered away from home in the middle of the night and physically fought me when I stopped him. After weeks, I found a nursing home where he settled into a routine. I settled into one as well, visiting him three times a week. Miserable that his mind did not work like he expected, for most of two years he had little to say to

me except for strings of cuss words that seemed permanently lodged in his brain. To survive, I carried my beadwork with me, focusing on it while he cursed at me.

During his three and a half years there, he wore out four more beaded hats. The nursing home workers, most of them Indian women, complimented him on his headgear. Their praise was one of the few things that lifted him from anger and confusion and made him smile.

One day, a nurse's aide stopped me at the end of my visit. "What tribe are you?" she asked.

"I'm not Indian," I responded.

"But your father is." She looked puzzled.

I shook my head.

"I noticed his hat," she said. "When I asked him, he said that, yes, he's sure he's an Indian, he's one of us, but he forgot what kind."

After that exchange, the aides began lavishing him with kindnesses that extended far beyond humoring this member of a lost tribe. Some called him Grandpa and others *Ate*, "father" in Lakota. They stopped in his room on their breaks, spending a few minutes to talk to South Dakota's oldest wannabe, to tease him and make him smile.

There is no smiling now in this overheated, stuffy room, with curtains tightly drawn against the glare of snow outside. Covered by a sheet, my father's gaunt frame lies propped against a row of pillows. The only sounds are his soft breathing and the rhythmic whoosh of the oxygen machine that has helped him breathe for five years. He told me several days ago, when he could still speak, that there is nothing left for him, that he is no longer afraid.

Nothing has prepared me for this. I *am* afraid, but my hand, with a will all its own, moves in time to the steady pumping of the machine. Pick a bead up on the needle. Raise the hand. Push the needle through the bead of the row below. Pull it tight. Pick up another bead. Circling round and round, I cover a piece of cord to decorate a cap that I know my father will not live to wear. I do not miss a beat.

I wish I could take apart the bad patches between us, work backward and dismantle my ungratefulness, his angry words, and the knotted emotions that marked many years of our relationship. I cannot. I remember my childish insistence so long ago, that he was obligated to take the burden of my illness from me, and I wonder if he felt as heartbroken by his helplessness then as I do now about my own.

He sleeps more now, refusing water as well as food. Already I feel a foreboding, dark emptiness waiting in the corner to pounce on me when he takes his final breath. Two yellow beads, one light orange, one dark orange, then red and blue, red again, dark orange—my fingers work their way past

the valley of the shadow to the light part of the pattern, then set it off with the rows of blue as dark as midnight sky. I draw the thread tight, stitch back and forth between the beads, and then cut it, finished. In the hallway outside his room, Sunday school children sing Christmas carols. After a time, two aides stop in to admire the hatband.

That night at home, I gather up all the key chains and earrings and bracelets I've made during the years of sitting beside him at the nursing home, the years of sitting for hours on my own sofa recovering from the wrenching sadness of those visits. The next morning, I begin giving them away to the orderlies, secretaries, cooks, housekeepers, nurses, and aides. "Merry Christmas from my father," I tell them, holding the shoebox so they can choose what they want to remember him by. "These are beautiful," they tell me. "Thank you."

"Don't thank me," I say. "Thank my dad. They're from him." It is true. Without that bead loom so many years ago, without the nursing home vigil, without the desperate need to keep myself from going crazy from the sadness, the box would be empty.

Throughout the morning, the nursing home workers slip into his room to hug him, to kiss his forehead, hot with fever, and to hold his hand as a thank-you for his beadwork. A few even tell him they love him. He is so weak now, he cannot move his arms, but he looks up at the women who stand at his bedside and smiles, eyes brimming with love and tears. They cry. Finally I cry, too.

Three days later, he quietly dies.

Although the hospice nurse, who arrives minutes after this, says that she will ready his body for the funeral home, the nursing home aides gather around his bed and I politely refuse her offer. She persists.

"He is our relative," one of the aides announces then, her obsidian eyes snapping. Slowly, she closes the door, leaving the hospice lady to stand in the hallway alone.

We four remaining women set to work, each dipping a washcloth into the basin of warm soapy water that one of them has brought. We clean him gently as we would a baby, lifting his arms, turning him so that every inch of his flesh, still hot from the fever, smells of soap instead of sickness. As our white hands and brown hands move across his soft, wrinkled skin, I am overwhelmed with gratitude at this pattern of diverse women my father has woven into family. His heart was strong, and he did good work.

LAURIE M. GREIG ✐ *Colorado Ritual*

We four women squeeze into a dirty pickup cab
and wind up the side of Vision Mountain

witness one hundred elk crossing the road
at once left, then right
full moon lights our September tipi
we form a first-time circle
around the fire on earthen floor
and a Cherokee crone guides
our offerings
foot-high crystals stand in east, south, west, north
we stroke a chunk of black meteorite
two hundred years old
and pass the white fossilized antler of a deer
we sing deep belly songs together
burn cedar, sage, sweetgrass,
juniper, tobacco
sprinkle holy water on the dirt under our feet
outside, coyotes call
and wind billows
as the graying smoke rises
through the high flap
sending our prayers for healing
ourselves and the earth
straight away to the stars.

ELLEN VAYO Cowgirl Up, Cupcakes

When housing was in short supply after World War II, my father moved our family into a deserted adobe homestead down the road from my aunt and uncle's farm near Penrose, Colorado. Even though most of the farms in the area had failed, my father, a city boy who couldn't grow moss on the north side of a tree, was confident he would wrest a profit from the land. Dad's reign as a country squire lasted about a month before he took off on one of his misadventures, leaving my mother, brother, and me to fend for ourselves.

Mom was no stranger to the land or to hardship. She knew the unpredictability of farming, and since we had no income, at the age of five I was moved into my aunt's home. While there, I shared the back-porch bedroom with my cousin, Velva, my aunt Ruby's wringer washer, and my uncle John's prized bantam rooster.

I loved the farm, but both Velva and I dreaded Monday mornings. We snuggled under the covers and prayed for chickenpox, prayed to become invisible, prayed the world would end. We prayed for any calamity that would keep us from spending the day at Charities, "doin' for the less

fortunates." For two 5-year-olds who were too young to sew, cook, or do handwork for the needs of others, there wasn't a thing to do at Charities except pick putty out of the windowpanes and hope for a strong wind.

During the summer, Charities was especially hard. The idea of all that sunshine and of us being locked in the basement of a musty church with a bunch of old ladies who clucked their tongues and smelled of "the ointment" was more than our little minds could handle. We begged to be left at home. Whining, we promised not to throw Uncle John's rooster down the two-holer, promised not to ride the pigs, promised not to get into another egg fight or graze Aunt Ruby's salad garden.

When our promises were again ignored, we screamed, cried, and pitched a royal fit by rolling across the floor, banging our heads as we flailed, but Aunt Ruby would not bend. She had wrapped her heart around the idea of caring for those in need and insisted we do the same. "Cowgirl up, cupcakes," she'd say, "the Lord's waitin' with business that needs doin'; 'sides, gotta show up, gotta protect your good name. Mind now, I don't fault them ladies for speakin' what they feel is truth." Aunt Ruby would drop to our level, gather us into her arms, and whisper, "Those old hens'll peck ya to death with their words." She'd quickly justify the Ladies of Charities with, "But be assured, if ya had a need, they'd give ya the paint right off their walls."

With faces scrubbed and hair pulled into tight pigtails, we shuffled along in the wake of Aunt Ruby's ever present horsetail trail of cigarette smoke. Throwing rocks and spitting for new distance records, we sulked past the stench of henhouses, past neighboring farms, wheat fields, rows of yellow sunflowers, and inviting irrigation ditches to the old whitewashed Baptist Church on the hill.

Aunt Ruby, who entered the church only on Mondays for Charities, referred to the structure as the guardian angel of the valley. She loved that church, but preachers were a different story. "Now about preachers," she'd say, "nothin's as stupid as ignorance. Preachers beat folks over the head with nonsense brimstone and di-lute the weight of my Lord's cross with poppycock hellfire."

At exactly 7:00 A.M., the five Ladies of Charities gathered inside the church. The first order of business was to get lunch under way. Aunt Ruby fired up the old Majestic cookstove, while the others chopped, peeled, and sliced veggies and chicken into bubbling pots of soup and kneaded flour and water into bread and something delicious with cinnamon. The scent of baking cinnamon still carries me back to the days of the First Baptist Church and the Ladies of Charities.

While the old Majestic did its magic, and while Velva and I made faces at each other and ate the peeling paint off the walls, the ladies stitched quilts for orphaned babies, crocheted afghans for the elderly, knitted socks

and mufflers for the imprisoned, and put up canned goods for emergencies and for those in need.

In the course of their duties, the Ladies of Charities imprinted our minds with stories of events that came about because of their alms giving. The spinster sisters, Miss Emily and Miss Louise, swore, week after week, that they wouldn't be "knittin' to this day" had they not recognized the socks worn by two convicts who held them hostage after a Cañon City prison break. "One of them old cons was holdin' a kitchen knife not a second from Emily's Adam's apple. Not bein' able to bear the sight of that old knife at my sister's throat, I looked down at the floor. And the next thing I hear is my mouth yellin', 'I knitted that pair of socks on those worthless feet of yours. How dare you be about threatenin' our lives when we gave our time and 'sources for your ingrate comfort.'" As Miss Louise told the story, her sister's head bobbed in agreement. In harmony, the spinsters always ended their tale with, "Had it not been for our work in Charities, we wouldn't be here today. No ma'am, wouldn't be here this day knittin' for another stack of crap ingrates." Velva and I loved the word *crap*. We giggled and tried to be indifferent to Aunt Ruby's glare.

The Ladies of Charities told how their canned goods saw the entire community through "the worst winter in Colorado history," told how (that poor soul) Alta Mae's "out-of-wedlock" baby would have never been adopted had he "not been wrapped in one of Miss Thelma's blue-ribbon, hand-stitched quilts." After each story, the ladies put their work aside, placed their communal hands over their communal hearts, and sighed in perfect accord.

By lunchtime, the aroma of soup coaxed Velva and me away from our putty and peeling paint to join the ladies around the table. Fidgeting, we waited while they set out bowls, prayed, and built a shelter of sisterhood around us that would last a lifetime.

I now understand the significance of my time in that church basement. My life was indelibly marked by the laughter, the bragging, and the humility of those women who offered their Mondays for the good of others. Those women, along with my aunt Ruby, not only showed Velva and me that charity was best stirred in with a soup spoon, but they also taught us how to grasp at our hearts, gasp in unison, and cowgirl up like good little cupcakes.

JEANNE ROGERS ✐ *Re-entry: Homeward Bound*

Gone a week
 or a lifetime, who can tell?
My car eats up the miles

through arid Nevada, Utah salt
headlong into the winds
of Wyoming. And the countdown
begins.

Evanston Rawlins Cheyenne Lusk
I pass a bald eagle, Old Woman Creek
and a sign: SOUVENIRS GALORE: WALL DRUG
Mule Creek Junction Morrisey Road
Deer and sheep graze among the sage
and a sign proclaims:
CALICO CHARACTERS 4-H CLUB ADOPTS A HIGHWAY
Newcastle. Population 3003.

Forty-five miles from home.
Forty-five miles from sisters in prison, halfway houses
 unwed mothers
the alcoholics and addicts
hanging
from every branch of the family tree.

So this is heaven.
Forty-five miles in a car
 alone
singing to the radio
feasting on dill pickle potato chips and diet Coke
as I spin past sage and pine
red buttes and limestone draws
spiraling down on outstretched wings
freewheeling on air, until
once more
I am grounded.

Cambria Sand Creek
Four Corners and Highway 585
Twenty-eight miles from home.

LIESEL SHINEBERG ✐ *Liesel, You're a Good Christian*

I am often asked what it's like to live as a Jew in a non-Jewish community. I
have learned to shrug a lot. Although I want to answer, being objective is
not easy. Everyone seems to know my religion, but I may not know theirs.

Some of my friends are Catholic, some Protestant. I don't think about it unless I am having a dinner party on a Friday and wonder who eats what.

Before I married, I lived in Los Angeles and associated mostly with Jewish young people. When I mentioned a new friend, my parents usually asked, "Is he Jewish?"

Now I realize the question was a means of protecting me. Once, when I dated a nice Christian man, my father explained his fear that in a fit of anger Henry might call me a "dirty Jew!" Since Henry's parents were also upset about our association, we soon broke up. My husband, Edward, who came to Wyoming in 1948 to work in the family business, told a similar story about dating a young Catholic woman here.

In 1951, Edward visited friends in Los Angeles, and a mutual acquaintance arranged our blind date on a Monday night. We saw each other on Tuesday evening, he asked me to marry him on Thursday, we introduced our mothers at a luncheon on Saturday, and he left for Rock Springs, Wyoming, on Sunday. The next month, I visited Rock Springs for a dance sponsored by the Elks Lodge, and five weeks later Ed returned to Los Angeles for our small family wedding. Our parents were highly relieved that we were a nice young Jewish couple. We are now approaching our fifty-second wedding anniversary. Our children married out of our faith but have wonderfully understanding partners and are teaching their children our traditions.

Raising our four children in Rock Springs without a Jewish community became an adventure. We fussed over our Hanukkah celebration, lighting candles for eight days until the menorah was ablaze, but we also exchanged presents. Because the Jewish calendar is based on the twenty-eight-day lunar calendar, Hanukkah almost never coincides with Christmas, and our children sometimes resented not having a Christmas tree. It seemed to me Jesus was closer to sagebrush than to a pine tree, so one day I took the kids to the prairie and found a perfect sagebrush. We dug it up, brought it home, sprayed it white and silver, and decorated it with homemade ornaments. This became a yearly tradition. Our kids shaped Stars of David out of pipe cleaners, dipping them into glue and blue glitter. Every Christmas tree in the neighborhood sported at least one Star of David. Eventually, we let the kids hang up stockings on Christmas Eve until our son Jonathan hung up a pair of my pantyhose, expecting those to be filled.

Our children invited their friends for potato latkes (pancakes) during Hanukkah and matzo meal latkes during Passover. Even now, when I meet old friends, they tell me they remember. In return, my children recall invitations to help trim Christmas trees. On Rosh Hashana (Jewish New Year) and Yom Kippur (Day of Atonement), we prayed by ourselves, in our living room, sometimes joined by a few local Jews.

When I was first married, I asked the manager of the local grocery store if he had sour cream to serve with potato pancakes.

"Madam," he replied, straightening his back, "when our cream turns sour, we throw it out!"

I am a longtime member and past president of the Federated Women's Club here. Once Hanukkah coincided with our December international meeting and buffet supper prepared by the members. I was the featured speaker, discussing the meaning of our eight-day festival. The hostesses also invited foreign students attending the local community college. When the ladies discovered the guest list included three Arab students, they asked me about dietary restrictions. I was not sure what made me the expert, but I researched at the library. With no clue of the students' nationality, I decided a vegetarian dish would suit. I offered to make two kugels (casseroles made with noodles). I flavored one with onions, garlic, green peppers, and kasha, and the other with apples, cinnamon, nuts, cream cheese, and cottage cheese.

I started my speech by telling the audience, "All my life, people have said to me, 'You know, some of my best friends are Jews.' I am here to tell you that most of my best friends are Christians." I got a standing ovation—except for the three Arab guys, who were on their way back to the buffet table to get more kugel.

One does run into thoughtless folks. One couple, after attending several of our parties, informed my husband that they could never have us to their home because everything they cooked had pork in it. What a limited diet! The restriction originated because the sages noticed that people who ate pig often became sick. Now that the meat industry is so well regulated, avoiding pork is more a tradition. I always hope, when I have a BLT, that the Almighty is looking elsewhere for that moment.

Once, when my older daughter was about eleven, she came running into the house. "Mom!" she cried. "Helen told me that I killed him, and I don't even know who he is!"

"Who is she talking about, and where did she hear that?" I asked.

"I dunno, maybe school. Some guy named Jesus!"

"Oh, really! We'll just see about that!" I called the parochial school and asked if the principal was available. She was, so I drove to the school. Waddling down the hall, nearly nine months pregnant, I encountered the tallest nun I'd ever seen. She must have been six feet tall. I panicked for a moment, but not for long.

"Sister, I'm Liesel Shineberg, and I need to discuss something with you."

"I'm Sister Katherine Ann," she said with a wonderful, wide smile.

I was really upset, but she assured me no child had heard that in her school. We became friendly; she and another sister visited me in the hospital after the birth of my son David. My stock went up in the community the evening two nuns came to visit the Jewish Mrs. Shineberg.

A good friend gave me food for thought recently when, while exercis-

ing her dogs, she met a Jewish lady doing the same. The dogs disagreed, and the women grew angry. My friend told me later, "I yelled at her and called her the most terrible thing I could think of at that moment. I called her a miserable, dirty Jew!"

She was crying when she told me this and was still crying, according to her husband, that evening.

Yet I know this woman would walk through fire and water for me.

I often join my Episcopalian friends, helping to cook or clean for the local food kitchen. One day, after a heavy cleanup, one of the gals put her arms around me and said, "Liesel, you are a good Christian!" I am not often speechless, but this stumped me.

"Thanks," I finally told her. "I think you are a good person, too." Out of the corner of my eye, I saw one of my buddies who had overheard the exchange wink at me.

My blessings and lessons have been many. When my friends and acquaintances travel or poke through catalogs, they remember my plaintive cry that there are never any decorations for our holidays. Consequently, my home proudly displays Jewish and Hebraic items from many cultures. I have learned a lot about the various factions of Christianity and have come to understand why Jesus captured the imagination of people all over the continent. I read the Bible with friends every Monday morning. This group consists of one Baptist, two Catholics, one member of the Church of Christ, one Congregationalist, and two Episcopalians. Only in America could we do this. Our friends and acquaintances accept people as they are. They respect people of varied skin colors whether they wear long robes, side locks and black hats, burkas or turbans, spiked hair or habits. Many people here call me to discuss current problems or write letters to the editor of the newspaper in protest of unjust diatribes about Israel, gays, Muslims, and others. Many know and accept the worth of the individual. These are the folks who make this country and this city great. I'm blessed to live here.

PEARLE HENRIKSEN SCHULTZ
Sonnet for My Grandchild

Listen! Accents of language that we speak
Echo down ages to your little ears:
Felicities in French, fierce consonants of Greek,
Norse prayers and graces from my childhood years.
I hear the energy of German tones
Mingle with Swedish soft as summer rain
And mate with crisper British patterns blown

Like Queen Anne's lace across this Western plain.
Released from velvet prisons of the past
The splendid sunshine of the Latin tongue
Adds color, flavor to this rich repast
Of cadences that flow with sounds outflung.
Your native English speech is shaped by these,
Bequests of past and future legacies.

MARY ZELINKA ✒️ *Never Silent Again*

When I arrived in Oregon just days before Christmas, 1978, after leaving my violent husband in Colorado, I had never heard of a battered women's shelter. And no wonder—the first one in the United States had opened only four years before. Newspapers still reported woman battering, and the often resulting murder, as a "lovers' quarrel." Nobody talked about domestic and sexual violence. I sure didn't. Ashamed over all that had happened to me, which I believed was my fault, I was determined to put my ex-husband and former life behind me. I found a job and began building a new life.

But my new life was lonely. As I would later learn was typical in domestic violence, my husband had cut me off from my friends. The only three I had left were back in Colorado. Isolating me even more was what my mother had taught me: women cannot be trusted.

Still, loneliness and anger over my abuse got me moving, and in October 1980 I signed up for hotline training at the local rape crisis center. I had no idea that I had just joined a grass-roots movement that would forever change not only our nation's definition of violence but also my life.

Accustomed to keeping quiet and listening to others lecture, I was surprised when the women leading this training asked me to say something. They said each of us has wisdom and answers, that our job as hotline workers was not to tell the caller what to do but to listen and help her find her own truth. Heresy!

My voice quivered so much the first time I spoke in that training that the trainers and other volunteers had to lean forward to hear me. But instead of laughing at my stuttering as my husband had done, they waited while I stammered through my thoughts. No one finished my sentences for me. They nodded or shook their heads, and they listened.

I had found community.

We had no training in establishing programs or challenging norms. In fact, for the most part, we were women who believed ourselves to be powerless. We had been forced to leave our homes to keep ourselves safe. Many of us had lost custody of our children either through the legal system or by willingly giving them up because we believed our batterers when they said

we were bad mothers. We were scared. We met in those early centers and discovered our own strength by listening to each other's stories. And once we started speaking out, we were never silent again.

We worked jobs during the day to support ourselves, but our nights and weekends were spent training more volunteers, stuffing newsletters, and typing training materials on old manual typewriters. We spoke to whatever civic group would listen. We marched in Take Back the Night marches and held candlelight vigils. We sat in courtrooms and listened to judges. We wrote letters to our congressional representatives and the editors of our local newspapers. We handed out leaflets on street corners. We went back to school to earn more acceptance for our voices. We held all-you-can-eat spaghetti dinners and researched grants. And we spent endless nights in hospital emergency rooms with raped and battered women we had just met yet knew to our bones because their stories were our own.

In the midst of creating this different world where women and children have worth, we created community for ourselves—a place where each of us can be honored for her own wisdom and truth. I learned to love and trust other women, just as I learned to love and trust myself. And somewhere along the way, I lost my stutter.

KAYNE PYATT *The Drumbeat Continues*

We are at retreat. We have come to the mountains, to a cabin, to reflect and restore our sense of balance in the world. Although we have ceased drumming, we remain seated in silence, reluctant to break the tranquil state.

Finally, one woman raises her hand and begins to speak. "I am struggling," she sighs. "I love my family, my husband, my children, but I feel so alone, so unfulfilled. I want to work, but at the same time, I want to be at home for my kids."

As her tears fall from her face onto her drum, I am tempted to rush to console her, to give advice. But we vowed to remain in a silent circle, sending loving energy and support with our silence. Only then do we really listen and allow the one speaking to struggle through to the answer that lies within. Only then can a woman tap into her own inner wisdom.

She continues to speak—crying, laughing—as we smile, nod our heads. When she is silent once again, we ask her what she wants of us.

She asks for a hug and we respond, crawling on our knees to her, giving her hugs and then returning to our places in the circle.

Someone else begins to speak. Her request may be different. Maybe she will ask our advice. Another may want to sit in the center of the circle while we place our hands on her in silent healing prayer or meditation. We have learned to honor diverse spiritual beliefs.

Another woman in the group speaks about a recent work change. "I love the challenge of my new job. It is an opportunity to express myself, a time to stretch, to really try new skills. I want to drum out my joy."

"Yes, yes," we shout and immediately begin drumming again.

This time the beat is lively and loud. A celebration. A young woman jumps up and begins to dance around the circle. Her long blond curls bounce in time to her body movements. I laugh and join her. Soon all of the women rise. We raise our drums above our heads, tapping out a beat our feet mimic. We laugh, sing, and eventually fall exhausted to the floor.

After catching my breath, I speak. "Now I want to give you a task. As important as togetherness is, so is solitude. I have a journal assignment for you. I want you to go on a walk alone and find the messages from Mother Earth and her species. You will find answers to the questions that have arisen as we sat in our circle or that you brought with you from outside. Take your journal with you and walk or sit with the earth. Observe your surroundings and write in your journal. Your answer will come to you in the silence and solitude. Come back when you are ready. We'll fix a meal together then."

The women quietly move about, putting on jackets and hats, picking up their writing tools and notebooks. Two walk into the woods, another down the dirt road; others have scattered over the hills. They are gone, and I follow suit.

I walk toward the beaver pond below the cabin. The leaves on the aspen trees are beginning to turn their brilliant autumn gold. The air is chill, but the expanse of sky and warm sun causes me to want to linger forever in the outdoors. I have just lost a dear friend. My heart is hurting, and my spirit is in despair. I sit beside the little stream flowing from the beaver pond and listen to its song.

Water is my healer. In my history, a hot bath has soothed me many times. The breath-catching cold of the Bear River has renewed me when my friend and I go skinny-dipping. The hot tub in my home has been an oasis of warmth for my women friends and me in the dead of winter. I can get lost in thought when my hands are immersed in hot dishwater.

I am alone here with only the water. I spread out on the grass and cry, luxuriating in the freedom to do so. I close my eyes and soon sleep. When I wake, I dip my fingers into the stream and splash my face. The water is cold, and I smile with life and feeling. I begin to write and write and write. When I can write no more, I rise to rejoin the circle of women.

When I return to the cabin, several of the women have started to prepare the evening meal, another is building up the fire in the wood heater, and a few rest in the loft above. Within minutes, the others return as if called by some silent bell. Noisily now, we prepare the meal together and then eat, as we share stories of wildlife viewed on walks and personal re-

flections. After our meal, we automatically gather in a circle on the floor and begin to drum. Thoughts and longing pour out through our fingertips and palms into a rhythm that binds us.

In the next day and a half, we share and reflect on our journal entries, take more walks alone, and make picture collages of our personal lives and dreams. We write and we explore what it is to be a woman in the wild, to live in a patriarchal world and still be able to speak out. We explore our connection with nature and what we can do to help Mother Earth survive. We make promises to ourselves knowing full well the commitment that will be required. We know when we leave this mountain and return to our homes, it will be difficult, because the daily grind can wrap us in its tentacles and strangle our good intentions. We discuss simple steps we can take to keep our circle of community with us.

"I can build an altar to nature in my bedroom—a place where I can put some of the objects I've found on my walks," one woman offers.

Another remarks, "I'll rise an hour earlier than my family and spend time writing in my journal."

"And drumming," the woman next to her adds.

We all smile and nod. I speak. "And we will close our eyes and envision our circle here. Women, strong and powerful in their intuition, their resilience, their knowledge, we will thrive, and we will make the world a better place. Each will make a difference. Each may make only one small change, but when you multiply that by the number of women here, that becomes a powerful change. Our drumbeat will be heard across the world because there are other women doing the same thing. That is powerful."

"Women power," one woman shouts, and we all join in. "Women power, women power."

Our moment together as a community will sustain us. It sustains me as I reenter my own world of work and obligations. In our hearts and minds, we can return to this weekend and gain renewed commitment, knowing we are not alone in our desire for a peaceful and balanced world.

The drumbeat goes on. The circle is open but unbroken.

NANCY CURTIS *Checkup, Checkout*

From: <Nancy@DiamondARanch.com>
To: <Mindy@stpaul.com>
Date: March 2, 2003
Subject: Checkup, checkout

Hi—Thought of you this morning when I was out in the cold, bottle-feeding the new bum calf. Wish you were here getting slobbered on—like last year—instead of me.

This afternoon I had appointments in town for my least favorite thing—annual medical checkups. Getting to town wasn't a problem. The drive was fine for the first 20 miles; the last 10 were slushy, but not bad.

But the first thing that happens when I go to the hospital for my mammogram is they ask for my insurance card. I open my purse, and my wallet is not there. I can see it in my mind's eye, sitting back home on the kitchen table where I'd written a check. But they let me in w/o the card, because, really, how many unauthorized women are forcing their way into hospitals to get mammograms these days? ;->

Sheila, the x-ray tech—yeah, the same Sheila who dated my brother in high school—can't get a good picture, though she takes two extra ones with super-firm compression. She apologizes and worries about squishing me until I say, "Do you ever get tired of being nice to people? Don't you sometimes just want to shout, 'Stand up straight and hold still!'" She says no, but then she grins and says, "Well, there IS this one woman . . . She begs me to only take two pictures, and I think, 'If you aren't going to let me do it right, why do you even come in here?'"

Sheila says the x-ray-reading doctor, who only comes there a couple of times a week, will probably want to order an ultrasound. She says not to worry; they'll call me. Sure, "not to worry."

Before I leave the hospital, I search my purse, and tucked in the side pocket I find one tattered old check, the kind with the account number printed on the bottom but w/o any name and address, the temporary kind they give you at the bank when you run out of real checks. Good thing, b/c my mother has given me a long list of groceries to pick up for her, and she'd be miffed if I came home without her V8.

I borrow $5 from my aunt who's volunteering in the hospital gift shop so I can refill my eyeglass cleaning solution, which costs a dollar at the eye doc's office. I remembered to bring the little bottle along this time, and if I don't do it now, I may never remember the empty bottle again. At the eye doc's, Kathy gives the bottle to a new girl to refill. I pay Kathy the dollar, and we joke about me borrowing money to make this big purchase—and now I'm down to $4. Then the girl brings the bottle and says, "That'll be a dollar." Kathy and I laugh, and Kathy explains I've already paid and I don't have a dollar to spare. It's beginning to look like one of those days.

Then I go to see Doc Brown for a Pap test. Doc says I need to watch my blood pressure. He gets the speculum and the swab and asks me if we are calving yet—a diversionary tactic, I'm sure. I am not distracted from the matter at hand. :-) He says his cows should start calving in about a week. And later when I tell him that I've been walking two miles a day, sure that he'll be delighted, he says, "Great,

now work up to five miles." "Five miles! Every day?" says I. And he says, "Well, four if you're on a treadmill because it's all uphill."

He asks if exercise is helping me lose weight, and I say, "I'm waiting for that to happen." Then when I stand up to go he says, "Well, it looks like it's rearranged some." Then he tells me he's pleased that my mother keeps perking along, even though she's 85 and has some health problems. "You must be doing everything right," he says, "helping her keep her independence and all." I say it isn't a matter of "helping" her do anything; she does exactly what she wants, with or without our help. Before I leave, I get a new prescription for cold sore medicine b/c my lip is puffed out like a meatball. :-*

Then I go and buy $140 worth of groceries. In the aisle I see Tom—remember him from the historical society? "You're looking exceptionally fit," he says. I thank him, but I should have thrown my arms around him and hugged him.

When I check out, I admit I don't have my Club Card and start to write my check. I say, "I suppose you want me to write my name in the corner, since it's not printed on here." The new manager says, "We don't take counter checks." "This isn't a counter check," says naive Nancy. "It has my account number down here; it just doesn't have my name."

"It's Safeway policy," says the new manager. "And it's posted right here." Thump, thump, thump, his finger goes on the little check-writing stand. "Only preprinted checks."

So I explain it's all I have—my wallet and my checkbook are at home, 30 miles away. He explains they are cracking down. He raises his eyebrow, looks down his nose, and says, "Do you have a credit card?" My meatball lip sneers as I say, "That would be in my wallet."

Hell's bells, now what? I tell him I can go to the bank and get money. The carryout girl Kim, who is Sally and Ray's daughter, points to my groceries. "Do you need help with these?" And the new manager, recognizing that I fit the profile of a grocery thief—shifty eyes, fat lip, squished boobs—holds up his hand to Kim and says, "No, we'll just keep her groceries here until she comes back with the money."

So I tear up the half-written check and go to the bank. I tell my story to Barbara—she's a good friend of my ex-sister-in-law Judy, the one we ran into with Judy in the Mexican restaurant once. Anyway, Barbara seems quite happy to give me money, even though I have no ID. But then bank robbers have a different profile—mask of Zorro, bulge under overcoat, deposit slip scrawled with "Give me money." ;> I decide that if my checking account is short for some strange reason, I'll say,

"My ice cream is melting. I don't have time for this. Just reach in your teller drawer and loan me some money, quick." It will be like a test; we'll see if they really do have friendly personal banking. "How would you like this?" asks Barbara. "Twenties?" I say I wish I knew what was most inconvenient for Safeway. I'd take it like that.

Back I go to get the groceries. There they sit, alone in a basket by the door. New manager is not in sight; bag girl Kim is not in sight. I could roll the cart out the door, throw the sacks in the car, and speed away. Maybe cops would speed after me with flashing lights. But I find Kim, who mumbles, embarrassed, about the new manager and his policy. I pay and push the basket out through the slush.

Next I go to the drugstore, where Charlene charges my account without blinking an eye. "Just sign here." Our families have had this connection ever since her father-in-law, Robert, the pharmacist and a leading citizen, went to federal prison because of a drug accounting problem. When he came back, they lost some customers, and others wouldn't look Robert in the eye.

Right after that, I took my dad in to get a prescription. My dad, who was in the early stages of something like Alzheimer's, boomed out: "Well, did they have you making license tags in the pen, Robert?" Customers stopped what they were doing and waited for the answer. After a pause, Robert said actually they had him typing forms. "Make much money?" my dad shouted. "Seventy-five cents an hour," Robert shouted back (my dad was hard of hearing). Then Robert said quieter, "But I didn't want my family to have to send me money for toothpaste, so I was glad to do it." Charlene and I had listened that day with our mouths hanging open a little. But my dad had broken the ice, and after that they had a bond. Charlene and I both remember that. And she knows that we've paid our bills there for fifty years.

So all in all, I got out alive and with over $140 worth of groceries, $180 in drugs, $4 in cash, AND eyeglass cleaner after starting with no cash, checks, cards, or ID. And I got the mammogram and Pap test out of the way, which must be a good thing. Plus a bonus stress test, in a way. Not a bad day after all, thanks to a lot of help from the neighborhood.

Old Mudd misses you. I'll give him a pat on the head from you. Love, nnc

PHYLLIS WALKER *Plant Sale Grows Roots*

The flames climbed higher, fingers of orange and red reaching into the night sky. Our house was on fire, and we were helpless to stop it.

My mother and seven of us children huddled together in the old station

wagon, cried, and prayed. A light sleet began to fall, and from a distance we heard the sirens. God had heard our prayers and dispatched angels. These angels of mercy, bumping at breakneck speed down the dusty country road toward us with flashing lights and screaming sirens, had familiar faces. As I watched them run past, I recognized men from the community all rallying together to help us.

As dawn came, the smoldering remains of our home stood black and forbidding. The flower beds that had surrounded it were trampled and muddy, morning glory vines hanging limply on the metal poles that had supported the porch.

My family was taken to the home of the insurance man, where his wife comforted my mother, gave us blankets, and let us rest. I lay quietly on the floor beside my siblings, not wanting to wake anyone but much too anxious to sleep, and I remembered. Nine years. Nine years to the very day, we'd come to the valley to start a new life, a life of contrast to what we'd known. We'd come from the desert of Utah—hot, flat, and barren. The only animals we ever saw there were horned toads and an occasional jackrabbit. Here the mountains rose from the valley floor so close you felt as if you could touch them. Animals were everywhere on green velvet fields, and pools of clear water dotted the land. It seemed we'd moved to paradise, and I wondered if the people would be as wonderful as the country.

We'd barely had time to get moved in when winter came with a fierce blast of cold. Our ranch, like others of the valley, became an island in a sea of white snow. Solitude was nothing new to our family, as we'd lived thirty miles from the nearest town in Utah, but it felt unnatural to live only three miles out and not feel knit into the community.

A chinook came eventually, and with it came the promise of spring. As subtly as the snow melted into the land, our lives began to melt into the community. The first sign of this change began with the annual Leon Ladies plant sale. We filled the back of the station wagon with little pots containing "starts" from every yard and garden in the area. Like adventurers from foreign lands returning home with treasures, we brought these little jewels to our ranch and began transplanting them. It was an amazing feeling to know that you'd brought home a part of your neighbors' world and incorporated it into your own. These plant sales were much more than fundraisers—they were the community women's way of exchanging bits of their lives. We had something to talk about now, a reason to call, and after the sale, the strands of our lives began mixing with theirs.

"How are those pansy plants doing for you? My tiger lilies seem a bit slow to come out this year, but I believe they'll do just fine once they get established. Say, speaking of getting established, how are the kids fitting into the school?"

Like the morning glory vines we bought at that first sale, our place in

the valley started small but grew through the years until we were so intertwined with this community that when one hurt, all hurt, and when one rejoiced, all were glad. Nine years.

The men of the community stopped the destruction of the fire that night, but it was the women who helped us rebuild our life. It was not just plants they brought this time, but even bigger parts of their lives—blankets, sheets, towels, clothes, shoes, furniture, housewares, and food. In the end, our lives had become so connected it was hard to see where one family stopped and another started. And yes, they brought plants; after all, there were so many things needing talked about.

PATRICIA WELLINGHAM-JONES ◈ One Panel of a Quilt

The AIDS Memorial Quilt contains 44,000 panels so far. It sends messages of remembrance and hope and is seen annually at thousands of displays around the world.

I watch your mother
bustle about the room,
fluff pillows, smooth
the afghan she made for your
first college dorm. Hands busy
so her eyes won't overflow.
She slides nourishing drinks
in rich hues of ripe fruits
into a mouth too sore to swallow.
Your friend visits almost daily.
Hot tears rain on white knuckles
clutching the footboard.
I sit like a quiet mouse
in a corner of your room,
snip and sew, search for the colors
you whisper from the bed.
We work together
on this summing up of a life.
I take my time assembling
the panel with your name, fear
that my final stitch
will signal
your last breath.

PAGE LAMBERT ✐ *One Word at a Time*

When I was a teenager and my family and I were visiting Russia, I fell in love with a wooden peasant doll. The dollmaker had painted a purple bodice and a bright red skirt; this wooden skirt formed the doll's base. The craftsman had depicted a smiling face, big blue eyes, rosy cheeks, red lips, and a scarf that only partially covered the doll's bright yellow hair. I remember gently lifting up the doll's top half and finding, hidden inside, another little doll, identically painted. And then nested inside of her, yet another doll—seven wooden dolls in all, each a tinier version of the previous. Dolls inside of dolls inside of dolls.

Thirty-five years later, I am reminded of the dolls as I sit among twenty delinquent girls at a group home in Wyoming. Some of the girls are as young as thirteen, the oldest no more than seventeen. Like the dolls, these girls are painted on the outside to look grown and worldly, yet inside each of them is a smaller—and, yes, sweeter—girl.

I'm doing research for a novel I'm writing, trying to create a realistic character—a runaway girl, raised on a sheep ranch, who finds herself homeless on the streets of Denver. I've named her Oakley. I am hoping these troubled girls will teach me something about her.

I meet with the girls in a small upstairs meeting room, the school's "group" room, reserved for low-key, heart-to-heart talks. The woman psychologist who works with them is with us. Some of the girls are sprawled next to me on an old lumpy couch; others are sitting on the floor leaning against the wall; a few are on the couch across from me, with unfinished afghans spread across their laps. They flick out strands of yarn as we talk, their crochet hooks fluttering awkwardly in their unskilled hands.

At first their stories come to me hidden within small, offhand comments that aren't offhand at all. One girl has been sexually abused since she was two, the abuse continuing until she arrived here. Many are drug users. Most admit to, and even brag about, being sexually active. Most have committed crimes. This group home represents their last hope. For many, it's here or jail. Or worse—back to the environment that damaged them in the first place.

Here they learn to seek answers through prayer, education, and sharing. The rules are strict: no bad language, no piercing, no unkind actions.

They are eager to talk about Oakley. "I think Oakley's running away from something," says one girl. "Maybe she's done something that will disappoint her parents."

"Or maybe she doesn't want to be under her parents' thumbs," pipes up another.

"Do you think Oakley has ever run away before?" I ask.

"She probably just stayed out one night." This young girl reminds me of

my own teenage daughter. She continues, "And then maybe she figured her parents would be so mad that she couldn't go home. So she just ran away. It just kinda happened."

Ah, a good girl caught in the momentum of growing up.

Then another girl, perhaps the oldest, says, "When you're on the streets, there's all kinds of pressure to strip and stuff. Older guys will tell you stuff, and it sounds good 'cause it's the kinda stuff you wish your father would've told you—like they love you and stuff."

How could a father withhold those words? I wonder.

Then all at once, the girls start talking.

"I think Oakley just ran away for the rush—you know, the adrenaline of just doing it."

"No, I don't think so. I think she didn't like living in the country, and she thought she could get a job in the city easier than in some hickville town. She was probably tired of not having any money."

They chatter for a few minutes while I scribble notes, then the enthusiasm wanes and they retreat into themselves, growing quiet. The talk shifts to the books I have written and what it's like to be a writer. They invite me back.

The second time I visit the home, the girls greet me by name and with enthusiasm.

I want them to know that I, too, am willing to share intimate things about myself, so I read them a story about the weekend my beloved black Labrador died and how our family mourned him. When I finish, they are unusually quiet. "How many of you have loved an animal?" I ask. Of the twenty girls there, at least fifteen raise their hands. I know they will be able to help me shape Oakley's story. She, too, has suffered loss and abuse at the hands of her fictitious track coach. I read them an excerpt from the novel, where Oakley is alone at the ranch trying to cope with the death of a lamb and the sadness she feels.

"I think she's compassionate," says the girl from Hickville. "Like sensitive, you know. But she can be tough when she wants to be."

Then a girl sitting in the corner speaks up in a soft voice. "If her coach abused her, maybe she's like the lamb in the story, and he's like, you know, the coyote." She drops her head and doesn't say anything else. I'm writing notes like crazy.

"I think she wants to trust people," says another, "but then this bad thing happened, and she can't share it with nobody. She trusted the coach; now she can't trust anything."

Then the girl from Hickville asks, "Does she have any friends? Has she told her friends? If she lives in the country, she might not have any friends, 'cause it's such a hassle to go anywhere 'cause she might not be able to drive yet."

Then a long-legged and graceful girl asks, "Did she *cause* it to happen?" I notice the psychologist is paying especially close attention. Two more girls speak up.

"I think she wants to protect her grandmother. She has emotions, but she's not showing them."

"I ran away," says the second girl, "because the guy who raped me said he'd hurt my family if I said anything. Maybe Oakley ran away to keep her family safe." She speaks casually, as if this occurrence is as commonplace as buttered toast.

Then another girl, who has not yet spoken, offers, "She could be pregnant." She looks up and adds, "From the rape. And then her parents accused her of being sexually active, but she wasn't, but she didn't tell them, 'cause they just kept getting mad at her about it."

I ask, "Is it more painful to stay where you are than to run away?"

"It's easier," says a longhaired blond. "It's easier to run away from your problems."

"Maybe," guesses another, "maybe Oakley doesn't realize how much the rape is affecting her—causing her to argue with her parents and stuff. Was she sexually active before the rape?"

Good question. I shake my head. "I don't know," I answer.

"I think you need to know if she was," comments the blond, "'cause that's a real important part of how she acts and everything."

The youngest-looking of the girls speaks up again. "I think the rape made her grow up really fast."

The dark-haired girl says, "It changes how she feels about her body. She feels dirty now. She wants to get control back, but she can't."

Then one of the girls adds a twist. "I think it happened once before, when she was really young, but she doesn't remember it until it happens again. Then it all comes back."

Next a girl who had talked earlier about avoidance and fighting says, "I think it only happened one time, but she lives in a small town, so she couldn't avoid the coach at school or anyplace. She probably can't handle being around him. So she runs."

We are all quiet; even the girls crocheting the afghans are still for a moment. The session draws to a natural close. As I am gathering my notebooks, one of them says, "I like helping you write your book."

Then another says, "Yeah, come back." She grins and adds, "Come during study time, though, so we don't have to study." They all laugh.

The others join in. "Yeah, that'd be cool."

I say goodbye to all of them, visiting privately for a moment with the counselor as I walk to my car. We talk about my novel and the writing process, and the counselor mentions how glad she is that the girls had a chance to visit with a real writer. As I'm driving away, I think of Oakley and how

her character embodies so many of their struggles. These girls are not wooden dolls, easily and neatly put back together and made whole. They have been torn asunder and, like Oakley, must be re-created—one gesture, one hug, one word at a time.

BARBARA WALLACE *Dealing Uno and Life*

Our Uno team plays in public once a month. The same three players always show up: Norma, Dionne, and me. Bev often watches and joins in the friendly banter while getting things done around us. Uno is a child's card game, where the object is to gather sets of cards by color and number. The rules are relatively simple; a little judicial strategy, however, can balance the luck of the draw. As our summer progresses, we discover other factors that also influence winning or losing.

It all begins with Norma picking me up at my house and driving across the river to northwest Portland. The day is hot and sunny, and her car has air conditioning, which we enjoy without really noticing. Our game is scheduled for just after one o'clock. Norma drops me off and parks the car. I head inside, sign in, and wait for my card partners to arrive. Dionne comes in with hugs, a sweet smile, and more snacks. Norma and I have carried in our bags and backpacks loaded with snacks, books (which we rarely seem to get to), a humorous video or two, and the Uno cards. We walk together into the long room full of recliners, chattering and greeting Bev as we find a spot and settle in. Some days, we rearrange the chairs and low tables so we can spread out.

Other people are here, too. They sit alone, read, watch TV, visit quietly with a friend, and sleep. Our exuberant entrance never seems to bother anyone, and it brings smiles to some, so we keep it up, respectful yet cheerful.

Bev, one of many phenomenal oncology nurses, comes over and gets the chemo concoction of Adriamycin and Taxotere started in the port in my chest. Dionne, Norma, and I hunker down to play Uno for most of the next four hours. During the first couple of hours, I'm able to strategize and win fairly frequently. Norma and Dionne bide their time. Bev checks on us every so often, laughing and chatting and sitting with us when she isn't busy. We all tease and laugh as cards are drawn and discarded, remembering we needed just that one red eight under the last two cards, gathering huge handfuls of cards that are almost hopeless to get rid of.

Even though we've consumed bananas, cheese and crackers, and plenty of juice and water, we are still hungry after a couple of hours. I can keep food down but can't eat much at a time, so I eat fairly constantly. Dionne and Norma keep eating right along with me. None of us seems to

put on weight, though. So Dionne takes our orders and walks down the block to a bakery to get roast turkey sandwiches with plenty of ripe tomatoes, crisp cool cucumber slices, and sprouts. When she returns, we take a break from card playing and share chips, more juice, and sandwiches. It is the last food I'll be able to taste for the next couple of weeks, so I really savor the flavors and the crunchy, luscious veggies.

The afternoon begins to wear on, my energy waning. I can still smile and laugh, but I can feel the effort it begins to take. Norma and Dionne keep up their cheerful interactions, sharing stories of the past three weeks, gently kidding me as I fade, and keeping a watchful eye on how I am. Bev continues to check with us, more quietly now. We play a few more games of Uno. Against all my efforts, Dionne and Norma begin to win most of the Uno games. Inside myself, I laugh at the struggle it takes just to maintain a sitting position, let alone think about cards—or anything else. The challenge for me at this moment has become an internal physical battle against breast cancer. I slowly let go of any real control I have and trust these dear women to care for me body and soul, sinking gratefully into their chuckles as they continue to win at Uno.

ELLEN WATERSTON ✑ **Anaconda Copper Dreams**

The mothers bring their children
In oversize clothes of no particular color,
Their eyes crusted from interrupted sleep,
To breakfast at the Headstart Center
In the shadow of the naked
Slopes of the Anacondas.

After toast and Tang
They are lined up for a photograph,
Holding their artwork under their eyes,
Large, dark circles mimicking
The place their fathers
Go every day to mine.

The mothers leave, drive around to the store.
Their forefingers draw a thick
Line through the dust on the shelves,
Wistfully recalling what the TV
Had promised, but for the strike.
Their men held out long as they could,
Sandwiched between cardboard

Placards of protest, before caving in
To the copper king.

The women cross the street to gather
In Rayleen's living room,
Moving the plastic red flowers
Off the coffee table, tucking
The purple afghan around their feet.
They lay out the supplies: neat stacks of
Styrofoam trays washed and saved
From packages of chicken breast or
Ground chuck, black velveteen
Ordered from a catalog, and Elmer's glue.

They fashion white stallions rearing,
Pawing the plush night,
Roses with exquisite white petals
Carefully planted in a dark velour bed,
Or ballerinas twirling on a tiny
Pointed slipper of foam.

The fathers don't come to the art show.
Just the mothers, who hang back
Against the wall,
Next to their Styrofoam dreams
And their children's drawings of the black hole in the ground
From which their fathers would never emerge.

KAY E. KONZ *Where They Know My Name*

I grew up a farmer's daughter in a small town in Iowa where everyone
knew who I was. Our church community circumscribed the people I knew:
we attended Mass where my parents were married and where we were all
baptized. We went to the same Catholic elementary school that my mother
had attended as a child. My classmates were the children of her old class-
mates, the same friends with whom my parents still played cards.

Since my parents had seven daughters (and four sons), some people
couldn't distinguish me from another of my sisters. But apparently we all
looked like our parents, because everyone knew that I was one of John and
Irene's girls. Much of our extended family lived in the same small farming
town, went to the same church, and attended the same school.

We had less intimate relationships with others in the town, those who

did not belong to the Catholic Church. My parents tried to patronize the Catholic businesses in town, so the man who put gas in the old station wagon was the same man who took up the collection at Mass. And the butcher and the grocer and the druggist were on the same committees with my parents. I never knew which one reported it to Mom and Dad when I was driving too fast down the street or dawdled for too long after school in my school uniform.

Of course, growing up in a small town was oppressive at times, although I didn't know anything different. Children were safe, as everyone knew what everyone else did. And everyone knew that John and Irene were strict, so of course I had to decline when my friends suggested anything remotely risky.

At times I relied on my parents' friends to advise me with difficult situations I couldn't talk about with Mom. And frequent family get-togethers provided opportunities to talk things over with my cousins or aunts or even an uncle. Someone would always help if I had a problem, even if it was only a flat tire.

We took care of our own in our small town. The retarded adult man who still lived with his parents relished his role in the back of the church shaking hands. Everyone understood that Frank's boys were "kinda wild" after their mother died. We all just accepted that Tom's wife was "nervous" and couldn't do the things the other women did.

If a tornado wrought its havoc on a local farm, everyone gathered to clean up and fix things. After all, we never knew if our family would be the next to need help or understanding.

We buried our own dead. For years, my mother and her best friend were co-chairs of the funeral committee. When someone in our parish passed away, the funeral director called Mom, and she called the family and arranged for the funeral dinner. The committee made sure that the grieving household had plenty of ham and pies to sustain them. And if neighbors had a hard time after a death or loss, someone made sure that they talked to the priest.

I was the first of the daughters in my family to truly leave home. I planned to become a school counselor, even though the only counselor I had ever met was the priest who filled that role in my high school. I was going to college, although it was not an aspiration encouraged by many in that community. Still, I was expected to come home and teach in the local school.

Dad thought I should settle down and marry a local farmer.

I never did return to live in that small town and work in the local school. I had learned a little about different people, lifestyles, and ideas in college, and I studied to be a school psychologist, so I could fuse my two passions: psychological assessment and children. I learned even more teaching in an inner-city school, with children who often came to school in order to eat

and rarely shared the same surname as the parent they lived with. I felt that I had graduated to the "real" world, and I wasn't going back.

Since then, I have worked in farm communities, urban areas, psychiatric hospitals, and mental health clinics, most often with children and adolescents. I have had experiences with grief, school crises, and teenage suicide, rape, and sexual abuse. I was surprised when I first realized that my mother and her funeral committee provided a model for my work. We enter the situation with professional credentials, not food, but we come with the same purpose—to provide support. Sometimes I worry that I have become too callous, and sometimes I long for a simpler life, one not quite as "real." My lifestyle now is that of the urban professional woman, but I am still a product of the small farming community where I grew up.

I know when I visit there that I can cash a check at the grocery store because they know that I am one of John's girls. The old grain elevator is gone, but I can still get a calendar every year from the farm supply store. And when I visit the cemetery, I sometimes feel that I know more people there than anywhere else.

I was grateful for that small town when Mom died. The house filled with old friends and family bringing pies and hams—at least half a dozen hams. They knew what needed to be done and helped me do it.

Many of my adolescent clients have never experienced that sense of connection to a community. No one besides their parents has ever held them accountable for the rules. They have no sympathetic older friends to talk to, to help them make decisions, and to make sure they follow through. No community grieves with them or supports them during crises.

My young women clients often don't know how to develop or maintain relationships. They don't have to be polite to the clerk at the convenience store because she doesn't know their mothers. No one in the bank questions them or tells their parents if they withdraw all the money from their account. When they experience trauma, they don't have anyone to talk to except the person in the online chatroom, who seems to be a nice teenager from Kentucky, because they don't know the parish priest or Aunt Sue.

I often tell young women clients about growing up in a town where I didn't dare break the rules. I tell them about a community that watched over its members, whether they wanted to be watched or not. These young people listen intently and often appear wistful when they tell me of their own struggles with a sexualized environment and transient relationships.

I sometimes equate the adult mentors in small towns with today's counselors, hoping my clients might think of me as a kindly—and maybe eccentric—aunt with some training in psychology; one who believes children are our most important resource, not so different from the people in that small town of my childhood.

Thank you, John and Irene, Saint Patrick's Church, and the community of Neola.

LYDIA GONZALES ᕲ *La Mujer y Su Cultura*

The Mexican woman brought her customs and traditions when she came to the United States. Despite the struggles in her life, she focused on the celebrations with pride and spirituality. She celebrated birthdays in the family with special Mexican food, music, and a piñata. She celebrated baptism, confirmation, and other sacraments in honor of the children, selecting *padrinos* (godparents) with care. Big events were *quinceañeras* (fifteenth birthdays) for the daughters, followed by *la boda* (marriage). When a family member died, *velorios* (prayers for the soul) were held in the home all night long. Friends and family reflected on the life of the one who had died. With stories told to each generation, the Mexican woman passed on the importance of love, religion, and pride in her family and community, teaching them to celebrate the triumphs of their lives.

SUSAN MINYARD ᕲ *On Watermelon and Stout Roads*

The cotton farm at Watermelon and Stout Roads was the one place on earth that felt as if I belonged to it as much as it belonged to me. Although we were two miles away, I adopted the nearby town, population always shy of two thousand. The words came easily when someone asked me where I was from. "A small town in southern Arizona—Gila Bend," pronounced the Spanish way: *Heel-ah* Bend.

I found that hometown sense of belonging, that like-mindedness, three more times: in a school system, at writing events with other women, and with a lively spirit group. Yet none of these communities was tied to the land as farming is. Members came, members left, all unremarked upon, all forgiven, forgotten, gossip-less, unstoried. No one climbed over the pilings of bodies of dead wishes and done dreams; I did not feel in those groups that I was adding to the muck.

We lost the farm—it was the only farm foreclosure in decades in Arizona. I've been through bitterness, and that dry stink is not a place I wished to linger.

The town constable was directed by the justice system to post the auction notices on the electric poles along Watermelon and Stout Roads. She followed orders, and she never said anything to me, but she carefully stapled each of the white placards so the black printed words faced away from the road, so no one would ever see them.

CHARLOTTE BABCOCK ✑ *A World Apart*

An article in today's paper caught my eye: a junior high school history teacher is taking her students to the local cemetery to learn about the history of their community. I applaud her effort. A wealth of history can be gleaned in the cemetery. I visit cemeteries whenever I get the chance. I like cemeteries—and why not? I expect to be a resident of one someday.

On Memorial Day, I place flowers on a number of graves. At the cemetery, people spill from cars to find their destinations among the tombstones like arrows aimed at familiar targets. Above, on the highest hill, the city band tunes up in preparation for the eleven o'clock ceremonies. Men and women in colorful uniforms carry flags and wreaths up the hill, careful not to let the flags, attached to their long standards, drag on the ground. They carry bright red wreaths made from the same red paper poppies that decorate the white crosses, which sit in precise rows atop the graves of servicemen. The hum of voices rises sedately to the treetops that shield this place from the hot sun and from the cacophony beyond the high steel-mesh fence, a fence that most days separates the living from the dead.

As I walk among the tombstones and look at the names etched into the stones, memories flood my mind—not sad memories, but endearing ones. There is a personality here, an untroubled and warming personality that I have sensed in many cemeteries. The ghosts, if ghosts there be, are kindly ones, and it is, somehow, a tranquil experience to mingle with them in that world apart.

The rounded tops of some of the tabletlike markers are so eroded that the bones lying beneath can't be identified by the inscriptions. The dates on the battered markers are sometimes more deeply engraved than the names, so I can tell that many people in this oldest part of the cemetery lived very short lives. Although many young people lie here, a sense of age permeates this ground. Through the mist of the morning, it seems as if very old men with flowing beards and watery blue eyes sit on the benches murmuring together. The spring flowers nod and rustle, creating a soft chorus, while those ghostly gentlemen discuss the civil strife of the era or the untimely death that brought them here.

Cemeteries hold an ambiance unlike anywhere else, and they keep me attuned to the past. A busy cemetery is a lovely commingling of two communities—the living and the dead. I hope that those junior high school children come away from the cemetery with a sense of the spirit of the past that can be found there—and they will if they look, listen, and wonder.

EVELYN I. FUNDA ✑ **Belongings**

My family and I lived for most of my childhood in a five-room farmhouse where, with regularity, the winter wind nudged the flimsy curtains in my parents' bedroom; where you had to be careful not to trip over the buckles and cracks in the ugly blue-flowered linoleum; where the toilet worked only part-time and we had an outhouse for the rest of the time; where my mother washed our clothes with an old-time wringer washer out on the porch, which was actually just plywood sheets laid over two-by-fours on the bare ground.

Even so, my parents never would say out loud that we were poor. We were, rather, "a little short" that day or that month or that year, a phrase that suggested the possibility that the next crop of wheat or corn or my father's next custom farming job would mean all the difference. As a result, I rarely thought about what we lacked.

Instead, I knew abundance and generosity. There was always surplus from the garden or orchard—corn and tomatoes and pears and plums that my parents heaped in the arms of friends who stopped by for coffee. Many times my mother turned a dozen fragrant loaves of rye bread out of their ringing metal pans in the morning, and by suppertime only one would remain for our own meal, the others having been passed out to people who came to buy my mother's fresh eggs, or delivered to a neighbor with whom my mother had a friendly rivalry about whose tomatoes would ripen first, or dropped off on the back porch of the woman who had once hosted my mother's wedding shower, where, with gifts of blankets and red rooster canister sets, ladies ceremoniously welcomed a stranger into a network of belongings. My parents were rich in friends, if not in possessions, rich in a community of people with whom they shared a common history. And "poor" was a term they reserved for people who kept, among their things, a sense of hopelessness—like the Freeman family, who spent the late 1960s and early 1970s residing in my rural hometown in Idaho.

Richard Freeman was in my class at school, and his sister Jacey was a year older. Richard frightened me with his stony silences, his wild-eyed stare and toothy grin, his indifference to low or failing grades in school. He was, as we said back then, "slow." Richard stared back at his accusers, seemingly unperturbed by the judgment passed on his intellect. When the year ended, our teacher passed him off to the next grade with the rest of us, certain that holding him back would be of no use, and once again he and I—Freeman and Funda—found ourselves placed next to each other on the new teacher's neatly organized seating chart.

Jacey, though, was intellectually bright, even though she often missed school because, as she told me, she had to stay home to take care of her sick mother or her younger siblings. She wore her dark, thin hair in long, greasy

strings around her face, and she often had on the same clothes day after day—a fact I tried not to notice.

I cannot honestly say that she was my friend, though I talked to her often enough as we sat out on the front step of Central Mesa Middle School during lunch break, when everyone else seemed busy gossiping or playing softball out back. As I recall now, we avoided talking too much about ourselves, our home lives, our dreams, choosing instead to untangle the knots of that particular day: whether we liked the Spanish rice the cooks had served in the basement cafeteria (I hated it, but Jacey—on a free lunch program—didn't think it was so bad), whether Mr. Bowers was the most handsome seventh-grade teacher ever at our little country school (on that we agreed), how much we both struggled with math (she less than I), how "uppity" my classmate Marisa seemed (though Jacey seemed to admire her "style," as she called it). Difference of opinion was accommodated. Nevertheless, I was wary around Jacey, more worried that my classmates might see me talking to "the retard's" sister than I was interested in a friendship. More troubling, though, was my worry that the sense of defeat that clung to her would somehow rub off. Already she had an attitude of concession, and that made me a bit frightened, not of her but of her acquiescence.

She spoke with a soft voice, and when she smiled, her crooked teeth showed, so she rarely smiled without a furtive hand to her lips. She accepted occasional jars of canned peaches and cherries from my mother with a murmur and a bowed head. She came to my house a few times after school, and once I invited her for a Halloween party I had begged my mother to allow me to hold in our old barn. But I am ashamed to say this invitation was a gesture of coercion more than one of sincere friendship. At my mother's insistence, I invited "that nice little friend of yours." While Jacey was taller than I, it was, I think, her deference—as if she expected a slap at any moment—that made my mother think of her in the diminutive sense, or perhaps it was because my mother, a refugee from war and poverty in her Czech homeland, understood the belittling power of loneliness in a way that I, as yet, did not.

Since they had appeared in town—seemingly arriving from no place—Jacey's family lived in a brown shack with a corrugated tin roof next to the sandy bluff that drops away precipitously from the town cemetery. Huddled on a dirt patch in that out-of-the-way place, their home seemed haunted by angry presences. Jacey invited me in only once—probably because my mother, bearing a foil-wrapped cobbler, was dropping her off, and the presence of an adult seemed to warrant entrance. We went in—I reluctantly, my mother with her usual graciousness, as if nothing were unusual about the house or its location—and what I remember now is the blackness, as if all the grief of the cemetery leached down into that house to

reside with the broken furniture, the smell of stale hamburger grease, and the yellowed shades drawn against the hot afternoon.

As we stepped outside, though, we were blinded by the sun, which reflected off the sandy bluff that rose behind the house. Swallows came fiercely screeching at our intrusion, dive-bombing our heads and barely missing, swooping down from the nests they had excavated under the grassy lip of the cemetery in a complex network of bluff-side holes. An instinct to protect their own from a perceived threat made them cruel.

"We can't let the little ones play outside," Jacey told me, almost apologetically. "The swallows pecked at Junior's head so hard once they drew blood." I didn't know how to respond to that kind of confession.

Their house stood right under the corner of the cemetery where Indian bones and artifacts had once been found, decades before either of us was born, when gravediggers had unknowingly unearthed an Indian grave. For a long time after the bones were found, I have been told, people of my town were superstitious about laying their loved ones in that bluff-side corner of the cemetery, as if the Indian grave made the place inhospitable. That section remained empty for years, even though it offered those visiting graves the best view of the tree-lined river below, the town, and Freezeout Hill beyond, where the highway exited the valley. I never heard what happened to the Indian bones, though I suspect they remained unclaimed, having lost to time not just muscle and sinew but the right to be claimed by kith and kin.

I never heard what happened to Jacey and her family. The swallows are still there—I see their nesting holes every time I drive up Cemetery Hill and turn in at the gates to place flowers at the graves of my parents. But the shack where Richard and Jacey lived fell down many years ago after the family disappeared from the valley. No one knew where they went, and no one seemed to care that they were gone. Theirs was a dejection so deep and pervasive that fruit cobblers and a party invitation could not mend it.

I tell this story as a confessional, that I may own up to my part in the failure of that community which had once enthusiastically welcomed my mother and had, just as vehemently, ignored the needs of Jacey's family. What made the difference, I am hard-pressed to say. I know only that more essential than the belongings we claim are those "belongings"—those interwoven communities—that claim us.

GAYDELL COLLIER ✐ AfterWord

I. February

Driving from the ranch, I see
the life-flight helicopter

tracking I-90
into the rising sun
bearing my daughter
car-crash injuries too multiple to count
too ferocious to contemplate

In town I gather grandchildren
from school, from home
we begin the eighty-mile drive east
the chopper ahead in my mind's eye

Behind us the community rallies
casseroles breads hams pies
dozen offers to care for her baby
a fund set up at the bank
the power company plans a benefit breakfast
in the basement of the courthouse
an artist donates a painting for a raffle
someone pays the electric bill
the gas station posts anonymous donations
to our account, gas money
for trips yet to come
friends buy gift certificates to the local Subway
for the older children
to the Hunan near the hospital for me
teachers pay school lunch, daycare fees
others offer to cook, clean, provide transportation

Prayers rise up—
Prayer chains, Latter Day Saints, Church of Christ
Methodists, Episcopalians, Christian Scientists
Greek Orthodox in Florida, Catholics in New York
Prayers from Oregon and Colorado, South Dakota, Wyoming
Wisconsin, California, Arizona, New Jersey, France

Gently the doctors tell us Do not hope
death or vegetable
which is more kind?
They do not trust the power
of prayer
of community
of poetry

II. April

I read poems to my daughter
not written by long-bearded men with pipes
nor by cloistered, rose-petal ladies
 in high-necked frocks
but by women who reach out
 from hearts shattered like her body
 who draw life from stones—
women whose anguish leaches into the soil
 rises again like smoke
 hovers eagle-winged

My daughter listens
 while her breath gurgles in the trach
 her hands wander
 her legs lie still
from one eye her soul seeps, reaches out

one eye tracks the sound of my voice
one eye writes her own poem

III. November

Late night at the care center
the upstairs lounge is lit up
 for the party
 a private celebration with
doors shut to muffle the ring of laughter

A nurse and the aides
 off-duty after a long day
 bring treats—
 candy, chips, crazy Ya-Ya hats—
surround my daughter in her wheelchair

Facing the big-screen TV
she nibbles popcorn, sips Pepsi
talks with them, teases, laughs
they are all laughing
Divine Secrets of the Ya-Ya Sisterhood
this is the one she wanted to see

Verse by verse, she is writing her poem

Contributors

LUCY ADKINS (page 101) attended country schools, then the University of Nebraska and Auburn University. Returning to Nebraska, she has taught junior high and high school English and has worked everywhere from offices to emergency rooms.

LINDA ALDRICH (page 151) moved in 1987 from San Francisco to a rural Colorado commune dedicated to the beliefs of an obscure religious group, where she lived for eight years. Although she was enriched there, she finds herself "writing about the things that caused me to leave that philosophy behind."

SANA AMOURA-PATTERSON (page 120) teaches at Metropolitan Community College in Omaha, including at a strip-mall campus in Fremont, Nebraska, next to a Walgreens—the setting of this poem. She and her husband, Bill, have two children.

BONNIE ANDERSEN (page 168) lived with her Air Force family in Germany, Scotland, and England before returning to the States at age fifteen. She has since lived in Scotland, England, and China with her husband and children. Between travels, she's taught at Wayne State College in Nebraska.

ANONYMOUS (page 171) lives on a hundred-year-old ranch that once was miles from the nearest neighbor but now may be right next door to your new subdivision.

CAROLINE ARLEN (page 7) grew up in the East but worked summers on dude ranches in the West. After college, she landed a job at *Time* magazine, and later *Sports Illustrated* and *U.S. News & World Report*. When she sepa-

rated from her husband, she returned to the big skies to begin her life anew, alone, and "somewhat ungracefully" in Durango, Colorado.

KAREN ARMSTRONG *(page 4)* grew up in western Oregon, with a passion for the outdoors and her Norwegian heritage. After teaching, she raised two sons in Hong Kong and then in Washington State. Now living in California, she's involved with mountain trails, spinning wool, house building, trips to Norway, and a lavender nursery.

BESS ARNOLD *(page 146)* is a freelance writer living in Cheyenne, Wyoming. She received her degree in journalism as a nontraditional student in 1990. She has written or cowritten three books relating to railroads.

CHARLOTTE BABCOCK *(page 273)* writes humor, children's stories, poetry, and fiction, but her favorite subject is Wyoming history. She is the author of *Shot Down!* a book about murders in early-day Casper, Wyoming; the editor of six collections; and a frequent winner of literary prizes.

DENISE BANKER *(page 73)* is a lifelong Nebraskan who, after her father's death, ran a family business with her mother and sister. She won the 2002 Gaffney Academy of American Poets award and is currently an assistant professor at Concordia University.

ROBIN BARKLEY *(page 71)* obtained her GED, which enabled her to take further studies in animal science at a community college. In 1977, she completed horseshoeing school, and she is now an AFA Certified Farrier. Married to a saddlemaker, she lives in Arizona close to the Mexican border.

BETTE-B BAUER *(page 206)*, a native Oregonian, has lived in Paris, Mexico, and the Caribbean. After careers as a jewelry designer, cook, and accountant, she currently teaches college English in Omaha.

VIRGINIA BENNETT *(page 4)* has performed cowboy poetry at the Smithsonian Institution, on PBS and National Public Radio (NPR) specials, and at gatherings across the West. For thirty years, Virginia has worked alongside her husband starting colts, showing hunter/jumpers, driving draft teams, and drawing cowboy wages on big outfits. They now manage the Bonel Ranch east of Paso Robles, California.

MARGARET BENSHOOF-HOLLER *(page 95)* lived in Wyoming; Colorado; northwestern Nebraska; Jakarta, Indonesia; Madrid, Spain; and Malmö, Sweden, before moving to San Francisco, where she now writes and teaches.

DANNY BERGIN (page 212) is the mother of eight adults scattered throughout six states and heaven, grandma of twenty-six, great-grandma of two, and friend to her stepson. She lives with her husband in the Black Hills of South Dakota.

KAREN M. BERRY (page 214), after many years in Wyoming, moved in 2000 to Denver and in 2002 to Tucson, Arizona, where she is learning to love the nuances of desert monsoons and a sticky 2:00 A.M. moon. She spends time at yarn shops selecting the perfect shades for her knitting projects.

HILARY BARTON BILLMAN (page 130) lives in Kemmerer, Wyoming, with her husband, Jon Billman, and their son, Sam.

DORIS BIRCHAM (page 91) has been partnered with the same man, same Saskatchewan ranch, and same prairie wind forever. Her nursing career and ranch experiences provide inspiration for her poems. She enjoys performing regularly at cowboy poetry gatherings and in schools.

MAUREEN HELMS BLAKE (page 51) recently began a new adventure as a college student in Spearfish, South Dakota. Although her studies focus on writing, she has been surprised by the joy of art classes.

WILLO BOE (page 116) spent her childhood in the small prairie town of Buffalo, South Dakota, where she was the only child of a housewife mother and a blacksmith/artist father. At forty, she completed her college degree, then taught for twenty years before retiring in Nebraska.

LESLIE I. BROWN (page 209) works in natural resources research, which has led to jobs on the Colorado River in the Grand Canyon, in the sagebrush hills of Nevada, and among the lodgepole pines of Idaho's Sawtooth Range. She now lives in Utah.

B. J. BUCKLEY (pages 13, 191) lives with her sweetheart, a blacksmith, in a tiny cabin with no running water or electricity in Montana. Her awards include the *Cumberland Poetry Review*'s Robert Penn Warren Narrative Poetry Prize.

MAURA T. CALLAHAN (page 105) lives surrounded by eighty-foot trees in the foothills of the Cascade Range of Washington State. She has the comfort of animals, wild and domestic, and lots of gray days for writing.

CLEO CANTLON (page 119) is a former farmer and English teacher who also commuted daily one hundred miles to work as a reporter, editor, and col-

umnist. Now retired in Minot, North Dakota, she is a theater nut, play-wright, and director.

VIRGINIA BIXLER CASSELLS *(page 155)* was raised on a homestead in western Nebraska and has been married for fifty-seven years. She worked as a registered medical technologist and on her son's archaeology crew. She raised, trained, and showed dogs and horses and now paints them.

ANNE FANTACI CLEMENT *(page 102)* was born in New York City. Since she left for college, she has lived in rural areas, first in Colorado and now in Montana. She and her husband have traveled thousands of miles on motor-cycles.

ASHLEY COATS *(page 90)* was raised in Hawaii, attended college in Cali-fornia, and has been happily living in Montana since she and her husband jumped feetfirst into ranching. She's often asked, "Do you work outside the home?" She answers, "Yes, but sometimes I come in for lunch!"

GAYDELL COLLIER *(page 276)*—a retired librarian, horse breeder, and cow milker—lives with her husband, Roy, on their ranch in Wyoming's Black Hills. There she reads, writes, and runs amok among two ancient geese, seven retired broodmares, an unretiring dog, and a herd of active cats.

SHELLY WHITMAN COLONY *(page 77)* lives on a small farm in northwest-ern Oregon with her husband and twin sons. Believing in the local produc-tion of food, she plans to raise organic strawberries, chickens, and sheep.

GERALDINE CONNOLLY *(page 187)* lives on the shores of Flathead Lake in Bigfork, Montana. She is a poet and codirector of the Plum Writers Retreat. Her awards include two National Endowment for the Arts (NEA) fellow-ships in poetry and the Margaret Bridgman fellowship of the Bread Loaf Writers' Conference. She is the author of *Food for the Winter* and *Province of Fire.*

STACY GILLETT COYLE *(page 243)* has taught at various colleges and uni-versities in Colorado and most recently in Wyoming. She recently took a year off to work on writing projects. She lives near Parker, Colorado.

NANCY CURTIS *(page 258)* likes arranging and rearranging words on pages, both her own and those of others. She runs a small publishing com-pany, High Plains Press, from the family ranch in Wyoming.

RUTH DANIELS *(page 186)* is the third generation to live on the family farm in the heart of the blackjack country of Oklahoma. Although she says she

has "had little formal education," she enjoys writing from her life experiences and rural roots.

LOU DEAN *(page 53)* grew up on a quarter-section farm in Osage County, Oklahoma. She says that in childhood pictures, she is "either on a horse or attached to a dog, lamb, pig, or kitten." She now lives in northwestern Colorado. She is the author of four books, including *Pawprints in My Soul* and *Angels in Disguise.*

MARILYN DORF *(page 143)* was raised on a Nebraska farm and now lives in Lincoln. She's published more than a hundred poems in various journals.

BETTY DOWNS *(page 181)* was married to a heavy-equipment mechanic for forty years. Now widowed, she lives in Black Hawk, South Dakota, where she enjoys baseball and her grandchildren.

SISTER HILDEGARD DUBNICK, OSB *(page 121)* was raised in a Catholic family that was not particularly devout. To her own great surprise, God called her to a life of prayer as a Benedictine nun. In 1987, she entered the Abbey of Saint Walburga, located near Virginia Dale, Colorado. She serves as Abbey organist and on the staff of the Abbey Retreat House.

CAROLYN DUFURRENA *(pages 87, 167)* is a teacher and geologist who writes from northwestern Nevada, where she lives with her husband, Tim. She is the author of *Fifty Miles from Home: Riding the Long Circle on a Nevada Family Ranch* and coauthor of *Sharing Fencelines.*

PHYLLIS DUGAN *(page 32)* attended a creative writing class just for fun after a lifetime of keeping personal journals. That spurred a writing career that has led to publication in newspapers, magazines, and books. She lives in Thayne, Wyoming (population 267).

NORMA NELSON DUPPLER *(page 179)* has been a reporter, humor columnist, and teacher of creative writing. She is currently the Barnes County, North Dakota, emergency manager. On the family ranch, she found a stone calendar that archaeoastronomers estimate to be four thousand years old.

SHANNON DYER *(page 113)* developed a strong passion for the land and its people after twenty years of living in the Nebraska Sandhills. As with any love, she learned to take the bad with the good. She now lives in Colorado.

SOPHIE DOMINIK ECHEVERRIA *(page 202)* is a poet, a singer, and a lifetime student of flamenco who lives in Wyoming. "All my politics are based

in art and agriculture," she says. Her large Basque sheep-ranching family is spread across the West.

FAYE EGGERT *(page 223)* is ninety-eight years old and spent her youth in Hiland, Wyoming. She's been active in the same church for eighty-three years. She attended the University of Kansas and the University of Wisconsin.

BARBARA A. ENGLE *(page 157)* has lived in southeastern Wyoming for twenty-four years and loves being a rural mail carrier. Animal welfare is one of her main interests.

KELLY MADIGAN ERLANDSON *(page 145)* lives in Lincoln, Nebraska. Her work has previously appeared in *Plains Song Review, Iowa Woman, Barrow Street,* and the anthology *Times of Sorrow, Times of Grace.*

GOOSE E. FEDDERS *(page 141)* was raised on the Red River in Texas's Tornado Alley, where "makin' up stories" is a long tradition. After studying art and literature, she became a design consultant and production artist in Santa Fe, New Mexico.

PAT FROLANDER *(page 35)* says, "After thirty-three years on my husband's fourth-generation ranch, if this were college, I'd have just completed my freshman year. Ranching is like my marriage: I can feel ambivalent but never detached."

EVELYN I. FUNDA *(page 274)* specializes in women's literature and Western American literature at Utah State University, where she teaches. She is writing a memoir about the deaths of her parents just three months after the sale of their family farm.

KATHERINE MANN GALEY *(page 235)* says that she wishes she could still "hand-crank the old ice-cream freezer and listen to my uncles and dad tell of horses they rode and bucks that got away." Living in the Sandhills of Nebraska and working with the cowboys there gave her a plethora of wonderful stories.

COLETTE "KOKO" KNUTSON GJERMUNDSON *(page 60)* earned a degree in mass communication with minors in animal science and general agriculture. She and her husband run a commercial cow-calf operation in North Dakota. She is also a freelance writer who enjoys public speaking.

LYDIA GONZALES *(page 272)* is a high school dropout who, at the age of thirty-eight with six children, returned to school. She retired from Garden

City Community College as assistant director of the educational talent search program. She was honored at the Kansas state capitol in Topeka with Lydia Gonzales Day.

KATHLEEN GOTSCHALL *(page 177)* lives on a Nebraska Sandhills ranch, where for years her goals were common things such as weaning the baby and trekking to town for groceries and a library stop. With her husband, she currently runs an organic beef, buffalo, and dairy operation and is a rodeo mom.

JANET E. GRAEBNER *(page 222)* moved to the mountain community of Conifer, Colorado, after pursuing a freelance writing career in Southern California. She and her husband, Peter, have a home built on Precambrian rock—a grounding influence, she says.

LAURIE M. GREIG *(page 247)* is a psychotherapist who works primarily with adolescents and women. She lives on Bainbridge Island, Washington.

LAURA HAWKINS GREVEL *(page 218)* is the granddaughter of Texas ranching families. She and her husband run an organic mountain farm in Austria near the Czech border (visitors welcome). Their goals are self-sufficient, sustainable agriculture and farming with horses.

JENNIFER GRAF GRONEBERG *(page 94)* lives in Montana with her husband of ten years, Tom; their three young sons; a cowdog; and two doleful cats. She is the editor of *My Heart's First Steps* and a past recipient of the Smith Corona Prize for short fiction.

TWYLA HANSEN *(page 78)* grew up with three older brothers and no television on a small farm in Nebraska, where the independence, isolation, and introspection shaped her sensibilities toward writing. Her latest book of poetry is *Potato Soup.*

A. J. HARNISH *(page 72)* is a family practice physician in Cheyenne, Wyoming. She says, "I love the many careers I have—wife to J.D., mother to Madi and Jack, daughter to Bennie and Joanne, and physician to many."

RUTH HARPER *(page 80)* is a wife, mother, friend, avid reader, counselor, educator, and occasional writer living in Brookings, South Dakota. She says that she is "blessed with a terrific book group and an encouraging 'writing buddy,' Ruby Wilson."

SUE HARTMAN *(page 182)* lives in rural Boulder County, Colorado, and the red rock country of Utah with her husband and two "worthless herd dogs."

Her short stories and nonfiction are anthologized in books, including *High Fantastic: Colorado's Fantasy, Dark Fantasy, and Science Fiction.*

MELINDA GREEN HARVEY *(page 17)* says, "Writing snuck up on me, causing me to turn my spare bedroom into a writing studio, making me take vacations away from family, tricking me into having a favorite dictionary! I never saw it coming." She once owned an architecture firm and currently works for the transit system in Lubbock, Texas.

LINDA M. HASSELSTROM *(page xv)* lives in Cheyenne, Wyoming, and conducts writing retreats for women on her western South Dakota ranch. Her Web site provides details on the retreats, lists her published poetry and nonfiction, and gives contact information. See www.windbreakhouse .com.

MARY ALICE HAUG *(page 226)* grew up in central South Dakota, where she divided her time between living on a farm/ranch west of the Missouri River and in a small town on the east bank of the Missouri. She teaches English at South Dakota State University.

CELESTE HAVENER *(page 17)* and her husband, Gary, built a log home in the Centennial Valley of Wyoming, where they are raising their son. Her education is in soils and ethnobotany, with an emphasis on indigenous agriculture.

LISA HELDKE *(page 126)* lives in St. Peter, Minnesota, where she teaches philosophy and women's studies at Gustavus Adolphus College. She and her partner host a monthly soup-and-bread night. In her next life, she will be an artisanal bread baker with her own brick oven.

MARCIA HENSLEY *(page 216)* worked in Wyoming when she was a college student, but it took her twenty years to get back. Now retired, she leads reading discussion groups and works with volunteers collecting area history in the small community of Eden/Farson, Wyoming.

YVONNE HOLLENBECK *(page 112)* felt lonely and unaccepted when she moved into the Clearfield, South Dakota, community after marrying a local rancher. Now she has bonded with a group of area women, and their friendships and accomplishments are noteworthy.

EMILIE HOPPE *(page 232)* and her husband are the parents of teenage triplets. She writes, "Except for my university years, I have always lived in the Amana Colonies in Iowa. Community is not something you belong to; it is

something you work for. Communities may be created by accident or by design, but they remain intact only if people are willing to work to make that happen."

KATHY HUNTER *(page 46)* moved to Kodiak, Alaska, in 1975 and wrote about Alaska's natural history, diverse cultures, and history for twenty-three years. After moving back to Oregon, she became a professional story-teller, writing fiction to provide material for her performances.

CHRISTINA HUTCHINS *(page 214)* holds a Ph.D. in interdisciplinary studies from the Graduate Theological Union in Berkeley, California. Her awards include a Villa Montalvo Biennial Poetry Competition prize, a Barbara Deming Memorial Fund for Women Poetry Award, and several residencies.

BARBARA JESSING *(page 139)* is a child and family therapist and the mother of two daughters with her husband, Timothy Butz. She lives in Omaha, Nebraska.

MARGARET EATON JOHNSON *(page 156)* lives on a Wyoming ranch settled by her husband's family in 1879. She celebrates the beauty of their Laramie River ranch and its wildlife in her art and photography.

JUDY ANN *(page 124)* is a Wyoming native, daughter of a Wyoming native, granddaughter of a Wyoming homesteader. She has two grown sons and one "almost there." She teaches, writes, and is involved in community theater.

KATHRYN E. KELLEY *(page 190)* says, "Writing about contemporary heartland subjects seems as natural as dandelions in the ditch to someone born in Iowa, educated in South Dakota, and living in Nebraska." Volunteer work with Free the Innocent is opening a deep vein of material for her.

DIANE KESEY *(page 30)* says she's "an old field-variety hippie," born in North Dakota and raised all over the West. She writes, homeschools, walks, and raises Cain, usually over the decimation of the West.

NANCY KILE *(page 45)* was born and raised near as the crow flies across the pine ridge from Fort Robinson, Nebraska. She writes, "I dedicate this piece to my daughter, Anna Rose Kile; my mother, Rosemary Clements; my grandmother Lucille Nancy Hat; and most respectfully to my great-grandmother Sarah Feather On Head."

JANE KIRKPATRICK (page 91) was a mental health professional before she and her husband, Jerry, stepped onto a cloud of faith believing they would not fall through. They began carving a ranch out of 160 acres along the remote John Day River in Oregon. Author of many novels and two nonfiction books, she speaks and teaches, returning to the ranch on Starvation Lane for the comfort of community.

NORMA THORSTAD KNAPP (page 84) lives in northern Minnesota, on a small lake with her husband, Byron, and her cat, Billy the Kid. Her hobbies include quilting cathedral window designs, bicycling, and downhill skiing.

JACKIE PUGH KOGAN (page 201) was raised in eastern Oregon on land homesteaded by her great-great-grandfather. Her writing is rooted in her family's records and manuscripts and her rural memories. She teaches literature and writing at California State University at Northridge.

BERNIE KOLLER (page 133) is a retired teacher who works as library director in Freeman, South Dakota. She is involved with her German-Russian ancestry, conducts tours to Hutterian colonies, and lectures at the annual Schmeckfest celebration.

KAY E. KONZ (page 269) is the seventh child of John and Irene Konz of Neola, Iowa. Currently transplanted to Lincoln, Nebraska, she is a licensed mental health counselor. She is domestically disabled but loves to have friends over anyway.

GRACE E. REIMERS KYHN (page 156) earned her GED at age fifty-one. Her first art and writing were published when she was sixteen, and she received one dollar in payment. She lives in Boelus, Nebraska.

PAGE LAMBERT (page 264), recipient of a 2004 Wyoming Arts Council Poetry Fellowship, is the author of *In Search of Kinship* and other works. A speaker and facilitator of writing retreats, she lives in the mountains of Colorado and the Black Hills of Wyoming, where she explores the inner and outer landscapes of a life in transition.

PHYLLIS M. LETELLIER (page 229) for years wrote and sold humor from Greybull, Wyoming, but she hasn't found much funny to write about since the death of her husband. She does bookkeeping for her son, who now runs the family's two-man farm equipment repair business by himself.

DARCY LIPP-ACORD (page 58) lives on a ranch near Ucross, Wyoming, with her husband, Shawn, and their five children. She teaches English part-time and works part-time as a freelance writer.

MARY LODE (*page 237*) grew up on her family's "small and dirt-poor ranch," which had only rare visitors and afforded her few trips to town. She loved it. After time in college, she returned to central Montana to buy her own small place, where she raises sheep and cows.

DOROTHY BLACKCROW MACK (*pages 160, 241*) is a spiritual midwife, a singer in Sisiwis and Indian Shaker healing traditions. The name given to her by Thich Nhat Hanh is Breathing Spirit of the Heart.

CLAUDIA F. MANZ (*page 106*) followed in the footsteps of her great-great-grandmother and came to Colorado, settling in the small mountain community of Lyons. She meets with "the four poetesses" once a week, who agree that a hike, a couple of hours of writing, and a strong cup of coffee cure most ailments.

B. LYNNE McCARTHY (*page 65*) was welcomed home to the family ranch after college, and her husband became a valuable partner. But after seventeen years, the ranch was divided and gone. Since then, she's been too busy surviving to write, but "now that we have electricity and running water, I'm hoping that changes." She lives in Missouri.

ELIZABETH KEOUGH McDONALD (*page 163*) works as a registered nurse in Gallup, New Mexico, to support her writing. An Air Force veteran, her recent work has appeared in *Intensive Care: More Poetry and Prose by Nurses*.

JANE McGARRY (*page 86*) lives in the North Fork Valley of the Gunnison River in Colorado, where she gardens, fills up a root cellar every fall, edits books, and writes poems and essays.

DONNA APPLEGARTH MENTINK (*page 172*) grew up thinking all girls worked in the hayfield, rode horses, and chased cattle. After college in Kansas and travel in the East and South, she married a Nebraska cowman. She now bales hay, rides horses, and chases cattle. "Life is good," she says.

SUSAN MINYARD (*pages 22, 272*) experienced displacement in her home state of Arizona when her family's farms did not survive. She is now the family matriarch, trying to become wise fast. For the first time in her life, she is content not being a student or a teacher.

DIANE MOLLESON (*page 18*) worked for ten years for literary agents and publishing companies in New York. In 1992, she moved to eastern Washington, where she has ghostwritten some of the Baby-sitters Club books and has written three nonfiction books for Scholastic.

PAT OGLE (*page 146*) had a nine-year career on the railroad before she married a railroader and raised three children. She enjoys bingo, playing cards, and an occasional gambling trip.

DIXIE PARTRIDGE (*page 57*) learned to irrigate fields, feed stock, put up hay, milk cows, and "winter in" while growing up on a farm homesteaded by her great-grandfather. She and her husband raised their family near the Columbia River in eastern Washington.

BETH PAULSON (*page 140*) lives and writes mostly in Ouray, Colorado, where she teaches a writing workshop. Previously, she taught college English for more than twenty years.

KATY PAYNICH (*page 63*) was born and raised in Bozeman, Montana. After college, she married her high school sweetheart and returned "home." She teaches at the high school and enjoys family and friends.

DIANE JOSEPHY PEAVEY (*page 173*) writes about the changing Western landscape and her family's Idaho sheep and cattle ranch. Her stories air on Idaho Public Radio and appear in her book *Bitterbrush Country: Living on the Edge of the Land.*

C. S. PEDERSON (*page 109*) divides her time between Missouri and Kansas, where her family still lives. She and her husband had a pond dug for her frog friends and are establishing a stand of native buffalo grass behind the pond.

LOREE PEERY (*page 224*) returns to the native grass pasture of her youth when she needs a break; there "the native land renews my spirit and my heart soars with the meadowlark's song." She works as a part-time editorial assistant at the University of Nebraska and values one-on-one conversations with her grandchildren.

MARIAN D. PETERS (*page 6*) is retired after thirty-four years with the South Dakota Department of Labor. Her activities now consist of writing, watercolor painting, playing bridge, and socializing with family and friends.

KAY MARIE PORTERFIELD (*page 224*) coauthored the *Encyclopedia of American Indian Contributions to the World*, which won a Colorado Book Award. She received a 2003 Colorado Arts Council Artist Fellowship to complete the book that contains "Beadwork."

KIM POTTS (page 81) announced that she wanted to be a cowgirl at age four and is still working toward that goal. She and her husband moved to Montana sight unseen and have never wanted to leave. She cleans a millionaire's log mansion and lives near Three Forks.

KAYNE PYATT (page 256) has developed seminars, workshops, and women's retreats on the subjects of feminine spirituality and intuition. Kayne also teaches at the community college in Rock Springs, Wyoming.

PAMELA RAMSEY (page 39) has worked as a waitress, secretary, sprinkler system installer, night watchperson, and public librarian. Talking, sharing, and laughing with her women friends give her a respite from contributing to the larger community. She and her family live in a small Colorado town at the base of Pikes Peak.

LORA K. REITER (page 195) was raised in the country and teaches college English in Kansas. Her first loves are the Kansas Flint Hills and the animals that surround her. Daughter of an essayist and poet, she was nourished by words along with milk.

MARY FRANCES RENSTROM (page 14) left Idaho to attend a women's college on the East Coast. She never fit in but had a marvelous time shocking her classmates and professors with her libertarian politics and stories of rural Idaho. She has now settled in Denver.

SARAH BYRN RICKMAN's (page 117) heart still resides in Colorado, although she writes books, short stories, and articles from Centerville, Ohio, where she now lives with her husband, Richard.

GAIL RIXEN (page 44) has worked as a carpenter, teacher, and health care worker but now farms with geologist Tim Kroeger in northern Minnesota.

JEANNE ROGERS (page 250) lives in Wyoming and has supported her community with various jobs over the years: waitress, gas station attendant, flagger, floral designer, bookkeeper, cashier, volleyball official, bus driver, construction laborer, weed sprayer, haying operator, draftsman, and writer.

TAMARA E. ROGERS (page 14) lives on the east slope of the Black Hills of South Dakota, sharing a small organic ranch with her sister.

GRETCHEN RONNOW (page 70) was raised in Nevada, was educated in Utah and Arizona, and now teaches in Nebraska. She's worked in Mexico,

Guatemala, and Siberia. Her professional fields are Native American Indian and contemporary Arabic literature.

WANDA ROSSELAND (page 137) has been fortunate to live in eastern Montana, making friends with ranchers, tough but tenderhearted women, deer, antelope, hawks, and cows.

JANIS RUSSELL-WILSON (pages 97, 164) has worked as a reference librarian in Oklahoma, Kansas, Missouri, and Arizona. She and her husband live in a country home, a haven for wildlife and orphaned pets, in Warrensburg, Missouri.

KATHLEEN RUTLEDGE (page 67) lives on sixty-two rolling acres near Garland, Nebraska. She is the editor of the *Lincoln Journal Star.* She and her husband, writer Ted Kooser, have a son and a granddaughter.

EDITH RYLANDER (page 229), born in California, has lived in central Minnesota since 1964. Her books are *Rural Routes: Essays on Living in Rural Minnesota, Dancing Back the Cranes* (poems), and, in collaboration with her husband, John, *Journeying Earthward.*

MARJORIE SAISER (page 207) grew up on the edge: the edge of a small town in Nebraska, even the edge of Nebraska. From the end of Main Street, she could see South Dakota. She is a poet living farther inland now, in Lincoln.

MARY LOU SANELLI (page 50) coordinates Port Townsend, Washington's Sunday at One Poetry Series and is artistic director of the Moving Arts Dance Company. Her commentaries have been heard on National Public Radio and published in the *Seattle Times.* She has published five volumes of poetry, and her work is widely published in journals.

MICHELLE M. SAUER (page 231) publishes in the areas of anchoritism, mysticism, asceticism, church history, and queer theory. Currently, her projects include a Cistercian sermon concordance and a book on the anchoritic movement in late medieval England. She is married to Adam Bures and lives in North Dakota.

MEGHAN NUTTALL SAYRES (page 31) lives in Valleyford, Washington, with her husband, three children, two sheep, and cat. She spins yarns for tapestries, dyeing her wool with native plants, and has studied this craft in Ireland and Turkey. She volunteers for Taipeis Gael, a tapestry-weaving cooperative in Donegal, Ireland.

PEARLE HENRIKSEN SCHULTZ *(page 254)* has been a teacher, a principal, the headmistress of a college preparatory school, and the curriculum supervisor in the Miami–Dade County Public Schools. Now retired in Big Horn, Wyoming, Pearle likes quiet evenings with her husband of fifty-nine years.

DAWN SENIOR-TRASK *(page 149)* lives with her husband, Juel, in the mountains of Wyoming, where they have collected a remuda of eight horses and ride with friends. As well as writing, Dawn creates bronze sculpture, oil paintings, and woodcuts.

LIESEL SHINEBERG *(page 251)* was born in Aachen, Germany, and immigrated to the United States, via Holland, in 1940. She joined her new husband in Rock Springs, Wyoming, after an eight-day courtship, and they've lived there for more than fifty years, raising four children.

BARBARA M. SMITH *(page 42)* has been published in collections such as *The Last Best Place,* an anthology of Montana writers, and *Drive, He Said,* an anthology about Americans and their love affair with the car. She teaches English at Western Wyoming Community College in Rock Springs.

CONSUELO N. SMITH *(page 238)* says making tortillas with her *abuela* (grandmother) and mama is the most significant of all her childhood memories. "The aroma. The flavor. The bread of life. You can buy tortillas by the dozen in any grocery, but you can't buy the history, the culture, the life."

JEANNIE P. SMITH *(page 69)*, a second-generation Nevadan, grew up on a dairy farm near Sparks. Her story is about her mother-in-law, who didn't want to give up life in the city for one in the country but made a success of her adventure.

MARY SOJOURNER *(page 240)* is a writer, radio commentator, and hardcore environmental and social justice activist. She writes, "What matters more than college degrees to me, or even family, is that my heart is broken. I signed on for that. It's how the truth gets in."

JENNIFER KAYL SOULE *(page 3)* is a retired social work professor who has returned home to South Dakota with her husband to write full-time on the prairie landscape that inspires her.

MARY K. STILLWELL *(page 159)*, a native of Nebraska, has studied writing in New York and on the plains and has published poetry in a wide variety of journals, including the *Paris Review* and *Prairie Schooner.* Her book of poems, *Moving to Malibu,* was published by Sandhills Press.

JO-ANN SWANSON (page 148) was raised on a farm in Armley, north-central Saskatchewan, and has lived in Montana for more than twenty years. An associate professor at the University of Great Falls, she is married and has an extended family of stray cats, a dog, rabbits, and too many deer!

SHAUNANNE TANGNEY (page 26) teaches at Minot State University in North Dakota. She publishes articles on apocalypticism and on the poet Robinson Jeffers. A native of California, she readily accepts the moniker a colleague recently gave her: "the West Coast apostle of the apocalypse."

ANITA TANNER (page 20) learned the value of hard work and a love of the land, nature, and animals on her family's small farm. She, her husband, and their six children made their home in Utah for many years before moving to Colorado, where she now works as a substitute teacher in Cortez.

JANIE TIPPETT (page 29) is a ranch wife near Joseph, Oregon, where she has written a weekly column for an agriculture newspaper for eighteen years. She is very involved with Fishtrap, a local literary organization, which she says "saved her life."

SUREVA TOWLER (pages 41, 132) abandoned the East for Steamboat Springs, Colorado, where she served on museum, library, and special district boards for more than thirty years. Her experiences generate books and a column in the *Denver Post*. She now divides her time between Kansas and Colorado.

ROSEMERRY WAHTOLA TROMMER (page 123) lives near Telluride, Colorado, where she is a trail runner, singer, and optimist. She travels often, speaking about how to live a more poetic, meaningful life. Visit her at www.word-woman.com to see her books and CDs.

CHRISTINE VALENTINE (page 166) is a retired chemical dependency consultant. She came to the United States from England in 1964 and put down roots in the little village of Birney, Montana.

ELLEN VAYO (page 248) lives with her husband in a high mountain basin near Casper, Wyoming. She has been a stay-at-home mom, a fitness instructor and belly dancer, a soda jerk, a shoe salesperson, and the literary editor of an award-winning anthology. The final chapters of her first novel are proving elusive.

JEAN VERTEFEUILLE-CUTLER (page 83) and her husband, Ron, are retired from raising horses in southern Colorado but still trail-ride in the mountains with their four dogs when they aren't traveling.

SHEILA VOSEN-SHORTEN (page 196) became friends with Jacqueline Stewart while teaching on the Northern Cheyenne Reservation, and Jacqueline's mother, Rose Marie, adopted her. After making mandolins and pottery in Bozeman, Montana, Sheila and her husband moved back to the Hi-Line, where she grew up.

PHYLLIS WALKER (page 261) lives in western Montana with her husband, four sons, and infant daughter. She writes children's books and teaches piano.

BARBARA WALLACE (page 267) worked on farms or ranches during summer breaks from her teaching job, while longing for her own place on the land. After months of treatment for breast cancer, she realized that she shouldn't wait. She now lives on fourteen acres in the foothills of the Cascade Range. "I am home," she says.

TRACY WANG (page 74) immigrated to the United States in 1997, moving from Canton, China, to Spearfish, South Dakota, where she and her husband owned and operated the Golden Dragon Restaurant until recently. She often interprets Cantonese or Mandarin for the police, the courts, and the hospital. This is her first essay written in English.

ELLEN WATERSTON (page 268) is a New Englander who married and moved to the ranching West. Her essays, poems, and short fiction have appeared in reviews and anthologies. She is the author of a memoir, *Then There Was No Mountain*.

HELEN M. WAYMAN (page 129) grew up on a Montana wheat farm in the Great Depression. A former nurse, she's lived all over North America with her geophysicist husband. Now living in Billings, she says, "I have never published anything, but have drawers full of writing at home."

PATRICIA WELLINGHAM-JONES (page 263) headed west as soon as she got her degree as a registered nurse and a car. She knew when she saw the mountains, she wouldn't be going back to New Jersey except to visit. She's been a Californian ever since.

JANE WELLS (page 176) lives outside Buffalo, Wyoming, with her husband, youngest child, and two granddogs. She's a "wrancher and a riter and has never ridden a wild bull intentionally."

JOANNE WILKE (page 152) spent three years as an editorial assistant at *Runner's World* magazine. Her work has been published in the *Christian Science Monitor, Pacific Review, Falcon for Kids,* and other publications. She

lives in Bozeman, Montana, with her husband, two children, and various chickens.

RUBY R. WILSON (page 25) is a native South Dakotan who lives on a small acreage near Bruce. She can sometimes be seen gathering seeds from the big bluestem and other native plants she nurtures.

MARIANNE HOFFMANN WOEPPEL (page 185) stored her works in boxes in her closet in Lincoln, Nebraska. She "came out" recently, during a gab session at her Ceili (Irish) dance class, when five people discovered a common interest in writing and started the Irish Writers.

CHERYL ANDERSON WRIGHT (page 77) works as a librarian in Cody, Wyoming. She raises a big garden that contains many herbs, which she uses in cooking and making gifts and as the topic of presentations.

PATTY ZEIGLER (page 37) grew up barefoot with big dreams. A career in television production couldn't sidetrack her love of the land, and she returned happily to her roots when she married. With her family, she farms and ranches near Highmore, South Dakota.

MARY ZELINKA (page 255) lives with her springer spaniel, Molly McGee (aka Wild Thing), in Albany, Oregon, where she is the client services director for the Center Against Rape and Domestic Violence. She likes hanging out with friends and solving the world's problems, laughing, or just being silly.

ACKNOWLEDGMENTS

We send thanks to the readers of *Leaning into the Wind* and *Woven on the Wind*, our earlier collections of women's writing. *Leaning* focused on women's relationships with the land, *Woven* on their relationships with each other. Your enthusiasm for these writings and your encouragement to continue this dialogue among women all over the country have inspired this third collection. *Crazy Woman Creek: Women Rewrite the American West* focuses on women's relationships to the communities in which they live. The work of more than five hundred women appears in these three anthologies, and we are grateful to every one of you.

We are grateful to the people who helped us arrive at the final shape of this book, even though their fingerprints may be invisible to others: Kathleen ("KD") Danker, Patty Myers, Shari Shaw, and Gertrud Goetz, along with the dozens of people who gave us ideas for the title, suggestions, inspiration, and encouragement. As we struggled with our vision for this collection, these folks entered into the spirit of creation; their good cheer helped keep us working during some dark days.

We appreciate the scores of writers who submitted their writing to all three collections, whether or not it was finally used. We also value the women among you who thought about the themes of each anthology and discussed our ideas, even if you didn't commit your words to paper. All of you have contributed to the ongoing efforts of women everywhere to open conversations about our lives, to find strength through our shared experiences, and to better the communities where we live.

Our thanks as well to all the women who contributed to this and the earlier works by forwarding e-mail messages, spreading word of the call for manuscripts and of publication, organizing autograph parties, contributing to the staggering collection of photographs and anecdotes in our archive, and in other ways demonstrating your dedication to the ideas these collections represent. Your enthusiasm, joy, and generosity in these endeavors have both humbled and energized us.

We thank those closest to us—the men in our lives, our families, our friends and coworkers—for their forbearance when we wandered around mumbling to ourselves, crazed with editing fever. Credit goes as well to Tamara and Tracy; we'd have been truly lost without you. We send blessings to Chet and Evelyn at The Bunkhouse Bed and Breakfast near Sundance, Wyoming, where we worked on all three books. Not only did they furnish us with comfortable beds and terrific, rib-sticking food, but they warmed us with fires both literal and metaphoric, and honored us with prayers and wisdom.

Marc Jaffe and his assistant editor, Mindy Keskinen, first accepted our work for Houghton Mifflin. Your vision has been carried on the wind outward from the High Plains to cover the entire West—and blown a few fresh breezes eastward as well. We're grateful beyond words.

We deeply appreciate our current editor, Susan Canavan, and the many hardworking people at Houghton Mifflin who have made this particular crazy quilt a reality.

CREDITS

"Quilting a Dissertation" by Bette-B Bauer. An earlier version appeared in *Friendly Woman*, vol. 13, no. 2, 1998; reprinted by permission of the author.

"The Non-Musicals Sing Their Last Song" by Willo Boe. First appeared in *Writing Our Stories II*, New Cassel Foundation, New Cassel Retirement Center, and Nebraska Humanities Council, 2000; reprinted by permission of the author.

"Nevada Firestorm" by Carolyn Dufurrena. First appeared in a longer version as "Cherry Pie" in *Sharing Fencelines: Three Friends Write from Nevada's Sagebrush Corner*, University of Utah Press, 2002; reprinted by permission of the author.

"In a Time of War" by Christina Hutchins. First appeared on the Poets Against the War Web site; reprinted by permission of the author.

"Crone Circle: Grandmothers Giving Wisdom" by Dorothy Blackcrow Mack. An earlier version appeared in *Our Turn, Our Time: Women Truly Coming of Age*, Beyond Words Publishing, 2000; with permission of the author.

"The Ramah Farmer's Market" by Elizabeth Keough McDonald. First appeared in the Ramah Arts Council newsletter, Summer 2003; reprinted by permission of the author.

"Cliff Dwellings: Mesa Verde" by Dixie Partridge. First appeared in *Dialogue: A Journal of Mormon Thought*, vol. 22, no. 3, 1989; also appeared in *Watermark*, Saturday Press, Inc., 1991; reprinted by permission of the author.

"At the Line Dance Café" by Marian D. Peters. First appeared in the *Vermillion Literacy Project* magazine, University of South Dakota, 2000; reprinted by permission of the author.

"Beadwork" by Kay Marie Porterfield. First appeared in an earlier form in the *Vermillion Literacy Project* magazine, University of South Dakota, 2001.

"Weeders, All" by Lora K. Reiter. First appeared as "Bonding" in the *Kansas Quarterly*, v. 18, no. 3, 1986; reprinted by permission of the author.

"Straightforward and Unafraid" by Wanda Rosseland. The Homemaker's Creed is a prayer written by Mary Stewart in 1904 originally titled "Collect for Club Women."

"The Living, the Warm" by Marjorie Saiser. First appeared in *Lost in Seward County*, Backwaters Press, 2001; reprinted by permission of the author.

"Sonnet for My Grandchild" by Pearle Henriksen Schultz. First appeared in *Wyoming Writing*, 1994, Wyoming Writers, Inc.; reprinted by permission of the author.

"The Circle Dance" by Mary K. Stillwell. First appeared in *Literal Latte*, reprinted by permission of the author.

"One Panel of a Quilt" by Patricia Wellingham-Jones. First appeared in *Thunder Sandwich*, no. 16, 2002; reprinted by permission of the author.

"The Brown Sofa" by Cheryl Anderson Wright. First appeared in *Visual Eyes, Verbalize*, 1999, Northwest College; reprinted by permission of the author.

Crazy Woman Creek

EDITED BY

Linda M. Hasselstrom, Gaydell Collier,
and Nancy Curtis

"Here is the essence of the West — not the myth, but the truth."

—W. MICHAEL GEAR AND
KATHLEEN O'NEAL GEAR

About the Editors

Linda M. Hasselstrom, born in Texas, divides her time between Hermosa, South Dakota, and Cheyenne, Wyoming. Her poetry, fiction, and nonfiction have been widely published. She is the author of eleven books, including *Between Grass and Sky: Where I Live and Work* and *Feels Like Far: A Rancher's Life on the Great Plains.* Hasselstrom was admitted to the South Dakota Hall of Fame in 1989 as Writer of the Year, and her book *Bison: Monarch of the Plains* was named the best environmental and nature book of 1999 by the Independent Publishers Association. She received a Wrangler Award from the National Cowboy and Western Heritage Museum in 2001 for her book of poems *Bitter Creek Junction,* which was also a finalist for the WILLA Literary Award from Women Writing the West. *Between Grass and Sky* was named a WILLA finalist in 2003.

Gaydell Collier, who was born on Long Island, New York, lives on a small ranch near Sundance, Wyoming, with her husband, Roy. A retired library director, she is the coauthor with Eleanor F. Prince of several books on horsemanship and horse care, including *Basic Horsemanship: English and Western.* Her work has appeared in periodicals and anthologies, including the *Christian Science Monitor, Smithsonian,* and *Flint-Edged Refrains.* She was a consultant on "Horses and Horsemanship" for the *Encyclopaedia Britannica* in 2000. Her interests include ranching, reading, dogs, horses, grand opera, and eating.

Nancy Curtis was born in Duncan, Oklahoma, and currently resides in Glendo, Wyoming, with her husband, Doug. She is the publisher and primary editor of High Plains Press, a company specializing in books about Wyoming and the West, which she runs from her family's ranch. High Plains Press has received three prestigious Wrangler Awards from the National Cowboy and Western Heritage Museum for publishing outstanding poetry books. Curtis and her cows were the subject of a photo essay on Western women in *Life.*

All three editors help manage working ranches.

For Discussion

We hope the following questions will stimulate discussion for reading groups and provide a deeper understanding of Crazy Woman Creek *for every reader.*

1. Community is defined in many ways in this anthology, with an understanding that "being part of a community is much more than owning property within its boundaries" ("I Like It That Way," 218). What does community mean to you? How do you define your place within your community?

2. How do the pieces in this anthology illustrate the ways in which a community originates and the means by which we can establish new ones? Is the more traditional notion of community becoming obsolete? What have these women done to preserve the communities and values people cherish? What can we do?

3. In her introduction, Linda M. Hasselstrom writes: "Can neighborliness survive even as our landscape is being bulldozed and paved over? Before we can answer that question, we need to get acquainted. In order to participate as members of any community, we need to exchange our stories, to teach, and to learn" (xxvi). In what ways can we exchange our own stories? In what ways do the women in these pages exchange stories?

4. Several stories express a newcomer's sense of belonging. See, for instance, "Path to a Small World" (58), "From Canton to Spearfish" (74), "A Haunting Experience" (109), "The Woman Who Didn't Fit In" (119), and "I Like It That Way" (216). How do the experiences of women who grew up in the West differ from those who came to it later in life? How do these differences affect their sense of community? How can you create community wherever you are?

5. The epigraph of *Crazy Woman Creek* states that vulnerability is what weaves a community together. Do you think that this assessment is accurate? How does facing adverse circumstances bring people together? See, for instance, "The Hippie Central Library Fest" (26), "The Logging Bee" (84), "Nevada Firestorm" (87), and "Ongoing Sustenance" (224).

6. Clubs and organizations play a large role within these communities. See, for instance, "Bingo Babes" (130), "Straightforward and Unafraid" (137), "The Caring Cleveland Club" (156), and "Crone Circle: Grandmothers Giving Wisdom" (241). How do organizations help strengthen commu-

nities? How does spontaneous community function along with structured community? What elements make a community successful?

7. In "The Far Side of Maple Street," Sophie Dominik Echeverria remarks, "Gossip is the great ancestor of the media, but much more interesting" (203). How does gossip both help and hinder a community? What role does communication play within a community?

8. Remote areas and bustling cities of the West are both represented in *Crazy Woman Creek*. How do rural and urban communities in the West differ? What aspects do they share?

9. In many cases, being part of a community entails a connection to the land as well as a connection to other people. How does the land become part of and affect a community? What other elements help form communities?

10. How do the part titles—"Women Driving Pickups," "Hallelujah and a Show of Hands," and "Cowgirl Up, Cupcakes"—represent women, community, and the West? How do you interpret these titles?

11. In "Well—You Told Me To," A. J. Harnish writes, "As women, I think we need to seize the opportunities we have to bond with those we encounter" (73). How do these stories depict women's general attitude toward forming communities? Do women have a tendency toward community that is particular in any way? How do men and women function differently in communities? Is this an accurate reflection of men and women in your own communities?

12. In her introduction, Linda M. Hasselstrom poses the question "Why weren't more mountains, statues, or government buildings named for women?" (xvi). What is your reaction to this question? How does this reflect what you know about the West? How are the women in this anthology rewriting the history of the West?

13. The editors compiled these anthologies in part to confront the stereotypes about rural women that they thought were misguided, untrue, or unfair. Are there stereotypes about women in your region? How do women respond to such stereotypes?

14. How do the voices here come together to create a more complete image of women in the West? How did this book change your image of women in the West?

Beyond Crazy Woman Creek

Prior to *Crazy Woman Creek,* the editors had two other anthologies published about and by women in the contemporary West — *Leaning into the Wind* and *Woven on the Wind.* Please see Linda M. Hasselstrom's introduction (xv) for background on this series of books. The following questions are meant to open the discussion about *Crazy Woman Creek* to include *Leaning into the Wind* and *Woven on the Wind.* Or they may simply be used to foster further discussion about *Crazy Woman Creek.* Either way, we hope that these questions will enrich your understanding of real women in the West — their particular challenges, opportunities, preoccupations, and hopes.

1. Looking at all three collections, do you think that women who arrived in the West later in life have a different relationship to the land and their neighbors—their community—than do women who are native to the area? Are these recent migrants any more or less "children of the land" than women who have lived in the West all their lives? Are they more or less likely to become involved in their Western communities?

2. In metropolitan areas, families may move frequently because of changing jobs or growing families. By contrast, some of the families that writers consider in these anthologies have lived on the same farm or ranch or in the same small town or rural community for generations. How are their relations with neighbors different from those of less rooted families? Can people who move from a metropolis learn the skills necessary to make them truly members of a new community?

3. Rural women are often faced with events beyond their control; however, women living in other areas also deal with unexpected events. Compare the importance of weather, transportation, emergency care, and other uncontrollable events in your life and in the lives of these Western women. How do such events affect community life? Might your community and its members learn and change as a result of observing how such events are handled in other communities?

4. Busy calving and harvest seasons make afternoon tea a difficult proposition for women ranchers and farmers. Indeed, the lives of women everywhere seem too busy, sometimes, for friendship and community involvement. How do women in your area reach out to their communities and bond with their friends and neighbors?

5. Have you lost friends because they moved or from some other cause? Have you been able to accept changes in friendships, to accept new neighbors? Can you discuss difficult and challenging issues with your friends? Is there a place or organization in your community that encourages such discussions?

6. How do you communicate most often with friends — by telephone, letter, e-mail, or some other method? How do changes in methods of keeping in touch affect our friendships? Our communities?

7. The editors compiled these anthologies in order to confront stereotypes about rural women that they thought were misguided, untrue, or unfair. Are there stereotypes about women in your region? If you asked women in your community to write about their lives, how would their evaluations differ from or conform to these stereotypes?

This reader's guide was written by Hal Hager & Associates, Somerville, New Jersey.

MARINER BOOKS / HOUGHTON MIFFLIN COMPANY
For information about other Mariner Reader's Guides please visit our Web site:
www.houghtonmifflinbooks.com

LEANING INTO THE WIND

Women Write from the Heart of the West

"Wise and honest and constantly surprising, a true work of art born of lived experience." — Teresa Jordan

An anthology of women's writing in the West that was the first of its kind, *Leaning into the Wind* brings together voices from more than two hundred women in six Western states. These memoirs, reflections, and poems tell of the rigors, glories, and ironies of Western life, offering a poignant glimpse into a lifestyle many of us will never know.

ISBN 0-395-90131-6

WOVEN ON THE WIND

Women Write About Friendship in the Sagebrush West

"An absolutely wonderful and touching collection, this book characterizes the ruggedness of the West and the resourcefulness of the women who inhabit it." — *Cowboy Magazine*

This second volume of women's writing from the heart of the American West expands to include stories, poems, and reflections from sixteen states and provinces. A communion of voices, *Woven on the Wind* tells of Western life and the ways in which it is enriched by friendship past and present. "Every woman needs to read this book for its wit and harmony, its near-biblical wisdom" (Ann Zwinger). ISBN 0-618-21920-X